Handbook of Adolescent Death and Bereavement

Charles A. Corr, PhD, is Professor, Department of Philosophical Studies, Southern Illinois University at Edwardsville, a volunteer with Hospice of Madison County in Illinois, and a former Chairperson of the International Work Group on Death, Dying, and Bereavement (1989–1993). In addition to numerous articles and book chapters, Dr. Corr's other Springer Publishing publications include: *Hospice Care: Principles and Practice* (1983), *Hospice Approaches to Pediatric Care* (1985), *Adolescence and Death* (1986), and *Sudden Infant Death Syndrome: Who Can Help and How* (1991). Some of his other publications include: *Helping Children Cope with Death: Guidelines and Resources*; *Childhood and Death*; and *Death, Dying, Life and Living*. Several organizations have recognized Professor Corr's professional work: the Association for Death Education and Counseling in 1988 for Outstanding Personal Contributions to the Advancement of Knowledge in the Field of Death, Dying, and Bereavement; Children's Hospital International in 1989 for Outstanding Contribution to the World of Hospice Support for Children and in 1995 for Life Time Achievement; and on five separate occasions the *American Journal of Nursing* for Book of the Year awards. In addition, Southern Illinois University awarded Professor Corr its Research Scholar Award (1990), its Outstanding Scholar Award (1991), and its Kimmel Community Service Award (1994).

David E. Balk, PhD, is Professor, School of Family Studies and Human Services, College of Human Ecology, Kansas State University, Manhattan, Kansas, where he teaches courses on death and bereavement, program evaluation, coping with life crises, the helping relationship, and middle childhood and adolescence. The College of Human Ecology at Kansas State University honored him in 1992 as Outstanding Teacher of the Year and in 1995 with its award for Faculty Excellence in Research. His 1981 dissertation about sibling death during adolescence is considered the seminal work in contemporary research into adolescent bereavement. The National Institute of Mental Health funded him in 1990 to study the efficacy of social support with bereaved college students. Professor Balk is the author of *Adolescent Development: Early Through Late Adolescence*. He is Book Review Editor for the journal *Death Studies*. His current interests include evaluating bereavement care programs for children and assessing further the efficacy of social support with bereaved college students. Dr. Balk is a member of the International Work Group on Death, Dying, and Bereavement.

Handbook of Adolescent Death and Bereavement

Charles A. Corr, PhD

David E. Balk, PhD

Editors

SPRINGER PUBLISHING COMPANY

Springer Publishing Company, Inc.
536 Broadway
New York, NY 10012-3955

Cover design by Tom Yabut
Production Editor: Pamela Lankas

96 97 98 99 2000/5 4 3 2 1

Library of Congress Cataloging-in-Publication Data
Handbook of adolescent death and bereavement / Charles A.
   Corr, David E. Balk, editors.
      p.   cm.
   Includes bibliographical references and index.
   ISBN 0-8261-9240-8
   1. Teenagers and death.   2. Grief in adolescence.
   3. Bereavement in adolescence.   4. Teenagers—Counseling
   of.   I. Corr, Charles A.   II. Balk, David E., 1943–   .
   BF724.3.D43H26   1996
   155.9'37'0835—dc20   95-42074
                                                               CIP

Printed in the United States of America

This book is dedicated to
Carol Ann Keene, Ph.D.
in gratitude for many years of friendship,
collegiality, encouragement, and support
and to
Marcian T. O'Meara
pastor, friend, priest, former Abbot of St. Pius X Abbey,
who offered a young man with promise but who was adrift
the chance to sink his teeth into reality.

Contents

Contributors

Leslie Balmer, Ph.D., is a clinical psychologist in private practice in Brampton, Ontario, Canada.

Ronald K. Barrett, Ph.D., is Associate Professor, Department of Psychology, Loyola Marymount University, Los Angeles, California.

Olivia P. Collins, Ph.D., is Assistant Professor, School of Family Studies and Human Services, Kansas State University, Manhattan, Kansas.

Lydia DeSantis, Ph.D., R.N., is Professor, School of Nursing, University of Miami, Coral Gables, Florida.

Ralph J. DiClemente, Ph.D., is Associate Professor, Department of Health Behavior, School of Public Health; Department of Pediatrics, Division of Adolescent Medicine, School of Medicine; and the Prevention Sciences Program, Center for AIDS Research, The University of Alabama at Birmingham, Birmingham, Alabama.

Julie C. Dunsmore, B.Sc. (Psych) Hons., M.P.H., R.N., is Director, Department of Health Promotion and Education, The Royal North Shore Hospital, St. Leonards, Sydney, New South Wales, Australia.

Stephen Fleming, Ph.D., is Professor, Department of Psychology, Atkinson College, York University, North York, Ontario, Canada.

Yvonne M. Foster, M.S., is a psychotherapist in private practice and also serves as a consultant to Lancaster Freedom Center in Lancaster, Pennsylvania.

David C. Hill, Ph.D., is Associate Professor, Psychology Department, Millersville University of Pennsylvania, Millersville, Pennsylvania, and a Pennsylvania Licensed Psychologist.

Nancy S. Hogan, Ph.D., R.N., is Associate Professor, School of Nursing, University of Miami, Coral Gables, Florida.

Mallory O. Johnson, B.S., is a doctoral candidate, Department of Psychology, School of Social and Behavioral Sciences, The University of Alabama at Birmingham, Birmingham, Alabama.

Anthony P. Jurich, Ph.D., is Professor, School of Family Studies and Human Services, Kansas State University, Manhattan, Kansas.

Marcia Lattanzi-Licht, R.N., M.A., is a psychotherapist in private practice in Boulder, Colorado.

Illene C. Noppe, Ph.D., is Associate Professor, Department of Human Development, University of Wisconsin—Green Bay, Green Bay, Wisconsin.

Lloyd D. Noppe, Ph.D., is Associate Professor and past Chairperson, Department of Human Development, University of Wisconsin—Green Bay, Green Bay, Wisconsin.

Kevin Ann Oltjenbruns, Ph.D., is Associate Professor, Department of Human Development and Family Studies, Colorado State University, Fort Collins, Colorado.

Robert P. Pack, M.P.H., is a doctoral candidate, Department of Health Behavior, School of Public Health, The University of Alabama at Birmingham, Birmingham, Alabama.

Ralph L. V. Rickgarn, Ed.S., is Coordinator, Student Behavior, Housing & Residential Life, and Lecturer, Department of Educational Psychology, College of Education, University of Minnesota, Minneapolis, Minnesota.

Michael M. Stevens, M.B., B.S., F.R.A.C.P., is Senior Staff Specialist and Head, Oncology Unit, The New Children's Hospital, Parramatta, New South Wales, Australia.

Eileen P. Stevenson, R.N., M.A., is a certified school nurse/health educator at Joyce Kilmer School in Mahwah, New Jersey.

Robert G. Stevenson, Ed.D., is a teacher at River Dell Regional High School, Oradell, New Jersey.

Katharine E. Stewart, M.A., M.P.H., is a doctoral candidate, Department of Psychology, School of Social and Behavioral Sciences, and Center for AIDS Research, The University of Alabama at Birmingham, Birmingham, Alabama.

Richard G. Tedeschi, Ph.D., is Associate Professor, Department of Psychology, The University of North Carolina at Charlotte, Charlotte, North Carolina.

Kirsten J. Tyson-Rawson, Ph.D., is Assistant Professor, Marriage and Family Therapy Program, Department of Child Development and Family Relations, East Carolina University, Greenville, North Carolina.

LaNae Valentine, Ph.D., is an individual, marital, and family therapist, Department of Psychology, Utah Valley Regional Medical Center, Provo, Utah.

Preface

This is a book about three principal topics: (1) adolescents who are coping with confrontations with death and dying; (2) adolescents who are coping with confrontations with bereavement; and (3) interventions designed to help these adolescents. The goal of this book is to contribute to improved understanding of the challenges and tasks that face adolescents who are coping with death, dying, and bereavement, and to guide efforts to assist such adolescents. In its topics, structure, and goals, this book is designed to stand alone and to serve as a companion to *Handbook of Childhood Death and Bereavement*, edited by Charles A. Corr and Donna M. Corr (Springer Publishing Company, 1996).

The first book devoted to a comprehensive survey of interactions between adolescents and death-related issues was *Adolescence and Death* (Springer Publishing Company, 1986), edited by Charles Corr and Joan McNeil. Before the publication of that text (and subsequently), many books and articles had addressed specific aspects of adolescent life and particular topics related to death (e.g., suicide among adolescents or the death of an adolescent's parent). In addition, many authors had mentioned adolescents in broader discussions of childhood and death. All of these specialized accounts of selected aspects of death, dying, and bereavement in relationship to adolescence are welcome, but they are not sufficient in themselves either to these subjects or to a proper appreciation of adolescent life in the late 20th century.

Moreover, since 1986 much has changed in our understanding of adolescence and in matters of death, dying, and bereavement. For example, we have come to realize more clearly the differences and the complex intersections between normative, developmental tasks in adolescence and the specific, situational tasks that are involved in coping with death, dying, and bereavement. Also, it has become evident that it is not sufficient merely to say that by the end of childhood most individuals will have acquired the cognitive capacities to understand the concept of death. True as that statement may be, one must go further to appreciate the real differences between children's understandings of death and those of adolescents, as well as contrasts that exist between central features of adolescent and adult understandings of death.

Suicide and life-threatening behavior in adolescents, along with coping with life-threatening illness as an adolescent, have been matters of substantial concern for some time. But much has been learned about these subjects in the last few years, even as increased attention has been devoted to homicidal violence involving adolescents and the new specter of human immunodeficiency virus (HIV) infection and acquired immunodeficiency syndrome (AIDS). All of these topics are examined in Part I of this book.

In the area of bereavement, it was common in the early and mid-1980s to bemoan the lack of research and insight informed by empirical data into distinctive features of adolescent grief and mourning. Such complaints are no longer valid—or at the very least they are not valid without significant qualification. Much has been learned during the late 1980s and early 1990s about adolescents and bereavement. The chapters in Part II of this book examine new information about the current state of our knowledge in this field and suggest ways in which present insights need to be expanded, enriched, or reexamined in the future.

Further, much has been learned since the mid-1980s about interventions that are appropriate to the specific needs of adolescents who are coping with death, dying, and bereavement. The chapters in Part III of this book draw together many ways in which to help adolescents and their families including modalities, such as educational programs, postvention or crisis intervention efforts immediately after a traumatic experience, support groups, and therapeutic communication.

For each of the chapters in this book, contributors were invited to explore a particular subject area related to death, dying, or bereavement that was important in the lives of contemporary adolescents. To do so, contributors drew on their own experience in the field in question, existing research, and relevant literature. Many of these contributors have conducted the research or written the literature that is most prominent in their respective fields. Whenever possible, contributors were asked to relate their findings to developmental issues or tasks in adolescence (i.e., to differences between early, middle, and late adolescents). In many cases that was feasible, and the result is an important feature of this book, even though the present state of our knowledge does not enable us to identify such interconnections in every topical area or to pursue them in extended detail across the board.

In the development of this book, its editors are indebted to many individuals who contributed to awareness of this field of study and to this particular project. Joan McNeil helped to sensitize both of us to the need for this work and to the benefits of working together on this endeavor. A former editor at Springer Publishing Company, Mary Grace Luke, first suggested this project. Many colleagues and friends talked with us about what should be involved in this undertaking, and a distinguished group of contributors found time in their busy schedules to write (and rewrite, often more than once) the chapters that follow. Southern Illinois University at Edwardsville and Kansas State University generously supported this project, as they have our separate professional endeavors over an extended period. Our wives, Donna and Mary Ann, encouraged us throughout the preparation of the manuscript and the work required for its production.

We have enjoyed working together throughout this project, and each of us has learned much in the process. We hope that readers will find the results to be helpful in enriching their understanding of adolescents who are coping with death, dying, and bereavement, and in guiding their efforts to improve assistance offered to such adolescents.

CHARLES A. CORR
DAVID E. BALK

I

Death

Chapters 1 and 2 are designed to establish a foundation for all that follows in this book. In chapter 1, David Balk and Charles Corr introduce us to distinctive features of adolescence as a special time in the human life cycle and to encounters with death that are characteristic of the adolescent years in our society. The first portion of that discussion seeks to contribute to an understanding of the meaning of adolescence as a distinctive era between childhood and adulthood, the normative life transitions that are typically experienced during adolescence, differences among adolescents, and developmental tasks that are typical of early, middle, and late adolescence, respectively. The second portion of chapter 1 examines encounters with death and bereavement that are most often found among adolescents in our society. In the case of deaths among adolescents, these encounters most often involve unanticipated or traumatic life events (accidents, homicides, and suicides); in addition, adolescents may also experience the deaths of significant others in their lives.

In chapter 2, Lloyd Noppe and Illene Noppe examine sources of ambiguity in adolescent understandings of death. If adolescents do encounter death and death-related experiences in their lives (as noted in chapter 1), what are the characteristic ways in which they conceptualize or think about such encounters? To say this another way, by contrast with children, it is clear that most adolescents have the intellectual capacities to understand the concept of death and its principal components. The issue for the authors in chapter 2 is to explore the central features of that understanding and the factors that may help to introduce ambiguity into ways in which adolescents think about death. The chapter focuses on four factors—biological, cognitive, social, and emotional—that are prominent in adolescent thinking about death.

With that established, chapters 3 to 6 discuss encounters with four specific types of death-related experiences that are prominent during the adolescent years. In chapter 3, Ronald Barrett examines the prevalence and some of the psychological consequences of homicidal violence in adolescent life with special attention to African Americans and Hispanic Americans. Barrett also explores a series of theoretical explanations that have been offered to account for adolescent violence and a set of recommendations designed both to improve efforts to help individual adolescents, and to create a better society within which adolescents and others can live more satisfying lives.

Next, in chapter 4 Anthony Jurich and Olivia Collins examine the phenomena of suicide and life-threatening behavior among adolescents. The discussion begins with a review of the demographic characteristics of adolescents who complete or attempt suicide, along with rates of incidence for these behaviors. To understand these phenomena, a theoretical model is offered to throw light on the tendencies of some adolescents at some times to turn to suicide as a way of coping with their life experiences. Within the model, five factors (physical, personal, family, peer, and community) are shown to tip the balance in adolescent behavior toward or away from suicide as a response to stress. Appreciation of these five factors can help adolescents and others both to understand adolescent suicidal behavior, and to strive to modify that behavior in constructive directions.

In chapter 5, Ralph DiClemente, Katherine Stewart, Mallory Johnson, and Robert Pack turn attention to a death-related threat that has only recently developed in the lives of contemporary adolescents: HIV infection and AIDS. The structure of the discussion is similar to that seen in chapter 4: a brief survey of the prevalence of HIV/AIDS among adolescents in our society is followed by an analysis of efforts to prevent HIV infection among adolescents and extended discussion of a model that is intended to illuminate adolescent reactions to HIV diagnosis.

Finally, in chapter 6, Michael Stevens and Julie Dunsmore explore the experiences of adolescents who are living with life-threatening illness. These adolescents encounter and grieve many losses as they live with their illnesses. In chapter 6, their experiences are illuminated through case histories and insightful comments on the implications of life-threatening illness for early, middle, and late adolescents. The authors also offer a depiction of typical features in an adolescent's journey through a life-threatening illness. This journey is described primarily in terms of experiences and reactions of adolescents with cancer, but comments are also added on several other life-threatening conditions, such as cystic fibrosis, severe brain damage, and catastrophic conditions with short life expectancy.

1

Adolescents, Developmental Tasks, and Encounters with Death and Bereavement

David E. Balk and Charles A. Corr

Adolescents delight and exasperate adults. Adolescent vitality, idealism, and romanticism get countered by maddening self-centeredness and frequent conflicts with parents. Adolescents offer adults a glimpse of the future and, at the same time, seem awkward strangers in our midst, living out what one parent called "the werewolf stage of human development." This chapter explores various ways in which to understand adolescence, developmental tasks that confront adolescents, the process of coping with unanticipated and traumatic life events as an adolescent, and encounters with death and bereavement during adolescence. The goal is to set the stage for an exploration of interactions between adolescents and their developmental work, on the one hand, and issues associated with death and bereavement, on the other hand. Those interactions are examined in detail in the chapters that follow.

DEFINITION OF ADOLESCENCE

The term *adolescence* derives from a Latin root *(adolescentia),* which refers to the process or condition of growing up and designates a "youth" or person in the growing age (Simpson & Weiner, 1989). In modern usage, "adolescence" designates the period in the human life cycle between childhood and maturity or adulthood. This "in-between" period in human development is a relatively recent component of the life cycle. Throughout much of human history, not to mention some contemporary societies or cultural groups, there was or is no such in-between period. Instead, children simply were seen as "coming of age" at some point or through some relatively brief ritual, after which they were regarded as full-fledged adult members of the community (Ariès, 1962). In North America and many other advanced, Westernized societies, however, adolescence is an extended, complex, changing, and distinct developmental era between the elementary school years and the achievement of full adult status.

In most modern societies, adolescents are considered capable of assuming responsibilities thought inappropriate for children. In the United States, for example, adolescents are normally given some choice in their educational curriculum, and they are taught by instructors with expertise in a particular subject matter, in contrast to the fixed, common curricula and single-classroom teachers that are more typical of the primary schools. Similarly, American adolescents are gradually regarded (with some limitations) as fit to take on work and wage-earning responsibilities, qualify to drive a motor vehicle, choose whether or not to enter into college or university education, vote, drink alcoholic beverages, and get married. In short, adolescents are no longer simply to be treated as children, but they may only gradually move toward the special privileges, responsibilities, and status of full adults.

In many modern societies, it may not be precisely clear either when an individual leaves childhood and becomes an adolescent, or when that same individual becomes an adult and is no longer an adolescent. It may seem simplest to equate adolescence with the teenage years, the period from 13 to 19 years of age. But chronological markers are not necessarily accurate indicators of developmental eras. For example, it might be better to identify the beginning of the adolescent era with the onset of puberty. However, different individuals arrive at puberty at different times (with females typically becoming pubescent at an earlier age than males), and puberty itself is more a series of related events than a single moment in time.

The transition from adolescence to adulthood may be even less clear because it lacks a biological marker like the onset of puberty. Many developmental psychologists define the end of adolescence as the point at which an individual leaves home and his or her family of origin. One can easily see how variable this may be in light of individual, cultural, and economic factors—not to mention the recent phenomena in which young people who leave home often return to live with their family of origin (cf., Goldscheider & Goldscheider, 1994).

Even when chronological age is accepted as the basic identifier for adolescence, many reports compile demographic data in 10-year age groupings (e.g., 15–24 years of age). These compilations are not consistent with a correlation between adolescence and the teenage years. They may mean that however we might wish to define adolescence, statistical data may not be available to us except in ways that only approximate our chosen definition.

NORMATIVE LIFE TRANSITIONS AND UNANTICIPATED EVENTS

Life-span developmental psychology distinguishes between normative life transitions and unanticipated events that evoke coping mechanisms and present life crises (Danish & D'Augelli, 1980; Danish, Smyer, & Nowak, 1980). A normative life transition is a turning point in individual development and is expected to occur at a certain time, in a certain relationship to other life events, with predictability, and to most if not all members of one's cohort. Entering the school system around the age of 6 is a key example of a normative life transition in the United States.

Unanticipated events are, as the phrase implies, not expected. They catch people unprepared. As the converse of normative life transitions, they occur unpredictably, with apparently random relationship to other life events, and to some but not all members of a cohort. A singularly ugly example of unanticipated life events is the growing incidence of date rape in the United States (FBI, 1992; Koss, 1988; Koss, Gidycz, & Wisniewski, 1987).

Many of the subjects addressed in this book would not fall into the category of a normative life transition. During adolescence in the postindustrialized world, the death of one's parent, sibling, friend, or oneself is not a normative event. Such situational occurrences are more properly understood as examples of unanticipated life crises. One might argue, however, that the prevalence of a situational crisis, such as the death of one or more grandparents during adolescence, could lead to considering such an event as an anticipated life transition during this era.

Normative life transitions and unanticipated, traumatic life events share a common characteristic. As life crises or turning points, they present "dangerous opportunities." They evoke growth and maturity if responded to well, but they presage harm and maldevelopment if re-sponded to poorly. Consequently, the occurrence of a traumatic, unan-ticipated life event in the life of an adolescent—such as the death of that individual's mother or father—might threaten healthy resolution of his or her developmental tasks.

DIFFERENCES AMONG ADOLESCENTS

Differences among adolescents may be as significant as differences between adolescents and children or adults. Obviously, adolescents differ among themselves as unique individuals; as males and females; as members of different social, cultural, religious, or economic com-munities; as a result of divergent life experiences; and in other salient ways.

In addition, as a group adolescents also differ in significant develop-mental respects. For example, it has been proposed (Blos, 1941; Flem-ing & Adolph, 1986) that it would be useful to divide this era of the life span into three more specific developmental subperiods: early, middle, and late adolescence. This tripartite division extends the era of adoles-cence by approximately 2 years before and after the teenage years. It thereby accords with a more extended transitional period in our society from childhood to adulthood. More important, understanding adolescence in terms of early, middle, and late subperiods permits a more detailed description of developmental tasks within the adoles-cent era.

DEVELOPMENTAL TASKS WITHIN THREE SUBPERIODS IN ADOLESCENCE

During adolescence, normative life transitions are usually described in terms of developmental tasks. These tasks represent the work that ado-lescents must undertake to navigate successfully the developmental challenges that confront them. For example, in a penetrating psycho-dynamic interpretation of adolescence Blos (1941, 1979) argued that *early adolescence* involves decreased identification with parents, increased identification with peers, fascination with hero figures, and interest in opposite-sex peers. "These early adolescent phenomena herald the efforts to form new ego ideals, separate from dependency on parents, gain more focused heterosexual relations, and develop a mature identity" (Balk, 1995, p. 18). For Blos, failure to cope with and surmount obstacles unique to early adolescence leads to ongoing difficulties with maturity.

Blos (1979) referred to *middle adolescence* as "adolescence proper." Challenges to be resolved during middle adolescence involve developing autonomy from parents and forging a distinctive, mature identity. Blos had an optimistic view of development, and thought the middle adolescent years offered each person a "second chance" (1979, p. 475). In other words, middle adolescents can develop greater ego resourcefulness by considerably reorganizing the values internalized from their parents. Blos (1979) called this reorganization a second individuation process. Such a concept provided a major break with orthodox psychoanalytic thinkers.

Late adolescence for Blos is that period following middle adolescence when individuals achieve a stable character formation. They achieve this character formation by meeting four distinct challenges: (a) the second individuation process; (b) traumatic life events; (c) historical continuity; and (d) sexual identity. Blos argued that achieving closure in the second individuation process was a critical task for late adolescents. He also saw that coping with traumatic life events provided late adolescents the means to achieve personal strength. Death and bereavement would certainly qualify as events of this kind. Further, historical continuity involves accepting one's past and thereby freeing oneself for growth and maturity. Finally, Blos differentiated sexual identity from gender identity. He asserted that gender identity occurred early, whereas sexual identity was only possible with physical maturity. Blos (1979) linked sexual identity to heterosexuality and did not mention that sexual identity could be homosexual.

Scholars interested in psychological disturbances of adolescents have found the demarcation of early, middle, and late adolescent subperiods to be useful (e.g., Weiner, 1977). The distinguishing aspects of each of these subperiods are the developmental tasks individuals are expected to master. In fact, several contributors to the *International Handbook of Adolescence* (Hurrelmann, 1994) consider poor responses to these developmental tasks to be signs of psychological problems during adolescence. Accordingly, we will employ this division of adolescence into early, middle, and late subperiods to provide a fuller account of selected developmental tasks that can be related to our concerns with death-related issues.

Early Adolescence

The early adolescent years begin around age 10 or 11 for most individuals, and last until the age of 14. The obvious marker of the start of this subperiod (and, thus, of the whole of adolescence) is the onset of puberty. Over the past 150 years, puberty has begun earlier in each generation (Birren, Kinney, Schaie, & Woodruff, 1981; Chumlea, 1982). This phenomenon is referred to as "the secular trend."

Increased interest in early adolescence emerged first in the school systems of the United States, which introduced the "middle school" in the late 1950s. The purpose of the middle school was to make easier the transition from elementary grades to high school (Noblit, 1987). Middle schools were supposed to provide a setting matched to the developmental tasks of early adolescents (Staton & Oseroff-Varnell, 1990). These developmental tasks were thought (Thornburg, 1980) to include becoming aware of physical changes; incorporating information for solving problems; learning sex and social roles; developing friendships; achieving more independence from parents; and realizing a tendency toward forming stereotypes. Research gathered in the 1980s and 1990s suggests, however, that middle schools have not provided early adolescents the easier transitions they were designed to achieve (Crockett, Petersen, Graber, Schulberg, & Ebata, 1989; Eccles et al., 1993; Hamburg, 1992; Staton & Oseroff-Varnell, 1990).

The dominant factor for early adolescent development is physical, and the timing of puberty can have profound effects. The onset of puberty is a normative life transition, but not all adolescents are prepared for puberty; some adolescents mature more quickly than others, and different psychological reactions have been noted for early-, on–time-, and late-maturing individuals. Many of these reactions show gender differences (Petersen, 1983; Tobin-Richards, Boxer, & Petersen, 1983).

As cases in point, consider the girl who matures more rapidly than her peers. She typically becomes self-conscious, loses self-esteem, and is thrust into a social context in which older boys "hit on her." Frequently, such early-maturing girls have not developed the emotional repertoire to cope well with looking older than they are. Evidence indicates, however, that by the start of late adolescence, such early-maturing girls develop sophisticated coping skills that overcome their few years of awkwardness (Tobin-Richards, Boxer, & Petersen, 1983). There are, unfortunately, data that show a positive correlation between early female maturation and delinquent behavior. The belief is that some early-maturing girls start running with an older crowd of adolescents who engage in deviant behaviors (Calhoun, Jurgens, & Chen, 1993; Rhodes & Fischer, 1993).

Against this, consider the case of the early-maturing boy. His peers look up to him, adults give him more respect than other boys his age, and he develops self-confidence and is usually seen as a leader. If he is athletically gifted, he is all the more a star among the adolescent crowd. Costs for such early maturation in boys have been noted: They seem less spontaneous, more somber, less flexible, and more deferent to authority than other males their age (Brooks-Gunn, 1987; Peskin, 1967). It is possible that "boys respond to early maturation with rigid attempts to be in control of what is happening to them, and they acquiesce more readily to goals and choices carrying adult approval. Another explanation is that having gained early acceptance by the adult world, the early-maturing boy has no motive to try alternatives" (Balk, 1995, p. 54).

Later-maturing boys show more interest in exploring alternatives and are less somber, more spontaneous, and more flexible than early-maturing boys. Unlike early-maturing boys who often adopt adult values before trying out options, later-maturing boys develop their own repertoire of skills to deal with choices they face during adolescence.

In summary, the data suggest initial and later reactions to the timing of puberty vary for early-maturing boys and girls. On-time maturing is seen as a positive experience for both males and females, whereas late maturation appears to cause distress for girls. (Several female college students who indicated they were late maturers have strongly challenged this assertion.) If so, early-maturing girls and late-maturing boys mirror each other in terms of turning initial distress into later social and personal competencies.

Chris was an early adolescent (age 13) when her brother died in a freakish motorboat accident. When asked how she responded in the first few weeks following his death, Chris recalled, "I felt like my life was just shattered. It was like this big jolt in my life, and I felt really little compared to the whole world. I had this feeling I was so empty inside. I hurt so bad, going numb was the only way to deal with it."

School and peers are central points in most early adolescents' lives, whereas for Chris "school wasn't the most important thing. I had to get myself back together." Chris noted she was "starting to study more again." Although not studying as much as she did before her brother's death, by age 14 a sense of purpose had reentered Chris's life. As she said, "I want to get into college. I know my directions better now, and I'm out of that shock."

Middle Adolescence

Discussions of early adolescence focus naturally on responses to physical maturation. By contrast, during middle adolescence—which roughly spans the years of 15 to 17 when most teenagers in the United States are in high school—the central issues for a young person concern experiences of growing pressure to gain greater skill at being independent and self-governing. Other prominent issues in the lives of middle adolescents involve what Erikson (1963) would have termed *identity and intimacy.* Adolescent identity formation during the middle adolescent years may reach closure, but most scholars would consider such finalization of identity to be premature and an indication of unreflective acceptance of the values and beliefs of others (Erikson, 1963; Josselson, 1987; Marcia, 1964, 1980).

Much current thinking about adolescent development during the middle and late adolescent years focuses on changes in cognition that both impel and signify normative transitions. This is evident in changes that occur in social understanding during the middle adolescent years. Elkind (1967, 1979) extended Piaget's (1929) notion of egocentrism to developments in social understandings that occur during adolescence. *Egocentrism* refers to the tendency to view situations from only one's own perspective and very possibly not even to consider there could be any other perspective to consider.

The development of formal operations or the capacity for abstract, conceptual thinking provides the means to overcome the obstacles of egocentrism by allowing adolescents to reflect on their own and others' experiences. However, Elkind noted that not until middle adolescence do individuals remove the shackles of egocentric thinking. Even though early adolescents possess the mental powers to consider other perspectives, their preoccupation with changes in their physical appearance often short-circuits any interest in testing whether their thoughts and feelings correspond to what other people think and feel.

Selman (1980) applied notions of advances in cognitive development during adolescence to explain qualitative changes in adolescents' interpersonal understanding. By middle adolescence, individuals have the capability to form complex, abstract, symbolic representations of reality. They appreciate that persons are more complex than words can sometimes explain. In other words, they accept that ineffability marks some of the more profound dimensions of interpersonal relations. From a practical viewpoint, adolescents who have reached this level of understanding realize many systems influence their social experience and appreciate that interactions with friends contain both moments of empathic self-disclosure and moments of frivolous "filler conversations." Admittedly, as anyone who has talked with middle adolescents knows, there are gaps in how they use their developing social understanding. Not infrequently, middle adolescents vacillate from short-term interest in what the other person is saying to a long-term preoccupation with turning the focus of conversation on themselves.

Fowler (1981, 1991b) extended the idea of perspective taking to explain the universal quest of humans to determine what gives existence ultimate meaning. He called this quest the development of faith. Faith can encompass religious beliefs but is not limited to them. Albert Camus would be a well-known example of someone whose faith development did not take on religious context or expression.

For Fowler, faith development occurs across the life arc in a series of stages and is dependent on progress through Piaget's stages of cognitive development. For adolescents, faith changes as egocentric limitations are overcome. The link of faith development to changes from egocentric thinking is most clear in the transformation of adolescents' widening world views.

During middle adolescence and into late adolescence, individuals have the capacity to attain what Fowler (1981) called "individuative-reflective" faith. This stage of faith consciousness depends on examining, evaluating, and restructuring one's beliefs and values. It also requires making choices about the roles and responsibilities one will assume in life. "In the individuative-reflective stage of faith, people seek foundations that underlie the roles and relationships in their lives" (Balk, 1995, p. 226).

Consider the example of changes in social understanding that emerged in the life of a middle adolescent whose brother had died from bone marrow transplant complications. One of the first things Rhonda learned was that most other people, especially her peers and teachers, were anxious around her after her brother died. They seemed unsure what to say and became noticeably uncomfortable when she was in their presence. Rhonda also learned "who my real friends were." They were persons who were with her when she needed support and who let her talk about her brother. She could cry around them, but she did not always have to be upset. She also found in herself a much greater empathy for other persons' pain and troubles. She no longer runs away either figuratively or literally when someone else is hurting.

A major transformation in social consciousness does seem to occur in the lives of bereaved adolescents, a transformation seen as a reaching out to and appreciation for the experiences of others. The experi-

ence of working through grief enhances their social perspective taking
and clearly propels them to grow up a bit faster than their unaffected
peers.

Late Adolescence

Many late adolescents (individuals who are roughly 18–22 years old) are
in college or have joined the world of work full time. During this subperiod middle adolescent concerns with changes in social understanding give way to such issues as making career choices, developing
intimate relations, and gaining autonomy from one's family of origin,
particularly from one's parents. There is some evidence that males and
females go about this decision making and commitment in slightly different ways. Raphael (1979) noted that late adolescent females felt issues of family and of career were intertwined, whereas males felt free to
focus singularly on career choices. There is evidence that males and females view success and achievement differently: The females who most
desire to achieve expressed the most fear of the costs of success,
whereas the males who most desire to achieve have the least fear of what
success will entail (Orlofsky, 1978).

Achieving separation from one's parents is a hallmark of late adolescent development and is a sign of becoming autonomous. Such separation is a normative life transition. For several adolescent researchers,
such separation is a matter of individuation (Blos, 1979; Collins, 1990;
Grotevant & Cooper, 1986; Hauser & Greene, 1991; Quintana & Kerr,
1993; Steinberg & Silverberg, 1986). Such individuation entails an aug-
mented sense of mastery over one's life (Blos, 1979) as well as ongoing
relations with one's parents based on mutual respect and attachment
(Youniss & Smollar, 1985).

Research suggests that most late adolescents attain separation from
their parents while maintaining warm and close relationships with them
(Bell, Avery, Jenkins, Feld, & Schoenrock, 1985; Campbell, Adams, &
Dobson, 1984; Moore, 1984, 1987; Sullivan & Sullivan, 1980). There
are, of course, counterexamples in which autonomy is achieved
through emotional detachment. In such cases, an adolescent may feel
distant from his or her family, break ties and communication with the
family, feel out of place when visiting, and see the family infrequently,
if at all.

Gender differences appear for adolescents who construe autonomy
in terms of emotional detachment from their parents. Males who associate separation from parents with emotional detachment express
greater loneliness, lower self-esteem, less life satisfaction, more prob-

lems leaving home, and more difficulty achieving a separate identity than do females (Moore, 1984, 1987).

One hypothesis about why females cope more effectively than males when autonomy is marked by emotional detachment is that socialization prepares females to be more capable to develop emotional intimacy and relationships in general. Females internalize richer emotional relationships with other people than do males. Thus, females can call on greater reserves of internalized personal relationships than can males, and these reserves "insulate later adolescent females during times of separation and make them less emotionally dependent (than males) on their parents" (Balk, 1995, p. 258).

A case in point is Justine, a late adolescent in college whose father died of leukemia in her freshman year. She had a particularly difficult bereavement, primarily because of her mother's decision to remarry within 6 months of her father's death. She got along poorly with her stepfather and his children, and she felt on shaky grounds with her mother. Achieving the normal developmental task of separation from her father became greatly complicated for Justine by her grief over his death and her ongoing ties of attachment to him. More work needs to be done to examine the complications involved with achieving the late adolescent developmental tasks of separation from one's parents when the adolescent is grieving a parental death. For example, a study by Tyson-Rawson (1993) of the experiences of college females bereaved over the death of their fathers led to the finding that such individuals expressed changes in how they think about the world as well as the salience of a sustaining spiritual belief.

ADOLESCENCE, TRAUMATIC LIFE EVENTS, AND COPING

Commonly, the adolescent years have been considered times of turmoil, disorder, distress, and other disruptive processes that were thought to be necessary to separate from parents and develop a unique identity. As Anna Freud (1958, p. 275) wrote, "to be normal during the adolescent period is by itself abnormal." This view was first articulated by Hall (1904), championed by Freudian psychoanalysts (A. Freud, 1958) and developed further by neo-Freudians (Blos, 1979; Erikson, 1963). Similar descriptions of adolescence in terms of "storm and stress" have been provided by Keniston (1965), who talked of the alienation of contemporary youth; Lewin (1939), who described adolescents as marginalized by adult society; Mead (1930), who thought of contemporary Western culture as laden with strife for adolescents; and Goodman (1960), who depicted growing up as an exercise in absurdity.

Other scholars have reported research that not only disconfirms the storm and stress view of adolescence, but that also makes a strong case for adolescence as a time of relative calm and stability (Bandura, 1980; Offer, 1969; Offer & Offer, 1975; Oldham, 1978). Thus, on the basis of their review of empirical research Offer and Sabshin (1984) observed that almost all researchers who have studied representative samples of adolescents "come to the conclusion that by and large good coping and a smooth transition into adulthood are much more typical than the opposite" (p. 101). Weiner (1985) concluded that the "storm and stress" theory of adolescence is essentially a myth perpetuated by psychoanalytic formulations, based on clinical populations, and then wrongly generalized to adolescents at large, but not supported by later research.

Offer's longitudinal research (Offer, 1969; Offer & Offer, 1975) and cross-national research (Offer, Ostrov, & Howard, 1981; Offer, Ostrov, Howard, & Atkinson, 1988) is particularly hopeful in relation to the resiliency of adolescents in the face of severe life traumas, such as the death of a parent. This research concluded that adolescents use such tragedies as means for growth; that is, coping with bereavement prompted the adolescents in question to proceed a bit more quickly than their peers into adulthood.

Coleman (1978) agreed that adolescent development was relatively calm and stable for most individuals. How is that possible, he asked, given the numerous significant changes occurring in the lives of adolescents: physical, emotional, social, cognitive, interpersonal? Coleman's answer was that most adolescents deal with stressors by concentrating on resolving one crisis at a time. He called this approach "focal theory." Troubles emerge for adolescents when they are unable to segregate their attention on one stressor, but must deal with multiple stressors, such as early physical maturation, parental divorce, and changing schools.

Here we must question how Coleman's ideas fit into an understanding of adolescents—early, middle, or late—who are coping with death and bereavement. Most studies indicate that coping with bereavement during adolescence leads to greater maturity, not regression or psychological disturbance (Balk, 1981, 1991, 1995; Guerriero & Fleming, 1985; Hogan, 1987; Hogan & Balk, 1990; Hogan & DeSantis, 1992; Hogan & Greenfield, 1991; Offer, 1969; Oltjenbruns, 1991). Rather than producing insurmountable obstacles to development, the trauma of bereavement more often promotes growth.

Blos (1979) asserted that facing such challenges was a task of late adolescence. We take this challenge back into the early and middle adolescent years as well. In so doing, we note, given the developmental tasks of adolescence, that there are no guarantees that any or all of these tasks will be resolved in adaptive ways. Nevertheless, we are impressed with the evidence that adolescents often do use trauma as a means to grow and to forge ahead into adulthood a bit more quickly than their unaffected peers. In any event, it seems obvious that all who would understand adolescents correctly must approach these youth with care and sensitivity. Adolescents are simultaneously unique individuals, members of a distinct developmental cohort, and persons who share the universal human situation. Especially when we make general statements about adolescence, we must be cautious not to stereotype an entire generation.

ENCOUNTERS WITH DEATH AND BEREAVEMENT DURING ADOLESCENCE

Deaths and Death Rates Among Adolescents

In modern societies, adolescents encounter death in many ways. In terms of deaths among adolescents, Table 1.1 provides data concerning deaths and death rates in the United States during the year 1992 for three age groups that are relevant to adolescence: individuals who were

TABLE 1.1   Deaths and Death Rates by Age, Race, and Sex: United States, 1992

Age (yr)	All races Both Sexes	Male	Female	White Both Sexes	Male	Female	Black Both Sexes	Male	Female
Deaths									
10–14	4,454	2,849	1,605	3,299	2,093	1,206	982	633	349
15–19	14,411	10,747	3,664	10,308	7,440	2,868	3,583	2,923	660
20–24	20,137	15,460	4,677	14,033	10,696	3,337	5,399	4,246	1,153
Death rates (per 100,000)									
10–14	24.6	30.7	18.2	22.8	28.2	17.2	35.3	44.9	25.4
15–19	84.3	122.4	44.0	75.6	106.0	43.3	135.5	218.4	50.5
20–24	105.7	159.4	50.1	91.0	135.4	44.3	200.7	321.0	84.3

Source: Kochanek & Hudson (1994).

10 to 14, 15 to 19, and 20 to 24 years of age (taken from Kochanek & Hudson, 1994). As is evident, numbers of deaths and death rates both rise rapidly during this 15-year period for all groups: the population as a whole, males and females, whites and blacks. In general, whites experience much larger numbers of deaths, but they also make up a much larger proportion of the population. Blacks have much higher death rates than whites, just as males in every group have significantly higher death rates than females.

From the perspective of the U.S. population as a whole in 1992, which experienced a total of 2,175,613 deaths and an overall death rate of 852.9, the numbers given here for adolescents (a total of just over 39,000 deaths and a death rate of approximately 72 per 100,000 deaths) are relatively modest. In other words, as a group adolescents are relatively healthy individuals whose encounters with death are far more rare than those of infants or adults in our society. Nevertheless, a total of some 39,000 deaths in a single year of individuals who were between 10 and 24 years of age is certainly substantial, and the death of any one individual in this age group will be an occasion of grief for his or her survivors.

Causes of Death Among Adolescents

In terms of causes of death, Table 1.2 provides data for numbers of deaths and death rates according to 10 leading causes of death for all individuals between 15 and 24 years of age who died in the United States in 1992. There are several significant observations that arise from the data in this table. First, the three leading causes of death for these young people are all human induced; none involves diseases or so-called natural causes. That is unique to adolescence; all other eras in the human life span include at least one (usually, two or more) disease-related cause among the three leading causes of death. In the case of American adolescents, more than 77% of all deaths in this group occur from accidents, homicide, and suicide.

The importance of these three leading causes of adolescent deaths can be illustrated in another way. If one adds together the total number of deaths and the death rates for the 4th through the 10th cause of death in this age group in 1992, the totals (4,550 deaths; a death rate of 12.3 per 100,000) do not equal those for suicide, the 3rd leading cause of death for this group. (Note also that if one sought out statistics for teenagers alone, including individuals younger than 15 and excluding

TABLE 1.2 Deaths and Death Rates (per 100,000) for the 10 Leading Causes of Death, 15–24 Years of Age, All Races: United States, 1992

Rank	Both sexes			Male			Female		
	Cause of Death	Number	Rate	Cause of Death	Number	Rate	Cause of Death	Number	Rate
—	All causes	34,548	95.6	All causes	26,207	141.8	All causes	8,341	47.2
1	Accidents & adverse effects	13,662	37.8	Accidents & adverse effects	10,253	55.5	Accidents & adverse effects	3,409	19.3
2	Homicide & legal intervention	8,019	22.2	Homicide & legal intervention	6,891	37.3	Homicide & legal intervention	1,128	6.4
3	Suicide	4,693	13.0	Suicide	4,044	21.9	Malignant neoplasms	725	4.1
4	Malignant neoplasms	1,809	5.0	Malignant neoplasms	1,084	5.9	Suicide	649	3.7
5	Diseases of heart	968	2.7	Diseases of heart	626	3.4	Diseases of heart	342	1.9
6	HIV infection	578	1.6	HIV infection	419	2.3	Congenital anomalies	170	1.0
7	Congenital anomalies	450	1.2	Congenital anomalies	280	1.5	HIV infection	159	0.9
8	Pneumonia & influenza	229	0.6	Pneumonia & influenza	126	0.7	Complications of pregnancy, childbirth, & the puerperium	110	0.6
9	Cerebrovascular diseases	197	0.5	Cerebrovascular diseases	118	0.6	Pneumonia & influenza	103	0.6
10	Chronic obstructive pulmonary diseases & allied conditions	189	0.5	Chronic obstructive pulmonary diseases & allied conditions	106	0.6	Chronic obstructive pulmonary diseases & allied conditions	83	0.5
—	All other causes	3,754	10.4	All other causes	2,260	12.2	All other causes	1,463	8.3

Source: Kochanek & Hudson (1994).

17

those older than 19, accidents, homicide, and suicide would still remain the three leading causes of death, although their relative order of importance would change to accidents, suicide, and homicide.)

Second, human-induced deaths most often occur suddenly and unexpectedly, and they are frequently associated with trauma or violence. More than three quarters of all deaths among adolescents are likely to possess these characteristics. For survivors, these deaths will probably be perceived as not only untimely but shocking in a way that is especially associated with swift and unanticipated disaster.

Third, the largest portion of the total of 13,662 deaths from accidents and adverse effects noted in Table 1.2 is made up of motor vehicle accidents (10,305 deaths versus a total of 3,357 for all other deaths in this category). In other words, in 1992 deaths associated with motor vehicles accounted for more than 75% of all accidental deaths in this age group. Like many deaths arising from homicide and suicide, many accidental deaths (especially many of those associated with motor vehicles) are in principle preventable with adequate education, care, and assistance. For that reason, survivors often find themselves angry at the behaviors that led to such deaths and anguished over what might have been done to forestall such outcomes.

Fourth, it is noteworthy that as early as 1988 HIV infection had advanced to being the sixth leading cause of death among adolescents in our society. That is deeply troubling. For adolescents, HIV infection is mostly associated with sexual behavior, and the use of alcohol and other drugs. It is linked to an epidemic of teenage pregnancies that distinguishes our society from many other contemporary communities, and it also highlights unacceptable levels of sexually transmitted diseases among American teenagers in the last decade of the 20th century. All of this flies in the face of social efforts to teach about the dangers associated with many forms of sexual behavior, automobiles, drugs, guns, and other lethal factors. When many, if not all, deaths among adolescents could be prevented, one must ask why they occur.

By and large, adolescents in America today and in many other developed societies are healthy young persons. Relative to other developmental groups, they enjoy a low death rate. This is because as a group adolescents have survived the hazards of birth, infancy, and early childhood, and they have not lived long enough to experience the degenerative diseases that are more characteristic of later adulthood. But as much as one half to three quarters of all deaths during the adolescent years might be prevented if we could only find effective ways to intervene before death occurs. That suggests just one of the many challenges associated with contemporary adolescence.

Two Variables in Deaths of Adolescents: Gender and Race

In addition to demographic data for adolescents as a whole, one can also consider comparative data by gender and by race. Table 1.2 contrasts deaths and death rates among all adolescent males in our society with those of adolescent females. Disparities are evident. More than three times as many of these young men die as do their female counterparts. Roughly the same rate of difference applies to accidental deaths in this cohort, although the difference is more than 6:1 for deaths associated with either homicide or suicides, and is nearly 3:1 for death associated with HIV infection.

Looking more closely at white versus black deaths (Tables 1.3 and 1.4), it is evident that although there are many more deaths of whites in this age group (24,341 vs. 8,982), blacks die at a far higher rate (168.4 vs. 83.7 per 100,000). Whites are somewhat more likely to die in accidents or from suicide, whereas blacks are far more likely to die from homicide, diseases of the heart, and HIV infection.

White males in this age group are more than three times as likely to die as white females (Table 1.3). Differences in death rates between white males and white females are at ratios of nearly 3:1 for accidents, 3:1 for HIV infection, more than 4:1 for homicide, and almost 6:1 for suicide. By contrast, black males in this age group are slightly less than four times as likely to die as black females (Table 1.4). And differences in death rates between black males and black females are at ratios of less than 2:1 for diseases of the heart, just over 2:1 for HIV infection, almost 4:1 for accidents, almost 8:1 for homicide, and more than 8:1 for suicide.

Deaths of Others Experienced by Adolescents

There are few reliable sources of data concerning the deaths of others that are experienced by adolescents. One study of more than 1,000 high school juniors and seniors disclosed that 90% of those students had experienced the death of someone whom they loved (Ewalt & Perkins, 1979). In nearly 40% of this sample, the loss involved the death of a friend or peer who was roughly their own age. In 20% of the sample, the students had actually witnessed a death. A similar study found that when asked to identify their "most recent major loss," 1,139 college and university students in New York State (average = 19.5 years of age) reported the death of a loved one or a sudden death (number = 328) was the most common loss among a total of 46 different types of losses (LaGrand, 1981, 1986, 1988). Clearly, it is not correct to think that con-

TABLE 1.3 Deaths and Death Rates (per 100,000) for the 10 Leading Causes of Death, 15–24 Years of Age, White Race: United States, 1992

Rank	Both sexes			Male			Female		
	Cause of Death	Number	Rate	Cause of Death	Number	Rate	Cause of Death	Number	Rate
—	All causes	24,341	83.7	All causes	18,136	121.5	All causes	6,205	43.9
1	Accidents & adverse effects	11,450	39.4	Accidents & adverse effects	8,546	57.3	Accidents & adverse effects	2,904	20.5
2	Suicide	3,935	13.5	Suicide	3,392	22.7	Malignant neoplasms	578	4.1
3	Homicide & legal intervention	3,179	10.9	Homicide & legal intervention	2,604	17.5	Homicide & legal intervention	575	4.1
4	Malignant neoplasms	1,467	5.0	Malignant neoplasms	889	6.0	Suicide	543	3.8
5	Diseases of heart	629	2.2	Diseases of heart	401	2.7	Diseases of heart	228	1.6
6	Congenital anomalies	369	1.3	Congenital anomalies	228	1.5	Congenital anomalies	141	1.0
7	HIV infection	290	1.0	HIV infection	225	1.5	Pneumonia & influenza	71	0.5
8	Pneumonia & influenza	164	0.6	Pneumonia & influenza	93	0.6	HIV infection	65	0.5
9	Cerebrovascular diseases	147	0.5	Cerebrovascular diseases	90	0.6	Cerebrovascular diseases	57	0.4
10	Chronic obstructive pulmonary diseases & allied conditions	107	0.4	Chronic obstructive pulmonary diseases & allied conditions	54	0.4	Chronic obstructive pulmonary diseases & allied conditions	53	0.4
—	All other causes	2,604	9.0	All other causes	1,614	10.8	All other causes	990	7.0

Source: Kochanek & Hudson (1994).

20

TABLE 1.4 Deaths and Death Rates (per 100,000) for the 10 Leading Causes of Death, 15–24 Years of Age, Black Race: United States, 1992

Rank	Both sexes — Cause of Death	Number	Rate	Male — Cause of Death	Number	Rate	Female — Cause of Death	Number	Rate
—	All causes	8,982	168.4	All causes	7,169	269.4	All causes	1,813	67.8
1	Homicide & legal intervention	4,625	86.7	Homicide & legal intervention	4,107	154.4	Homicide & legal intervention	518	19.4
2	Accidents & adverse effects	1,684	31.6	Accidents & adverse effects	1,328	49.9	Accidents & adverse effects	356	13.3
3	Suicide	536	10.0	Suicide	478	18.0	Malignant neoplasms	124	4.6
4	Diseases of heart	305	5.7	Diseases of heart	198	7.4	Diseases of heart	107	4.0
5	HIV infection	286	5.4	HIV infection	192	7.2	HIV infection	94	3.5
6	Malignant neoplasms	276	5.2	Malignant neoplasms	152	5.7	Suicide	58	2.2
7	Anemias	86	1.6	Anemias	50	1.9	Complications of pregnancy, childbirth, & the puerperium	53	2.0
8	Chronic obstructive pulmonary diseases & allied conditions	80	1.5	Chronic obstructive pulmonary diseases & allied conditions	50	1.9	Anemias	36	1.3
9	Congenital anomalies	70	1.3	Congenital anomalies	44	1.7	Chronic obstructive pulmonary diseases & allied conditions	30	1.1
10	Pneumonia & influenza	57	1.1	Pneumonia & influenza	29	1.1	Pneumonia & influenza	28	1.0
—	All other causes	977	18.3	All other causes	541	20.3	All other causes	409	15.3

Source: Kochanek & Hudson (1994).

temporary adolescents have no experience with death and bereavement.

In fact, adolescents do encounter deaths involving: grandparents and parents; neighbors, teachers, and other adults; siblings and friends; pets and other animals; celebrities and cultural heroes with whom they identify; and even in some cases their own children. Indeed, adolescence may be the first time in the history of the human life span in which an individual can experience the full range of possible deaths including members of older, same, and younger generations, along with one's own offspring (Ewalt & Perkins, 1979). In addition, adolescents report that they have encountered a wide variety of loss-related experiences that do not involve death, such as the ending of love relationships or friendships (LaGrand, 1981, 1986, 1988).

Many of these experiences with death and loss may have particular significance for an adolescent and his or her developmental work. For example, early adolescents who are striving to achieve emotional emancipation from parents may experience complications and conflict in those efforts if a parent (or sometimes a grandparent who is their surrogate parent) should suddenly die. Has such an adolescent been abandoned by the death of the older adult? Can one attain a feeling of safety in such circumstances?

Similarly, middle adolescents who are seeking to achieve competency, mastery, and control at a time when they enjoy some sense of autonomy may experience a substantial degree of jeopardy to their newfound independence if a member of their own generation should die. The great likelihood that the death of another adolescent will be sudden, unexpected, traumatic, and often violent may enhance the threat to the surviving adolescent's own prospects and security. Adolescents who have carried over from childhood the "tattered cloak of immortality" (Gordon, 1986) or who maintain a "personal fable" (Elkind, 1967) of invulnerability may be shaken when they realize that death can befall a person of their own age and similar circumstances.

Finally, late adolescents who are working to reestablish intimacy and commitment with those who are significant in their lives may feel thwarted and frustrated when they encounter the death of a person of a younger generation (e.g., a younger brother, sister, friend, or their own infant child). Dedicating themselves to a relationship with a person of this sort and achieving the kinds of closeness that it can involve are stymied when the other person in the relationship dies. Death rebuffs the older adolescent's efforts to reach out to the other in a painful and disempowering way.

We can conclude from this that adolescent grief responses and mourning processes are likely to conform to the distinctive developmental characteristics of adolescence and its subperiods. If so, adolescent grief responses and mourning processes may not exactly parallel those of adults. For example, it has been reported that although adolescent mourning may involve grieving that comes and goes, the overall process may extend over a long period (Hogan & DeSantis, 1992). In other words, adolescent mourning is paradoxically both continuous and intermittent (Raphael, 1983).

Perhaps it is most important to appreciate that mourning in adolescence involves situational challenges and tasks that overlay normative life transitions and developmental tasks. Especially in adolescence, typical developmental tasks of establishing emotional separation, achieving competency or mastery, and developing intimacy (Fleming & Adolph, 1986) echo in significant ways processes in normal adolescent mourning, which Sugar (1968) has described as involving protest/ searching, disorganization, and reorganization. This means that those who wish to assist grieving adolescents may be challenged to distinguish that which is associated with an individual adolescent's developmental work and that which is directly related to his or her experiences of loss (Garber, 1983).

CONCLUSION

It has been said that "death is a very remote event for most young people" (Jonah, 1986, p. 268). To the degree that this is true, perhaps it is because many adolescents may simply not have had enough salient experiences with living to perceive the personal dangers involved in behaviors that are open to serious consequences or that may actually put life at risk. In addition, adolescents may perceive value in acting in ways that reject adult and societal authority, attract applause from peers, or express frustrations and other strong feelings. Enriched experience may help adolescents to appreciate how and why some behaviors are potentially hazardous; greater maturity may enable individuals to find safer ways of coping with life and its challenges.

Alexander & Adlerstein (1958) suggested that death has "a greater emotional significance for people with less stable ego self-pictures" (p. 175). If so, it would seem that death-related threats would have greatest personal significance at times of significant transitions in the life span. During adolescence, critical points would appear to involve moments of decreased ego stability and self-confidence. Enhancement of an individual's sense of personal confidence and equilibrium, together with his or her level of maturity, may result in an apparently paradoxical combination of "greater sophistication and acknowledgement of the inevitability of death as well as . . . enjoyment of life and altruistic concerns" (Raphael, 1983, p. 147).

Thus, adults who wish to assist adolescents might do well to help them look beyond the immediate moment and learn lessons from experiences that they may not yet have had. The key issue is not just to acknowledge in an abstract and impersonal way some intellectual truths about death, but to develop these into a concrete, personal appreciation of the implications of death for life and living. This task asks adolescents not to abandon, but to enrich, the intensity of their lived experience. It suggests that they seek ways to give personal reference and meaning to impersonal facts and abstract concepts about death.

2

Ambiguity in Adolescent Understandings of Death

Lloyd D. Noppe and Illene C. Noppe

People of all ages have ambivalent feelings about the concept of death, but adolescents may be particularly vulnerable to conflicting tensions that distinguish their interpretations of death from those of adults. The traditional definition of a mature conception of death—universality, nonfunctionality, and irreversibility—has been thought to develop at the threshold of adolescence (Koocher, 1973; Speece & Brent, 1984; Toews, Martin, & Prosen, 1985). It is our contention that although such qualities may be attributed to adolescent understandings of death, there are certain tensions experienced by adolescents that compromise their truly mature grasp of, and ability to cope with, a more complete and mature approach to this complex phenomenon (Noppe & Noppe, 1991).

Of course, adolescents recognize that death can and will happen to everyone (universality); however, their high-risk activities often suggest that they operate according to the principle of "it can't happen to me." Clearly, there is a conflict between what many adolescents, in a rational moment, might sensibly perceive to be foolish behaviors, yet evidently choose to engage in despite the apparent risks. Jonah (1986) has described this problem as an imbalance between risk perception and utility. Perhaps adolescent analyses of personal mortality are clouded by stronger needs to express independence from adults, deal actively with various frustrations, or seek acceptance from peers (Corr, 1995).

Similarly, adolescents who can explain the physical cessation of life (nonfunctionality) and the implausibility of undoing the process of

25

death (irreversibility) may act as if these are not serious concerns. Fascination with various attractive alternatives to a permanent and total ending of life—an antimatter universe, an afterlife, reincarnation, and so forth—is certainly not exclusive to adolescents. However, adolescents may be so beguiled by these spiritual and intriguing possibilities that offer another world of the dead-existing parallel to the world of the living that they fail to contemplate the significance of death for bereaved survivors (Noppe & Noppe, 1991). Such notions only begin to illustrate how a teenager's understanding of death can be distinguished from more mature concepts.

This chapter provides several examples that indicate how a mature concept of death is not typically present among adolescents. The themes of the adolescent research literature are often organized into categories of biological, cognitive, social, and emotional development. A variety of ambiguities highlights these characteristic attributes of adolescent understandings of death. There are strong *biological* tensions between physical and sexual maturation, which also herald inevitable decline. A rich, *cognitive* explosion is found in young, logical minds that must also contemplate their own demise. *Social* conflicts among friends, between adults and peers, and among competing or diverse cultural pressures may introduce an increased sense of isolation. An *emotional* "roller coaster" of reworking attachment relationships, and the emerging sense of personal identity, contrasts with feelings of anxiety, depression, and the loss of self. The chapter concludes with considerations designed to assist parents, teachers, and other adults in helping to reduce adolescent ambiguities about death.

RISKING OF THE BODY UNNECESSARILY

Adolescence ought to be a time to celebrate the richness of biological development. Elements of physical growth and health stand in sharp contrast to considerations of death. Never again during the life span will the death rate be lower than it is during the adolescent years (Kochanek & Hudson, 1994), and the causes of death for teenagers are overwhelmingly unnatural, tragic, human-induced aberrations.

Should contemplating the finality of death really be expected to compete with the tremendous growth of height and weight during adolescence, the peak of strength and stamina, the onset of reproductive capacity, and the physical skills that depend on increased coordination and balance? The vibrancy of these biological transformations infuses adolescents with ecstasy, optimism, and joy. They permit a reveling in physical sensations and accomplishments that appear to be exactly the opposite of death. In fact, there has been a gradual decline in adolescent deaths attributable to natural causes, such as cancer and heart disease. Over the past 50 years, however, this decrease has been partly offset by rising mortality rates from accidents, homicide, and suicide (National Research Council, 1993).

Because adolescents have so much to live for and enjoy, it is curious that we have witnessed an increase in unnatural adolescent deaths. Therefore, we must attempt to discern the sources of tension and conflict that, consciously or unconsciously, underlie obvious physical risks so often acted out. Koocher and his colleagues (1976) have suggested that adolescents are increasingly aware of their inevitable biological decline. With each passing day of life, one does approach death more closely. The affirmation of life and physical development simultaneously leading toward death might serve to heighten anxiety. Aging parents and grandparents may provide a graphic image of the adolescent's physical future—a disturbing contradiction between feeling so alive yet knowing that one will cease even to exist some day (Noppe & Noppe, 1991).

Ambivalence about life and death may be represented by coping with the conflict through attempts to "cheat" death. Various high-risk outlets for adolescents include reckless driving (possibly under the influence of alcohol or other drugs), chemical abuse of the body, daredevil stunts (such as diving off a high cliff), and other forms of athletic endurance beyond safe physical limits. These biological risks allow adolescents to channel their energies from succumbing to the worries aroused by their physical maturation into death-defying behaviors. The thrill of victory in facing down their own mortality appears to be worth the unlikely potential failure, especially when combined with any peer approval that may accompany these contemporary rites of passage (Hankoff, 1975). In tempting fate with actions that seem to beg for death, these adolescents are also testing the limits of life (Gordon, 1986).

Gans (1990) pointed out that "the majority of adolescents engage in some risk-taking behavior but do not experience tragic consequences" (p. 17). Many adolescents compensate for their risky actions with a diversity of health-promoting behaviors, too; however, much luck and many close calls enable relatively low death rates during this period to continue dropping. In contrast, favorable attitudes toward risk taking seem to be common among adolescents. A well-known national survey, for example, reported that 35% of adolescents enjoyed doing things that were somewhat dangerous, and 45% indicated that they liked to test themselves by doing something a bit risky (Bachman, Johnston, & O'Malley, 1986).

Many adolescents do not take excessive physical risks or have done so only on rare occasions. This does not mean that they do not contemplate, and even yearn to attempt, acting out dangerous and careless activities. It is the tension between security, rationality, and morality versus excitement, impulsivity, and risk that may be the foundation for anxiety about death. Adolescents who act out these behaviors may feel under increased levels of stress compared with adolescents who merely think about engaging in risky activities. Whether or not a particular adolescent actually experiences a physical danger or simply imagines what it would feel like, he or she can flirt with the biological borderline between life and death.

The prevalence of eating disorders among adolescents—females especially—may reflect similar ambiguities about life (Bensinger & Natenshon, 1991). On the one hand, an eating disorder can lead to a fatal conclusion; conversely, physical control represented by anorexic or bulimic behavior, as well as the social reinforcement for maintaining a thin appearance, compensates for the threat of death. Teenagers with eating disorders may not always be aware of the deadly game they are playing (a slow form of suicide), but syndromes like these divert attention from other conflicts that adolescents may be feeling. Thus, difficulties in relationships with parents, challenges in school, or sexual pressures from peers and society, can be masked by binge eating, restrictive dieting, or compulsive exercise.

Another possible link between bodily changes and adolescent death conceptions is the loss of innocence that accompanies sexual development. Pubertal achievement may provoke anxiety regarding sexual expectations to perform in a more advanced fashion than an adolescent is ready to deal with at the time (Morrison, Starks, Hyundman, & Ronzio, 1980). Although few adolescents are apt to express overt concern over their emerging sexual status, they may long for the simpler days of childhood when they were not required to make decisions about behaviors that are fraught with social, emotional, and physical risks (Feinstein, 1981). Certainly, with increased sexual activity, adolescents are forced to ponder, at least to some extent, the possibility of having to face pregnancy, abortion, parenthood, or the contraction of sexually transmitted diseases. The loss, or "death," of prepubertal asexuality may raise discomfort and anxiety that parallels and is intertwined with the physical changes that eventually lead to actual death (Ariès, 1981).

The crisis resulting from the HIV/AIDS epidemic presents an instructive window for examining adolescent death conceptions. It might be expected that levels of sexual activity among adolescents would decrease because of fears of contracting AIDS. However, there is no compelling evidence to suggest that adolescents are less likely to engage in sexual intercourse now than they were 10 or 15 years ago. The good news is that a significantly higher percentage of sexually active adolescents have been using condoms in recent years (National Research Council, 1993). Nevertheless, despite some improvements in contraceptive practices, many adolescents continue to engage in unsafe sexual activities, and these behaviors are now occurring at even younger ages than before. Neither the availability of contraceptives, the proliferation of educational information programs, nor threats of sexually transmitted diseases appear to have sufficed to inhibit adolescent sexual behaviors.

Biological contradictions and ambiguities, as in the realm of sexuality, are evident among the many drug and alcohol abusers who risk their health or life to achieve chemical stimulation. Greater adolescent awareness of the potential for harm from various legal and illegal substances has been reflected in lower rates of drunken driving, smaller percentages of adolescents using illicit drugs, and less daily cigarette smoking (especially among male adolescents). In contrast to those positive signs, there has also been an increase in binge drinking (for a study of a representative, national sample of college students that defines "binge drinking" as five or more drinks in a row for men, or four or more drinks in a row for women, see Wechsler, Davenport, Dowdall, Moeykens, & Castillo, 1994), higher rates of inhalant usage, and more serious substance use at younger ages. These statistical disparities seem to indicate that many adolescents are confused about their possible encounters with death.

RATIONALITY AND ROMANTICISM

A fascinating historical analysis of loss and grief (Stroebe, Gergen, Gergen, & Stroebe, 1992) suggested that "assumptions of health and adjustment are by-products of cultural and historical processes" (p. 1211). The authors distinguished between romanticist, modernist, and postmodernist approaches to death in Western societies. In the 19th century, the romanticist view—emphasizing spirituality, eternal love, and the centrality of committed friendships—implied "holding on" to grief, public acknowledgment of a "broken heart," maintenance of "relations" with the departed, and expectations of ultimate reunion.

This view was replaced in the 20th century by modernist attitudes of rationality, efficiency, and functionality. "When applied to grief, this view suggests that people need to recover from their state of intense emotionality and return to normal functioning and effectiveness as quickly and efficiently as possible" (Stroebe et al., 1992, p. 1206). Thus, "breaking the bonds" with the past and acquiring a new identity, perhaps with the assistance of counseling or therapy, places a definitive limit on the bereavement process.

Although Stroebe and her colleagues (1992) did not discuss adolescent conceptions of death, they indicated that we are making a difficult transition to a postmodernist culture in which a multiplicity of acceptable alternative perspectives on death are embedded within both individual and cultural contexts. In particular, they pointed out the strains of attempting to adhere to a strict modernist view of loss and grieving. Adolescents—searching for their own initial identity, experiencing their first freely chosen love relationships, and adjusting to the intensity of their spiritual growth—must have an especially strong attachment to romanticist notions of death.

However, teenagers are simultaneously coping with the intellectual abilities that Piaget (1972) described as the onset of formal thought. Acquiring the logic of formal operations presents adolescents with a greater understanding of life's many possibilities. The increasing sophistication of an adolescent's reasoning power necessarily implies thinking about death as well as about life. Most adolescents begin to question their childhood ideas regarding religion, values, the future, relationships, and similar issues. As they reflect on what they have been taught, what they have read, and what they have observed in adult behavior, and what all of this means, teens are forced to confront the clash of life and death.

Despite cognitive advances permitted by formal thought, including the flexibility to consider various options for their lives, adolescents typically have trouble synthesizing contradictory perspectives in a mature form of relativistic thinking (Perry, 1970). Should they try to deny the romanticist approach to death and be stoic, unemotional, and practical? Can they accept the modernist view even though the popular culture extols heroic death and grief? Without a fully constructed sense of identity and without an ability to coordinate the discrepant values modeled in this society, is it any wonder that adolescents have a confused understanding of death?

Although a rational orientation toward the future seems to be a positive step for adolescents to take—planning ahead, setting goals, working out long-term strategies for personal growth—lurking in the background is the one aspect of the future that is the only certainty (Noppe & Noppe, 1991). Death may not easily be accepted by adolescents as the logical conclusion to life, but it must be faced nonetheless. Bearing this in mind, it is not so paradoxical that at a time when they can more fully contemplate the future, adolescents may withdraw into immersion in a vivid present (Kastenbaum, 1959) or try to manipulate their sense of time through the use of alcohol and drugs (Hankoff, 1975). Taking part in risky activities may be an effective strategy for distracting adolescents from coping with the realities of life and death.

Contemplating one's own death, as a teenager, may be an almost incomprehensible abstraction. Though adolescents may try to banish such thoughts to the extent possible, there is no perpetually avoiding the fact that life does end. Rarely do adolescents have to prepare for their own deaths, yet they may witness or be aware of others who do so. For example, making a will, purchasing a cemetery plot, selecting a casket, or arranging other specific funeral details may strike adolescents as disturbing, despite an enjoyment in playing with death phenomena in the abstract.

In ascertaining a concrete future for themselves, adolescents are dealing with a major challenge. On the one hand, there is the promise of happiness and success. This could include a sexual and marital partner, one of many potential careers, stimulating and satisfying friendships, giving birth to and raising children, cultivating new hobbies and skills, involvement in a community, traveling to distant places, and a host of other lively activities. Conversely, adolescents must also consider possible negative aspects of their futures. That is, they may face the death of loved ones, the destruction of the environment, the ending of friendships, disappointment or failure on the job, economic difficulties, health problems, and a variety of other unpredictable forms of loss (Raundalen & Finney, 1986).

Some researchers have voiced concern that the threat of nuclear war may be devastating to the well-being of adolescents (e.g., Austin & Mack, 1986; Zuckerman & Beardslee, 1986), although Diamond and Bachman (1986) found that such concerns were coupled with the belief that humans will survive, as they always do. This is a seemingly uncontrollable situation, similar to the probability of the earth being struck by a comet or an asteroid, that may become more likely with the recent rise of international terrorism. Thus, tension may be created by the juxtaposition of both optimistic and pessimistic components of the future (Cottle, 1972).

According to Elkind's (1978) notion of the "personal fable," adolescents become so wrapped up in their own thoughts and their own destiny that they fail to recognize just how ordinary and human they really are. This exaggerated preoccupation with their own lives may contribute to the conviction that they are beyond death and that risky behavior is not a reality for them (e.g., "My car will not crash"; "I cannot get AIDS"; "Smoking crack cannot harm me"; or "Getting pregnant happens to other girls"). Ignoring harsher versions of reality by flaunting adolescent egocentrism leads to irrational behavior, such as driving without seat belts or under the influence of alcohol or drugs, failing to use contraceptive devices to protect against pregnancy and sexually transmitted diseases, and not attending to other warning signs of danger that may herald an "impossible" death (Noppe & Noppe, 1991).

As Corr (1995) reminded us, although adolescents are capable of thinking about death in a mature fashion, they do not necessarily or frequently do so. Furthermore, having the intellectual capacities to conduct formal operations with concepts does not guarantee that an individual would ascribe to the belief that death is an irreversible state. An interesting research project that remains undone would be to analyze the attitudes about death exhibited by adolescents who have experienced loss and grief in comparison with their nonbereaved peers. Furthermore, comparisons between the extent of engagement in high-risk behaviors by these two groups could be equally revealing. Constructing a complete model of adolescent death cognition will require consideration of logical development and regression, cultural and historical contexts, and the social and emotional experiences of individual adolescents.

SOCIAL LIFE AND DEATH

Adolescents' perceptions of death are profoundly affected by the social context of their development. That is, their increased need for autonomy and self-definition occurs against a backdrop of the need for community. In Maslow's theory of human motivation (Maslow, 1970), the needs of belonging, or affiliation, are located at the midpoint in a hierarchy of needs. Relationships with others are significant to psychological and physical well-being throughout the life span. Interactions with parents, peers, and the larger community take on a new dimension that may occupy a large sector of an adolescent's life space. Although Maslow presented the basic drives as primary, when they are satisfied such needs recede in importance for all human beings; thus, the social needs of adolescents in our society may sometimes seem to take primacy over such basic necessities as food and drink.

The tension, then, that exists for adolescents involves creating a "social life" and avoiding a "social death." In the thanatological literature, social death (as distinct from biological or clinical death), involves the point at which an individual is treated as if he or she were dead, even though he or she may still be alive (Sweeting & Gilhooly, 1992). Such social death may be self-perceived ("I am as good as dead") or other perceived ("My friends or family treat me as if I were dead"). To be a "person" is, to a large extent, to be a person to others. When one is not treated as a living, breathing person by others, one becomes alienated and socially dead. In Sweeting & Gilhooly's analysis, modern Western societies often treat people as socially dead before their clinical death. This may happen when one is institutionalized in a mental hospital or a nursing home. The end result is that one is dehumanized and *depersonalized*. In contrast, many traditional societies do not consider a person dead until some sort of ritual formally acknowledges this person as dead in the eyes of the community (a process that may occur significantly later than the biological death).

In contrast to death in the biological sense, social death may be a transient phenomenon. Yet, social death can lead to much anguish and despair. Given the increasing significance of the peer group, is it no wonder that adolescents do so much to avoid social death amongst their peers? The consequence of unsuccessful relations with other people is that adolescents may have a deep sense of loneliness or alienation (Brennan & Auslander, 1979; Ostrov & Offer, 1978). The continual scrutiny of the peer group, and its concomitant demands for conformity often are a source of anxiety, but isolation from other adolescents (either self-imposed or resulting from rejection) can be even more devastating (Moore & Schultz, 1983). Even a series of small interpersonal difficulties of the type usually experienced by all adolescents can be felt as painful, "little deaths." It is extremely important to adolescents to develop a social life. Social death, either self- or other perceived, is always a risk. It presents adolescents with conflicting and scary situations ("I could have died when he saw me with my mother at the mall").

Adolescents' perceptions of death are also shaped by the broader social context of the school community. Herein, again, lie sources of ambiguities and growth-promoting tensions. First of all, the normative transitions from elementary to middle school, and then on to high school, coincide with so many other life-enhancing (and death-potentiating) experiences. The social field changes from one classroom with one teacher to the entire school. In the myriad different classes and extracurricular activities, adolescents have opportunities to interact with a greater variety of people than ever before, explore new topics and disciplines, and develop further awareness of the possibilities of the world and the future. The social context of the school provides powerful images of what adolescents' lives will be like beyond the context of the family.

Although social expectations are greatly increased during adolescence, feelings of self-efficacy can result from owning up to demands for autonomy and maturity. Yet this is also a time when adolescent idealism can be tempered by the limits of individual control and power. How much can we change the world to make it a better place? How can we stop the tidal wave of famine, disease, and violence, leading to premature death in so many inner cities and so many parts of the Third World? Certainly children are aware of death, but their self-involved lives often insulate them from many contemporary issues of death. By contrast, in many contemporary adolescent classrooms and organizations, heated discussions of abortion, the death penalty, and physician-assisted suicide are common. In addition, the ripple effects of peers' deaths are felt deeply and greatly. An entire school can go into mourning, as when high school students in Brooklyn, New York, went into shock and grief when five of their classmates died in an amusement park fire (Podell, 1989). Thus, life and death may become a dialectical theme whose synthesis may not be achieved until later on in adulthood.

Any awareness of death is profoundly influenced by cultural context. Thanatologists have become increasingly aware of the diversity of belief systems and practices that affect the construction of death concepts (Irish, 1993; Kastenbaum, 1992). Culture shapes beliefs about the nature of and transition to adolescence as well as the causes of death and the possibility or nature of an afterlife. Culture also determines procedures for body disposition and funeral rites, and affects the patterning of grief and roles of the bereaved (Ross, 1981). For example, traditional Hmongs (a recent immigrant group from Southeast Asia) believe that the spiritual world coexists with the physical world (Bliatout, 1993); many Islamic groups maintain a strong belief in the afterlife as influential on present existence (Gilanshah, 1993). For many, understanding death and coping with the aftermath of a significant other are mediated by cultural expectations and the support of one's own ethnic group (Counts & Counts, 1991). Because social support is such a significant factor in how grief is handled (Vachon & Stylianos, 1988), it is not surprising that bereavement is a time when most people conform to the expectations and behaviors of the group. These are, in fact, the behaviors that are most resistant to cultural change (Kalish, 1980).

Correspondingly, the cultural milieu has also been emphasized in current work on adolescent development (Allison & Takei, 1993;

Schlegel & Barry, 1991). The cultural context of adolescents and their families can provide a rich source of support for identity development, strength against peer pressures that could lead to failure, and a needed sense of belonging. Yet, cultural variations outside of mainstream America can also work against the need for autonomy and "fitting in" that is so important to adolescents (Allison & Takei, 1993). Once again, conflicts between social life and death may emerge.

Little has been said about how ethnic diversity affects an adolescent's understanding of death, and his or her participation in its rituals. For example, Chinese Americans have been noted to grieve privately (Halporn, 1992). How would this cultural practice relate to the coping of adolescent Chinese Americans, when it has been noted that adolescents in general tend to keep their grief private (Raphael, 1983)? If cultural practices associated with death are the most resistive to change, how does an adolescent with high needs for assimilation handle participation in these rituals? Do such rituals (e.g., burning gold paper, wailing, or chanting all evening), which may strike an assimilated teenager as highly stylized and "odd," become fraught with hypocrisy and meaninglessness? Conversely, some adolescents may be fortunate to find solace within their cultural group, which may not be available to their peers. Native-American, Hispanic-American, and African-American adolescents who follow traditional practices may have the support of their communities in helping them cope with their grief. In death, as in life, an adolescent's need to balance individuality and community is significant.

Interactions with other people, especially if they are positive, are one of the clearest indications of being alive. Flowering of adolescent social relationships, and the possibilities of social death, need to be considered within the context of peers, school, and the broader culture surrounding an adolescent.

BREAKING OF THE BONDS

A major source of tension in an adolescent's interpretation of death arises from the contemplation of death and the sense of loss that is inherent in the otherwise life-affirming task of identity formation. During childhood, one's identity is largely defined by one's family. Achieving individuation and autonomy is a major developmental task of the adolescent years involving cognitive, social, and affective dimensions (Harter, 1990). The process of adolescent identity development involves a reformulation of the parent-child attachment relationship begun in infancy. Separation from one's parents is a necessary component of the process, but it is a loss that may be construed by an adolescent as a form of death (Noppe & Noppe, 1991). Perhaps it is no coincidence that both adolescence and bereavement are viewed as psychosocial transitions (Parkes, 1988).

According to Bowlby (1980a), the psychological processes involved in grieving are initiated by separation and loss of the attachment figure. The sense of security that results from proximity to the attachment figure typically is relinquished during adolescence (Weiss, 1988). In a sense, adolescence represents a period of mourning for the loss of that parent-child attachment relationship (Bowlby, 1980a). (Ironically, parents are not "motivated" to relinquish such old attachment bonds to their children, and they, too, are mourning the loss.) For adolescents, coping with this grief involves a remapping of the parent-child attachment relationship onto one's peers (Holmes, 1993). This process is facilitated by a model of the self and significant others as reliable, lovable, and trustworthy—a secure, internal, working model (Bretherton, 1987). So, too, in grief, is the need to revise one's model of the world (Parkes, 1988). And, as with many forms of grief, the testing of an adolescent's internal working model of relationships via disengagement from the original figures of attachment can be accompanied by feelings of anger, as if one's parent's are deliberately not allowing the adolescent to be himself or herself.

> I can be my true self with my close friends. I can't be my real self with my parents. They don't understand me. What do they know about what it's like to be a teenager? They treat me like I'm still a kid. (Quote taken from a 15-year-old's self-description, as cited by Harter, 1990, pp. 352–353)

Attachment figures provide a secure base from which to explore the world. It is important to recognize that these parent-child attachments are not relinquished during adolescence. Successful negotiation of the affective ups and downs associated with the developmental transitions of adolescence is predicated on supportive and positive relationships between adolescents and their parents (Papini & Roggman, 1992). However, there is a qualitative change in the adolescent's perspective on these relationships. Transference of attachment relationships to the peer group provides a sense of security, particularly if the rules of conformity are not transgressed. But the peers of childhood and adolescence often can be fickle. In childhood, solace may be taken in the "holding environment" of the parents and the new friendships that occur the very next day. For adolescents, the loss of intimacy found in their friendships can trigger profound sadness and a sense of loss that resembles bereavement and grief.

It may be difficult to break or restructure these bonds, reflecting a more romantic notion that the significance of the relationship is lost if one "gets over it" and moves on to forge new relationships (Stroebe et al., 1992). Validation of one's sense of self, then, may involve holding on to these bonds, because to dissolve them would not only imply that the relationship was superficial but also one's own sense of self worth (Stroebe et al., 1992). Is there anything more painful and sad than the loss of a teenager's first love or rejection by one's best friend? In the case of loss through death, the depth of despair and feelings of abandonment may be much greater than adults are willing to acknowledge (Meshot & Leitner, 1993; Podell, 1989; Raphael, 1983).

An implicit assumption held by most adults is that their core self remains intact even when important others die—this aspect of death understanding is embedded within the modernist practices of the 20th century (Stroebe et al., 1992). For adolescents, however, contemplation of death involves the threat of losing a self that is intimately tied in with the other, a self that is in an active process of creation. When an adolescent grieves, the extent of identification with the deceased is significantly greater than what has been observed in adults (Meshot & Leitner, 1993). When an adolescent experiences the actual or threatened loss of a peer, his or her sense of romanticism and its spirituality involves as much a holding onto the self as it is a holding onto one's peer. Not being quite whole yet, the death and life of one's self and one's true love represent common themes in adolescent poetry and books. In music, the Romeo and Juliet syndrome is ever available on the airwaves; content analysis of the top-40 music from the 1950s to the present reveals that songs with death-related themes were the most popular (Plopper & Ness, 1993).

Identity development involves creating an anchor for one's self in the life cycle. According to Erikson (1968), adolescents must explore who they are within the context of their personal pasts, the present, and their anticipated futures. Embedded within this task are feelings of intensely being alive (Waterman, 1992). During adolescence, the concept of self is broadened so as to include a range of possible selves, some of which are ideal selves of what we would like to become, whereas others may be dreaded possible selves, such as the "alone self" or the "incompetent self" (Markus & Nurius, 1986). Such feared possible selves often reflect the unrealized potential that life may be disappointing (Cross & Markus, 1991). Thus, the "dead self" also becomes part of this landscape of possibility, and in the attempt to forge a unified identity, adolescents must reconcile their new identities with the prospect of nonexistence (Noppe & Noppe, 1991). The "unique self" also is another possibility, but it also comes with the price tag of loneliness and the loss of a direct connection to others (Harter, 1990).

These tensions between attachment, separation, and loss, identity, and death of self are uncovered in both empirical research and theoretical writings on adolescence. In general, self-esteem and ego identity have been found to be important sources of strength in adolescent coping and the management of stress resulting from loss (Harter, 1990; Hauser & Bowlds, 1990). For example, Sterling and Van Horn (1989) found that identity development is related to death anxiety. High school and college students who have higher self-esteem also have lower scores on scales of anxiety and fear of death (Davis, Bremer, Anderson, & Tramill, 1983; Neimeyer & Chapman, 1980).

We have, thus far, identified several sources of ambiguities that may affect adolescents' understandings of death and serve as reasons why their concepts are not as mature as those of most adults. One other important dimension needs to be considered—gender. Men and women experience death differently, as seen in research on responses to bereavement (Glick, Weiss, & Parkes, 1974; Parkes & Weiss, 1983), death anxiety (Dattel & Neimeyer, 1990), and willingness to think and speak about death (Da Silva & Schork, 1984). Yet, little has been written about how gender affects the development of death concepts during childhood and adolescence. Kastenbaum (1992) suggested that the roots of these gender differences come from early socialization within the family. Differences in the timing of puberty may also influence how and when male and female adolescents actively contemplate death. We suggest that it is during adolescence that responses to death diverge by gender and that these differences are linked to identity development.

Within the context of our culture, the desired outcome of identity development is an autonomous, independent persona. Yet, the evidence suggests that the pathways for development differ for male and female adolescents (Cosse, 1992). Erikson's (1968) concept of identity and later work on identity statuses (Marcia, 1987) seem to fit best with male adolescent development. An alternative description of female adolescent development has been provided by the work of Carol Gilligan and her colleagues (Brown & Gilligan, 1990; Gilligan, Lyons, & Hanmer, 1990). Relying on the life stories of girls and women who were between 6 and 18 years of age, Gilligan learned that girls are highly attuned to the rhythms and complexities of relationships, define themselves within the context of these relationships, and judge themselves in terms of their ability to care and maintain a sense of connection to others. What is the impact of these gender-related differences in identity and attachment on an adolescent's understanding of death? In the context of their need for connection, do adolescent girls find the threat of death to be a greater source of anxiety than do adolescent boys? Or is the threat of death with its associated loneliness and our culture's idealization of male autonomy and separation all tied together for the adolescent male?

Perhaps exploration of the potential isolation by death is part of the identity process for the adolescent male—in death, as in life, you are alone. For adolescent girls, however, the possibility of death may be perceived as a testing of one's ability to care for others as well as how one's self enters into a network of social support. Meshot and Leitner (1993) found that among a group of adolescents who lost their parents at around age 15, girls tended to identify more strongly with their deceased parent than boys, and they manifested stronger reactions of grief. These researchers suggested that unresolved grief may be more common for female than for male adolescents, although it is equally plausible that these findings reflect gender differences in how the context of relationships affects grief patterns.

In the affective domain, attachment relationships, self-concept development, romanticism, identity, and gender role development interact with adolescents' death concepts in significant ways. It is imperative that the complex dynamics of these factors be considered, not only in terms of normative issues in adolescent development, but also in terms of life-threatening situations involving depression, suicide, and death through violent means.

CONCLUSION

Parents, educators, and mental health professionals who work with adolescents need to recognize that their adult-like stance with respect to death is mediated by tensions that are unique to this period of life. It is not appropriate to expect the same intellectual or emotional responses to death from a 15-year-old as from a 50-year-old.

Previously, we (Noppe & Noppe, 1991) considered how development in the biological, cognitive, social, and affective domains present "dialectical dilemmas" for adolescents in coming to terms with an understanding of death. Merely to note that adolescents are aware of death's finality, universality, and irreversibility is not sufficient. Such "facts" are tempered by the need to synthesize reaching the apex of one's biological development with its ultimate decline, awareness of abstract logic and future potential with deadly realities, the need for peer interaction with the fear of loneliness and isolation, and development of an emerging identity with the fear of losing the self.

In this chapter, we have attempted to elaborate these dialectical themes further. The joy of metamorphosis into an adult may be tested with attempts to cheat death through risk-taking and health-compromising behaviors. The ability to perform logical, abstract analyses can be contradicted by a need for romantic and irrational, spiritualistic beliefs. On a social level, the need for autonomy is jeopardized by the need for validation through one's peers, the burdens of conformity and assimilation, and fear of social rejection (death). In the affective domain, adolescents frequently engage in a process of making and remaking the self, a process that involves as much undoing (as in former attachment relationships) as doing.

We have considered the preceding to be dialectical themes, as opposed to conflicts, because we take the optimistic view that syntheses in these realms can be achieved. The timing of such syntheses is a unique developmental issue. For adolescents, the dialectics of life and death are sources of ambiguities; they are one of many puzzlements that define this stage of life and serve to make adolescent understandings of death different from those of most adults. That is not to say that every adult has it all figured out, a factor frequently noted in descriptions of goals for death education (Feifel, 1990). An adult's understanding of death can easily resemble that of an adolescent's, even a child's! Yet, the ability to overcome death dialectics beyond knowledge of universality, finality, and irreversibility is part of the road map that comes with the wisdom of experience, the acceptance of contradiction and synthesis into more embracing wholes, and an understanding of how reality coexists with ideal constructions of life (Rybash, Hoyer, & Roodin, 1986).

Increasing awareness of the need for thanatological education for adolescents does not diminish the significance of opportunities that are not formally planned. Instead, lessons on life and death are found in the "teachable moments" of disasters in the news, deaths of significant others, or late-night conversations with teenagers when they should be studying for a midterm examination. Adults who work with adolescents need to recognize that adolescents do, and do not, sound like adults when they ponder death-related issues. Differences need to be understood and respected, and an appropriate balance must be achieved between the need of adolescents for privacy and separation from adults, and their need to talk openly and maintain a foothold on the secure base that an adult can provide. Use of peer groups for discussion and support can serve as effective bridges for adults who are dealing with adolescents on death-related issues.

Cutting across the dialectical themes involved in an adolescent's understanding of death are such individual difference factors as gender, race, ethnicity, and past grief experiences. Although the culture of adolescence may be a great leveler, death may heighten the differential responses of males and females, traditional and assimilated teenagers, and those who have already grieved deeply in their tender years. Adults must not be too quick to judge responses to death-related issues in a negative way. Teens who do not openly grieve may be private—not cold-hearted—and girls who display intense identification with a deceased significant other may be expressing their own identities within the context of their relationships—not unresolved grief.

Feifel (1990) wisely acknowledged that "acceptance of personal mortality is one of the foremost entryways to self-knowledge" (p. 541). The developmental tasks of adolescence are frequently described as involving identity formation, independence, vocational development, and peer relationships. Rarely, however, is it recognized that creating a meaning for death within the context of life may be the crucial achievement of adolescent development. The goal for adults who work with adolescents should not necessarily be to achieve a "mature" concept of death, but rather to provide a comfortable climate for an exploration of how death, in its threatening and fascinating biological, intellectual, social, and affective demands, serves to clarify one's personal position in the human life cycle.

3

Adolescents, Homicidal Violence, and Death

Ronald K. Barrett

Each of the three leading causes of death during adolescence—accidents, homicide, and suicide—typically leads to sudden, unexpected, and traumatic modes of death. This chapter examines deaths in the lives of contemporary adolescents that are associated with homicidal violence. It provides a description of the nature and scope of homicidal violence as it affects adolescents, discussed here in terms of differences in adolescent death rates associated with age, gender, and race (Fingerhut & Kleinman, 1989; Ropp, Visintainer, Uman, & Treloar, 1992; Sullivan, 1991). Subsequently, this chapter analyzes the psychological consequences of chronic violence for adolescents, theoretical explanations of violence in adolescent life, and recommendations for improved intervention and social policy.

THE NATURE AND SCOPE OF HOMICIDAL VIOLENCE IN ADOLESCENT LIFE

In 1992, homicide was the 10th leading cause of death for all Americans in the United States, accounting for a total of 25,488 deaths (Kochanek & Hudson, 1994). In the same year, homicide was the second leading cause of death in those who are 15 to 24 years of age, accounting for 8,019 deaths. Homicidal deaths among 15- to 24-year-old males in 1992

(6,891) substantially outnumbered similar deaths (1,128) among their female counterparts. Moreover, patterns of homicidal violence reveal that homicides are primarily "intramural" with most victims and perpetrators coming from the same ethnic or racial background.

Of the 1 million adolescent youth aged 12 to 19 who are victims of violent crimes each year in the United States, homicidal violence is an especially high risk for adolescent urban males of color (African-Americans and Hispanic Americans), with blacks who die by homicide outnumbering whites five to four. The rate of victimization of younger adolescent black males is 10 times higher than that of younger white males.

Regarding trends, one study (Ropp et al., 1992) of mortality rates among young people during 1980 to 1988, which grouped subjects by several variables (urban/suburban, age, gender, and race), reported a 50% increase in all causes of mortality in the urban population compared with no change or a slight decline in the suburban and national populations. The increase was found to be greatest in the African-American, urban population. Homicide showed the largest increase (252%), with firearm-related homicides accounting for most of the homicide deaths (Fingerhut, Kleinman, Godfrey, & Rosenberg, 1991).

More than one half of all serious crimes in the United States (murder, rape, aggravated assault, robbery, burglary, larceny, and motor vehicle theft) are committed by adolescents 10 to 17 years of age (Winbush, 1988). Within the United States between 1960 and 1980, juvenile crime rose twice as fast as adult crime. According to the Federal Bureau of Investigation (U.S. Department of Justice, 1990), in northern California persons aged 17 and younger are arrested for 57% of all felonies against people (homicide, assault, rape, etc.) and for 66% of property crimes. One study of homicides in Southern California for 1988 (Barrett, 1991) revealed that adolescents were most frequently both victims and perpetrators of these crimes. In addition, African-American and Hispanic-American males accounted for nearly 70% of all homicides in Southern California. In Chicago, the Federal Bureau of Investigation's Uniform Crime Report for 1990 (U.S. Department of Justice, 1990) reported that one third of all murders were committed by persons aged 20 or younger—a 29% increase over rates reported for 1975.

Throughout the United States, homicide is the number one cause of death of African-American and Hispanic-American adolescents (Kochanek & Hudson, 1994). Homicides occur at such a high rate among these young people that they have decreased the overall life expectancy of all African-Americans and Hispanic Americans. On this basis, some scholars (Barrett, 1993; Fingerhut & Kleinman, 1990; Sullivan, 1991) have concluded that homicide should be regarded not as a criminal justice issue but rather as a public health crisis.

Homicide—particularly involving firearms—is a significantly larger problem in the United States than in many other countries. Research findings in the United States (Barrett, 1993; Ropp et al., 1992) have called attention to the marked increase in firearm-related homicides among children and adolescent youth. For example, a 1991 study (Fingerhut et al., 1991) reported an alarming pattern of escalating lethal violence for adolescent youth during the period 1979 to 1988. In 1988, 77% of homicides among adolescents 15 to 19 years of age were associated with firearms; the rate was 88% among African-American males. Among 20- to 24-year-olds, 70% of homicides related to firearms; the rate was 81% among African-American males.

Although adolescents who kill have largely been characterized as urban adolescent males 15 to 25 years of age, typically from socially disadvantaged environments, there is a growing trend of parallel violence in middle-class, suburban family settings among "advantaged" adolescent youth as well (Lacayo, 1994). Erik Menendez at age 19 of Beverly Hills, California, and Amy Fisher at age 17 of Merrick, Long Island, are just two examples of infamous adolescents of the 1990s—both from mostly white, advantaged communities that do not fit the stereotypical pattern of teenagers who engage in homicidal violence.

Across the nation there is a growing public concern about the new phenomenon of a rise of violence among girls, often in complicity with violent male significant others (Barrett, 1993; Hamburg, 1992). The percentage of girls convicted of violent crimes rose from 15% in 1987 to 38% in 1991 in Massachusetts (Press, McCormick, & Wingert, 1994). Experts on gangs suggest girls are increasingly joining previously all-male gangs and all-girl gangs are modeling the violent behavior of all-male gangs. This growing trend suggests that no segment of society is immune from the social and public health concern of an escalating pattern of adolescents who kill (Press, McCormick, Wingert, 1994).

In addition, national data trends suggest that the profile of adolescent youth who kill is also rapidly changing, with increasing numbers of preadolescent youths being identified as perpetrators of homicidal violence (Lacayo, 1994). During the years 1988 to 1992, there has been a significant increase in juvenile crime in the most serious categories: murder, rape, robbery, and aggravated assault. Homicide arrests for youth aged 10 to 14 rose from 194 to 301 between 1988 and 1992. In

1986, most cases in New York City's Family Court were misdemeanors; today more than 90% are felonies. Though killers under the age of 15 are still relatively atypical, over the past 3 years in Los Angeles, for instance, those 14 or younger accounted for nearly 17% of the 460 homicides committed by youths under 18 (Lacayo, 1994). Recent cases included 12-year-old Manuel Sanchez and John Duncan who were arrested for the murder of a migrant worker in Wenatchee, Washington, and the short and violent life of 11-year-old Robert "Yummy" Sandifer of Chicago who was allegedly a drug-related hit man and who himself was later executed by a group of adolescent gang members. It is estimated that adolescent males 14 to 17 years of age and younger, whose participation in lethal violence has jumped 161%, will continue to be increasingly represented in such acts (Press, McCormick, & Wingert, 1994).

Given the nature and incidence of homicidal violence in poor, socially disadvantaged, urban, nonwhite (i.e., African-American and Hispanic-American) communities, it is not surprising to see evidence of trauma, distress, and violence in the lives of young people from these communities. Homicidal violence is a significant fact of life in these communities, with homicides ranked as the leading cause of death for adolescent, urban, nonwhite (i.e., African-American and Hispanic - American) males 15 to 24 years of age.

Even as they are more likely to become perpetrators of lethal violence, youngsters in urban environments are increasingly at risk of becoming "primary victims" of homicidal violence. In a demographic study of homicides over a 12-month period for Los Angeles County for 1988, Barrett (1991) found the highest risk for victims of homicidal violence to be younger, adolescent, male nonwhites (i.e., African-Americans and Hispanic Americans) ages 15 to 24 years. Similar findings have emerged from an examination of national statistics in urban homicides in several larger metropolitan centers (Barrett, 1993).

In recent years, it has become increasingly evident to human services workers and those who work routinely on the "front line" with young people that more and more urban youngsters are "secondary victims" of trauma and violence (Garbarino, Dubrow, Kostelny, & Padro, 1992). Most often these urban youngsters witness and are impacted by a barrage of routine acts of violence in their immediate social environment. A growing body of evidence (American Psychological Association, 1993; Garbarino et al., 1992; Pynoos, 1985) has begun to document the consequences of community violence for the psychological functioning and well-being of these young people.

ADOLESCENTS AND THE PSYCHOLOGICAL CONSEQUENCES OF CHRONIC VIOLENCE

An emerging body of data reported by trauma specialists and others who work with adolescents suggests that those who witness chronic violence—so-called secondary victims—are characteristically (but not solely) poor, inner-city, socially disadvantaged, nonwhite (African-American and Hispanic American) youngsters from dysfunctional families. Scholars concerned about this emerging reality have warned of the possibility of a generation of young people at risk (Garbarino et al., 1992; Pynoos, 1985).

A typical day for urban adolescents might, more often than not, begin in the context of a dysfunctional home environment that is a setting in which they experience and witness countless acts of domestic violence and abuse (Sullivan, 1993). Far too many adolescents also live in violent communities besieged by gang- and drug-induced criminal activity that poses serious threats and fears for their health and well-being. In addition, many urban youths must negotiate safe passage as they travel to and from school through routine dangers that are real and potentially life threatening.

For a growing number of young people, the school environment is no refuge from the dangers of the streets (Kantrowitz, 1993). Many American adolescents find the quality of their learning environments to be seriously compromised by the intrusion of abuse, assaults, and random violence (Evans, 1992; Glassman, 1993; Portner, 1994). For example, a 1993 study of 720 school districts by the National School Boards Association (Glassman, 1993) found that 82% of these districts reported an increase in violence in their schools over the past 5 years. According to Richard W. Riley, the U.S. Secretary of Education, each year about 3 million thefts and violent crimes occur on or near school campuses, averaging approximately 16,000 incidents of violence per school day (Portner, 1994). Educators and juvenile crime statistics have also reported that urban adolescents are bringing firearms to school in increasing numbers and at younger ages than previously witnessed. One study suggested that one in 25 high school students carries a gun (Fingerhut et al., 1991). Witnessing repeated acts of victimization and violence understandably increases levels of fear and mistrust among adolescents.

Pynoos (1985) warned that the greater the personal impact of violence on the youngster, the greater the likelihood a traumatic state will occur. Violent injury or victimization by a parent in itself may impose a severe stress and sense of trauma on the youngster and serve as a psychic disorganizer profoundly altering the individual's view of the world. Reports from the American Medical Association (Ropp et al., 1992) have estimated that approximately 2 million children experience physical abuse or neglect each year. There is concern that such abuse or neglect may influence them to be at risk of becoming perpetrators of abuse and violence themselves. Estimates of physical abuse of children and adolescents suggest that as many as 10% are assaulted by family members and caregivers each year. In addition, the casual and vivid portrayal of violence in virtually all aspects of American society from the national news on television to entertainment videos, games, and sports clearly reflects our societal romance and esteem for violence. Chronic violence that victimizes the developing adolescent in this sociocultural context is redefining the meaning and reality of adolescence for a growing number of contemporary youngsters.

THEORETICAL EXPLANATIONS OF ADOLESCENT VIOLENCE

Theories of violent behavior among adolescents are as varied as those who offer them (Winbush, 1988). The main reason for this variation is that crimes committed by adolescents appear to be a function of economic, political, racial, sex role, and other factors. As a result, it is difficult to articulate a single, comprehensive, theoretical explanation of adolescent violence because of the ubiquitous and varied situational contexts in which these behaviors occur (Barrett, 1993). This section reviews some of the most important theoretical explanations that have been offered to shed light on the phenomena of adolescent homicidal violence.

Little Men/Big Men Thesis

The little men/big men thesis directs attention to the role of the social environment in increasing violence among adolescent youth. In particular, this thesis takes note of the fact that youthful aggression and homicidal violence in such forms as drive-by shootings, gang violence, muggings, assaults, or robberies characteristically occur in situations of peer and social influence. On their own, adolescents rarely engage in these behaviors; within groups, however, many contemporary adolescents appear to find acceptance from peers through acts of aggression and violence. As a result of this fact, most criminal justice experts and researchers agree that motivation for murder usually is different in youth and adult offenders.

Nevertheless, insufficient attention has been given to the role of peer and social influence on acts of adolescent aggression and homicidal violence. This influence may range from the passive indifferent observer to the active coperpetrator of aggression and violence. That is, brute physical aggression, violence, fear, intimidation, and dominance appear to be regarded by some adolescent peers as essential to a kind of "rite of passage" into their group. In these ways, the sanction received from such peers serves to promote rather than inhibit behaviors regarded as socially unacceptable by the larger society.

Increased risk of homicidal violence among nonwhite (African-American and Hispanic-American) males supports the little men/big men thesis by suggesting that violence and aggression are esteemed in some subcultures as an essential attribute in the rite of passage to manhood and masculinity (Majors & Billson, 1992; Staples, 1982; Wilson, 1992). According to this perspective, young males are especially at risk during adolescence because of their developmental dependence on social esteem to sanction and validate essential aspects of their becoming as a means of self-acceptance and male identity formation.

Even among adolescents who have not privately endorsed or internalized the complex value system of the contemporary urban youth subculture, many have come to recognize the survival value of publicly imitating those values in such matters as dress and behavior. This may help to explain a phenomenon in some white adolescent males who have come to favor the seemingly fashionable life style, music, and personal presentation of nonwhite urban youth. In all of these ways, "little men" are those males who may be seeking the social esteem of peers and older men in hopes of becoming "big men."

The fact that all nonwhite adolescent males do not behave violently or manifest socially unacceptable levels of lethal aggression—just as all white adolescent males are not found to mimic the behaviors or life styles of their nonwhite counterparts—suggests limits to this thesis as an explanation of homicidal aggression. More empirical research on the relationship of individual differences, such as personality, social class, and socioeconomic standing, to homicidal violence may be illuminating and useful.

Subculture of Violence Thesis

Wolfgang and Ferracuti (1967) proposed the sociological thesis that the overrepresentation of assaultive violence in African-Americans may be attributed to the unique ecological dynamics of ghetto life and a sub-culture that models and sanctions violence as a way of life. Implicit in this thesis is the belief that certain sociological groups are more prone to violence because violence is a value sanctioned by the group. Bo-hannon (1960) and Silberman (1978) also suggested viewing the prob-lem from a subcultural perspective, arguing that the propensity for violence is not part of the cultural heritage African-Americans brought from Africa. Not everyone agrees with this point. For instance, Mazrui (1977) documented a warrior tradition that characterizes tribes throughout all parts of Africa and that has produced a legacy of cultural indoctrination of African violence against Africans.

Many African-American scholars (e.g., Hawkins, 1986; Rose & Mc-Clain, 1990; Staples, 1976) are critical of this "sub-culture of violence thesis." These critics stress the importance of viewing urban violence in its proper socioeconomic and cultural context. Others (Curtis, 1975) reject the subculture of violence thesis as overly simplistic. For instance, Curtis (1975) built on the thesis of the African-American culture of poverty and provided a "multidimensional value space" model to ac-count for important interactions between race, culture, poverty, and vi-olence in urban settings. Similarly, Hawkins (1986) argued that the subculture of violence tradition underestimates (if not ignores) the im-pact of the legacy of slavery and racism on the etiology of African-Amer-ican crime today.

The thesis that there is a subculture of violence among contempo-rary African-Americans has some conceptual appeal. But the model (Wolfgang & Ferracuti, 1967) as proposed is overly simplistic and of questionable utility in explaining the unique dynamics of African-American male homicidal violence. Thus, Huff-Corzine, Corzine, and More (1986) questioned the traditional assumptions of ecological mod-els of homicide and their suitability in explaining African-American homicidal violence. Models and related findings that provide support for the assumed role of a Southern subculture of violence to explain white violence may simply not be adequate to explain African-American violence (Rose & McClain, 1990). Similarly, African-American scholars (Barrett, 1993; Hawkins, 1986; Staples, 1976) critical of this thesis have stressed the importance of viewing the problem of African-American male homicidal violence in its proper socioeconomic and cultural per-spective.

Gouldner (1973) noted that the study of criminology ought to in-volve a critical understanding of the larger society and cultural context in which the behavior occurs. Staples (1976) viewed African-American homicide as "normative" not because of a unique African-American subculture of violence, but rather because it is a fundamental aspect of the larger pattern of American culture and especially its historical and traditional styles of relating to its ethnic minorities. Consequently, to characterize this behavior as a sociopathological component of the American cultural experience is an exercise in blaming the victim. Consideration of cultural, socioeconomic, and political influences, as well as the historical legacy of slavery and racism in their varied forms and manifestations, is important in tracing the etiology of African-American homicidal violence in the historical and cultural ecology of the American experience.

Another major flaw in the ecological thesis is that it implicitly suggests that a subculture of violence is a response to poverty among African-Americans in general. This overlooks findings that document homicidal violence as a predominantly male phenomenon. According to the thesis, one would expect all members of the socially disadvantaged subculture to be violent in response to their condition. Findings that show a discrepant pattern in the incidence of expressed lethal violence in ethnic minority women do not support this view. In fact, by comparison with other groups, African-American females are more likely to be victims of homicide, more likely to be victimized in the home, and less likely to be "primary offenders" and accomplices (Block, 1986; O'Carroll & Mercy, 1986).

More work needs to be done if the claim is to be supported that there is among African-Americans a subculture that supports and nurtures violence. Barrett (1993) has argued that particular emphasis should be placed on the social and ecological variables that lead to this behavior in a "male subculture of violence." Empirical findings that homicidal violence is generally a form of criminal behavior dominated by males are especially worthy of more study. This is particularly true given the fact that this pattern of homicidal violence is specifically acute (for victims and offenders of intra-age homicide) among teenage and young adult males. This suggests that correlations with gender should also be accompanied by developmental and maturational factors (Block, 1986; Conrad, 1985; Goodman, 1960). A more complex model for the consideration of variables of race, sex, and poverty may assist in explaining the observed pattern of elevated violence in younger African-American (and other minority) males in urban settings.

Black Rage Thesis

According to this view (also referred to as the psychoanalytic thesis), the high incidence of violence among African-Americans and Hispanic

Americans may be a function of "poorly developed" mechanisms for coping with the anger and rage caused by situations of economic deprivation, poverty, and discrimination (Fanon, 1967, 1968; Grier & Cobb, 1968; Poussaint, 1983). The eruption of violence and externalization of anger is particularly associated with the developing nonwhite male youngster's emergence from the social context of the family. As that adolescent begins to venture into the larger society, he is confronted with potentially emasculating encounters with racism and discrimination—from individuals, institutions, and the larger society.

Consistent with this thesis is the premise that males are sex-typed to be more assertive and aggressive than females, and also more likely to cope more poorly with frustrations. This thesis is in agreement with the research of Weaver and Gary (1993) who found that younger adolescent African-American males may experience developmental distress in coping with daily life hassles and stressors that are better handled by older African-American males. The black rage thesis seems especially relevant for explaining the explosive rage and violence of younger adolescent nonwhite males who also have less supportive resources for coping with chronic interpersonal, societal, and systemic frustrations evident in daily living.

The black rage thesis also includes consideration of the socialization process in producing "socialized criminals" who are likely to choose convenient scapegoats in their immediate environment (Gibbs, 1988). This combination of unsublimated anger and low impulse control, coupled with the easy availability of handguns and easy victims (i.e., other African Americans or Hispanic Americans), creates potentially violent situations for young adolescent African-American and Hispanic-American males to explode at the slightest provocation. The high incidence of black-on-black homicide reflects this displacement of affect by African Americans who are presumed to have low self-esteem and high levels of hostility and frustration in response to their limited social and economic possibilities (Poussaint, 1983). According to this argument, the chronic and severe frustrations experienced by African-American males in American society may engender understandable levels of frustration, rage, and aggression which are likely to be displaced on victims of convenience in their immediate environment (Gibbs, 1988; Grier & Cobb, 1968).

This approach contends that people exposed more to antisocial influences than to law-conforming influences may reflect antisocial responses in their personalities and modes of interpersonal behavior (Flowers, 1988). The black rage view of adolescent nonwhite male homicidal violence makes sense and has great intuitive appeal. Barrett

(1991) has offered a similar thesis in the interpretation of African-American male homicidal and suicidal patterns in a study of Los Angeles homicides for 1988. The interpretation is that African-American (and Hispanic-American) males who experience a greater sense of "loss of personal effectance" and possibilities for self-actualization, which are critical to their sense of well-being and identity as masculine members of society, are more likely to respond with indiscriminate rage and violence in their social and interpersonal behavior. However, a major drawback to black rage research is that it cannot easily be tested empirically. The hypothetical concept of personality is unobservable and difficult to measure. Consequently, this claim is essentially the analyst's interpretation of a patient's interpretation of what is occurring in the subconscious (Sheley, 1985). This presents methodological problems for researchers undertaking empirical attempts to test and explore the black rage thesis of violent criminal adolescent behavior.

Economic Deprivation Thesis

Merton (1952), a conservative sociologist, has long advocated the capitalist view that crime among adolescents in America is an understandable consequence of individuals seeking status, recognition, and esteem via the acquisition of material rewards associated with success and prosperity. However, Title, Villemez, and Smith (1978) have challenged the assumptions of this view in a review of 35 studies of juvenile delinquents, which reported a significant decline in the relationship between crime and social class over the past 40 years. Nevertheless, social class has been significantly correlated with the incidence of violent crimes. Typically, poorer individuals are more likely to commit violent crimes against persons, whereas the more affluent are more likely to commit white-collar crimes. Little, if any, empirical evidence supports the view that property crimes are linked to class.

It seems reasonable that socioeconomic status impacts on a variety of factors that may indirectly influence observed patterns of homicidal violence. Thus, many researchers attribute some significance to the role of poverty, unemployment, and racism on the level of violent crimes in American society (Block, 1985; Gibbs, 1988; Hawkins, 1986; Miller, 1958; Rose & McClain, 1990; Winbush, 1988). Nevertheless, the existence of violence among middle-class, ethnic-minority adolescents weakens this position (Lacayo, 1994). In short, the relation of economic conditions to homicidal violence is complex and worthy of further study.

Politics of the Economics of Crime Thesis

According to this position, the escalating level of violent crime in American society is intimately linked to an economic system that benefits directly from violent criminal behavior (e.g., security systems, the criminal justice system, treatment and prevention programs, and firearms). Consider the following. The U.S. Department of Justice has reported that between 1987 and 1991 juvenile arrests for weapons violations rose by 62% (Press, McCormick, & Wingert, 1994). Black youths under the age of 18 are the group most frequently involved in violence. In 1991, black youths were arrested for weapons-law violations at a rate triple that for white youths, and they were murdered at a rate six times that for whites. According to Millstein, Petersen, and Nightingale (1993) the median age of first gun ownership in the United States is 12½ years of age; often the gun is a gift from a father or other male relative. Experts on firearm-related crimes argue that in part because of the ready availability of firearms, guns are involved in more than 75% of adolescent homicides.

Compare these facts with data (Brazil & Platte, 1994) that cheap inexpensive handguns produced by a few leading manufacturers in the United States were associated with nearly 20% of all criminal acts of murder, robbery, assault, or firearm-related crime between January 1991 and May 1994. Handguns produced by just five U.S. manufacturers and priced as low as $25 have increasingly become the weapons of choice for criminals, crime-fearing citizens, and American youth.

The easy accessibility of firearms is a critical factor in escalating patterns of lethal adolescent violence (Barrett, 1993). In a 1993 survey of 2,508 students at 96 public and private elementary, middle, and senior high schools, Portner (1994) reported that 60% of the youth said they could get a handgun; one-fifth claimed they could do so within an hour, and more than one-third said they could do so within a day. Nevertheless, social advocacy efforts for gun control in America to curb adolescent violent crime are at best stalled at the level of political debate and inaction.

Social–Psychological Thesis

Criminal violent behavior among urban youth may be easily modeled, learned, and sanctioned during a developmental era when many adolescents often seek counterculture expressions in their struggle for individuation and identity. This is a traditional belief in much of the theorizing about rebellious youth who become juvenile delinquents. Barrett (1991) argued that conformity and peer pressure of gangs and "posses" may play a significant role in explaining the expression of violent behavior of urban youth. The social pressure and apparent attraction are visibly evident in the counterculture of heavy metal and rap music, and other forms of self-expression, including dress, that have radically changed the appearance and presentation of American urban youth.

In addition, the influence of alcohol and drugs plays a significant role in criminal behavior (Bartol, 1991; Fitzpatrick, 1974). Gary (1981) reported that more African-American males between 15 and 30 years of age are victims of alcohol-related homicides than any other race/sex/age group. Also, 50% of murder cases in the low-income, African-American community in 1979 involved alcohol and drugs. Drug abuse among African-American youth has increased over the past 25 years, spreading from the inner cities to the suburbs and has become increasingly linked to "hard drugs" (i.e., heroin and crack cocaine), which are, in turn, inextricably tied to violent street crime (Kerr, 1987). Alcohol and drugs are associated with the three major causes of death among African-American males (homicide, suicide, and accidental deaths) because they lower inhibitions, increase feelings of frustration, and fuel resulting aggression. Situational risks of acquisition, use, and sales are highly correlated with increasing rates of lethal violence.

The observation that increased homicidal violence and criminal behavior appear to be correlated with specific social and environmental conditions lends some support to the social–psychological thesis. However, many theories of urban violence and gang affiliation are too simplistic. More careful study is needed to understand better the social-psychological factors that influence gang involvement. Studies of individuals who have made the choice of gang involvement and those who become socialized in correctional institutional settings do seem to favor the values and virtues of groups of which they become a part. Barrett's (1991) observations of Los Angeles gangs and ensuing violent behaviors identified a pattern of socialized behaviors supporting the social-psychological view. The overrepresentation of young, nonwhite males in survival struggles in both urban community settings and correctional institutions may place them at greater risk of modeling and conforming as a means of masculine survival, thereby sanctioning violence (Staples, 1976).

Dysfunctional Systems Thesis

A growing body of evidence suggests youth at risk of murder are products of family and educational systems that have failed them. These dysfunctional systems increase the victimization of adolescents to neglect, physical and sexual abuse, and critical educational skill deficits (Busch, Zagar, Hughes, Arbit, & Bussell, 1990; Kessler, Burgess, & Douglass, 1988). Short and Stodtbeck (1955) posited the existence of an important relationship between school failure and gang affiliation; when school is rejected as a means of socialization, choosing an alternative system for survival and social esteem is a predictable outcome. Conversely, those whose socialization skills equip them to compete with the demands of middle-class achievement choose otherwise. Against this, Miller (1958) dismissed the view that gang membership results from a rejection of the majority culture and simply viewed the individual's behavior as more a function of rewards acquired via conformity to in-group standards and values.

More recent theories of gang affiliation and counterculture behaviors consider a wide variety of social and environmental influences on the individual's choices, suggesting that forces outside the individual impact on the probability that he or she will engage in criminal behavior (Gabor, 1986; Gibbs, 1988; Jacks & Cox, 1984; Jenkins & Crowley, 1981). One sample of 1,956 delinquent adolescents (Busch et al., 1990) found that adolescents who kill have a tetrad of characteristics including criminally violent family members, gang membership, severe educational difficulties, and alcohol/drug abuse. Kessler, Burgess, and Douglass (1988) documented a similar pattern of formative events for youth at risk of violence.

The dysfunctional systems thesis is consistent with numerous observational studies that correlate juvenile delinquency with failure in educational and related achievement institutions. However, the startling observation that a significant proportion of violent youthful offenders come from traditional families with an atypical achievement history cannot be rationally explained by this thesis alone. The relative influence of achievement failures in dysfunctional institutional settings provides some insights about the emerging pattern of elevated lethal violence in urban youthful offenders. At the same time, it raises some disturbing questions about how we have traditionally conceptualized and measured "achievement." For example, as a society, should we continue to think of a "successful family" as one that shows evidence of material means or as one that raises healthy, well-adjusted, and productive members of society?

Declining Value of Nonwhite Life Thesis

Although it is reasonable to expect fairness in the criminal justice system, a growing body of evidence suggests that nonwhites do not receive fair treatment and justice in that system (Waters, 1990; Wright, 1990). According to this view, the lack of consistency and fairness in the treatment of young, nonwhite felony offenders has cheapened the value of life for nonwhites (Waters, 1990; Wright, 1990). Even the young can see the inconsistency in valuing the life and welfare of whites more than nonwhites, thereby increasing the probability of victimizing members of one's own reference group.

According to Hawkins (1986), the idea of a racial hierarchy for the treatment of criminal homicide offenders is well documented in the social sciences research literature. Johnson's (1941) classic study of racial differences in sentencing in three southern cities between 1930 and 1940 reported that a greater proportion of African-Americans who killed whites than whites who killed whites were executed upon being sentenced. In addition, African Americans who killed other African-Americans were least likely to be sentenced or executed.

Garfinkel (1949) produced similar findings, although Radelet (1981) reported finding no overall racial differences in sentencing or probability of an indictment in his analysis of a sample of 637 homicide cases. However, Kleck (1979) found racial differences and a racial bias in his analysis of homicides in the South and speculated about their generalizability to other areas of the country. Hawkins (1986) concluded that race is a crucial variable, even though other factors are considered in determining the seriousness of a homicide case (e.g., the race of the offender, the victim's and the offender's relationship, the degree of premeditation).

According to this thesis about the declining value of nonwhite life, the response (or lack thereof) of the criminal justice system toward African-American offenders and victims of homicide has created a racial hierarchy of homicide offenses such that cases involving white victims are regarded more seriously than homicide cases involving nonwhites. The existence of such a hierarchy of homicide offenses would result in an inadvertent but significant impact on black-on-black crime (Poussaint, 1983), thereby explaining the curious pattern of elevated homicidal violence witnessed among African-Americans and other ethnic minorities in urban America.

This thesis and its related data are an essential link which is missing in the subcultural, ecological, and psychoanalytic views. According to these viewpoints, one might expect not only violent assaultive criminal behavior to occur but also that it would occur indiscriminately. And if the behavior is not indiscriminate, it would be reasonable to expect it to target those who are the source of one's sense of struggle and frustration rather than those least responsible (i.e., other African-Americans and nonwhites).

The finding of a significantly higher incidence of intraracial homicide (black-on-black criminal homicide) and significantly lower levels of interracial homicide (black-on-white homicide) lends support to the theory of the existence of a hierarchy of homicidal violence sanctioned by the criminal justice system, one that is inadvertently understood and internalized by the members of the larger society (Barrett, 1991). Several recent studies of homicidal violence in urban centers report similar findings of increasing rates of African-Americans and Hispanic Americans killing members of their own communities (Gibbs, 1988; Hawkins, 1986; Rose & McClain, 1988).

The theorized hierarchy of homicide offenses is deeply rooted in the social history of African-Americans in the American experience of slavery, the victimization of African-Americans, and the devaluing of African-American life (Flowers, 1988). Hindus (1980) noted that within the institution of slavery in America it was not uncommon for white slave masters to kill and injure their black slaves and suffer no criminal offense or social sanctions. Within that social and historical context, however, the act of an African American killing a white person was considered one of the most heinous offenses.

The constant fear of African-American insurrection led to the organization of a swift and cruel response style to punish African-American offenders (Hawkins, 1986). This response was similar in style and severity to the response of the present-day criminal justice system that severely sanctions African-American criminal behavior targeting white victims and less severely sanctions African-American criminal acts targeting African-American victims. If Black's (1976) view of law as a form of governmental social control is applied here, it is reasonable to conclude that the larger society's relative devaluation of black-on-black homicidal violence is an often ignored and overlooked dynamic that is a part of the problem.

Situations involving "peace officers" constitute another area of homicidal deaths among African-American males which desperately needs more detailed study. In a Chicago study, Harding and Fahey (1973) reported disproportionate racial differences (i.e., more nonwhite victims) in police-involved shootings. A national study of all 50 states (Kania & Mackey, 1977) revealed similar findings. Similarly, Fyfe (1981) analyzed police shooting deaths for the period 1971 to 1975 and reported that although police-shooting victims were generally younger, a greater proportion of African-American males of all age groups was considerably more likely to become police-shooting victims than were their white or Hispanic-American contemporaries. In a study of homicidal deaths in Los Angeles for 1988, Barrett (1991) reported similar findings of a greater risk of officer-involved shooting for younger (15–34 years of age) African-American males.

While the number of police-involved shootings of African-American males may not appreciably impact the total incidence of homicidal death for African-American males, the reality of differential treatment within the criminal justice system and the observed pattern of officer-involved deaths (however infrequent) may serve as a significant means of social control (e.g., curbing the probability of victimization by whites, the police, and other authority figures). Recent examples of officer-involved lethal violence seemingly targeting nonwhite males (e.g., Rodney King of Los Angeles and Malic Green of Detroit) communicate a devaluing of nonwhite life and raise some reasonable doubt about fairness and justice for nonwhites in the criminal justice system. This type of social control may in turn reduce the value of African-American life and increase the probability of rage (e.g., the 1992 Los Angeles riots), as well as intraracial (black-on-black) homicidal violence.

In addition, the inability of the criminal justice system to adequately rehabilitate youthful offenders increases the risk of these youngsters returning to society more skilled and enraged to repeat the pattern of violence. In a 1945 Philadelphia cohort study, both race and social class differences were reported by Wolfgang, Figlio, and Sellin (1972) in the decision to arrest juvenile offenders being processed in the juvenile justice system. Whether a youth was a one-time offender or a recidivist, he was more likely to be arrested if he was nonwhite. Forty years later, Gibbs (1988) reported a similarly disproportionate rate of arrest for African-American male youths, placement in detention centers, and commitment to public juvenile correctional facilities. A national survey of juvenile facilities shows that African-American youth under the age of 18 account for approximately 13% of the total in U.S. jails, although they represent only 10% of the U.S. population in that age group. As of February 1, 1988, more than 30% of the residents of public and private juvenile custody facilities were African-Americans (Flowers, 1988).

The declining value of nonwhite life thesis is supported by a growing body of empirical evidence that documents that crimes involving both nonwhite victims and perpetrators receive different responses from the criminal justice system. This difference needs further careful study and analysis to shape social policies that will reduce the level of lethal violence in the African-American community and address the escalating violence that has become a public health concern for all Americans.

In summary, the research on psychological influences underlying homicidal violence in urban adolescents has arisen from a variety of theoretical frameworks. All of the explanations presented are of some value and provide some insight into the complex phenomenon of homicidal violence among urban adolescents. No one explanation is adequate to account fully for and explain the varied dimensions and scope of this phenomenon. Without exception, all are worthy of additional thought and empirical study. With few exceptions, better data-gathering and management techniques are needed to develop descriptive causal models that will ultimately impact on social policy and guide intervention strategies.

The persistent and alarming pattern of premature deaths among adolescents in the United States calls attention to the need for a well-articulated national youth agenda. There is a need for a multidisciplinary approach across institutional settings bringing together researchers and behavioral scholars, social policy advocates, politicians, law makers and law enforcement personnel, youth leaders and ministers, educators, and parents. Our youth are our future and clearly represent one of our most precious resources. The current level of chronic community violence impacts the quality of life for all. This justifies its priority as an urgent public health crisis in the United States.

RECOMMENDATIONS FOR IMPROVED INTERVENTION AND SOCIAL POLICY

Community Empowerment

First and foremost, it is of the utmost importance that African-Americans and Hispanic Americans come to terms with the seriousness of the problem of progressive homicidal violence within their communities. In a clear voice, these groups must say that the level of homicidal violence and varied forms of self-destructive behaviors witnessed is unacceptable. In neighborhoods where youthful gang violence is not only life-threatening to young, nonwhite males but also to the community at large, this criminal behavior should be labeled as being clearly unacceptable and not to be tolerated. Giving voice to such a protest must also be coupled with a collective commitment to social action, social change, and multilevel intervention.

The church has historically been a major institutional resource in the struggles of African-Americans and Hispanic Americans. Churches can provide essential leadership in the interventions that are required. Churches can also be a viable platform for educational campaigns and socialization efforts to discourage propagation of brutality and violence. In many instances, the family and domestic environment are another important place to begin intervention attempts to reduce social violence (Zimring, 1984).

African-American Male Agenda

Within the African-American and Hispanic-American communities, African-American and Hispanic-American males must assume some responsibility for the insidious progression of criminal violence. In doing so, they must serve as leaders in taking back control of their communities. The posture of finding fault and looking for others outside of one's community for answers only psychologically lessens the chances of African-Americans and Hispanic Americans ever feeling empowered to effect the necessary change that must start within these respective communities. Others have no vested interest in these communities; they cannot and should not be depended upon to resolve this social and public health crisis that particularly victimizes young African-American and Hispanic-American males by identifying them as "an endangered species" (Barrett, 1991; Gibbs, 1988).

There is a growing, national, grass roots movement among African-American males to reclaim the inner cities and to develop innovative social and community programs to serve younger African-American males. There is a real need for programs in virtually every segment of the community (home, school, church, social clubs, athletics, entertainment, etc.) to establish an "African-American male agenda—nurturing and cultivating future leadership." Although the assistance and support of caring and committed females is necessary and valued, the leadership and impetus must come from caring and committed older African-American males to mentor, work with, and empower younger African-American males—many of whom are victims of a complex array of social and environmental conditions that place them at perilous risk of self-destruction and lethal violence.

Socialization Agenda

Although there is a crucial need to hold educational institutions more accountable for the care and development of African-American and Hispanic-American youth—especially African-American and Hispanic-American males—to assure their personal and professional development, there is also a critical need for a "survival education and socialization agenda" for these nonwhite, male youths. At every level in the educational process, the evidence is clear that when and where parents show interest, their children are more likely to succeed. The level of apathy and passive involvement of African-American and Hispanic-American parents must change. African-American and Hispanic-American fathers (as well as mothers) must become actively involved and not entrust the education and socialization of their children to others.

Historically, educational institutions lacking a vested interest in and appreciation of our youth often have failed them miserably. More often than not, blame for such failures has ultimately been put on the victims—usually young African-American and Hispanic-American males. As argued by contemporary African-American visionaries (Gibbs, 1988; Kunjufu, 1985; Madhubuti, 1990), perhaps alternative educational and socialization systems are necessary for the development and salvaging of young African-American and other nonwhite males. A crucial part of this educational and socialization agenda should address Afrocentric and Hispanic cultural values, enhancement of self-esteem, drug and sex education, a sense of community and collective accountability, and political and social strategies for survival in a multicultural and racist environment that is often hostile to the well-being of these adolescents.

Lethal Confrontation Skills

Given the reality and probability of lethal confrontations for younger African-American and Hispanic-American males, it is imperative to educate young, nonwhite males in a systematic way about the risks of lethal confrontations with other nonwhite males and to develop orderly skills for managing those situations. For example, if there is a real risk of homicide associated with robbery (as research data suggest), then teaching skills to handle lethal confrontations is in order. If given a choice in a robbery, young African-American and Hispanic-American males should be instructed to choose life over the value of material possessions or saving face. In addition, self-defense skills and skills in conflict management may hold some promise for reducing the incidence of homicidal violence among young African-American and Hispanic-American males.

Lethal confrontations between law enforcement officers and nonwhite, young males should be regarded realistically as situations of risk for all involved. Adolescents need to develop an awareness of the potential risk in these encounters, an understanding of skills to be used in managing confrontations with police and peace officers, and a knowledge of legal rights for recourse. Everyone needs to acknowledge that the propensity for violence and use of firearms manifested by many of these male adolescents presents lethal risks when police confront them.

Reforming Correctional Systems

Community empowerment is urgently needed, along with a collective effort to address the inequities and discriminatory practices in the criminal justice system that are cited to excuse black-on-black criminal behavior. These factors unwittingly encourage the propensity for homicidal violence in the African-American and Hispanic-American community. Laws and the operation of the criminal justice system must be made equitable, not just in theory but in practice. On a broader level, there is also a need to make correctional programs more effective in rehabilitating and counseling young, nonwhite males who are involved with criminal activity. Unless we begin to take some responsible actions of this sort to impact the level of criminal violence, our future looks bleak. At the same time, although it is important to correct the overvictimization of African-American and Hispanic-American males within the various components of the criminal justice system, it is also urgent to hold African-American and Hispanic-American criminals more accountable, particularly when other African-Americans and Hispanic Americans are victims.

Social Justice Advocacy

At the societal level, we must address the problem of socioeconomic inequities that create conditions of poverty and social stress that place the poor and underprivileged at greater risk of criminal violence. Social policies that do not address these issues of inequity cannot reduce crime. Unemployment and economic inequality appear to lead to crime only when they occur within a cultural context that infuses them with an acute sense of "failure" and "rejection." In turn, these produce a sense of "relative deprivation" and "thwarted ambition" (Box, 1987). In many ways, the unskilled and unemployable ethnic minorities in urban America are being excluded from the legitimate economy. All too often, younger people are finding a window of opportunity in the illegitimate economy at an astronomical cost to themselves and the local communities in which they reside (Athens, 1989; Rose & McClain, 1990). At the federal level, juveniles convicted of violent crimes should expect high retribution and punishment by the law and increased use of highly structured boot camp programs for youthful offenders. A greater priority for primary prevention youth outreach efforts should be supported to prevent youth at risk from turning to crime and related violent behaviors.

Domestic Violence Research and Intervention

More and better research data are essential on the nature of homicidal violence involving African-American and Hispanic-American males. These data will help to identify the types of homicides experienced in minority communities, situations leading to homicidal violence and battering, familial and relational influences, demographics of victims and offenders, the influence of alcohol and drugs, and other important socioeconomic variables. Conditions and correlates associated with the incidence of domestic violence are also worthy of further study. At present, data are lacking to test some of the theoretical explanations offered.

Firearms Control

There is a serious need for policy changes at the federal level to limit the easy access to, availability of, and use of automatic assault weapons. Such a legal framework could help curb the level of lethal violence in American urban areas, especially where gang-related violence and indiscriminate use of these weapons result in increased deaths and injury to more and more victims annually. The laws should hold equal penalties for the possession and sale of these lethal instruments. Along with these policy changes to outlaw automatic assault weapons, social and community efforts to offer amnesty to individuals to encourage them to surrender these weapons are a valuable undertaking. Invariably, the politics and the economics of manufacturing and distributing inexpensive handguns must also be confronted.

Refining Clinical Interventions

There is a desperate need to develop, refine, and implement effective models of counseling and clinical intervention when working with victims and offenders of brutal and violent crimes. New theoretical models and therapeutic interventions are required for work with populations that have special needs related to ethnicity, age, gender, and social class. The ultimate goal of psychological counseling should be to assist individuals to gain insight into their behavior, maximize their coping skills, and explore more socially acceptable coping mechanisms.

A Worthy American Agenda

Attempts at curbing violence within the African-American and Hispanic-American communities are futile if the broader American culture of violence is not addressed (Graham & Gurr, 1969). Ultimately, there is a need to examine violence and acts of brutality as issues at a national and societal level. A critical examination of the conditions and societal influences that nurture violence as a way of life is a worthy agenda for American society. With these insights, improved efforts at both rehabilitation and remediation can be realized. However, our greatest prospect for the future is in prevention. As higher standards of living are developed in our society, we should examine the destructive consequences of a rather primitive and maladaptive way of living that nurtures violence and ultimately threatens the quality of life and existence of humankind.

CONCLUSION

The unprecedented nature and scope of both the incidence and lethality of violence among contemporary adolescents warrant its priority as a major public health concern. Homicidal violence is a major cause of death for American youth 15 to 25 years of age. In addition to the primary victims who lose their lives to homicidal violence, there are also secondary victims who are affected and traumatized by witnessing chronic community violence. The extent of the trauma for youthful secondary victims may be significantly undermining a sense of safety and hopefulness in contemporary youth. This loss of hopefulness may influence many behaviors that reflect a sense of fatalism, pessimism, and self-destruction. In many instances, this may lead to behaviors in which those who were secondary victims themselves become primary victims and even perpetrators of violence. Note that young people who commit acts of violence experience losses in that very behavior, because violence invariably has demoralizing and demeaning consequences for its perpetrators.

4

Adolescents, Suicide, and Death

Anthony P. Jurich and Olivia P. Collins

Kurt Cobain, driving force behind the grunge rock group Nirvana, appeared to have "made it big," with wealth, fame, and the adoration of millions of adolescent fans. On April 8, 1994, the world discovered the pain behind this image when, shortly before 9 A.M., the lifeless body of Kurt Cobain was discovered in a greenhouse above the garage of his Seattle home. Kurt Cobain was dead at the age of 27 from a self-inflicted gunshot wound (Strauss, 1994). Within days, Cobain's picture was on the cover of most major news magazines, with articles that reminded us once more about that little secret we hide in the closet—suicide among the young.

This chapter analyzes the phenomenon of suicide among the young. It does this by: setting forth the demographic characteristics and rates of incidence of adolescent suicide; describing a theoretical model of the stressors, resources, and perceptions that may lead a young person to choose suicide; identifying five factors—physical, personal, family, peer, and community—involved in adolescent suicide; and applying the model to show how these factors are involved in processes of maladaptation and bonadaptation as they apply to the suicidal crises of young people.

PROFILE OF ADOLESCENT SUICIDE

Adolescents Who Complete Suicide

Regardless of headlines and statistics, the topic of suicide among the young, especially adolescents, always arouses feelings of disbelief, sorrow, and confusion. Almost 5,000 adolescent suicides occur in the United States each year (Henry, Stephenson, Hanson, & Hargott, 1993). Between 1960 and 1988, the suicide rate for adolescents, aged 15 to 19, increased from 3.6 to 11.3 per 100,000 population, an increase of more than 200%, compared with a general population increase of 17% (Garland & Zigler, 1993).

Suicide is now the third leading cause of death among adolescents, behind accidents and homicide (Kochanek & Hudson, 1994). Suicide accounts for 13% of all deaths in the adolescent population, but only 1.5% of the number of deaths in the general population. These numbers are shocking, especially when one considers that many suicides are not reported because of "religious implications, concern for the family, and financial considerations regarding insurance payment restrictions" (Garland & Zigler, 1993, p. 169). In addition, many accidental deaths (e.g., vehicular deaths) would be found to be suicides if the accidents were examined more closely (Hafen & Frandsen, 1986).

Suicide is prevalent in early, middle, and late adolescents. However, some demographic characteristics appear to be important when discussing adolescent suicide rates. Suicide rates rise as young people enter into middle adolescence (Pfeffer, 1986) and rise again as middle adolescents reach late adolescence (Berman & Jobes, 1991). With more autonomy comes a greater likelihood of ending one's life. At every age, white adolescents are more vulnerable to committing suicide than black teenagers (Berman & Jobes, 1991) or Hispanic teenagers (Kochanek & Hudson, 1994). For every 100 white teenage suicides, there are 53 black and 62 Hispanic adolescent suicides per 100,000 population. Native Americans have the highest rates of suicide among any ethnic groups, with rates ranging from 12 per 100,000 for the Navajos to 43 per 100,000 for some Apache groups (Berlin, 1987).

In all categories of adolescents, males have a higher suicide rate than females. There are more than three completed male suicides for each completed female suicide (Kochanek & Hudson, 1994). Although there are many speculations as to why males have a higher suicide rate than females, the two reasons most often cited are the greater propensity of males for using more lethal means of suicide and their greater fear of failure (Kirk, 1993).

Adolescents Who Attempt Suicide

"Although the exponential increase in suicide completions for adolescents causes alarm, the increase in suicide attempts is mind-boggling" (Kirk, 1993, p. 9). During 1990, 3.6 million young people in the United States considered suicide (Centers for Disease Control, 1991). Although there is conflict among the data, studies typically find that between 6% and 13% of adolescents have reported at least one suicide attempt in their lifetime (Garland & Zigler, 1993). One group of researchers (Rubenstein, Heeren, Housman, Rubin, & Stechler, 1989) reported a high rate of 20% of adolescents in the study had tried to "hurt themselves." In a survey on teenage suicide, Gallup (1991) reported that 45% of the randomly selected teenagers, aged 13 to 19, knew someone who had attempted suicide and failed, and 15% knew someone who had completed suicide. In a midwestern high school sample, 62.6% of the adolescents surveyed had reported some type of suicidal ideation or behavior (Smith & Crawford, 1986).

Although male adolescents are more likely to complete suicide, female adolescents are three times more likely to attempt suicide (Kochanek & Hudson, 1994). Part of this gender difference may be due to the method of data collection, which typically gathers "attempt" data from mental health or health facilities, which are used more frequently by females (Berman & Jobes, 1991). However, the main reason for the more successful suicide completion rate among males is their use of more violent and immediately lethal means, such as firearms or hanging. Female teenagers are more likely to use the ingestion of substances, which may or may not be fatal, and which, even if the dosage is lethal, allows time for emergency treatment. In all of these methods, whether the adolescent is younger or older, regardless of which ethnic group and gender, and despite the fact that the suicidal thoughts may not have as yet been acted on by the young person, these adolescents are in a great deal of pain. The remainder of this chapter focuses on the factors contributing to that pain.

THEORETICAL MODEL

The phenomenon of adolescent suicide has been viewed through many lenses. Some theorists have sought to find the genesis of adolescent suicidal tendencies in the biophysical realm. They have hypothesized that suicide is generated by psychiatric disorders that have biological foundations (Holinger & Offer, 1981), biological transmission of suicidal precursors (Hawton, 1986), or biochemical fluctuations and changes that predispose an adolescent to suicidal vulnerability (Shaughnessy & Nystul, 1985). Others have sought "the answer" in individual pathology and the quest for the "suicidal personality" (Holinger & Offer, 1981). Others, such as Durkheim (1951), have postulated a sociological theory of adolescent suicide, focusing more on the degree of integration of adolescents into social institutions and the regulation of adolescents by these social structures.

Social psychological theorists have focused on the identification of situational factors rising out of the social environment of the adolescent including family, school, and peers (Henry et al., 1993). In 1949, Hill proposed his classic ABC-X theory, in which he proposed that a crisis (X), such as adolescent suicide, was produced by an interaction among stressor events (A), interacting with both the family's resources (B), and the perceptions and meaning the family attaches to the event (C). Mc-Cubbin and Patterson (1982) improved on Hill's model by introducing the elements of pile-up, coping strategies, adaptation, and feedback loops into the model. They hypothesized that once crisis was reached there would be a "pile-up" of stressors (Double A). The family's coping strategies would then come into play and either change perceptions and meanings (Double C), deplete or enhance new resources (Double B), or both, resulting in either bonadaptation (good adaptation), thereby strengthening the family against the next onslaught of stressors, or maladaptation (bad or poor adaptation), spiraling the family toward more crises.

Further developments on the Double ABC-X model (Burr et al., 1994) have introduced different levels of abstraction in family stress. The Double ABC-X model has been successfully applied to the field of

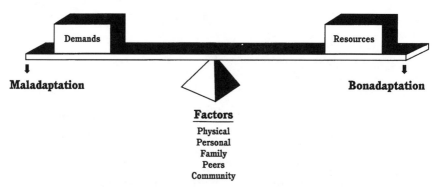

FIGURE 4.1 Balancing resources and demands.

adolescent suicide (Collins, 1990). A human ecological approach attempts to draw from all these previous theories to develop a comprehensive approach to adolescent suicide (Henry et al., 1993).

Drawing on the preceding theories in an attempt to be truly ecological in scope, we propose the following formulation of adolescent suicidal crisis. For most adolescents, life consists of an attempt to balance the demands of living with the resources on which an adolescent can draw. Figure 4.1 shows how this balance can be visualized as a "teeter-totter."

The research literature has focused on five factors that play a role in the phenomenon of adolescent suicide: (a) physical; (b) personal; (c) family; (d) peer; and (e) community. Each of these factors may put demands on adolescents, but each may also serve as a resource. If these five factors place more demands upon an individual adolescent than they provide resources, the demand side of the teeter-totter swings down and the adolescent experiences maladaptation (suicidal ideation, suicide attempts, and suicide). If, however, the five factors provide an adolescent with a wealth of resources in comparison with a minimum of demands, the teeter-totter swings down on the resources side of the model and the adolescent experiences bonadaptation (self-satisfaction and satisfaction with life).

As any individual who has ever played on a teeter-totter knows, it is the person whose feet are on the ground in the "down" position who has power over the situation and controls the motion of the apparatus, whereas the person on the "up" end of the teeter-totter sits helpless and powerless as his or her feet dangle in the air. Consequently, it is the

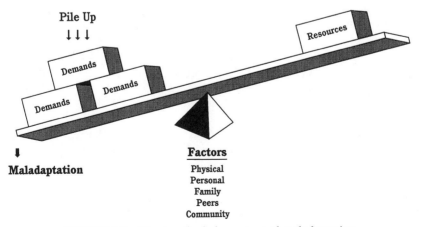

FIGURE 4.2 Tipping the balance toward maladaptation.

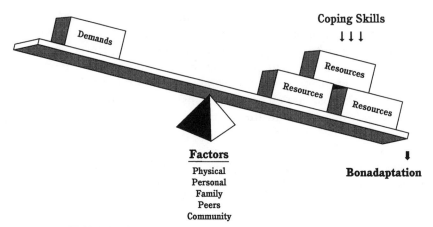

FIGURE 4.3   Tipping the balance toward bonadaptation.

"down" position of the teeter-totter pictured in Figure 4.1 that controls the situation and tends to accelerate the adolescent either toward maladaptation or bonadaptation.

Drawing on McCubbin and Patterson's Double ABC-X model (1982), there are two courses of action that will tip the teeter-totter down, either on the left or right. As can be seen in Figure 4.2, a pile-up of either normative or nonnormative stressors (McKenry & Price, 1994) will tip the balance toward maladaptation. Likewise, Figure 4.3 demonstrates that, if good coping skills can be employed either to increase resources or to change the adolescent's perception of the crisis, the balance will be tipped toward bonadaptation and the adolescent will increase his or her resilience to resist the temptations of suicide. This model provides the outline for the remainder of the chapter.

FACTORS IN ADOLESCENT SUICIDE

Physical Factors

Several researchers (e.g., Mann, DeMeo, Keilp, & McBride, 1989), predominantly in the medical and psychiatric fields, have explored the biological correlates of adolescent suicide. This research includes post-mortem brain studies, cerebrospinal fluid studies, experimental drug studies on neuroendocrine transmitters, and peripheral blood studies. Although much of the data are incomplete and contradictory, some physical factors have been associated with adolescent suicide.

A series of studies have identified biochemical factors in suicide (e.g., Lester, 1988). Most of these studies found alterations in the chemistry of neurotransmitter chemicals, such as serotonin. It has been suggested that this leads to an adolescent's greater vulnerability to psychiatric problems and suicide (Shaughnessy & Nystul, 1985). There also seems to be a correlation between low levels of growth hormones and suicidal behavior (Ryan et al., 1988). These studies have led researchers to consider the possibility that a genetic predisposition to suicide may be passed down through the generations (Roy, 1986). This possibility dovetails with research focusing on the biochemical foundations of mental illness, with the hypothesis that it is the presence of psychiatric illness that predisposes an adolescent to contemplate suicide (Holinger & Offer, 1981).

A second set of studies has focused on the reactions of adolescents to physical illness. Suicide has been correlated with medical illness in late adolescents but not in early adolescents, where the psychosocial factors seem to mask any adolescent response to physical illness in suicide (Hawton, 1986). However, when the illness is extreme, like epilepsy, the stressor of a long-term physical condition is highly associated with suicidal thoughts and behavior of adolescents at all ages (Brent, Crumrine, Varma, Allan, & Allman, 1987). Similarly, adolescents with AIDS have been found to be at very high risk of suicide (Marzuk et al., 1988). Added to the suffering of the disease, AIDS is a terminal illness with a great amount of fear and social stigma attached to it. Often adolescents feel so out of control over their condition that the only thing they do feel control over is the taking of their own lives.

A third level of physical stress is the reactions of adolescents to their own physical development (Ladame, 1992). When an adolescent's developed body does not measure up to his or her ideals and expectations, suicide may seem like the only way to change things. Although this may sound extreme (and it is), to an adolescent, who has no independent perspective on his or her own development, the finality of his or her own physical development, especially sexual development, may be overwhelming enough to trigger suicidal ideations.

Kurt Cobain, with whom we began this chapter, manifested several physical factors in his life (Mundy, 1994). His family had a history of suicide, he was diagnosed with bronchitis, and he had a mild case of scoliosis. He was given Ritalin at an early age to counteract hyperactivity. As he grew into his teenage years, he suffered from severe gastrointestinal pain (Handy, 1994). He obviously suffered from the demands placed on him by several physical factors that helped push him into maladaptation.

Personal Factors

Among the personal factors that influence adolescent suicide, many studies have focused on the psychiatric symptoms of young people who either complete or have attempted suicide (de Wilde, Kienhorst, Diekstra, & Wolters, 1993). Some researchers claim that there is only a small minority of suicidal adolescents who are free from any discernible psychiatric symptomatology (Shaffer, 1988).

The psychiatric diagnosis most often linked to suicide among adolescents is major clinical depression (Ladame, 1992; Wodarski & Harris, 1987). In fact, it has been asserted that depression is the most powerful discriminant of whether or not an adolescent completed suicide (Triolo, McKenry, Tishler, & Blyth, 1984). Estimates are that three out of every four adolescents were depressed at the time they completed suicide (Allberg & Chu, 1990), despite the fact that Ryland and Kruesi (1992) found major depression as the "official diagnosis" in only 17% to 38% of the cases in the studies they reviewed.

Kurt Cobain's major depression was diagnosed as early as high school (Strauss, 1994). Symptoms arising from adolescent depression that led to suicide are sleep and appetite disturbances, inappropriate affect, social withdrawal, complaints of boredom and fatigue, pathological guilt, lasting mood changes, lack of spontaneity, and anhedonia (the incapacity for experiencing pleasure) (Allberg & Chu, 1990). When elements of borderline personality present themselves with a major depression, adolescents engage in impulsive actions, uncontrolled and inappropriate anger, chronic feelings of emptiness, overinterpretations of the behaviors of others as signs of rejection and unlovability, and a preoccupation with death (Berman, 1985). Rural adolescents, because of their isolation and time alone, may be especially vulnerable to loneliness and suicidal fantasies (Forrest, 1988). When an adolescent is in the pain of a major depression, the specter of death no longer seems frightening; instead, it may begin to look attractive, seducing the adolescent into considering death as an alternative to that pain.

Some professionals do not consider depression itself as the major precipitating factor in adolescent suicide but point to feelings of hopelessness as the salient variable within the depression (Hawton, 1986; Rubenstein et al., 1989). When adolescents who are trying to achieve autonomy are faced with the hopelessness of depression, they feel as if they have no control over their lives and may desperately seek some form of control. For example, a depressed adolescent may turn to an eating disorder (Allberg & Chu, 1990), or may seek to self-medicate and control his or her pain through the use of drugs (Kirk, 1993). This only causes a further downward spiral toward maladaptation, because the drugs may lead to further depression or drug addiction, providing a ready means of suicide or possibly even an avenue by which the adolescent could kill himself or herself unintentionally through an accidental overdose (Allberg & Chu, 1990; Garland & Zigler, 1993; Ryland & Kruesi, 1992). Kurt Cobain was a notorious drug user who always described his drug use as self-medication for his physical maladies and as a way of numbing him from his psychosocial problems (Mundy, 1994). In this regard, he chose a maladaptive coping technique like so many young people have done before him.

Some researchers have shown that depression may lead to other problematic behavior, such as panic disorders, aggression, and both personality and psychotic disorders (Ladame, 1992). Studies of diagnosed disorders of suicidal adolescents often cite affective disorders as a typical diagnosis (Berman, 1985; Ryland & Kruesi, 1992). Other diagnoses cited frequently by mental health professionals include substance abuse, conduct disorder or antisocial personality, personality disorder, adjustment disorder, and schizophrenic disorder (Ryland & Kruesi, 1992). Such diagnosed problems not only add stress to an adolescent's life, but they also lead adolescents to make poor choices in coping strategies. Suicidal threats become a method of coping (Shafii, Carrigan, Whittinghill, & Derrick, 1985). These may escalate into suicide attempts (Berman, 1985; Garland & Zigler, 1993; Shafii et al., 1985). Tragically, suicidal threats and attempts often escalate into a completed suicide. The words of Kurt Cobain's music were a precursor to his ultimate suicide (Strauss, 1994). He gave voice to many troubled young souls, but the voice was also the cry of his own pain.

Some personal factors are not nearly so dramatic as serious mental illness. An adolescent's main task is to achieve an independent ego identity which is differentiated from his or her parents (Jurich, 1987). If he or she is unable to achieve a differentiated identity, the adolescent remains in an "identity diffused" state (Sands & Dixon, 1986). This may lead to an inhibited personality (Shafii et al., 1985) as well as higher state and trait anxiety (de Wilde et al., 1993). In any case, such an adolescent will have a lower sense of self-esteem because he or she is not achieving his or her principal developmental task. Low self-esteem has been strongly associated with greater suicidal risk in adolescence (Collins, 1990; de Wilde et al., 1993).

Using Freud's work as a foundation, self-psychologists have emphasized the role of "shame" in the process of identity formation (Shreve & Kunkel, 1991). They define "shame" as a sense of personal inadequacy stemming from a perceived failure to reach one's own internalized ideals. In adolescence, this shame can lead to a lack of cohesiveness in the newly formed self. Suicide may seem like a good coping strategy but is instead a maladaptive effort to ameliorate that shame. Because of this pain, together with some maladaptive coping techniques, an adolescent's judgment is skewed when he or she thinks about suicide.

Although cognitively capable of intellectually understanding the finality and universality of death, adolescents often fail to grasp that, in taking their own lives, they will die and will not return to life (Hawton, 1986). If we remember how prevalent egocentrism is to the newly forming adolescent identity (Jurich, 1987), it is questionable if adolescents who use suicide as a coping technique really know they are going to die in the full meaning of what death is.

Family Factors

Some researchers have stated that the family may be the single most influential factor in the suicidal thoughts, attempts, or actions of any adolescent, but especially in younger adolescents (Triolo et al., 1984). Models that emphasize family interaction focus on normal family processes that have become pathological in families that have produced suicidal adolescents (Orbach, 1988). For example, research has shown that moderate degrees of connectedness or cohesion are present in healthy families (Olson, Sprenkle, & Russell, 1979). Extremes in cohesion were found to be associated with problems. The family that is too distant or disengaged often had members who felt isolated or rejected, whereas the family that is too close or enmeshed often had members who felt smothered.

Several studies of suicidal adolescents found their families to be either enmeshed or disengaged (Collins, 1990; Corder, Page, & Corder, 1974) or found both extremes in the same family by vacillating back and forth between the two (Pfeffer, 1986). Families that have had a suicidal adolescent and that are described as disengaged are characterized by a lack of warmth (Corder, Page, & Corder, 1974), a lack of empathy (Miller, King, Shain, & Naylor, 1992; Wodarski & Harris, 1987), and a lack of supportive adults in the home (Morano, Cisler, & Lemerond, 1993). Families with suicidal adolescents who were enmeshed were overly controlling (Corder, Page, & Corder, 1974) and stunted the adolescent's quest for individuation from the family (Pfeffer, 1986; Wenz, 1979). In this way, a factor such as cohesion, which is typical of healthy families if moderate, becomes associated with families with suicidal adolescents if the closeness is too intense (enmeshed) or too distant (disengaged).

Likewise, the dimension of adaptability in families is associated with healthy families when moderate but with pathological families when it is extreme, either rigid or chaotic (Olson, Sprenkle, & Russell, 1979). Both of these pathological extremes in adaptability have been associated with families who have suicidal adolescents (Collins, 1990). Chaotic families with suicidal adolescents tend to be disintegrating, multiproblem families with few functional coping skills (Miller et al., 1992). Rigid families who have suicidal adolescents do not have the ability to adjust to these changes within the family, especially those brought about by a maturing adolescent (Pfeffer, 1986). Therefore, the developmental needs of family members, especially those of adolescents, go either unrecognized or unmet.

When rigidity is combined with disengagement, a suicidal adolescent experiences both the pain of isolation and an inflexible family system, which limits the possibility of change to lessen the pain (Miller et al., 1992). Suicide may seem like the only way out. When rigidity is combined with enmeshment, decisions are made by the parents, without the input or involvement of the adolescent (Corder, Page, & Corder, 1974). The adolescent feels little power over his or her involvement and, therefore, feels trapped in a child-like developmental stage. Because any individuation is viewed as betrayal and disloyalty by the parents, the adolescent feels powerless to change his or her stunted growth (Pfeffer, 1986). Suicide may be an adolescent's desperate act to restore some sense of personal power in an attempt to meet his or her own developmental needs (Wenz, 1979).

Extremes in such basic family dimensions as cohesion and adaptability make it dangerous to speak openly and honestly within the family system (Olson, Sprenkle, & Russell, 1979). In families with suicidal adolescents there is either a scarcity of communication (Corder, Page, & Corder, 1974; Wodarski & Harris, 1987) or there are poor communication patterns (Pfeffer, 1986). Secrecy, incongruent and disqualifying messages, nonsupportive statements, and double-binding messages are the family's typical patterns of communication. This increases the level of hostility within the family of the suicidal adolescent (Pfeffer, 1986; Rubenstein et al., 1989; Wodarski & Harris, 1987). A suicidal adolescent may have been subjected to emotional, physical, or sexual abuse (Allberg & Chu, 1990; Hawton, 1986; Shafii et al., 1985; Slaby & McGuire, 1989). Regardless if the hostility was directed toward the adolescent or not, 43% of all adolescent suicide attempts were preceded by a family fight (Litt, Cuskey, & Rudd, 1983).

Because of the degree of hostility, many families seek to close off their boundaries in an effort to shield the family from the critical gaze of outsiders (Leigh, 1986). Although this does eliminate, at least to some degree, outside criticism, it also cuts the family off from any external resources (Sands & Dixon, 1986). As a result, suicidal adolescents see the family as being totally alone with no hope of change from a very painful situation. In those circumstances, suicide may seem to be the only option available to force the family to open its boundaries.

Much of this hostility and the closing of the family boundaries seems to stem from the inability of the parents to accept and perform parental roles (Pfeffer, 1986). The parents of suicidal adolescents often demonstrate an inability to deal with their own childhood trauma (Sands & Dixon, 1986). These parents seem to be so egocentric in their needs that they have a difficult time understanding the normative expectations placed on them by society (Wenz, 1979). Therefore, they are in no position to offer much clear-cut guidance about values or coping skills (Peck, 1982). Because of norm confusion, adolescents may attempt, through trial and error, to create techniques for coping with stress that are maladaptive (Wenz, 1979). Suicide may become one of these maladaptive techniques that is explored by adolescents who are trying to make sense of a highly confusing world.

Many parents of suicidal adolescents not only have problems with their parental roles but with their spousal roles as well (Pfeffer, 1986). Families with suicidal adolescents often have severe marital discord (Berman, 1985; Sands & Dixon, 1986). In many cases this can lead to marital separation or divorce (Allberg & Chu, 1990), and life in a single-parent household (Garland & Zigler, 1993). In the case of Kurt Cobain, his parents divorced when he was 7 years old (Mundy, 1994). Subsequently, he lived with his father, grandparents, and mother, never again finding a stable home environment and always feeling a profound sense of loss.

It is this sense of loss that characterizes many suicidal adolescents when they speak about their families (Henry et al., 1993; Morano, Cisler, & Lemerond, 1993). This loss may be due to a parent's death (Allberg & Chu, 1990), the parent's suicide (Rubenstein et al., 1989), parental absence because of work (Shafii et al., 1985), or drug or alcohol use (Henry et al., 1993). A parent may have a chronic illness (Hawton, 1986) or may be trying to cope with his or her own emotional problems (Berman, 1985) so that he or she is unable to meet the emotional and interpersonal needs of the adolescent.

Even if both parents are present and are seemingly unburdened by these stresses, they may be psychologically absent and unavailable to the suicidal adolescent (Hawton, 1986). The adolescent may feel ignored (Henry et al., 1993), unwanted, or unloved by his or her family (Triolo et al., 1984). In such families, the suicide or suicide attempt may be a symptom of the family dysfunction, diverting attention away from the family's problems (Henry et al., 1993) and pushing the family further toward the side of maladaptation.

Peer Factors

Although peers are important to all of us, they are especially important to adolescents in that they provide a counterpoint to the influence of the family in an adolescent's quest for self-definition (Jurich, 1987). Therefore, peers are inordinately important to adolescents, and young people can be hypersensitive to messages of nonacceptance from their friends, associates, and the peer group as a whole (Kirk, 1993). The adolescent seems trapped by his or her own inability to internalize peer acceptance to validate himself or herself. Once adolescents are without that peer acceptance, belonging, and affirmation, they may find their self-esteem diminishing and their minds turning to thoughts of suicide (Sands & Dixon, 1986).

When adolescents fail to differentiate from their parents, they often do not identify with their peers (Sands & Dixon, 1986; Wodarski & Harris, 1987). Adolescents who function inadequately in social situations but feel that they are surrounded by socially competent peers are likely to decrease their self-esteem (Holinger & Offer, 1981; Sands & Dixon, 1986). Suicidal adolescents expressed less satisfaction with their peer relationships and needed to belong to a social group of peers to enhance their self-esteem (Forrest, 1988; Rubenstein et al., 1989). Younger suicidal teenagers also expressed a wish for their parents to approve of their peer group (Triolo et al., 1984).

When these adolescents do come into social contact with their peers, they are often lacking in social communication skills (Allberg & Chu, 1990). Peer contacts may be awkward or even humiliating (Blumenthal, 1990). Consequently, an adolescent may isolate himself or herself (Allberg & Chu, 1990), and become a "loner" (Wodarski & Harris, 1987). This leaves the adolescent with fewer interpersonal resources and poor social supports (Blumenthal, 1990; Slaby & McGuire, 1984). Such adolescents begin to feel the "emptiness in their lives" (Hawton, 1986), which can lead to loneliness, depression, and a further withdrawal from peer contact (Allberg & Chu, 1990; Forrest, 1988). A suicide attempt may be an adolescent's only way of dramatically and drastically attempting to communicate his or her pain to peers (Allberg & Chu, 1990). Thus, a suicidal adolescent may become a victim of his or her own alienation, conflicting social pressures, and his or her own social marginality (Sands & Dixon, 1986; Young, 1985).

Several situations make adolescents more vulnerable to these peer stresses. Adolescents who view their romantic relationships as being unstable and problematic are susceptible to this type of peer stress (Berman, 1985; Henry et al., 1993). Adolescents whose romantic relationships have broken are even more susceptible to the kind of peer stress that ends in suicide (Blumenthal, 1990; Hawton, 1986; Sands & Dixon, 1986). However, even if these young people do not break up and attempt to raise a family in their teen years, the stress of doing so also makes them more likely candidates for suicide (Henry et al., 1993).

Sexual identity problems have also been linked to a higher risk of suicide because of peer group censure (Ryland & Kruesi, 1992). Drug use supported by peers may lower inhibitions and lead to more impulsivity, which may lead an adolescent with poor self-esteem to seek an immediate release from his or her pain by suicide (Garland & Zigler, 1993; Shaffer, 1988). Delinquent adolescents, who seem so independent from society's rules, might, in reality, feel trapped by the rules of the peer group or gang, and look to suicide to escape (Sands & Dixon, 1986).

When there is a difference in development between the intellectual and social abilities of adolescents, they may feel "immature" in their social skills and not identify with their peers' needs and values (Delise, 1986). It is for these reasons that gifted adolescent females have been found to be at higher risk for suicide attempts (Delise, 1986; Shaughnessy & Nystul, 1985). Declining grades or failing in school can also be a source of personal and peer embarrassment, leading to a suicide attempt (Henry et al., 1993; Rubenstein et al., 1989; Wodarski & Harris, 1987).

Even the simple fact of residential mobility may disrupt relationships with peers, forcing an adolescent into being the "new kid on the block" and inducing new peer stress without the assistance of familiar resources to help the individual cope (Henry et al., 1993). This was the situation with Kurt Cobain, who moved multiple times with his family and between his father, mother, and three sets of aunts and uncles (Mundy, 1994). This can increase the vulnerability of adolescents to turn to suicide to cope with their pain.

The most dramatic example of the influence of adolescent peers on each other is the phenomenon of "cluster suicides" (Davidson, 1989). For example, on February 19, 1983, a 17-year-old boy was killed in what was reported to be a drag racing incident in Plano, a suburb of Dallas, Texas. Within the next 8 weeks, three other Plano teenagers, including the 17-year-old's best friend, took their own lives (Gelman & Gangelhoff, 1983). Three other examples of cluster suicides among adolescents are provided by Collins (1990), and three more examples are provided by Davidson (1989).

Studies have shown that just knowing somebody who has committed suicide (Blumenthal, 1990) or somebody who was murdered (Berlin, 1987) was enough to increase suicidal risk. However, in cluster suicides an initial adolescent suicide seems to breed a contagion among other adolescents who knew the deceased in a manner that follows the model of an infectious disease (Gould, 1990). There appears to be an identification with the person who most recently committed suicide and, especially among young people, a strong modeling effect (Davidson, 1989). Such a major peer influence can tip the teeter-totter toward maladaptation not only for one suicidal youth but for many. If this force could be harnessed in positive directions, it could turn the tide toward bonadaptation.

Community Factors

At its broadest level, the term *community* refers to the culture in which a suicidal adolescent lives. We are not alone in the United States when we have concerns over adolescent suicide. In the *International Handbook of Adolescence* (Hurrelmann, 1994), excluding the United States, one half of the 30 countries about whom a chapter was written felt the need to have a section on adolescent suicide. Each country responds differently to the phenomenon of suicide among its adolescents (Hawton, 1986). A key factor appears to be the speed of change within a given culture, with rapidly changing cultures creating more turmoil for their adolescents (Ryland & Kruesi, 1992).

Within the boundaries of our own country, there still exists a number of subcultures that view death, dying, and suicide in different ways (Irish, Lundquist, & Nelsen, 1993). Certain tribes of the Native American population have the highest suicide rate in the United States (Berlin, 1987). Contributing to the stress of Native American adolescents is the impact of poverty and economic hardship, the problems of life on the reservation when compared with what the young person might see of the culture at large on television, the displacement of being sent to a boarding school, and the paradoxical and often conflicting messages of the culture of his or her heritage and the culture at large (Henry et al., 1993). Added to these are the prejudice suffered at the hands of the majority culture and the fact that many Native American tribal cultures do not have the same negative view of suicide that is generally found in the larger society. It is little wonder that, for some Native American young people, the suicide rate is so high.

However, even in the ethnic group that has one of the lowest suicide rates, the African-Americans, there are problematic conditions that have caused the suicide rate of their young people to rise also (Murry

& Bell-Scott, 1994). The African-American community has often felt a sense of alienation from the majority culture, and its people have sought to distance themselves from society because of it. Although this may lessen stress, it also cuts off many African-Americans from needed resources. This situation is worst in the urban ghetto, where poverty, overcrowding, crime, violence, and social isolation from mainstream society create feelings of powerlessness, depression, and despair among young people. Thus, for subcultures at either end of the suicide rate continuum, there are still pressures that can lead to suicide and other forms of maladaptation.

Within the larger society, communities vary in the degree to which they value their young people and support them through the very difficult period of adolescence. If a community is quick to arrest an adolescent (Kirk, 1993), it will be viewed by adolescents as being a hostile environment in which to live. If the community is a highly transient community in which many families locate and then relocate, it will cause stress to the adolescent population (Kirk, 1993). If there are no social supports to help adolescents cope with these stressors, the adolescents will be more likely to become maladaptive (Hawton, 1986). If the community's adolescent population is large, there may be more competition for such prized commodities as jobs, good grades, and status positions (Holinger & Offer, 1981; Ryland & Kruesi, 1992). Young people may find themselves courted by community merchants to spend money but chased out of the mall if they "loiter too long."

Some of a community's values are taken from the greater society. The greater society condones taking medications to cope with illness, either physical or psychological, and this attitude has been thought to increase the likelihood of suicide by drug overdose (Hawton, 1986). The societal acceptance of violence creates an atmosphere which is ripe for suicide as a problem-solving technique for young people (Berlin, 1987). The society at large allows for the widespread availability of firearms (Boyd & Moscicki, 1986), and researchers have shown a positive relationship between the accessibility and use of firearms and suicide rates (Garland & Zigler, 1993; Lester, 1988). Since 1950, the number of firearms per person in the United States has dramatically risen, and the number of suicides by firearms has increased three times faster than all other methods (Boyd & Moscicki, 1986). In addition, there is a greater availability of firearms in the homes of adolescents who commit suicide (Brent, Perper, Moritz, Baugher, & Allman, 1993).

How a community newspaper or television reports an adolescent suicide may also have a major effect upon whether any more young people also commit suicide (Henry et al., 1993). Suicides seem to rise sharply if there is more media coverage of that event (Blumenthal, 1990; Garland & Zigler, 1993), and the suicide rate in that broadcast or circulation region tends to increase for 1 or 2 months after a suicide has been covered by the media, especially among people who are similar to the suicidal victim (Phillips, Carstensen, & Paight, 1989). How an individual community responds to these societal values will determine, at least in part, that community's adolescent suicide rate.

Kurt Cobain, as noted earlier, had problems arising out of all four of the types of suicide factors previously mentioned in this chapter (physical pain, psychological distress, family disruption, and social stress). He also felt pressure from his community, Aberdeen, Washington (Gilmore, 1994). Aberdeen is a lumber town halfway up Washington's outer coast that has fallen on hard economic times from lumber industry cutbacks. In part, Cobain learned how to hate life because of the scorn he received from the Aberdeen community. Aberdeen's suicide rate is twice the national average. It also has high incidences of unemployment, domestic violence, alcoholism, and drug usage. Cobain got into trouble at school, dropped out, drifted around the town, and finally left. But he still carried his community in his pain. When he finally sought release from that pain by shooting himself with a gun, a friend remarked, "I hate to say it, but it was the perfect Aberdeen death" (Gilmore, 1994, p. 45).

APPLICATION OF THE MODEL TO THE FACTORS

Although each of the five factors can affect either the demands or resources side of the model, the preceding discussion has focused on these factors as demands. This is partly because of the methodology used in discovering these factors. The stressors in these factors were identified through their association with the acts or attempts of suicide as correlates or causes of suicide. Hence, they were tied to the demands portion of the model by the methodology used to identify them in the literature. The resources side of the model for each factor would be the absence of that variable in the adolescent's life. Therefore, each of the above five factors points to stressor variables that may give the reader information on either the demands or resources side of the model.

Tipping the Balance Toward Maladaptation

The presence of any of the stressors cited within the preceding five factors will push down on the demands side of the model toward maladaptation. An accumulation of stressors is referred to as "pile-up." This pile-up of stressors may come from one factor, such as a multitude of physical injuries or conditions, or may come from two or more factors, such as a psychiatric disorder and a dysfunctional family problem. Our example of Kurt Cobain demonstrated a young man with a pile-up of stressors from all five factors. These stressors may be normative, such as the typical developmental stressors of adolescence, or they may be non-normative (i.e., situational), such as the suicide of a close relative. Regardless of their origin or type, this pile-up of stressors makes the maladaptive outcome of suicide more likely (Hawton, 1986). The cumulative effect of a pile-up of stressful events and conditions can cause a pathological response by overtaxing the normal adaptive capacities of an adolescent (Rubenstein et al., 1989). Thus, the pile-up of stressors tips the balance toward maladaptation, increasing the likelihood of suicide.

Tipping the Balance Toward Bonadaptation

If there are stressors piling up on the demands side of the model, for an adolescent to choose bonadaptive means of dealing with these stressors, there must be resources from which the adolescent can draw to counterbalance those demands. According to the Double ABC-X model (McCubbin & Patterson, 1982), a key element in determining how an adolescent reacts to these stressors is the adolescent's coping skills. If the level of coping skills is high, it will tip the model toward bonadaptation.

Some coping skills help adolescents perceive stressors or contextual situations differently. The first perceptual step is an acknowledgment of the problem (Wodarski & Harris, 1987). At this point, helping an adolescent see the situation differently, with hope and a new perspective, will allow the adolescent to recognize and use the resources he or she has available (Triolo et al., 1984). With the help of this change of perception away from shame and self-blame, a suicidal adolescent can engage in a more problem-solving course of behavior (Shreve & Kunkel, 1991). Thus, the ability to change perception can be, in and of itself, an important coping skill.

Other coping skills involve the pursuit of resources to counterbalance the pressure from stressors. Although resources are often plentiful for children and adults in our society, they are often scarce for the adolescent population. We seem to think that adolescents are neither as needy as children nor as important as adults. Consequently, adolescents must develop the ability to seek out resources to help in coping with stress. One such coping skill is physical fitness. Though it may not eliminate an adolescent's physical stressors, physical fitness can help ameliorate their effects. Personal resources, such as healthier self-esteem or an internal locus of control, can also reduce the risk of suicide (Collins, 1990).

Working to build on family strengths and peer support can also serve as protective mechanisms to lower the probability of suicidal behavior (Rubenstein et al., 1989; Wodarski & Harris, 1987). In addition, drawing on resources from the community, including professional helpers, can lessen the strain of an intolerable situation for an adolescent (Sands & Dixon, 1986). These resources may emphasize the prevention of suicidal ideation and situations (Hawton, 1986; Kirk, 1993), or focus on therapy with an adolescent who is already considered to be suicidal (Blumenthal, 1990; Pfeffer, 1986).

The ability to use these resources is crucial because a suicidal adolescent may view the environment, defined by the five factors of the model, as hostile and unsupportive. If the family, peers, and community can provide resources to an adolescent, and the young person can recognize and use those supports at his or her disposal, the weight will shift from the demands side to the resources side of the model, moving the adolescent toward bonadaptation, thus avoiding suicide as a solution to stress.

CONCLUSION

To cope with the crisis of suicide among the young people of our society we must understand the genesis and processes that lead adolescents and young adults to pursue suicide as a maladaptive coping technique. This chapter sought to increase understanding of the reasons young people choose suicide by exploring the five factors that can influence an adolescent to consider suicide as an option. To facilitate that task, a "teeter-totter" model was employed. Stressors, resources, and the perceptions of those two elements were found to lead adolescents to maladaptive coping strategies, such as suicide, when stressors were high (pile-up), resources were low, and the perceptions of both stressors and resources were extreme and negative. Likewise, when adolescents had few stressors, many resources, and viewed their stressors as manageable and resources at least as adequate, they were more likely to choose bonadaptive coping strategies and avoid suicide as an option. By applying this model of five factors (physical, personal, family, peer, and community), readers can understand the major dynamics that lead adolescents to suicide.

Adolescents who suffer from physical illness or stress, have psychiatric difficulties (especially depression), come from families with dysfunctional coping patterns, are vulnerable to peer-induced stress (e.g., cluster suicides), and receive little community support are more likely than adolescents who do not have such experiences to consider suicide as a method of coping with what they believe to be a hopeless situation. This chapter also suggested a blueprint for influencing young people toward more bonadaptive coping techniques by expanding physical resources, enhancing self-concept and changing self-perceptions, working with families of adolescents by utilizing family therapy techniques, working with adolescent peer groups, and enlisting community support. In this way, readers may use the model and the information in this chapter not only to understand suicide among adolescents, but also through both prevention and remediation, to work to minimize the use of suicide as a coping technique and to maximize more bonadaptive coping mechanisms.

5

Adolescents and AIDS: Epidemiology, Prevention, and Psychological Responses

Ralph J. DiClemente, Katherine E. Stewart, Mallary O. Johnson, and Robert P. Pack

Adolescents have only recently emerged as a risk group for HIV infection, the virus associated with the pathogenesis of AIDS. Though the prevalence of HIV infection among adolescents is undetermined, surveillance data indicate adolescents are one population experiencing an increase in AIDS cases (Bowler, Sheon, D'Angelo, & Vermund, 1993; Hein, 1992). Moreover, epidemiological data identifying the high rate of risk-taking behavior among this age group suggest that the future rate of HIV infection in adolescents may continue to increase (DiClemente, 1990, 1993a).

At present, there is no cure for AIDS. Recent advances in the development of antiretroviral therapy have produced promising, new therapeutic agents (Worth & Volberding, 1994). Some agents, like azidothymidine (AZT) (also known as ZDV or zidovudine), have shown an ability to inhibit viral replication. Other new and more potent pharmacological therapies are currently undergoing extensive clinical trials. Similarly, a vaccine to prevent HIV infection is currently not available, although concerted efforts by public and private biotechnology laboratories are progressing rapidly. It is difficult to project when a vaccine will be available, in large part, because of the complex, mutagenic nature of the virus. Thus, in the absence of an effective therapy or vaccine, a coordinated and systematic public health education effort may represent the only practical approach for preventing the spread of HIV infection (DiClemente, 1993b; DiClemente & Peterson, 1994; Institute of Medicine, 1986).

This chapter addresses three issues critical to understanding the threat and the impact of the HIV epidemic for adolescents. First, this chapter describes the epidemiology of HIV and AIDS among adolescents. Second, we describe the state of the science of behavioral interventions designed to prevent or reduce HIV-associated risk behaviors. Finally, we propose a hypothetical model describing adolescents' psychological reactions to HIV diagnosis, disease progression, and, ultimately, death.

AIDS SURVEILLANCE AMONG ADOLESCENTS: AIDS CASES IDENTIFIED BY THE CENTERS FOR DISEASE CONTROL AND PREVENTION

AIDS is relatively uncommon among adolescents. Individuals between 13 and 19 years of age account for less than 1% of all diagnosed cases of AIDS in the United States (Centers for Disease Control, 1994). However, recent data indicate that the rate of AIDS among adolescents has increased over the course of the epidemic (Hein, 1992). Moreover, AIDS is not uniform among adolescents. Minority populations, in particular African-American and Latino adolescents aged 13 to 19, are 5.1 and 4.3 times more likely, respectively, to be diagnosed with AIDS than are white adolescents (DiClemente, 1992). Gender-specific analyses of case surveillance data have identified African-American and Latina females as 11 and 5 times more likely, respectively, to be diagnosed with AIDS than similar-age white female adolescents.

AIDS case surveillance data, although useful, are not a timely or accurate measure for evaluating the magnitude of the health threat HIV poses for adolescents. Given the lengthy latency period from infection to clinical diagnosis (Bacchetti & Moss, 1989; Lui, Darrow, & Rutherford, 1988), an undetermined proportion of adults diagnosed with AIDS in their 20s will likely have been infected during their teenage years. Thus, AIDS surveillance data may markedly underestimate the risk of disease for adolescents. A more useful measure of disease impact is HIV seroprevalence.

HIV SEROPREVALENCE AMONG ADOLESCENTS

Currently, there are no representative population-based studies for estimating HIV seroprevalence among adolescents as existing estimates of seroprevalence are based solely on selected adolescent populations. A recent review (DiClemente, 1992) has identified seroprevalence rates ranging from a low of 0.17 per 1,000 (for white military applicants) to a high of 68 per 1,000 (for Latino youth in homeless shelters in New York City). As with Centers for Disease Control (CDC)-defined AIDS cases, HIV infection is not uniform across ethnic groups. African-American adolescents have a substantially higher prevalence rate of HIV infection relative to white and Latino adolescents. Seroprevalence rates among African-American adolescents are generally 3 to 5 times higher than those of white adolescents (see Table 5.1).

As the epidemiological data in Table 5.1 demonstrate, although adolescents may not represent a large proportion of diagnosed AIDS cases, this may be more a reflection of the long latency period between infection with the HIV and onset of case-defining symptomatology than the absence of a real threat. Clearly, adolescents are being infected with HIV and, unless prevention programs are urgently developed, many more are likely to become infected.

STATE OF THE SCIENCE FOR PREVENTION OF HIV AMONG ADOLESCENTS

Many adolescents engage in sexual and drug-related behaviors that increase the risk for HIV infection (DiClemente, 1990; Hein, 1992,

TABLE 5.1 Prevalence of HIV for Selected Surveys by Ethnicity[a]

Study (yr)	Sample or Site	Black	Latino	White
Burke et al. (1990)	Military applicants	1.0	0.29	0.17
Kelley et al. (1990)[b]	Active-duty military	5.1	4.0	1.25
St. Louis et al. (1991)	Job Corps entrants	5.3	2.6	1.2
St. Louis et al. (1990)	General hospital	8.3	4.9	2.7
Stricof et al. (1991)	Homeless shelter	46.0	68.0	60.0
D'Angelo et al. (1991)	Ambulatory clinics	3.7	—	—

[a] All findings have been converted and are presented as rate of seropositive adolescents per 1,000 to permit comparability with other surveys. [b] Sample of active-duty military personnel is not exclusively composed of adolescents.

1987). Although sexual abstinence is the most effective method to prevent the transmission of HIV as well as other sexually transmitted diseases, few adolescents adopt this HIV-preventive behavior once they have become sexually active. An alternative prevention strategy for male adolescents who are sexually active is to use condoms consistently during sexual intercourse and for female adolescents to insist that their male partners use condoms (Hein, 1993; Roper, Peterman, & Curran, 1993). Although condoms prohibit the transmission of viral pathogens, including HIV (Cates & Stone, 1992; DeVincenzi, 1994), their effectiveness as a risk-reduction strategy is dependent on appropriate and consistent use. Unfortunately, increasing consistent condom use, as well as other HIV-preventive behaviors among adolescents, has not yielded widespread reductions in risk behaviors.

Many adolescents continue to report a high prevalence of HIV-related risk behaviors (Anderson et al., 1990; Kann et al., 1991). Recent findings from the 1991 CDC youth risk behavior survey indicate that 54% of high school students are sexually active, with more than one half (52%) reporting that they did not use a condom the last time they engaged in sexual intercourse. Moreover, 19% report four or more sexual partners over their lifetime (CDC, 1992). Developing effective programs that promote the adoption and maintenance of HIV-preventive behaviors is critical to avert an escalation in HIV infection among adolescents (DiClemente, 1993a, 1993b).

The development and implementation of programs designed to reduce high-risk behaviors associated with HIV transmission may, at present, and perhaps for years to come, be the only effective strategy for controlling the spread of HIV infection (DiClemente, 1990, 1993a, 1994; DiClemente & Peterson, 1994). However, the HIV epidemic poses unprecedented challenges for the development of effective interventions. Modifying well-established behaviors, particularly sexual behaviors is a formidable task. One obstacle to developing more efficacious interventions has been our lack of understanding of the factors that affect sexual behavior. For example, it is clear that this is not a simple behavior; rather, it is the outcome of a multifactorial decision-making process in which many influences—biological, social, developmental, and psychological—underlie the willingness of adolescents to tolerate and accept risks. Unfortunately, there is little empirical information available about the factors that reinforce adolescents' sexual risk taking and, more important, less information is available about those factors that influence adolescents' use of health-protective behaviors. Although the empirical data base for developing behavior change interventions is limited, there is some evidence to suggest that promoting the adoption and maintenance of HIV-preventive behaviors among adolescents is achievable.

Theory-Based HIV Prevention Programs

Social psychological theories serve as excellent building blocks for HIV prevention programs. However, no single theory explains or predicts the myriad behaviors linked to HIV infection (Leviton, 1989). Thus, many different theories are being evaluated regarding their utility for HIV prevention interventions. Indeed, many new theories are being developed specifically to prevent adolescents' HIV risk behaviors (Fisher, Misovich, & Fisher, 1992; Rotheram-Borus, Koopman, & Rosario, 1992).

In the past, many risk-reduction interventions for adolescents, considered first-generation programs, were based on education and information alone (DiClemente, 1994). Although these constructs would seem to have utility for understanding and preventing HIV-associated behavior, informational programs on their own are often not sufficient to motivate adolescents to adopt HIV-prevention strategies. More recently, social psychological theories such as social learning theory (Bandura, 1992), the theory of reasoned action (Fishbein, Middlestadt, & Hitchcock, 1994), and diffusion theory (Dearing, Meyer, & Rogers, 1994) have been proposed as being useful in guiding intervention efforts. This has spawned a new generation of HIV-prevention programs. Unlike their predecessors, these new programs not only emphasize an informational component, but also stress the need for changing adolescents' normative perceptions and social skills necessary to avoid or resist risk-taking situations and demands (Jemmott, Jemmott, & Fong, 1992; Main et al., 1994; Rotheram-Borus, Koopman, Haignere, Davies, 1991; St. Lawrence, Brasfield, Jefferson, Alleyne, O'Bannon, & Shirley, 1995; Walter & Vaughan, 1993). We briefly describe successful school- and community-based prevention programs for adolescents.

School-Based Interventions. The most obvious choice for an intervention site and target population is the school, as the overwhelming majority of children and adolescents attend school. Indeed, there are more interventions being implemented in schools than perhaps in any other site. Recently, several studies have appeared in the literature that suggest a rigorous methodological, theoretical, and evaluable trend (DiClemente, 1993a, 1994; Howard & McCabe 1990; Kirby, Barth, Leland, & Fetro, 1991; Main et al., 1994; Walter & Vaughan, 1993). One study, for instance, has demonstrated a statistically significant effect in reducing adolescents' sexual risk behaviors (Walter & Vaughan, 1993).

There are several key elements that contribute to this intervention's success. The HIV-prevention curriculum is based on established psychological models of behavior change. Moreover, the investigators were able to target key psychosocial constructs which directly affect adolescents' decision making and sexual risk taking based on a needs assessment and recent empirical data. In particular, the HIV prevention curriculum emphasized risk information, self-efficacy, and sexual negotiation skills, beliefs about perceived susceptibility, barriers and benefits to engaging in HIV-preventive behaviors, and perceptions of the acceptability and norms for involvement in HIV-preventive behaviors. Finally, teacher inservice was provided to familiarize teachers with the curriculum.

Based on a 3-month follow-up, findings indicate that the intervention was effective in increasing HIV knowledge, changing adolescents' beliefs, enhancing self-efficacy, and, most important, in reducing high-risk sexual behaviors. Adolescents in the intervention group reported a lower frequency of sexual intercourse with high-risk partners, decreased number of sex partners, and an increase in consistent condom use relative to their peers in a control group. This study may provide the impetus for the development of a new generation of school-based HIV prevention programs: those that are theoretically based, empirically driven, and systematically evaluated.

While findings from recent school-based prevention interventions are encouraging, the small effect sizes observed suggest that other innovative and effective strategies are urgently needed to increase the proportion of adolescents who adopt HIV-preventive behaviors (DiClemente, 1993b). In a recent review of school-based HIV prevention programs (Kirby & DiClemente, 1994), several key elements were identified which may enhance program effectiveness. These include (a) using social learning theories as a foundation for program development (e.g., social learning theory, cognitive behavioral theory, and social influence theory); (b) maintaining a narrow focus on reducing sexual risk-taking behaviors; (c) using active learning methods of instruction; (d) including activities that address the social and media influences and pressures to have sex; (e) focusing on and reinforcing clear and appropriate values against unprotected sex (i.e., postponing sex, avoiding unprotected intercourse, and avoiding high-risk partners); and (f) providing modeling and practice of communication or negotiation skills. Furthermore, to maximize program effectiveness, HIV prevention programs must also be tailored to be developmentally appropriate and culturally relevant (Wingood & DiClemente, 1992; in press). Although school-based intervention programs will undoubtedly be a key risk-reduction vehicle, community-based prevention efforts are also crucial.

Community-Based HIV-Prevention Programs. Schools offer great promise for developing and implementing adolescent HIV prevention interventions. However, the impact of schools as agents of change, promoting the adoption and maintenance of HIV-preventive behaviors, should not be exaggerated. Schools alone will not achieve maximal effectiveness if adolescents live in environments that counteract newly acquired HIV-prevention knowledge and skills. There is ample evidence, for instance, that adolescents who do not attend school are at disproportionately greater risk for HIV infection (CDC, 1993). Thus, community-based HIV-prevention interventions may be better able to access this difficult-to-reach adolescent population.

Community-based organizations such as the YMCA, the Boys Club, runaway shelters, recreation centers, and physician offices are all possible places to implement an HIV-prevention intervention. Several of these community-based organizations were used in the three studies that have significantly reduced adolescents' sexual risk behaviors (Jemmott, Jemmott, & Fong, 1992; Rotheram-Borus et al., 1991; St. Lawrence et al., 1994). One study (Jemmott, Jemmott, & Fong, 1992) tested the effectiveness of an HIV risk-reduction intervention with African-American male adolescents. One hundred fifty-seven African-American male adolescents were recruited from a local medical center, community-based organizations, and a local high school, and assigned randomly to an HIV risk-reduction condition or a control condition on career opportunities and to a small group of about six boys led by a specially trained male or female black facilitator.

Adolescents in the HIV risk-reduction condition received a 5-hour intervention involving videotapes, games, and exercises aimed at increasing AIDS-related knowledge, weakening problematic beliefs and attitudes toward HIV risk-associated sexual behavior, and increasing skill at negotiating safer sex. Adolescents randomly assigned to the control condition received a 5-hour placebo-attention intervention. Structurally similar to the HIV risk-reduction intervention, it involved culturally and developmentally appropriate videotapes, exercises, and games regarding career opportunities.

At 3-month follow-up, adolescents in the HIV risk-reduction condition reported less risky sexual behavior in the 3 months postintervention than did those in the control condition. For instance, they reported having coitus less frequently and with fewer women, they reported using condoms more consistently, and fewer of them reported engaging in heterosexual anal intercourse.

Rotheram-Borus and her associates (1991) have developed and evaluated HIV prevention programs for high-risk runaway and homeless adolescents. Over a 2-year period (from 1988 to 1990), consecutive recruitment of adolescents at two residential shelters in New York City (one designated the nonintervention site and the other the intervention site) resulted in 79 and 188 runaways available for enrollment in the program at the intervention and nonintervention sites, respectively. After attrition, the final sample was comprised of 78 adolescents in the intervention condition and 67 adolescents in the nonintervention condition.

Runaways participating in the risk-reduction program were exposed to a multiple session intervention administered by skilled trainers. The program addressed the following: general knowledge about HIV/AIDS, coping skills, access to health care and other resources, and individual barriers to use of safer sex practices. General HIV knowledge was addressed by having adolescents participate in video and art workshops and review commercial HIV/AIDS videos. Coping skills training addressed runaways' unrealistic expectations regarding emotional and behavioral responses in high-risk situations. Additional medical, mental health care, and other resources were made available to address specific individual health concerns. Individual barriers to adopting and maintaining safer sex practices were reviewed in private counseling sessions. Participants in the nonintervention condition were exposed to individual counseling from staff; but this counseling did not specifically address HIV prevention. Condoms were available and staff members, on an unsystematic basis, discussed condom use.

Runaways in the risk-reduction program demonstrated a significant increase in consistent condom use and less frequently reported engaging in a high-risk pattern of HIV-associated behaviors over 6 months. A high-risk pattern of sexual behavior was defined as consistent condom use occurring in fewer than 50% of sexual encounters, 10 or more sexual encounters, or three or more sexual partners. A greater proportion of adolescents (22%) in the control group reported this high-risk pattern of sexual behavior compared with those adolescents (9%) who received between 10 and 14 intervention sessions, and those (0%) who received 15 or more intervention sessions. Reports of consistent condom use increased from about 32% of runaways at initiation of the project to 62% 6 months after receiving more than 15 intervention sessions. A 2-year follow-up of the same sample continued to show significant reductions in risk acts among those who received the intervention.

To help understand the dynamics of designing interventions in the community setting, Bowser and Wingood (1992) offered a stage model for implementation of community-based HIV intervention for adolescents. This model describes the different levels of communication and analysis that are possible in the community setting as well as examples of applied intervention procedures. In addition, the model calls for high levels of community visibility and involvement.

Other means of accessing adolescents with HIV-prevention information and skills training are needed. One underused and underevaluated avenue is physicians' interactions with their adolescent patients (DiClemente & Brown, 1994). In one recent report (Mansfield, Conroy, Emans, & Woods, 1993), the effects of physicians' assessment of adolescents' risk behaviors and counseling about HIV risks and prevention were evaluated in an inner-city, hospital-based adolescent clinic. Ninety adolescents (mean age, 17.6 years) seeking care were randomly assigned to one of two groups: a standard care group in which physicians interviewed adolescents about high-risk behaviors related to HIV disease and a counseling group in which physicians provided discussion of HIV risks and prevention.

Approximately 2 months after baseline assessments and randomization, 25% of adolescents reported less sexual activity; 32% and 18%, respectively, of the standard care and counseling group reported less sexual activity. Consistent use of condoms also significantly increased among adolescents in both groups (standard care, $p = .03$; counseling $p = .02$). Use of condoms at last intercourse increased in the counseling group from 37% to 42% ($p = .03$).

These findings suggest that physicians, in the process of conducting interviews about risk behaviors, may have a motivational impact on adolescents to reduce HIV-related behaviors over a brief follow-up period. Although more remains to be learned, these findings are promising and suggest that physicians have an important role to play in HIV prevention. Overall, the findings from school-, community-, and hospital-based studies suggest that behavior change, although difficult, is attainable.

Despite prevention efforts, there are and will continue to be adolescents who are infected with HIV. More and more doctors, teachers, therapists, and social workers will be confronted with the situation in which one of their young patients, clients, or students faces HIV infection. How should the needs of this very special population be best addressed?

A HYPOTHETICAL MODEL OF ADOLESCENTS' REACTIONS TO HIV DIAGNOSIS AND DISEASE PROGRESSION

This section outlines a hypothetical model aimed at understanding adolescents' reactions through a series of phases, beginning with the decision to seek HIV-antibody testing and counseling, disease progression, diagnosis of AIDS, and eventual death. Several authors have made reference to various phases of HIV disease (Nichols, 1985; Sande & Volberding, 1992; Tross & Hirsch, 1985), although a model of psychological reactions to the spectrum of HIV disease in terms of psychosocial functioning is unavailable. We must reiterate, however, that in the absence of empirical data, we are relying heavily on our clinical impressions, insights, and experience in counseling persons affected with HIV. And, although the model will be described primarily in the context of adolescents, its general concepts are also applicable to adults and children facing HIV disease and, to a lesser degree, their loved ones.

The progression of HIV disease follows a highly unpredictable course. An adolescent testing positive for HIV may live free of symptoms for 10 years or longer, or may develop AIDS and die within a short period (Osmond, 1994b). Such an uncertain disease course may further exacerbate psychological distress of the individual, making the development of a model a complex task. For this reason, we point out that this model is not one which outlines the exact phases followed by adolescents who become infected. Rather, the model is intended as a heuristic tool, useful in considering the range of responses of adolescents to HIV infection. It cannot consider individual differences in underlying physical or psychological health, or social and familial support that may be available, which could affect the course of the disease or adolescents' adjustment.

Not all adolescents will enter the model at the initial phase of deciding to seek HIV testing. For example, all military recruits routinely receive HIV testing and active duty military personnel receive repeat HIV testing every 2 years. Thus, adolescents who have no intention of seeking an HIV test may learn of their serostatus as a consequence of involuntary testing. In other instances, adolescents may be told that they are HIV-positive and have AIDS at the same time, because they sought treatment for an AIDS-defining condition. In this case, the psychological and physical distress may take a much different course. Despite the difficulties of prediction in this area, our purpose is to provide some insight into the concerns and coping mechanisms involved as adolescents face various aspects of HIV infection and death.

Figure 5.1 shows the proposed pattern of physical and psychological distress as hypothesized by the model. As the figure suggests, adolescents in the process of deciding to seek HIV-antibody testing are likely to experience increased emotional and psychological distress that can have physical sequelae, such as sleep disruption and gastrointestinal disorder, which are not related to their infection. Distress is projected to escalate on learning the positive results of the test. After this phase, there is often a lengthy time interval in which symptoms of HIV disease

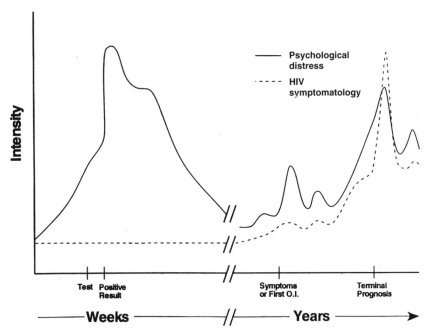

FIGURE 5.1 Hypothetical model of response to HIV infection.

are absent and the adolescent feels healthy. Psychological distress, at this phase of disease, may also go into "remission." However, the appearance of opportunistic infections or other symptoms may again exacerbate psychological distress. As the disease progresses, physical disabilities and psychological distress may alternate in their relative impact on the adolescent. Separating these two becomes increasingly difficult, as changes in mental and physical functioning from the time of the diagnosis of AIDS and up to the point of death are not uncommon. Each event and phase described in the model will be addressed in turn, beginning with the decision to seek HIV testing.

Seeking the HIV Test

The decision to seek HIV testing and actually going through the testing process is, in general, anxiety provoking. Our model suggests that in this phase, which may be lengthy, going to the test site and then waiting for the test results may be marked by moderately high levels of psychological distress. However, this distress may be mediated by several factors including disclosure to others about the test and individual coping styles.

Disclosure to Others.   If parents are coercing their adolescent to be tested, the youth may feel varying amounts of distress related to the extent of familial pressure centering on testing. Conversely, an adolescent seeking testing of his or her own volition may experience more anxiety, because this decision is based on an assessment of the individual's perceived personal risk. There are also likely to be differences between those individuals who tell a friend or family member about their HIV test compared with those who tell no one. If loved ones are supportive and assure the adolescent of care regardless of the outcome of HIV testing, this will certainly minimize fear of rejection. However, if members of the social network are rejecting or judgmental, fear may escalate, even to the point that adolescents do not return to obtain their test results. Failure to return to obtain HIV antibody test results is common, especially in public health centers, and may be related to these aforementioned fears.

Disclosure must also be made to individuals who are not in the adolescent's social network but who may be involved with obtaining the HIV test. An adolescent often must approach school, public health center, or other health care personnel about how to be tested. In the process, the adolescent may fear that these adults, who may be perceived as in positions of authority and thus able to report back to parents or friends, are judging their queries as a tacit admission that the adolescent has been engaging in unsafe or socially proscribed behavior. Issues of confidentiality also arise, because different geographic areas and agencies have diverse policies regarding testing of minors.

Individual Coping Style.   The mental functioning and coping styles of the adolescent are also important for understanding the decision to seek HIV testing. The adolescent may have been fearful of obtaining an HIV test for some time before actually seeking testing. Some adolescents may feel so sure that they are infected that being tested might remove any last vestige of hope that they are HIV negative. These fears may be grounded in realistic concerns over past sexual or drug experiences, or they may be unwarranted and rooted in a lack of understanding of HIV transmission.

The fear and anxiety associated with HIV testing, whether recently developed or long term, may result in interpersonal and school-related problems and physical symptoms. Likewise, shame and guilt over previous high-risk or suspected high-risk behaviors and over the possibility of disgracing themselves and their family may be experienced. These problems may, in turn, increase anxiety and fears about being HIV positive.

How adolescents cope with the stress of deciding to seek HIV testing can range from a firm belief that there is no possibility that the test will be positive to certainty that they are infected with HIV. Adolescents in denial may disregard the seriousness of testing and may even joke about it, whereas others may view testing as a catastrophe and experience high levels of associated anxiety and depression. Some adolescents may also express intense feelings of anger directed at themselves, the individual(s) they feel exposed them to HIV, or the world in general. In coping with these decisions, adolescents may or may not share their fears with others.

Interventions for adolescents deciding whether or not to seek HIV testing are limited by a lack of knowledge of their intentions and fears. For this reason, school- and community-based efforts to improve adolescents' knowledge of alternative testing protocols and the community resources available are valuable forms of intervention. As noted, adolescents may unnecessarily worry about their level of personal risk. For example, in a survey of college-aged individuals, more than one half expressed fears that deep kissing could transmit HIV (author's personal files). Thus, provision of accurate and comprehensive education about HIV transmission may be an effective strategy to decrease unnecessary worry.

For the adolescent whose parents are involved in the testing decision, intervention is made more direct and feasible. Assessing adolescents' risk of infection and providing counseling focused on their fears and expectations would be appropriate. Getting adolescents to anticipate their reactions and the decisions they would make if they received a positive HIV test would also be helpful to increase their coping ability. For adolescents who do not inform anyone of their intentions to be tested, pretest counseling at the test site can be an extremely important intervention.

Positive Test Result

Adolescents who test HIV positive may do so in any number of contexts. Variations in setting, test anonymity, the presence of significant others, expectations of the result, and degree of choice about testing may all alter to some extent the degree of their reaction to the result. We expect few will argue, however, with the premise that this is a stressful and difficult time for an adolescent. As hypothesized in Figure 5.1, the period immediately following a positive HIV test may be the most distressing, because strategies and personal resources to cope with the issues surrounding being HIV positive have typically not yet been mobilized. However, primary concerns at this point may include recovering from shock, obtaining additional information about HIV disease, and beginning to disclose the news to others.

Recovering from Shock.   Initial reactions to the news of a positive HIV test span a broad spectrum of emotional reactions. They might include denial, depression, and anger. However, it is just as likely that adolescents may experience an emotional numbing or shock. Feelings of hopelessness for the future, guilt, or shame may also become immediately apparent. Often, in this highly emotional and confusing time, expressions of rage and even desire for revenge directed toward the sexual or drug-using partner who they believe infected them may be prevalent (Winiarski, 1991).

Concern about Disclosure.   Intense worries and fears about how family, schoolmates, and friends will react when their HIV status is disclosed may be among adolescents' first thoughts and feelings. Interventions at this phase include posttest counseling to clarify the meaning of the test results. As mentioned earlier, adolescents initially may not be able to attend to or understand explanations. If this is the case, it is advisable for a counselor, friend, or family member just to be with an adolescent until he or she regains equanimity. Initial reactions, which may include self-destructive or suicidal ideation, should be assessed and appropriately addressed. Finally, after a period when initial reactions have subsided, a more thorough assessment of the adolescent's understanding of HIV transmission is important to reduce the probability of being reinfected or infecting others. Depending on the community, personal, and family resources available, suggestions for further counseling, therapy, and support groups may be appropriate at this time. For example, a local support group for youth infected with HIV may be an appropriate resource.

Asymptomatic Period

The "asymptomatic period" of HIV disease refers to the time interval between being infected and before the immune system deteriorates sufficiently to allow the development of opportunistic infections (Osmond, 1994a). Depending on when an adolescent learns that he or she is HIV infected, the asymptomatic period may be nonexistent (i.e., the adolescent may be diagnosed as HIV positive on the presentation of an AIDS-defining opportunistic infection or CD4 count <200 per mm^3), or it may last for years. This period is characterized by an absence of significant physical symptoms and a concomitant ability to function relatively normally in day-to-day activities. However, the HIV-positive adolescent may experience a sense of hypervigilance in anticipating the appearance of symptoms. This period has been characterized by one adult HIV patient, for example, as "waiting and watching, and trying somehow to just get on with life" (author's personal files).

Our proposed model of adjustment to HIV disease suggests that in the face of "waiting and watching," psychological distress slowly decreases during this period. The initial shock of the HIV diagnosis subsides over a period. Simultaneously, a return to the daily routine of school or work as well as the use of various coping mechanisms, ranging from denial ("I'm one of those patients who just never gets sick") to sublimation (becoming active in HIV-prevention or advocacy organizations), allows the adolescent to function relatively well. However, the asymptomatic period presents its own challenges, often related to the fact that the adolescent can effectively "hide" his or her HIV status.

Disclosure. Depending on the adolescent's age, parents may or may not have been informed about the HIV diagnosis by health care personnel. For most adolescents, however, there exists a host of extended family and friends that will be unaware of the diagnosis. Infected adolescents face choices about disclosure across the domain of their social network. Younger adolescents may simply be told by their parents "not to tell anyone," or they may get caught up in their parents' conflicts about disclosure and possible social stigmatization and repercussions.

Because they are asymptomatic, HIV-positive adolescents are unlikely to encounter many queries about changes in appearance or hospitalizations. However, the level of distress that they experience when initially diagnosed may be sensed by some family members or friends, prompting questions about their psychological state. Whether these questions are answered truthfully or not, or whether family and friends are told of the HIV diagnosis at all, may be a frightening decision for the adolescent, especially in the context of special friendships or romantic relationships.

A particularly upsetting situation that may exist for the person, particularly likely for older adolescents, is the prospect of informing present or past sexual or drug-using partners of their diagnosis. Because public health officials may press adolescents to name these individuals, there may be considerable worry that the health department will contact them before the adolescent can do so, or that the health department will identify the positive adolescent to these contacts. There is potential for considerable anxiety as the adolescent copes with the simultaneous possibilities of painful rejection and loss of relationships as well as suspicion because of health department inquiries.

Discrimination and Social Rejection. HIV disease in the United States is traditionally associated with two groups: gay/bisexual men and intravenous drug users. Both of these groups are stigmatized in the society, and it has been argued that, in fact, the HIV epidemic has increased hostility toward them (Turner, Miller, & Moses, 1989). Regardless of how adolescents are infected, they face the specter of discrimination, stigmatization, and rejection, often based on the assumption that they have engaged in homosexual or drug-using behavior. Thus, the decision to disclose one's HIV status involves the risk of immediate social rejection or punishment.

A strong attachment to a peer group (Lewis & Volkmar, 1990) may potentiate the effect of the threat of rejection's causing substantial distress. The case of Ryan White, who faced a full-fledged campaign by parents in the school system to bar him from attending classes, is illustrative of the extent to which this rejection can be carried (Walker, 1991). Of note is the fact that Ryan White's family was supportive of him, which may or may not be the case for every adolescent. Surveys of homeless youth, for example, reveal that many runaways left home after being rejected or attacked by parents because of the revelation of their sexual orientation, drug use, or HIV status (Rotheram-Borus, 1991). As with HIV-positive adults, adolescents who have supportive families and friends are, we hypothesize, more likely to avoid significant psychological difficulties over the course of the disease. However, the threat of rejection from members of the social network is ever present, and hostile jokes or remarks about HIV patients or AIDS will impede an adolescent's ability to feel completely acceptable, trusting of others, or at ease.

Infection of Others. Sexuality becomes a major issue, especially for older adolescents (Lewis & Volkmar, 1990). For HIV-positive adolescents, what may already be an anxiety-provoking topic has additional complexity. Contrary to some accounts of newly diagnosed individuals deliberately attempting to infect others out of anger (Winiarski, 1991), this appears to be a highly transient wish. Most HIV-positive persons report a great deal of concern about the possibility of infecting a loved one.

Misinformation about the modes of HIV transmission may lead to overly cautious behavior, even in the context of zero-risk activities, such as sharing drinking glasses or eating utensils in the household environment, as well as anxiety about sexual contact with others. Also, even for

HIV-positive adolescents who are aware of appropriate risk-reduction behavior, such as condom use, the prospect of discussing these behaviors with potential sexual partners may be anxiety producing as they wonder whether insisting on safety measures will lead to questions about their HIV status or simply to ridicule.

HIV-positive adolescents who are active in athletic activities with the potential for injuries or who are engaged in sexual relationships may experience anxiety as they attempt to sort through the deluge of information about HIV prevention, or may become despondent about the possibility of losing these aspects of their lives and identities. Again, a supportive and well-educated social environment may mediate these concerns and allow an adolescent to confidently continue his or her activities in a safer manner.

In much the same way, sexual or drug-using behavior by the HIV-positive person not only potentially places others at risk but puts the seropositive person at risk for reinfection with HIV and increases the potential for exposure to other infectious diseases. Because it has been suggested that exposure to several different strains of HIV through reinfection may lead to a more rapid deterioration of immune competency (Osmond, 1994b), an adolescent who learns and practices safer behaviors not only protects others, but also himself or herself.

Maintaining Health.   Avoiding behaviors that increase the risk of exposure to other strains of HIV or to other infectious agents is only one of myriad recommendations that will likely be made to a newly diagnosed adolescent. During the asymptomatic period, the immune system's functional level may stay relatively stable, decline slowly, or "roller coaster" (Osmond, 1994b). HIV-positive persons are often advised to take several preventive measures to enhance their immune performance including a healthy diet, regular exercise, and stress management (Worth & Burack, 1994). In addition, literally hundreds of alternative treatments and therapies exist that purport to prolong the asymptomatic period of disease. Taking many vitamins, watching their diet, or practicing stress-reduction techniques may be an additional burden and reminder of being "different," especially for adolescents who may have been unconcerned with health matters before their diagnosis. Adolescents who live away from family or who are in low socioeconomic groups may have limited access to information about health maintenance or limited financial resources to engage in some of these activities, causing additional frustration and the potential for a more rapid disease course. Finally, it should be noted that many healthy adolescents adopt a deliberate focus away from their bodies and physical concerns because of discomfort with natural but dramatic bodily changes (Lewis & Volkmar, 1990). This poses a developmentally related challenge to HIV-positive adolescents who may be encouraged or feel compelled to focus intensely on physical symptoms and changes as they "watch and wait" for signs of disease progression.

Planning for the Future.   One of the most vexing aspects of HIV disease, as reported by many HIV-positive individuals (Winiarski, 1991), is the lack of certainty about the future. Because the duration of the asymptomatic period is undetermined, planning for a questionable future may prove confusing and create frustration. For adolescents who may still be in school or planning for entry into vocations, this uncertainty may be even more frustrating. Questions about whether to finish high school, attend college or technical schools, get married, or begin a career may become seemingly unanswerable. Unlike the stereotypical image of adolescents as lacking a "future orientation," most adolescents do tend to have a plan or expectation about what they wish to accomplish during their adolescence and young adulthood (Kastenbaum, 1986). The diagnosis of HIV may radically alter those expectations, leading to concerns, grief, or anxiety about the likelihood of reaching important goals or life events.

The asymptomatic period of HIV disease offers a considerable opportunity for reorganization and use of coping mechanisms, leading to a decrease in overall psychological distress for HIV-infected adolescents. However, the issues discussed above all hold the potential for problematic adjustment. Appropriate education, including an understanding of the course of HIV disease and risk-reduction techniques, and a supportive social network will be primary interventions that will assist adolescents in facing these issues.

Health care personnel or other professionals who are aware of an adolescent's diagnosis may be in a position to provide much-needed counseling after the initial posttest shock about disclosure and health maintenance, allowing the adolescent an opportunity to take some control over these aspects of the disease. Given the extraordinary sense of loss of control that often accompanies an HIV diagnosis, provision of this information and these choices may facilitate the adolescent's adjustment and encourage a proactive stance toward disease management.

Development of Symptoms

As HIV disease continues its attack on the immune system, risk increases for opportunistic infections that capitalize on the immunosuppressed state. Common opportunistic infections include *Pneumocystis carinii* pneumonia, cytomegalovirus infections of the retina or gastrointestinal tract, tuberculosis, and Candida infections of the mouth and esophagus (Sande & Volberding, 1992). The appearance of these illnesses, or other physical symptoms (such as recurrent diarrhea or flu-like episodes), signals disease progression.

For most HIV-positive patients, adolescent and adult alike, the appearance of the first opportunistic infection is a major stressor. Fears of illness and death that had been managed relatively well during the asymptomatic period may be reawakened and become more severe (Winiarski, 1991). In our model, we hypothesize that this period of initial symptomatology is likely to be marked by an increase in psychological physical symptomatology. An adolescent, perhaps now for the first time accurately described as a "patient," faces several hurdles including further disclosure concerns, management of complex medical regimen, and confrontation with HIV-associated disabilities and functional impairment.

Disclosure. Whereas in the asymptomatic phase of disease, adolescents are able to function well, generally arousing little concern or suspicion about their health, the overt appearance of symptoms or hospitalizations may evoke questions from members of their social network who are unaware of their diagnosis. Many HIV patients continue to avoid disclosing the true nature of their illness, telling friends or even family that they are suffering from cancer or some other serious illness (Stewart & Haley, in press). Although adolescents who are living with family members may be unable to avoid health care personnel's disclosing their diagnosis to parents, they may still have a choice whether to inform others in their social network.

Most of the concerns surrounding disclosure at this stage are identical to those confronted during the asymptomatic phase; however, adolescents may experience a heightened sense of urgency about disclosure because of the presence of obvious illness. They may simultaneously desire more intimacy or social support from friends or loved ones, but fear social repercussions of disclosure or feel that telling more people somehow indicates that the disease is progressing irreversibly. How adolescents react to these difficult choices may be affected by the support of their immediate family and other health care personnel, the nature of their social network prior to illness, and their perceptions concerning their peers' attitudes about HIV and AIDS.

Medical Management. As HIV disease progresses, typical medical management dictates a complex regimen of antiretroviral medication (such as AZT, ddI [didanosine], or ddC [zalcitabine]) and prophylactic therapies to prevent opportunistic infections (Sande & Volberding, 1992). In addition, other therapies may be required for the management of symptoms. As more medications and treatments are added to their regimen to manage existing disease symptomatology and prevent the occurrence of new ones, the likelihood of drug interactions and problematic side effects increases (Lee & Safrin, 1992). Adolescents may be forced to cope with chronic problems, such as nausea, diarrhea, or strict dietary restrictions, as well as be expected to adhere to a medical regimen that often requires precise timing of medications. For adolescents who, before their diagnosis, were accustomed to relatively few restrictions on their activity, adherence to strict medical regimens may be a distressing disruption of their lifestyle.

Confronting the "Patient Persona."   Once a HIV-positive adolescent's immune system has deteriorated to the point that he or she develops opportunistic infections, there often follows a period in which symptoms and illnesses exacerbate and wane with appropriate treatment, creating unpredictable cycles of relative wellness or malaise. However, symptoms rarely disappear altogether; even in well periods, the person may continue to be easily fatigable or experience mild symptoms or medication side effects. Unlike the asymptomatic phase of HIV disease, it now becomes increasingly difficult to avoid the perception of oneself as "an AIDS patient."

Adolescents who are facing this phase of the disease may have additional difficulty adjusting to the sense of being different or separated from their peers. Repeated hospitalizations may interrupt academic or social progress, and obvious symptoms or disabilities may be embarrassing to adolescents who are concerned about their standing within a peer group. Younger adolescents may be more confused than older teens about the "up and down" nature of this period, or may become considerably more dependent on their parents.

Meanwhile the appearance of serious symptomatology or opportunistic infections is likely to precipitate a psychological crisis in many HIV-infected adolescents. Most important, because of the increase in symptoms, the adolescent is more likely to have contact with health care providers. Thus, the opportunity for detection of serious cases of depression, anxiety, or other adjustment problems is increased if staff are sufficiently sensitized to these issues. Additionally, counseling about disclosure and management of medical regimens, as well as about the losses of independence and, often, of positive self-image, can be provided not only to the adolescent, but to his or her family at this stage.

Terminal AIDS

At some point in the course of the disease, the AIDS patient's immune system is simply unable to mount a response to any threat. More serious or repeated life-threatening opportunistic infections are likely to occur and responses to treatments become more limited. However, HIV disease is often unpredictable. Patients who were thought to have only weeks to live may make remarkable recoveries and live several more months; patients who appear to be doing well may suddenly develop a serious infection and die within days (Stewart, unpublished manuscript). Thus, to speak of a "terminal period" in AIDS is perhaps an artificial construction. It may best be thought of as the time in which the patient is aware that there is little time left, or that he or she is unlikely to recover from the next infection. It is the period for HIV patients most similar to descriptions of persons with severe or terminal cancer. Primary issues to be addressed by adolescents at this phase include maintaining hope, grieving about loss of loved ones and life roles, and maintaining integrity and dignity.

Maintaining Hope. Because HIV disease is so unpredictable, it may be the case that physicians or other health care providers pronounce a brief prognosis only to have the patient live significantly longer than their prediction. As Adams and Deveau (1986) noted in their review of adolescents with terminal cancer, adolescents may be particularly resilient and future oriented; thus, an adolescent with terminal AIDS may be capable of maintaining a belief that at least partial recovery is possible, giving the person strength to manage high levels of medical intervention.

Grieving and Loss. As it becomes clear that an adolescent is truly in the terminal stage of the illness, he or she may abandon the last vestiges of denial about imminent death and begin letting go of various relationships and life roles. Adolescents may now face the reality that there will be no return to school or friends, and that life is coming to an end. Adolescents may differ in their approaches to these processes, some facing them directly or with ritualistic goodbyes to important people; others becoming more withdrawn and isolated as they cope; and still others relying on religious or spiritual beliefs to provide assistance with their grief, fears, or concerns.

As in all of the phases of HIV disease, one of the most important variables at this phase is the presence or absence of supportive family or friends who can provide assistance. Additional time to talk or allowing more private time, giving the adolescent control over visitors or some medical decisions, and being open and honest can be invaluable means of social support. As Adams and Deveau (1986) have suggested, nurses and other health care staff may play an increasingly important supportive role for the adolescent and his or her family.

CONCLUSION

Adolescents continue to engage in HIV-associated risk behaviors. The urgency of the HIV epidemic demands that behavior change interventions be rapidly developed to curb new HIV infections. Moreover, the most effective research interventions should also be conducted on a scale broad enough to yield direct public health benefits. Ultimately, preventing HIV infections will depend not only on the development and evaluation of innovative behavior change approaches, but also on the translation of intervention research into credible community programs.

Understanding adolescents' reactions to HIV diagnosis and disease progression is critical to developing and implementing effective phase-appropriate counseling and supportive strategies. Although identification of an effective treatment and vaccine is in the distant future, psychological distress, physical pain and suffering, and social discrimination and stigmatization are frequent consequences of HIV disease. Though the magnitude of psychological distress and physical impairment varies among individuals, there is a high degree of certainty that HIV-infected adolescents will confront a spectrum of emotional reactions. Understanding the range of factors influencing these emotional reactions is crucial to developing effective strategies designed to enhance quality of life.

6

Adolescents Who Are Living with a Life-Threatening Illness

Michael M. Stevens and Julie C. Dunsmore

Life consists not in holding good cards
but in playing those you do hold well.
—Josh Billings

This chapter offers an analysis of the situation of adolescents who are living with life-threatening illnesses. The analysis includes some remarks on how adolescents react to a crisis; an outline of losses experienced by a young person on developing a life-threatening illness; case presentations to illustrate how life-threatening illness is experienced differentially in early, middle, and late adolescence; and a description of common reactions and experiences of young people with cancer in the form of a journey through a life-threatening illness.

Despite advances in treatment, cancer remains the most common cause of death from disease in childhood and adolescence (Bleyer, 1990). Accordingly, this chapter draws heavily on young people with cancer. However, many of the principles discussed can be applied to

The authors thank the young people who are mentioned in this chapter; their families; David Bennett, Margaret Burgess, Katrina Douglas, Pam Jones, Mary Mirabito, Rhondda Rytmeister, and Anthony Schembri for their helpful comments; and all staff of the Oncology Unit at the Royal Alexandra Hospital for Children and CanTeen for the care and support they provide to young people with cancer and their families.

107

terminal illnesses and life-threatening conditions other than cancer. Some comments on distinctive qualities of three life-threatening conditions other than cancer are provided in the concluding section of the chapter.

HOW ADOLESCENTS REACT TO A CRISIS

Cognitive development involves the acquisition of formal thought processes and the ability to think in an abstract manner (Piaget & Inhelder, 1969). During adolescence this process does not occur in a linear fashion. When a young person is in crisis or under threat, regression to a more concrete way of thinking often occurs. Frequently, adolescents are able to say the "right" thing and discuss complex issues with a maturity beyond their years, yet behave in a very different manner. Interruption of the developmental process by illness may interfere with the adolescent's developing abilities to perceive the future and to understand the consequences of behavior. Because cognitive development is so influenced by psychosocial maturity, the choices adolescents make may not be easily understood by adults.

In times of crisis most adolescents require support to some extent from their parents but also sufficient freedom to be able to experiment with coping with the challenge by themselves. Their response, typically, is that they want to be loved and supported, but not "wrapped in cotton wool."

Adolescents with a life-threatening illness may welcome the support from parents developed during the crisis, yet feel confused as to how best to be a "normal adolescent" when an opportunity arises to spend time away from their parents. Rather than confide in parents, they may prefer to confide in their peer group, particularly with peers who are in a similar situation, about their needs to experiment and for discussion of personal issues (Deem, 1986).

Much of the usual stress experienced by well adolescents is related to an inevitable struggle with developmental tasks, social changes, and relationships with family and peers. Adolescents with a life-threatening illness must deal not only with these challenges, but also with additional stresses associated with their illness, its treatment, and side effects of therapy. How those around them react will have a significant effect on how successfully adolescents with a life-threatening illness cope and on their freedom to make their own choices.

Working with adolescents, such as those introduced in the case histories that follow confirms that, despite being ill, they react to crises occasioned by the normal process of growing up in a similar manner to their well peers. Their resilience and soundness of mind have been noted by several authors (Carr-Gregg, 1987; Chesler & Lawther, 1990; Koocher, 1986; Smith, Ostroff, Tan, & Lesko, 1991). For example, most adolescents with a life-threatening illness desire information about their disease, involvement in the planning of treatment, and participation in decision making (Cassileth, Zupkis, Sutton-Smith, & March, 1980; Dunsmore & Quine, in press). Further, terminally ill adolescents are usually more concerned about how their family and friends will be affected by their death than about themselves. They are not so much afraid of death as of the dying. With patient and attentive listening, an accurate understanding can be acquired of these young persons' perceptions of death and of their own prognosis.

ADOLESCENTS WHO ARE GRIEVING FOR LOSSES AS THEY LIVE WITH A LIFE-THREATENING ILLNESS

Being an adolescent and living with a life-threatening illness involves significant grieving at the onset of the illness, during its course, and in its terminal phase. Not all of the losses are related to death or dying. Many are related to the process of having a chronic or debilitating illness. For example, some significant losses mourned by adolescents with cancer follow.

Losses Mourned by Adolescents With Cancer

Prediagnosis Person. Adolescents with a serious illness often find themselves grieving for their former healthy selves. The onset of their illness prevents them from living in the style they enjoyed while well. The sick role makes them different because of feelings of weakness, lack of energy, and physical changes to their bodies. This can lower their standing within their peer group. One young person remarked, "People don't treat me like the person I used to be." Spontaneity is reduced and many young people, after diagnosis, question their place in the world, as in "I wish it could just go back to the way it was."

Body Image. Amputation, hair loss, weight gain, weight loss, and other side effects of treatment alter the young person's body image at a time when concerns about physical attractiveness and prowess are greatest. Compared with other age groups, adolescents feel most the unpleasant and upsetting side effects of radiotherapy and chemotherapy. Adolescents report how upset they felt when their hair fell out. This upset may not be evident to a casual observer at the time because many patients put on a brave front, but the pain of the experience is often felt for many years. Loss of hair and related side effects may have an isolating effect on the adolescent, because of the resultant self-imposed restriction on socializing and, sometimes, rejection by peers. Use of cosmetic aids, such as artificial limbs and wigs only superficially restores an adolescent's composure and confidence: The insult to body image is internal and cannot be restored properly by an external prosthesis.

Health.   Young people describe losing the perception by others that as a healthy person, one is independent, in control, and not unreasonably vulnerable to physical harm or emotional upset. This altered perception results instead in their being regarded as "precious." As one young person said, "It's the 'wrapped up in cotton wool' syndrome. My parents are paranoid about me catching infections and relapsing. 'Don't be too late,' they say, 'You'll get sick.'" Some continue to experience avoidance by others, including friends and parents of friends, long after treatment is completed because of fears of contagion.

School Life.   Young people are upset by missing out on developmentally important milestones associated with day-to-day life at school, such as taking tests, dating, poking fun at authority figures, and participating in group experimentation with risky behavior (e.g., smoking or skipping school). Young men report their most disturbing losses are associated with loss of prowess, loss of energy, not being able to take part in sports, and being seen as wimps. Girls experience losses resulting from school absence most strongly in a social context, e.g., isolation from their "group," missing out on the latest gossip, and being unable to join in activities with best friends.

Independence.   Most adolescents test out and establish their independence between the ages of 12 and 18 years. In so doing they seek to identify their capabilities. The onset of a life-threatening illness during this period makes it difficult for adolescents to become independent of parents and other authority figures. Ill adolescents are ambivalent about having to depend on parents for even their most basic care (e.g., changing of beds, toileting, washing, dressing, feeding). Considerable anger may be generated by the helplessness they experience over the loss of their independence. Matters are made worse if adolescents are unwittingly treated by staff of pediatric units in the same way as younger children. The dying adolescent's frustration may be taken out on a parent, usually the one that has been constantly at the bedside, by attempting to drive the parent away. If the attempt succeeds, or even seems likely to succeed, there is often an immediate plea for the parent to return.

A young man aged 21 who was dying said, "I hate to see the sadness in my mother's eyes. She is also not well, and yet she tries to do everything for me and fusses over everything like I'm 5 years old again. I want to scream at her, but then I get scared she will leave me and no one will care for me then."

Prediagnosis Family.   Following diagnosis of a life-threatening illness in a young person, family relationships may deteriorate or improve. Life in the family is no longer the same as it used to be. There is often a plea for life to return to the way it was. There is a common and erroneous perception that cancer leads to breakdown of families. Twenty-five of 51 adolescents (49%) with cancer in a recent survey reported that they had become closer to their families; a further 21 (41%) reported no change (Dunsmore, 1992).

Relationships with Parents.   Ill adolescents are often attempting to deal with feelings of anger and ambivalence about their parents. There is now doubt that eventual independence from parents will be achieved. There are often concerns about the commitment of time and expense required of their parents, and about the demands placed on their own relationship. Roles within the family are often threatened.

Relationships with Siblings.   Siblings of ill adolescents may experience feelings of hostility and guilt. They may become angry because of all the attention given to their brother or sister and the various secondary gains that this can bring. They may be afraid of developing a similar illness. They may feel guilty, believing they have caused their brother's or sister's disease because of some crisis that might have occurred at an earlier phase in their family life.

Relationships with Girlfriends/Boyfriends.   Deterioration of the young person's appearance causes embarrassment. Ill adolescents frequently prefer to break off friendships, rather than risk causing their friends embarrassment or being abandoned by them. Their interest in sex appears to be similar to others their age (Dunsmore, 1992), although those in relapse have commented on missing out on sexual experiences because of their physical appearance and low energy levels.

Lack of opportunity for sexual intimacy is often not addressed by parents or caregivers of adolescents with a terminal illness. Girls have reported more difficulty forming or maintaining relationships than boys. Young men with a life-threatening illness appear to be more accepted by girls; some are seen as heroes and in need of looking after, whereas girls in similar conditions may be regarded as "damaged goods" (Koocher & O'Malley, 1981).

Young women may frequently structure their use of free time around opportunities for relationships with young men. If, through disability, an adolescent girl is unable to take part in strenuous activities, she may also miss out on opportunities to meet males (Deem, 1986). It appears that well young men are threatened by the heightened assertiveness and confidence of chronically or terminally ill young women, who have acquired a maturity beyond their years through coping with a life-threatening illness (Dunsmore, 1992).

Uncertainty about the future may adversely influence the development of a new relationship. The terminally ill young person may choose to break off a relationship with a partner to try to protect the partner from the pain of separation associated with death. Young people with a life-threatening illness do not want to be pitied. Their biggest fear is that someone may stay with them only because of pity.

Certainty About the Future.   Adolescents have a more mature concept of death and dying than do younger children, being able to see the permanence of death and the finality of separation which it involves. Thus, terminally ill adolescents mourn the loss of the future as well as of the past. It is in adolescence that life goals are becoming more strongly established in one's mind. Adolescents sense this loss when confronting the possibility of death. It is difficult to predict with certainty who will be cured of their disease. Adolescents with cancer are left in a limbo of uncertainty about the results of treatment, often for many years after diagnosis and commencement of therapy. "Living one day at a time" is a common motto of adolescents who are living with a life-threatening illness.

Indicators of the Future.   A sense of worth in adolescence is linked to experiencing milestones along the journey to adulthood. If milestones such as examinations are missed due to illness, a young person's sense of worth may deteriorate. Adolescents who have been given a poor prognosis may experience difficulty in resuming studies after completion of treatment, if they perceive the likely duration of their survival to be limited. Other milestones include planning what one will do after leaving school, planning to have a family, planning for travel, and the attainment of increasing economic independence.

Hope. Young people living with a life-threatening illness have the same developmental needs as well adolescents. Young people facing death require opportunities to develop peer relationships, experiment with different sides of their personalities, and interact in the manner of their well peers. Frequently, young people who have been told that they may die soon report that people start to treat them as if they are already dead. As one 18-year-old said, "They treat me like a nonperson. It is as though I am in the coffin already and they are waiting to hammer in the final nails." Hope becomes an essential ingredient for living successfully for these young people. Their hopes may not necessarily be for a cure or magical recovery, but more often for joy and for success with the challenges of living. One can be very clear about the implications of one's life-threatening illness and still maintain hope. One adolescent had on her bedroom wall, "Be realistic. Plan for a miracle."

IMPLICATIONS OF LIFE-THREATENING ILLNESS FOR EARLY, MIDDLE, AND LATE ADOLESCENCE

Adolescence has been divided into early, middle, and late phases. Although in practice the boundaries between these phases may be blurred, some differences between phases are evident in key issues, behaviors, and relationships with peers, and in the impact of a life-threatening illness. Characteristics of adolescence and implications of a life-threatening illness in adolescence are summarized in Table 6.1. Typical reactions of young people in each of the three phases of adolescence to having cancer as an example of a life-threatening illness are presented in the case histories that follow.

Early Adolescence

Early adolescence generally occurs between the ages of 12 to 14 years in girls and 13 to 15 years in boys. This is a time of rapid physical growth and the onset of puberty. Early adolescents focus strongly on the development of their bodies. Membership in a peer group is important.

TABLE 6.1   Characteristics of Adolescence and Implications of a Life-Threatening Illness in Adolescence

Period/Age	Early Adolescence: 12–14 Years (Female); 13–15 Years (Male)	Middle Adolescence: 14–16 Years	Late Adolescence: 17–24 Years
Key issues and characteristics, focus	Focus on development of body Most pubertal changes occur Rapid physical growth Acceptance by peers Idealism Mood swings, contrariness, stubbornness, temper tantrums Day dreaming	Sexual awakening Emancipation from parents and authority figures Discovery of identity by testing limitations, boundaries Role of peer group increases	Defining and understanding functional roles in life in terms of careers, relationships, lifestyles
Social/relationships, behavior	Skills in abstract thinking improve Foreseeing of consequences, planning for future Physical mobility prominent Energy levels high Appetite increased Social interaction mostly in groups Membership in a peer group important	Relationships narcissistic Risk-taking behavior increases Intense peer interaction Most vulnerable to psychological problems	Increasing financial independence Planning for the future Establishment of permanent relationships Increasing time away from family
Relationships with adults	Parents and other authority figures still mostly respected As part of adjustment to new "adult" bodies, may assert themselves as adults while still dependent on parents and caregivers Some testing out (eg, with time away from home)	Parental relationships strained Separation from family begins Some hero worship	Culmination of separation from family Increasing financial independence Sense of being equal to adults

Relationships with peers	Peers used as standards for measurement of developmental progress and assessment of "normality" Comparisons of strength and prowess Friendships with same sex generally more important	Interaction with peers increases Questioning increases concerning who are one's friends and one's own identity and value Sexuality and sexual preference of more concern	Increasing experimentation with intimacy outside family
Impact of life-threatening illness	Concerns about physical appearance and mobility Privacy all important Possible interference with normal cognitive development and learning (school absence, medication, pain, depression, fatigue) Comparison with peers hindered, making self-assessment of normality more difficult Possible lack of acceptance by peers Reliance on parents and other authorities in decision making Hospitals perceived as disturbing	Illness particularly threatening and least well tolerated Compromised sense of autonomy Emancipation from parents and authority figures impeded Interference with attraction of partner Fear of rejection by peers Limited interaction with peers may lead to social withdrawal Dependence on family for companionship and social support Hospitalization, school absences interfere with social relationships and acquisition of social skills Noncompliance with treatment	Absences from work, study Interference with plans for vocation and relationship Difficulties in securing employment and promotion at work Unemployment hinders achieving separation from family and financial independence Discrimination in employment and health/life insurance Loss of financial independence and self-esteem Concerns about fertility and health of offspring

Wendy was a 14-year-old girl with a cerebral tumor. Until the onset of her illness and its treatment, Wendy had been an attractive, outgoing, and popular adolescent. When introduced to her counselor (author JCD), Wendy had just undergone further surgery to lower intracranial pressure caused by the tumor, together with radiotherapy and medical treatment with steroids. Wendy pretended she was not in the hospital, spoke little, ate little, and constantly asked about going home.

Wendy agreed to talk only after the counselor was introduced as someone from outside the ward who worked with other teenagers with cancer. Initially, she requested that her mother be present but soon welcomed the chance to talk alone. She disclosed that she disliked the hospital and felt very distressed about her shaved head, the effect of the steroids on her face, and her weight gain. She particularly disliked being confined in the one room. She reported difficulty walking, was distressed about having to rely on others to get around, and was pleased when a wheelchair was arranged for her personal use.

As trust developed, she confided that she had pet names for almost all the staff and had also developed a code with her mother which enabled them to get someone to leave if she did not like them or if she was tired. Her sense of humor was wry. She had become astute at working out which staff she could trust. Refusing to use the word "cancer," she always referred to her tumor as her "lump," explaining that her grandmother had died of cancer, and she was not going to die.

Her tumor progressed despite a further nine months of treatment as an outpatient. Her parents were informed by her specialist that nothing more could be done for her. She was not seen again by her specialist after her initial operation. A series of house staff reviewed her in the outpatient clinic. It seemed to her that no one was coordinating her treatment. She reported feeling sad that her doctor had given up on her but was going to show him that he was wrong. Despite the "what ifs" often being discussed, she remained positive that she would survive. She enjoyed taking part in guided imagery and drawing with her counselor, and these techniques were used to assist communication.

When palliative care commenced, she refused to be readmitted to the hospital and was pleased that nursing at home could be arranged. She supervised the decoration of her room at home. Posters of her favorite horses and dogs were prominent. Her family purchased a special canopy bed of which she was proud. If her mother attempted to discuss dying with her, Wendy would change the subject. She confided how worried she was about her mother and about who would look after her mother when "you know . . . I'm not here any more." She avoided using the word "death" in her discussions but seemed content to refer to her own death in "what if" terms.

In imagery sessions she described thoughts and feelings of a character who was dying. After a session in which her character was reported as feeling very sad, Wendy was asked how sick she thought she was at the moment. She answered, "Well, you know I am going to die. You can't get much sicker than that!" In exploring what that meant to her, she explained that she had a number of goals she wanted to achieve before she "you know," including going horse riding, going on a special camp that was being organized for teenagers with cancer, and, lastly, a number of private goals to do with her family.

Even though she was becoming increasingly disabled Wendy accomplished all of these goals before she died. At the camp, although unable to spend much time out of bed, she still enjoyed swapping stories about treatment, telling jokes, and being with others. She was proud of her horse riding, and everyone was shown photos from the camp afterward. Despite her appearance being considerably affected by the side effects of treatment, she reported that she felt accepted at the camp and not embarrassed. As she said, "They understand." She regarded the camp as the best time she had had since her diagnosis.

By now most of her school friends were staying away and no longer visiting her. She was told of a rumor going around her school that she had died. Although feeling hurt, she responded with humor. She contacted one of her fellow students by telephone saying she was "calling from the grave."

Despite continuing deterioration in her condition, Wendy remained at home. She considered her local doctor and her home nurses as very caring, referring to them as "my angels." After lapsing into a coma, she regained consciousness several times, calling for certain people to say goodbye to them. After she lost consciousness for the last time, her family continued to talk to her, holding her hand, making jokes, and telling stories. Initially, some members of her family were distressed on witnessing Wendy's Cheyne-Stokes respiration, but this was explained to them as periodic breathing observed immediately before death in patients dying of cerebral tumors. Such breathing is characterized by rhythmic waxing and waning of respiration (i.e., by intervals of deeper breathing at an increased rate alternating with intervals of suspended respiration). This clarification anticipated the family's distress on presuming Wendy had just died only to see her resume breathing, and on erroneously perceiving her to be in pain and requiring more analgesia during phases of heightened respiration. Fortified with this explanation, Wendy's family stayed by her bed until she died. After Wendy had died, her mother helped prepare her body with the assistance of a community nurse who had shown much caring for her over those many months.

Life-Threatening Illness and the Early Adolescent.   Early adolescents with a life-threatening illness are most concerned about the effects of the illness on their physical appearance and mobility. Significant distress is common in adolescents with cancer if treatment results in weight gain, hair loss, scarring, or similar alterations to their physical appearance, which are perceived as drawing attention to their disability (Carr-Gregg & White, 1987; Kagen-Goodheart, 1977). Because privacy is all important to early adolescents, large ward rounds are often excruciatingly embarrassing (Dunsmore & Quine, in press; Carr-Gregg & White, 1987). Being less assertive than older adolescents, their concerns about such issues may go unrecognized.

Just as Wendy asked for her mother to be present initially, most early adolescents are still reliant on authority figures and are content to let parents act on their behalf (Levenson, Pfefferbaum, Copeland, & Silverberg, 1982). They do, however, wish to be involved in decisions and to have opportunities to talk with their doctor on their own (Carr-Gregg & White, 1987).

Because many early adolescents are very disturbed by hospitals, the presence of familiar, friendly staff is all important. Younger adolescents tend to rely on nursing or social work staff and parents to be their advocates, particularly with doctors.

The use of symbolic language is common in this age group. Frequently, just giving voice to their thoughts reduces their anxiety. Encouraging them to do so will often be beneficial by helping them regain some control over their situation and feel less overwhelmed. There is no need to force young people to confront their situation. If a caregiver listens to what is said, a gentle easing into the truth of the situation is possible. Wendy practiced denial and avoidance of information at certain times during her illness, yet at other times seemed preoccupied with acquiring and recounting information about drugs used in her treatment and their side effects. She experienced avoidance from both caregivers and peers.

Her mother worried that Wendy was not discussing her impending death with her. She decided that because they had such a close relationship that it was sufficient just to keep providing opportunities for this discussion without forcing the issue. Wendy may have preferred not to discuss this openly with her mother to avoid upsetting her further, as did children reported by Bluebond-Langner (1978). Instead, Wendy chose to refer to her own death symbolically, in her stories.

With support from her health caregivers, Wendy's family was able to stand by her and care for her through the terminal phase of her illness, despite the pain that was involved.

Middle Adolescence

This period is defined as approximately 14 to 16 years of age for both females and males. Midadolescents most commonly focus on attracting

a boyfriend or girlfriend, emancipation from parents and authority figures, and increasing interaction with peers.

*Michelle developed an osteogenic sarcoma of the leg at age 16 years. She
was the eldest in a family that included a younger sister and four younger
step-siblings from her father's second marriage. She had spent most of her free
time caring for the younger children of whom she was very fond. Michelle was
referred (to author JCD) by the ward's nurse unit manager because she had become withdrawn, appeared depressed, and was refusing further treatment.*

*It was evident immediately that Michelle intended to remain withdrawn
and uncommunicative. After a week of daily visits, Michelle would still merely
nod, then look down or away. Her unwillingness to communicate was considered not only attributable to shyness but also an attempt to retain some
control. Her father explained that after her surgery, she had been informed
that 12 months of treatment would be required. She complied until 12 months
had elapsed, whereupon she said no further treatment was to be given. Having reviewed her case history, her specialist now recommended that an additional nine months of treatment be given. Despite pleas from both family and
caregivers to consider the possibility of relapse, Michelle remained resolute that
she would not accept further therapy, as was her legal entitlement. She believed
that she was now free of cancer. When pressured to permit her treatment to be
extended, Michelle seemed to shut herself off totally from those around her. She
confided later that this was the one time that she felt that she was in control.*

*When Michelle was visited again the following week, a different approach
was adopted: risking being seen as a little "crazy," the counselor (JCD) sat
with Michelle and conducted a conversation with herself, asking questions
and answering them herself. After several of these one-sided conversations,
Michelle became irritated and told the counselor, in no uncertain terms, to
leave. With humor, the counselor exclaimed that Michelle could talk. Before
long, Michelle chose to see the humor also and a close relationship with the
counselor soon developed.*

*Michelle had not had an opportunity to meet other young cancer patients
during her hospitalization, and was encouraged to join CanTeen (the Australian Teenage Cancer Patients Society, Inc.). Attendance at her first Can-
Teen camp brought about a wonderful transformation in Michelle. The
previously introverted and shy adolescent in hospital became a gregarious and
extroverted teenager at the camp. She teamed up with a young man who
had had a leg amputated on the opposite side. According to Michelle, they
made a perfect match. She reported learning at the camp from others her age
that plans for treatment were often altered and that very little was ever certain
in the treatment of cancer. By listening to other young people who were confronting similar difficulties, she reported realizing for the first time that she*

did not feel so alone. Over the following 6 months, Michelle's hair eventually regrew and she mastered the use of an artificial leg so that she could walk without a limp.

Sadly, at the time Michelle consented to have more treatment, her cancer was found to have recurred. Palliative care was commenced. As her condition deteriorated, a particularly challenging consultation occurred when, with her family present, she asked for the first time if she was dying. She deflected attempts to be drawn out on her own perceptions of what might be happening and asked again, insisting on a direct and honest answer.

When informed that such was indeed the case, and that her death was expected soon, possibly within days, she immediately screamed and began crying out loudly in anger and defiance, weeping and banging her good leg repeatedly and violently on her bed, while her family looked on helplessly. It was as if she was discharging all the pent-up negative feelings about her illness and her situation in one torrid outpouring. To their credit, her family and staff chose not to try to stifle her protest. After she had settled, Michelle said she felt very peaceful, as if a huge load had been lifted, and she was ready to face what was to come. She cried for the first time with her family, but was also able, for the first time, to tell them what she felt and what she wanted. At her request, her care was continued at home, in a rural district away from Sydney. To the surprise of her treatment team, she survived another three months. During this special time, she kept in touch by telephone each week. These conversations would begin with her saying "Hi. It's me. I'm still here!"; after these comments, both patient and counselor would dissolve in laughter. A few days before she died in a small rural hospital, her horse was brought to the hospital for a visit. Michelle died in the company of her family, her younger siblings, and some trusted and supportive staff.

Life-Threatening Illness and the Middle Adolescent.   Midadolescents with a life-threatening illness are most concerned about the effects the illness will have on their ability to attract a girlfriend or boyfriend, on their emancipation from parents and authority figures, and about being rejected by their peers. Time in hospital, and away from school, can severely interfere with social relationships and the acquisition of social skills (Katz, Rubinstein, Hubert, & Bleu, 1988).

Social standing within a peer group can be threatened. The ability to attract a boyfriend or girlfriend can be reduced if illness or treatment affects the way a young person looks. Being different within a peer group can signal disaster for an adolescent. Fear of rejection by peers can lead to many adjustment problems, including a lowering of self-esteem, withdrawal, depression, and acting-out behaviors (Bartholome, 1982; Bennett, 1985).

Noncompliance with medical treatments and lifestyle changes is highest in this age group. To young people in this age group, side effects of treatment may be much more alarming than the threat of death. They understand the threat of death, but often appear to make choices, as Michelle did about cessation of treatment, based on an unrealistic view of their invincibility.

With a life-threatening illness, midadolescents often find themselves totally dependent on family again. This dependence and accompanying regression reduce self-esteem. A sense of personal autonomy is often compromised by hospitalizations and frequent trips to clinics and specialists involved in routine treatment. Many adolescents report frustration over loss of control over their life, and a sense of being taken over by institutions and health professionals (CanTeen Focus Groups, 1991–1993). This loss of independence can be met with rebellion, noncompliance, or further regression. As control issues are so important in midadolescence, informed consent and open communication with authority figures involved in management is vital.

Michelle considered the loss of her hair even more upsetting than the loss of her leg. Until she became a member of CanTeen she had remained at home not wanting to be asked questions about her bald head. The formation of friendships and particularly the interest shown by a member of the opposite sex, did much to increase Michelle's self-esteem.

At the camp, she became sufficiently confident to leave her bald head uncovered and to venture into the city, well prepared to deal with any questions she might be asked about her missing leg or the absence of her hair. (In dealing with tactless questions about amputations, an answer favored by these young people, at least on the Australian coast, is that the leg has been taken by a shark.)

The manner in which Michelle was befriended and encouraged to discuss her feelings might be considered unconventional. However, there is always scope for both intuition and creativity in working with ill adolescents. Creative or new ways of working with young people utilized by health professionals may not always succeed, but are usually valued by the young people as an indication of willingness to communicate.

Late Adolescence

This period is defined as approximately 17 to 24 years for both females and males. Significant issues for the late adolescent include defining of careers, permanent relationships and life styles, increasing financial independence where this is possible, and separation from family.

David had developed acute lymphoblastic leukemia at age 16. He had met author JCD during his initial illness. He had undergone a bone marrow transplant. He had relapsed 5 years after diagnosis and was preparing for a second bone marrow transplant. He was a rather shy young man. Having considered himself socially awkward at school, a significant change occurred after becoming involved with CanTeen. He appeared to thrive on having what he described as a purpose, to help others. During his illness, he served as a national president of CanTeen, became an accomplished public speaker, and represented Australia at an international conference on adolescent health held in Switzerland.

David expressed needs for independence. He reported that he felt close to his family and that they were very supportive of him. He described being frustrated that, on the one hand, he wanted to live away from home, but, on the other, he needed his family's assistance. This became particularly frustrating as he became weaker and needed more assistance. Options to assist him in retaining a sense of independence were frequently discussed with him. One was for him to take a risk and tell people what it was he wanted. Because he was so used to putting everyone else first, David found this difficult. Rather than explaining what was really worrying him, he would instead become angry and focus on more minor details. He would become particularly upset by what he called incompetence in staff. He would observe new staff critically and question their every move. However, overall, he enjoyed positive relationships with staff, and special relationships with many of his carers including the physicians supervising his treatment.

David frequently wanted to discuss his life and the possibility of his death, but also to be able to choose when, and with whom, he would talk. He became vocal about the rights of patients and would often recount the story of how he had made his own choice of counselor. He reported suffering recurring nightmares and would telephone his counselor in a panic to discuss their meaning, fearing most that they were premonitions of his death.

David resigned from his employment immediately when he relapsed, saying he did not think it was fair to his employer to hold his position for him in such circumstances. To help prepare for the possibility that he would not survive the second transplant, he went on a special holiday with his mother. He also bought a "flash" car that he "hooned around" in as much as he could prior to admission for the second transplant.

Over the 9 months before his death, David participated in the filming of a documentary about young people with cancer (The Topic Of Cancer, ABC Andrew Denton Series Money or The Gun, 1993). David died before the final segment of the documentary was filmed. In discussions about the possibility that he might not survive to the end of filming, David had been adamant that his death be discussed in the documentary rather than glossed over or ignored. He firmly believed that young people needed opportunities to discuss death, and especially to talk about the person who had died. Being remembered and expressing feelings were both important to David. He was very aware of how discussion of these issues was avoided by so many, and of how attempts had been made to prevent some young people from joining an organization like CanTeen "because people would die and that would upset them." As the young people themselves relate in the documentary, they would not have forsaken knowing David and experiencing the fun, the special closeness, and the friendship involved, just because he might die. When discussing attempts to protect young people from emotional upset associated with the deaths of peers, the most common response is, "But hey, that could be me! Surely I have a right to be a normal teenager. Just because I might die, don't shut me out!"

David died just after his 22nd birthday, after a prolonged hospitalization for management of complications induced by the second transplant. Until his death, David continued to hope for a miracle or even for a reprieve, yet also seemed resigned to his impending death. His need to retain control was maintained by approving who could visit him. Motivating photographs were displayed all around his hospital room including images of him with his family, prized car, and special friends. His relatives were generous in allowing his friends time with him, especially in the last weeks of his life. They would allow friends to sit and talk with him alone, while he lost and regained consciousness. David was concerned about the possibility of losing control of his body's functions. He panicked if he thought the staff had taken his pajamas off for ease of care. He was modest and attempted to do things for himself whenever possible, or with the least amount of help from the nursing staff. Privacy was important for him and having a private bathroom was a big comfort. He resented casual inspection of his medical record, and discussions that ignored him, being held over his bed while being transferred from one part of the hospital to another.

Toward the end, David became ambivalent about continuing his struggle for survival. At times he would insist that his doctors and nursing staff relay information to him promptly, as if he was committed to continuing with curative treatment, yet at other times he expressed regret that a second transplant had been attempted, and also dismay at his repeated resuscitations. A particularly painful comment to his mother was "I've just turned 22, but look at me—I'm like an old man of 86." David's zest for life, humor, and generosity in supporting other teenagers with cancer will not be forgotten by those with whom he came in contact.

Life-Threatening Illness and the Late Adolescent. Late adolescents with a life-threatening illness are most concerned about the effects of the illness on their plans for career and relationships, and on their lifestyle. Time off work or away from study can interfere with work promotion and academic achievement (Chang, Nesbit, Youngren, & Robinson, 1987). This in turn can have ramifications on economic independence and self-esteem. Job discrimination has been widely reported, and life insurance and health insurance rejection is also common (Koocher & O'Malley, 1981). Illness and treatment can cause major social disruptions, increased dependence on parents (Chang et al., 1987), and consequent interference with the formation of intimate relationships. Some late adolescents with a life-threatening illness have to return home after having lived independently for a number of years.

Reproductive capabilities are reduced in some conditions, causing concern in this age group about intimate relationships and having children. Low energy or weakened physical capabilities can interfere with independence, economic security, and social flexibility. Questions from ill adolescents about fertility are common, even in the terminal stages of their illness. Sadness about possible loss of fertility, and thus loss of the chance to live on through their children, can displace sadness over the prospect of death.

JOURNEY THROUGH A LIFE-THREATENING ILLNESS: EXPERIENCES AND REACTIONS OF ADOLESCENTS WITH CANCER

Just as adolescents who are healthy are a heterogeneous group, so too are adolescents living with a life-threatening illness. There are, however, common threads in the reactions experienced by young people living with cancer, as an example of a life-threatening illness. Knowledge of these reactions will assist those working with ill youngsters to be better aware of their needs. Adolescents themselves can be our best teachers, if the time is taken to listen, to find out from them what their needs are, and to show that one cares.

Any threat of death or disability is deemed by today's adolescents to be incongruent with the desirable lifestyle of a young person portrayed by the media. Images of fit, healthy, beautiful, youthful individuals are visible everywhere. There is a mythologic inference that the young can conquer all, including death. Adolescence is a time for experimentation, for expanding one's limits, for seeking new experiences. A sense of invulnerability is strong in adolescents. Only by experimentation can the boundaries of one's potential be learned. It is only through trial and error while learning how to manage conflict and deal with intimacy that a young person learns how to navigate successfully in the world of adults. The capacity to solve problems is predicted by the individual's exposure to multiple new experiences throughout the preadolescent and adolescent years (Inhelder & Piaget, 1958). The more restricted a young person's range of experiences, the fewer resources can be drawn on to solve problems.

At Diagnosis

When confronted with a diagnosis of cancer, young people so often respond with disbelief: "That happens to old people, I'm too young!" The adolescent and family often assume the worst, that the young person is going to die and soon. They will be stunned, disbelieving, shocked. Soon after, feelings of anger, guilt, sadness, and depression set in. Reactions are similar to those seen in parents of younger children with cancer (Stevens, 1995). However, Dunsmore (1992) reported the great majority (96%) in a study of 51 adolescents with cancer considered they were coping well; 62% perceived themselves as coping very well both with the diagnosis and subsequent treatment.

One of the goals in initial consultations is to readjust the adolescent's and parents' expectations to a more hopeful level, in keeping with the patient's actual prognosis. Effective communication with the adolescent and parents at diagnosis is vital in laying the foundation for effective palliative care later, should that become necessary. Adolescents prefer the conversation to be directed toward them rather than their parents. If information, friendly encouragement, practical support, and hope have been made freely available to the patient and family by the treatment team from the time of diagnosis, they will be much more likely to cope successfully with treatment, and with palliative care if required, than if they feel uninformed, misunderstood and unsupported. Suggestions for more effective communication with ill adolescents and their families are provided in chapter 17.

How Adolescents with a Life-Threatening Illness Feel Different from Healthy Peers

Young people with a life-threatening illness are often denied the opportunity to experiment. They are "protected." Decisions are made for them. This leaves them feeling somewhat powerless and less able than their well peers to make experienced decisions.

The resilience observed in young people living with a life-threatening illness is often marveled at by those around them. Most of these adolescents do not see themselves as being either extraordinary or brave, rather, as normal adolescents making the best of a difficult situation. They do, however, perceive themselves as being different from their well peers, as a result of coping successfully with what has happened to them. They perceive themselves as being more mature, more sensitive, more positive about life, less interested in the trivial, and less interested in worldly possessions, money, and power (Chesler & Lawther, 1990; Dunsmore, 1992).

Reactions When Completing Treatment

When planned treatment is completed and no further evidence of the cancer can be detected, the adolescent may initially be euphoric, but, later, may be left with a lingering uncertainty about the future. On the one hand, there is hope for cure based on the promising response to treatment and the encouragement provided by the treatment team. On the other, there is fear based on awareness of a poor outcome for peers with a similar diagnosis, who frequently have become close friends during the course of treatment and follow-up.

Denial

Because well adolescents often behave as if personal death is unlikely, denial or avoidance are common strategies for coping with a life-threatening illness (Carr-Gregg, 1987; Cohen & Lazarus, 1979; Goss & Lebovitz, 1977). The purpose of both denial and avoidance (Van Dongen-Melman, Pruyn, Van Zanen, & Sanders-Woudstra, 1989) is to ward off disruptive levels of anxiety and to allow, instead, for maintenance of normal functioning and self-image. Fluctuating episodes of denial and avoidance by adolescents with cancer have been observed both by the authors and others (Carr-Gregg & White, 1987; Bluebond-Langner, 1978).

The preference for use of denial by adolescents is understandable, because one requirement in adolescent development and maturation to adulthood involves recognizing the certainty of dying, and, as Spiegel (1993) says, "hence the need of defences to help us manage that terror" (p. 134).

Living with Uncertainty

The situation of survival being obtained at the cost of continuing danger has been described by way of a metaphor, the "Damocles Syndrome" (Koocher & O'Malley, 1981). Just as in the story of Damocles, adolescents with a life-threatening illness (e.g., cancer, cystic fibrosis, or HIV/AIDS) sit uneasily at the banquet of life, forever aware of the sword that hangs by a thin thread over their heads. Certainly, the reality for some of these adolescents is that they are either dying or will die soon. But they prefer to perceive themselves as living and intending to live well.

Confronting the Possibility of Death

Most adolescents with cancer will feel more in control if they have opportunities to discuss the "what ifs" and to evaluate their priorities in living. Some adolescents with life-threatening illness will decline a proffered opportunity to consider the possibility of their own death. Others become more willing to consider the issue later in the course of their illness, especially when they have been restored to apparent health, and are attempting to reshape their plans for the future.

Overprotection and Its Problems

Most adolescents living with a life-threatening illness describe their willingness to confront the illness directly. They speak of their belief that honesty is the best policy. In two surveys of CanTeen members, all participants in the surveys responded to the question on bad news. Ninety-six percent said categorically that they would want to be informed of adverse events in their management, such as failure of treatment or other setbacks, and, most important, if they were dying (Dunsmore & Quine, in press). It is evident from these surveys and from responses provided within other discussion groups and workshops conducted regularly by CanTeen, that young people who live with a life-threatening illness feel strongly about this issue. Typical responses include the following (Dunsmore, 1992):

> "I have a right to know; it's my body."
> "I'm a real person. It's my life."
> "It's my body, not the doctors', not my parents'."
> "There are some things I want to do. I need to know how much time I have."
> "I don't want to spend all my time worrying they aren't telling me the truth."

Providing Bad News

When asked whom they would prefer to provide them with bad news, 48% of CanTeen members said that it should be the doctor, 35% their parents and their doctor together, and 12% their parents alone (Dunsmore & Quine, in press). The manner in which such news is provided is vital if satisfactory relationships with the adolescent are to be maintained. Adolescents often comment on whether or not they think the news meant anything to the caregiver who provided it. As one said, "She really cared. She said she would continue to be my doctor, she would make sure I was looked after." Honesty, continuity of care, and feeling supported rather than abandoned, are important issues for those facing death. Continuity of care may be adversely affected both by the patient moving from pediatric or adolescent units to facilities caring for adults, and by transfer into palliative care.

At Relapse

Contrary to reactions at diagnosis, those who had relapsed felt that having the cancer recur was more upsetting than the initial diagnosis, because of the poorer prognosis after relapse, the loss of hope entailed in relapse, and awareness and fear of what lay ahead. Young people with cancer who have experienced a recurrence of their disease will frequently speak of their fear of what lies ahead. As one 16-year-old said, "I sailed through treatment the first time. I always believed I would make it. This time it's more difficult. I see the pain and fear in the faces of my family. I see the pity in the eyes of my nurses and doctors. I am just so confused. One doctor tells me, 'Keep your chin up, keep fighting. We still have tricks up our sleeve—more chemotherapy, more radiotherapy, maybe a bone marrow transplant.' Another has told my parents to prepare for the worst. I'm not a fool. I'm not a child. Be straight with me!"

Avoidance by Health Professionals

Avoidance is practiced not only by adolescents with a life-threatening illness, but also by their health professionals and parents (Foley & Whittam, 1990). The truth may be perceived as devastating by those surrounding the young person. Many health professionals have said they feel at a loss to know what best to do in these circumstances. When treatment goals are oriented toward cure, there may be a perception of having failed. The death of a young person is tragic and may provoke in a caregiver much sadness and reassessment of priorities, relationships, and of personal mortality. As Spiegel (1993) says, "You must bring the unmentionable out into the open so everyone can deal with it" (p. 186).

Control of Visiting Rights

The terminally ill adolescent's family may seek to prevent visits by friends and peers in the belief that whatever time is left for their child deserves to be spent just with them. There may also be a conviction that this policy spares the friends from becoming upset. It is likely, however, that the adolescent does want his or her special friends to be permitted to continue to visit. The young person's wishes should be respected. Tom, an 18-year-old confined to bed in hospital, spoke of his frustration with his mother who he believed was preventing his friends from visiting him. His mother had left strict instructions with the nursing staff that Tom not have any visitors other than herself and his grandmother. He became depressed, refusing to talk to his mother or to eat. Despite his mother's instructions, a friend managed to visit him, staying with him for a few hours. His mood improved immediately. He spoke with his mother and negotiated an agreement with her about ways in which he could share what time he had left with his friends, as well as with his family.

Attempts to Mask Reality

The implications of the situation in which these young people find themselves cannot be concealed from them. For example, it is not uncommon for them to witness the death of a fellow patient while in hospital. Staff may attempt to disguise such an event by closing curtains around the bed, whisking away the deceased person's body, avoiding discussion about the deceased person, and ensuring that a new patient occupies the bed promptly. These ruses are described by young people as simply unrealistic. It is as if the young person who died vanished, or worse still, never existed. In group discussions, young people commonly describe in emotional terms how disposable they feel. Rather than vanish or cease to exist, they would prefer to be remembered and to be missed. They equate the manner in which they may be treated after death to their perceived worth and to the degree to which they were loved.

Despite a conspiracy of silence by staff, news of a patient's death manages to spread quickly and effectively by word of mouth through a ward of young people. Other patients may not be given an opportunity to discuss their feelings or to openly grieve for the death of a fellow patient, because of a conviction that to do so would admit defeat or cause distress. Most of the other patients, in fact, already know what has happened and need an opportunity to express their feelings and to acknowledge the person who has died. Adopting a closed approach is more likely to increase, rather than decrease, young people's distress.

Misinterpretation of Health Management Initiatives

Wards may have what adolescents at several hospitals refer to as "the dying room," a single room into which they perceive patients are moved when death is imminent. Understandably, this perception causes significant anxiety for a young patient moved into such a room merely to assist with provision of a better night's sleep, because of a fear that the real reason for the transfer is not being disclosed. One such young person in this unfortunate situation was encountered the following morning, sitting upright in bed having not slept all night, wide-eyed and visibly shaken, scared of falling asleep and not waking up!

Privacy

Privacy is more significant for ill adolescents in comparison with older or younger patients because of their preoccupation with physical change, their awakening sexuality, and normal shyness. Further, young people fantasize about the potential for more intimate relationships with many other people with whom they come into routine contact, however little the potential may actually be for such relationships to develop. When caregivers are of similar age as the patient, these thoughts and feelings, and associated embarrassment, may be heightened. Being cared for by a healthy young person may result in an ill adolescent feeling humiliated, if the ill young person perceives differences between himself or herself and the carer, and especially if the ill young person believes the carer is making an unfavorable comparison. Young people want to be regarded as people, not objects.

Young people who are chronically or terminally ill have the same need for quiet contemplation as others their age. Such opportunities cannot be provided without attention to privacy and provision of time to be alone.

Young people commonly have thoughts, feelings, and secrets that are not normally revealed to their families. That privilege may suffer after developing a life-threatening illness because of the perceived expectation that the patient with a serious illness must disclose all to the authority figures providing care. Recognition of the need for private time with a boyfriend or girlfriend is also important. Opportunities for physical closeness, for kissing and cuddling, are often denied during a life-threatening illness.

Caregivers should ensure that adolescents are not unduly or unnecessarily exposed during medical examinations and nursing procedures, by appropriate use of curtains and provision of garments providing privacy. Discussion of what is required and what will happen should occur beforehand. Teenagers should be allowed to undress or get changed for examinations in private. The number of people observing them while undressed, or during physical examinations, should be minimized. Care should be taken to involve them in discussions. Young people appreciate private discussions being removed to private areas, "away from prying ears." Young people should be asked what information they have provided can be disclosed to others and what they want kept confidential.

Terminally ill adolescents also value having some control over who can enter their personal space, whether at home or in the hospital. This control helps maintain a sense of privacy and dignity at a time when control over bodily functions may be failing.

In the Terminal Phase

The death of each adolescent is unique, because of differences in the natural history of each teen's disease, differences in personalities of patients and families, the variety of preferences for style of care expressed by patients, and varying requirements for technical support related to their palliative care. Some adolescents will choose to die in denial. Some will request lots of noise; others want peace and quiet. Some will want their family around them, whereas others will not. Some will want to remain alert as much as possible to the end, even though in pain. Others will prefer to be heavily sedated.

It is the process of dying, especially loss of control, that adolescents fear most, rather than being dead. They fear becoming vegetative and totally dependent on others. They fear becoming dependent on others for their personal hygiene. They fear the embarrassment of becoming demented, helpless, and child-like. They express concerns that their pain may increase, that the truth will be withheld from them, that they will not have an opportunity to achieve their goals in life. When in the hospital, many express concerns that they will not see their own room or their home again, or that they will not be able to say goodbye to their pets. Their greatest distress is their concern for their loved ones. Young people have commonly worried excessively about the effect their dying was having on a sibling or a parent (Foley & Whittam, 1990). They also fear separation from their families and from their special friends. These concerns are more commonly expressed to carers or friends than parents, and even then only if the confidant is perceived as being willing to listen, honest, and trustworthy.

Denial

Young people who are terminally ill commonly use denial as a way of escaping temporarily from the brutal reality of their situation. Passing into and back out of denial assists them in adjusting bit by bit to their impending death. Further, they will not want to spend their whole time talking about death, rather, preferring to talk about other nonthreatening subjects as a way of reducing their anxiety. This is often misinterpreted by caregivers as denial. One 17-year-old with osteogenic sarcoma of the pelvis said, "My life is short enough without having to spend all my waking hours talking about dying."

Adolescents' Preparations for Death

Adolescents who are seriously or terminally ill commonly take steps to put their affairs in order. A patient of one of the authors (MS) with relapsed acute myeloid leukemia prepared for the probability of not surviving an impending mismatched bone marrow transplant by asking that the family have a holiday together before the transplant. She asked if she owned her bedroom furniture and her piano, and about her right to make a will. Those attending her funeral were to wear bright colors. The service was to be held in her school chapel and the madrigal group of which she was a member was to sing a favorite hymn. She selected a white coffin, named the clothing for her burial ("not a nightie, under any circumstances"), and asked that a family photograph, a bible, and her rosary beads be placed in her coffin. She purchased a remembrance gift for her parents and wrote them a personal letter. She recorded herself playing a special piece of music on the piano. She asked her parents not to remain sad, to be kind and loving to each other, and always to stay together. Examples such as this are common and indicate that young people who are dying may respond in a manner well beyond their years.

Needing Permission to Die

Young people who are dying may linger, close to death, for prolonged periods. They may simply need permission from their loved ones to die and will often die promptly when such permission is given. One of the author's (MS) patients, an 11-year-old boy with osteogenic sarcoma, was dying at home after a 5-year illness. Throughout his illness, he had demonstrated a notable tenacity to survive and willingness to endure continuing and painful treatment as long as it entailed some hope for further quality survival. After his death, his father reported that as the boy's death drew close, he lingered on in a coma for more than 7 days. An aboriginal community nurse who was caring for the patient spoke with his father, informing him that the boy needed his parents' permission to die. The father and mother ushered the boy's grandmother and other relatives out of his room, sat down alone by the boy's bed, spoke to him of their love for him, and gave him their permission to die. The boy died peacefully a few hours later.

Even at the point of death, adolescents may still choose to censure behavior that upsets them. One of the author's (JCD) adolescent patients was prostrate in bed, close to death. His family and friends chatted on among themselves, talking about him over his bed. He appeared to hold his breath, then let out a long sigh. His family reasonably assumed he had just died. He suddenly opened his eyes and said with a laugh, "That'll teach you! I'm not dead yet. Talk to me!" He died 8 hours later.

LIFE-THREATENING CONDITIONS OTHER THAN CANCER

Many concerns of adolescents who are coping with cancer also apply to young people with other life-threatening conditions. In this section, we note some modifications that apply to adolescents with cystic fibrosis, severe brain damage, and catastrophic illness with short life expectancy.

Cystic Fibrosis

A diagnosis of cystic fibrosis is commonly established earlier in childhood. Thus, young people with cystic fibrosis learn at an early age that their life span is expected to be limited. Issues of dependency and of attaining goals in adolescence are experienced, as by young people with cancer. Denial is a common reaction in adolescents with cystic fibrosis, evidenced, for example, by noncompliance with physiotherapy, diet, and other important components of long-term therapy.

Severe Brain Damage

Issues affecting the family of an adolescent with severe brain damage may be more significant than those affecting the young person. Families of patients who are vegetative, apparently unresponsive, and totally dependent on them, may exhaust their reserves of energy in caring for such young people. From the family's perspective, it is not easy caring for such a child: The strain and loneliness can be great. These families will benefit from the patient receiving periodic respite care, to assist them in recharging their spiritual batteries. Families of such adolescents should be encouraged to remember that the patient may still be able to hear despite being unable to respond, and to continue talking to the young person at the bedside, even if about simple matters, such as what one is doing at that moment. These families may describe being in a dilemma of wanting the adolescent to die in order to be released, yet experiencing guilt over such feelings. Opportunities are required for these families to work through their anticipatory grieving. Just being able to discuss their feelings will assist them in the grieving process. Others will remain adamant that miracles do happen.

Catastrophic Conditions with Short Life Expectancy

When a catastrophic illness or life-threatening condition (e.g., motor vehicle accident, acute cardiomyopathy, viral meningitis or overwhelming sepsis) occurs in a previously well adolescent and death is imminent, issues of honesty with the young person become important. Young people in this situation are likely to suspect that they are about to die. They deserve honesty from their caregivers to ensure, for example, that something they want to say or have done can be accomplished. Families in this situation are often required to make urgent and painful decisions about treatment or organ donation. Additional support may be required in such painful circumstances, particularly relating to opportunities for grieving after the adolescent's death and removal of the deceased's body to the mortuary. The aftercare of such families is as important as would have been the ongoing care of the young person, had he or she survived.

CONCLUSION

Many imagine that caring for young people with cancer or other life-threatening illnesses must be depressing, stressful, and unrewarding. Undoubtedly such work is stressful at times, but those working in such fields will attest that they enjoy caring for their patients and families, and that the work is frequently rewarding and affirming. It is commonly described as a significant privilege to be afforded the opportunity of working with young people such as those introduced in this chapter, and their families, because of the opportunity provided, by caring, to experience enriching friendships and human contacts, and to witness the transformations that occur in empowered young people living with life-threatening illnesses. In confronronting the possibility of death, and in dying, they teach us with humor and with love, about the preciousness of life and living. The message for caregivers from adolescents with cancer who participated in the Eighth Children's Hospice International Pediatric Palliative Care Conference in Sydney, Australia, in mid-1993, was "be honest, . . . have a sense of humor . . . talk to us . . . we are normal, treat us that way . . . and let us have hope!"

II

Bereavement

The chapters in this section describe encounters with bereavement during adolescence. This involves death-related losses that are most likely to occur during the adolescent years in our society, factors that influence bereavement in adolescence, grief reactions that are typical of adolescents, and efforts by adolescents to cope with loss and grief. In Chapter 7, Stephen Fleming and Leslie Balmer provide an overview of these subjects by offering a theoretical framework that notes parallels in tasks confronting adolescents coping with bereavement to the normative work of coping with developmental tasks in early, middle, and late adolescence. Thereafter, chapter 7 concentrates on a critical review of empirical research concerning the impact of death-related losses on adolescents, emphasizing three independent variables (time since death; age and gender of the adolescent survivor; and family environment) and two dependent variables (school performance and self-esteem).

Following that introduction, chapters 8 to 10 explore three bereavement experiences that are most likely to be encountered by adolescents in our society. In chapter 8, Kirsten Tyson-Rawson examines adolescent responses to the death of a parent. In chapter 9, Nancy Hogan and Lydia DeSantis discuss adolescent sibling bereavement and set forth elements in a new theory of this type of bereavement. In chapter 10, Kevin Ann Oltjenbruns examines the death of a friend during adolescence. Each of these discussions is sensitive to the importance of an adolescent's relationship(s) with the deceased person, the significant features of the bereavement experience that follows such a death, and ways in which interested persons can help adolescents to cope effectively with their losses. In addition, each of the chapters in this section offers suggestions for future research that can enhance our understanding of these and other bereavement experiences during adolescence.

7

Bereavement in Adolescence

Stephen Fleming and Leslie Balmer

Since the introduction of Freud's theory of mourning (Freud, 1957), there have been countless theoretical and empirical publications exploring various aspects of bereavement. Several trends within this literature are noteworthy. Investigations have focused for the most part on parental responses to the death of a child (Klass, 1988; Martinson, Davies, & McClowry, 1987; Rando, 1986), or on adult loss of a spouse (Parkes, 1985; Robinson & Fleming, 1992). It is only relatively recently that there has been sustained attention to bereavement during adolescence as a serious life crisis (Balk, 1991). This chapter offers a critical review of empirical research examining the impact of death on adolescent adjustment. After briefly sketching a theoretical framework for understanding adolescent grief, the authors consider the influence of the following independent variables on adjustment: time since death; age and gender of the survivor; and family environment. The chapter concludes with a discussion of the impact of death on two dependent variables (school performance and self-esteem) and offers suggestions for future research.

The authors gratefully acknowledge the support of the Hospital for Sick Children Foundation, Toronto (Grant XG 88-55) in the preparation of this manuscript.

THEORETICAL FRAMEWORK

If theories of adolescent development have been characterized by conflicting conceptualizations and predictions (see chapter 1), until recently theories of adolescent bereavement have been virtually nonexistent. One exception to this is the model formulated by Fleming and Adolph (1986), which integrates theories of adjustment to loss (Bowlby, 1973; Sugar, 1968) with theories of adolescent ego development (Laufer, 1980). In this conceptual framework, adolescence is chronologically defined as the years from 11 to 21, and for each of three maturational periods spanning these years, there are specific tasks and conflicts (see Table 7.1).

Briefly, in phase one (early adolescence) adolescents struggle with separating from their parents in an attempt to determine their own identities. Phase two (middle adolescence) involves the development of one's sense of competency, and phase three (late adolescence) addresses challenges involved in risking interpersonal closeness. The principal feature of this theoretical framework is the attempt to incorporate in a comprehensive theory of adolescent bereavement aspects of both adolescent development and grief theory. As Fleming and Adolph (1986) have noted:

> During adolescence, the loss of a profound relationship—whether an internalized object or a person in the external world—may interfere in what seems to be the natural progression of intellectual-emotional-psychological "growing up." Changes that are normally expected may be averted, avoided, or may not even take place. Such an arrest of developmental unfolding may put the adolescent "on hold" in one phase, and thus inhibit the energy and skills necessary to meet subsequent phase-ap-

TABLE 7.1   Tasks and Conflicts for Adolescents by Maturational Phase

Phase I	Age:	11–14
	Task:	Emotional separation from parents
	Conflict:	Separation vs. reunion (Abandonment vs. safety)
Phase II	Age:	14–17
	Task:	Competency/mastery/control
	Conflict:	Independence vs. dependence
Phase III	Age:	17–21
	Task:	Intimacy and commitment
	Conflict:	Closeness vs. distance

Source: Fleming & Adolph (1986).

propriate demands. A developmental arrest may also have the opposite effect, that is, of increasing the intensity of prior phase-specific behavior in a following phase. (pp. 101–102)

In suggesting age-typical thoughts, feelings, and behaviors for developing adolescents, this model encourages the matching of age-appropriate conflicts and tasks with emerging grief responses as a reflection of how the adolescent survivor's developing personality may be shaped and colored by loss. Accordingly, this developmental model of adolescent grieving emphasizes differential responses of adolescents in their attempts to cope with a life crisis. In other words, this model proposes that adjustment to the death of a significant object or person will, in part, be determined by such variables as the adolescent's developmental phase and the major interpersonal tasks with which he or she is struggling when the death occurs.

ADOLESCENTS AND LOSS: INDEPENDENT VARIABLES MEDIATING ADJUSTMENT

Empirical research examining the impact of loss on adolescent adjustment is plagued by several dilemmas. One of the most problematic issues, as Fleming and Adolph (1986) have noted, is the confusion regarding the definition of "adolescent." Haslam (1978) referred to children from 10 to 19 years of age, while Laufer (1980) embraced the period from "puberty to about the age of 21" (p. 265). With few exceptions (e.g., Balk, 1981, 1983; Guerriero, 1983), one finds that adolescence is either considered an extension of childhood or part of adulthood. More specifically, Caplan and Douglas's (1969) research participants were "children" between the ages of 2 and 16 years, while Van Eerdewegh, Bieri, Parrilla, and Clayton (1982) included children between 2 and 17 years of age. Finally, Hardt (1979) included participants with an age range of 13 to 26 years.

The following review of empirical research on independent variables influencing adjustment (time since death, age, gender, and family environment) will exclude research combining both children and adolescents in the analyses. Emphasis will be placed on the impact of parental and sibling death because, as Balk (1991) has noted, in the literature there has been an unfortunate lack of attention paid to the effects of a friend's death.

Adjustment and Time Since Death

Guerriero (1983), in one of the few studies to include a control group, looked at the impact of the death of a family member on physical health, self-concept, and death anxiety. Time since death predicted level of self-concept for one third of the sample; unexpectedly, the more recent the bereavement, the higher the self-concept score. In addition to reporting no significant health differences between the bereaved and nonbereaved adolescents, Guerriero found no evidence in support of previous research on depression as a common affective response for bereaved adolescents. Guerriero's results suggested that such adolescents had slightly, but not significantly, higher levels of depression.

Balk (1981), in his study of 33 sibling-bereaved adolescents, did not find that time since death influenced the nature and dynamics of one's grief. (Note: These findings are also presented in an abridged form more readily accessible to readers in Balk [1983a].) Balk did, however, report the majority of bereaved adolescents experienced a variety of responses, such as shock, numbness, confusion, depression, fear, loneliness, and anger. Although in most cases these reactions dissipated somewhat, about one half of the sibling-bereaved participants still reported one or more emotional reactions to the death by the time of the interview (on average, approximately 24 months later). These responses included feelings of guilt, confusion, loneliness, and anger as well as sleep difficulties, loss of appetite, and suicidal ideation (although none of the respondents had made any serious attempt at self-harm).

The relationship between manifestations of grief and time since death is far from clear in the research by Guerriero (1983) and Balk (1981). However, there are significant methodological problems that may have contributed to these conflicting and inconclusive results. For example, as Guerriero herself has suggested, the finding of higher self-esteem early in the grief process was not expected and may be peculiar to a limited sample of 22 bereaved adolescents. In other words, the small number of sibling-bereaved participants, as well as the inclusion of various other kinds of losses, may have contributed to this unexpected and apparently contradictory finding.

Similarly, although Balk's (1981) study offered some unique insight into adolescent sibling bereavement, it has serious methodological limitations. For example, the reliance on retrospection to establish one's emotional responses at the time of a death many months or years previous calls into question the accuracy of some of the results, as does the problem of the great variability in time since death (4 months to 7 years in this study). Similarly, the use of a nonrepresentative sample and the lack of a control group limit one's ability to draw inferences based on this study.

In contrast to this early work, more recent research (Balmer, 1992; Hogan & Greenfield, 1991) has revealed the time-since-death dimension to be a salient predictor of adjustment in bereaved adolescents. In their study of adjustment to the death of a sibling, Hogan and Greenfield (1991) found the reported frequency and intensity of grief-related experiences dissipated slowly over time, although even those most removed in time continued to report some degree of these experiences.

The use of a matched control group, relatively large sample size (bereaved group $n = 40$), and brief time since death (within 36 months) allowed Balmer (1992) to scrutinize closely the time-since-death variable and its impact on sibling-bereaved adolescents. Respondents in their first year of bereavement were significantly less well adjusted in terms of their depressive symptomatology, self-esteem, and somatic symptom scores when compared with their matched controls. Significantly, by the second or third year of bereavement, the adjustment scores of the bereaved and nonbereaved participants in this study were indistinguishable.

In summary, there is limited support for the finding that time since death is a salient predictor of adjustment as measured by depressive symptomatology and self-esteem (Balmer, 1992; Hogan & Greenfield, 1991). However, the task of comparing more recent studies with previous research characterized by retrospective, cross-sectional methodology, no baseline data, a wide range of differences in the time-since-death dimension, retrospective, semistructured interviews, the absence of control groups, and the failure to use standardized measures, makes comparing and contrasting results a somewhat hazardous enterprise. Finally, one must exercise caution when interpreting grief-specific results gleaned from semistructured interviews, because such interviews may not reflect overall levels of adjustment but the distress accompanying the recall of painful memories.

Age and Gender Differences in Adjustment

The clinical and theoretical literature on adolescent bereavement implies and hypothesizes that there are age- and gender-related differences in adjustment. For example, Raphael (1983) suggested that male and female adolescent responses to death are different, with males behaving aggressively, testing authority figures, and likely to self-medicate with drugs and alcohol. By contrast, Raphael indicated that females tend to reach out for support and consolation. Fleming and Adolph (1986), in supporting Raphael's contention that gender differences play a powerful role in determining how an individual will express feelings, noted "with the possible exception of anger, when distressed or frustrated, males encounter more prohibitions against emotional expression than do females" (p. 116). Consequently, males may have fewer outlets than females to express their grief. Similarly, from a developmental perspective it would seem logical that age differences would be an important variable in terms of differential responses, as clearly noted in the model proposed by Fleming and Adolph (1986).

However, as previously mentioned, one of the major methodological problems in existing empirical research is that researchers view their bereaved samples as a homogeneous group rather than attempting to highlight within-group differences. Consequently, few age and gender differences have been reported in the literature.

Age. Balk (1981) noted some interesting age differences in affective responses to the death of a sibling. Older respondents (17–19 years of age), compared with younger ones (14–16 years of age), reported feeling significantly more angry at the time of their sibling's death. Against this, Guerriero (1983) did not find significant age-related differences on any of the variables addressed in her research. Finally, Gray (1987a) reported bereaved adolescents 15 years of age or younger at the time of a parent's death reported lower mean scores on their most recent report card than adolescents who were older at the time of death.

Balmer (1992) found age to be a significant predictor of adjustment with older bereaved adolescents experiencing greater psychological distress, whereas younger ones reported greater physiological distress following the death of a sibling. One could hypothesize that younger respondents are more sensitive about appearing to be different from their peers. If so, younger bereaved adolescents may be less likely to discuss death-related concerns openly with their friends. If a death occurs at a time when they are also attempting to separate themselves emotionally from their families, they are left feeling isolated and with fewer options for the expression of their grief (Fleming & Adolph, 1986). As stated by Deveau (1990), if an adolescent's emotions cannot be expressed or resolved, the resulting anxiety may be internalized and eventually displayed in physiological symptoms, such as headaches, stomach pains, and insomnia.

By contrast, older adolescents, more independent in their thinking and with a stronger sense of personal identity, may have more peer options in terms of discussing their losses. However, the cost of increased maturity may be less denial, a fuller appreciation of the short- and long-term impact of their sibling's death (Deveau, 1990), an increase in depressive symptomatology, and lowered self-esteem. Moreover, the death of a sibling at a time when an adolescent is preparing to leave home physically can lead to many developmental dilemmas including questions like, "Who will take care of my parents when I leave?" Because the data are far from unequivocal, however, further research is needed on the relationship between the nature and the dynamics of grief and the age of the adolescent survivor.

Although there appears to be a discrepancy between these data and the suggestions of many authors about age-related responses to loss (Fleming & Adolph, 1986; Raphael, 1983), one must be aware that the few studies addressing the issue of age differences among bereaved adolescents have numerous methodological problems. These include the lack of a control group (Balk, 1981; Gray, 1987a), the lack of a representative sample (Balk, 1981; Balmer, 1992; Gray, 1987a; Guerriero, 1983), and the significantly large variability in the time-since-death dimension (Balk, 1981; Gray, 1987a). It is likely that all of these factors impact on, and in part are responsible for, the lack of solid and consistent findings in this area.

Gender. Balmer (1992) found that gender emerged as a significant predictor of adjustment for sibling-bereaved adolescents, with female respondents exhibiting lower self-esteem and higher anxiety/insomnia levels than their male counterparts. This suggests that adolescent females may be more prone than adolescent males to adjustment problems following the death of a sibling. An alternative explanation is that such males experience a similar drop in self-esteem and increased anxiety/insomnia, but they are less willing to admit these vulnerabilities as a result of sex-role stereotyping, which tends to restrict expressions of grief among males. If this were the case, however, one would expect a similar trend to have occurred in the nonbereaved group, but that was not observed.

As stated earlier, because empirical investigations of adolescent bereavement have used a wide variety of assessment tools, it is difficult to compare and contrast their results. For example, Balk's (1981) finding that females were more likely to report feeling confused about the death of their sibling at the time of the interview was not supported by Balmer's (1992) research. Similarly, Guerriero's (1983) finding that females in both the bereaved and nonbereaved groups reported poorer health also contradict's Balmer's conclusions. Once again, however, comparisons are difficult because different scales were used to measure health. Balmer's results, though, are consistent with much of the clinical and theoretical literature on adolescent bereavement, which implies that gender plays a role in determining how an individual will express grief-related feelings (Fleming & Adolph, 1986; Raphael, 1983). Nevertheless, there was no evidence supporting Raphael's contention that bereaved males are more prone to self-medicating with drugs and alcohol.

Family Environment and Adjustment

The enormous influence of the family during one's developing years is undisputed. That is, the family milieu acts both to create stress and to mediate it, depending on a variety of factors (Bell, 1978). In fact, the family's role in facilitating or hindering adjustment to the death of a family member had been noted in the bereavement literature (Walsh & McGoldrick, 1991b). This granted, one might expect bereaved adolescents to be a high-risk population not only because of factors related to their own grief, but also because of issues related to potential maladjustment in their parents and families. It would seem imperative that any investigation of adjustment in bereavement include an exploration of the mediating effects of the family environment. Unfortunately, few empirical studies have addressed this issue.

Gray (1987a) found that parentally bereaved adolescents who reported a good prior relationship with their surviving parent had lower mean depression scores than those reporting a poorer connection. Balk (1981) found that sibling-bereaved adolescents scoring low on a family coherency scale were confused and angry after their sibling's death. They were also significantly more likely to feel guilty at the time of the interview. In contrast, those participants who scored high on the family coherency scale tended to feel more depressed. In interpreting these results, Balk (1981) suggested that coherency in some families acts as a resource for adolescents as they work through problems, and depression may be the price paid when death severs close bonds. Against this, adolescents who do not have close family ties may be insulated somewhat from depression, but they may feel guilty and later confused about the death.

Regarding signs of depression, Balmer (1992) found that family climate—and more specifically levels of cohesion, conflict, and expressiveness—acted as a protective factor for sibling-bereaved adolescents and, to a lesser extent, nonbereaved participants. This would appear to contradict Balk's results. On closer examination, however, it is likely that differing measures of family coherency might account for this discrepancy, because Balk's family coherency scale is qualitatively different from the one used by Balmer (The Family Environment Scale [FES]; Moos, 1974). Finally, Balmer also reported that lower levels of parental attachment were predictive of higher self esteem and lower anxiety/insomnia scores.

Balmer's data not only support the view that family plays an important and powerful mediating role in adolescent bereavement, they are also consistent with research reporting that the "Family Dimensions" subscale of the FES was a salient predictor of adjustment in 250 potentially high-risk adolescents (Felner, Aber, Primavera, & Cauce, 1985). Also, Farber, Felner, and Primavera (1985) found that the levels of cohesion and conflict (as measured by the FES) were the most prominent predictors of adaptive outcome in a group of 65 adolescents who had experienced the separation/divorce of their parents.

When all of these factors are considered, it is plausible that a bereaved adolescent could view the family environment as helpful in adjusting to death if that family unit is cohesive, allows for members to express opinions, and is low in conflict. At the same time, it is reasonable to assume that a healthy reaction to observing intense levels of distress in one's parents, a distress unlike anything witnessed before, may be to distance oneself psychologically until such time as one is better able to cope. As Fleming and Adolph (1986) have cautioned, however, there are interpersonal as well as intrapersonal costs when developmental tasks and family demands collide.

Finally, Balmer (1992) conducted one of the few assessments of the relative helpfulness of family members and significant others after the death of a sibling. For the adolescent survivors, *mothers* were viewed as most helpful because, in verbalizing their own pain and anguish, they validated and normalized their children's grief. *Fathers* were found to be less helpful as a function of their perceived unavailability and their restricted expression of grief within the family. Balmer was quick to point out, however, that the question asked of participants regarding helpfulness was specific to grief-related issues. Cook (1984) has suggested that fathers tend to share their grief less for they feel a responsibility to support other family members; thus, they may play an important role indirectly by maintaining financial stability and providing a sense of ongoing routine and emotional security.

There is also evidence that fathers may be more objective than mothers in their perceptions of their children's adjustment to sibling death. Hogan and Balk (1990) reported that mothers perceived the grief reactions of their adolescents to be more problematic, and their self-concepts to be more mature, than did fathers and the adolescents themselves. Fathers, then, may be in a better position to assess the situation objectively and to react appropriately when adolescents are having difficulties adjusting to the death of a sibling. This finding may bring into question the validity of studies in the child and adolescent literature that base their findings on the reports of grief-stricken mothers.

Given the voluminous literature on the impact of death on adolescents, it is surprising to find that the quality of the surviving siblings' relationships has not been systematically examined. One might assume that bereaved adolescents would find support and comfort from their siblings, but Balmer (1992) found no support for this position. In fact, *siblings* were reported to be the least helpful family members. Most sibling-bereaved participants expressed an inability or unwillingness to share their grief with their surviving siblings, and many reported feeling alienated from them. When expressions of grief were not forthcoming from siblings, several participants interpreted this as indifference. Examples illustrating this point include: "My sister only cried once, and she doesn't talk about it at all," and "My brother is never around any more . . . it seems as if he doesn't even care." Because sibling relationships may have been problematic before death, it is unclear whether this sense of alienation and lack of support characterized their relationship before the death, or whether the death was a contributing factor.

Extended family members were as helpful as mothers, and significantly more helpful than fathers and siblings. Frequently, adolescents found extended family members easier to talk with for they shared a common bond, knew the deceased, and were perceived to be in less visible pain. Familiarity with the deceased was also important when it came to their *friends.* Several participants in Balmer's research expressed a feeling of comfort while interacting with the deceased sibling's friends, oftentimes preferring to be with this group than with their own peers. It was not uncommon for participants to recount incidents where such friends continued to have contact with their family by coming for dinner, attending informal gatherings, or simply dropping by to visit. For some bereaved adolescents, spending time with friends of the deceased involved talking about grief-related concerns, but, just as often, there was an unspoken understanding that the deceased was missed. Conversations, when they occurred, focused on the discussion of shared, treasured memories. In general, friends were considered most helpful when the bereaved felt they had "permission" to respond freely, to discuss grief-related concerns, or to "escape," however temporarily, from their pain and that of their families. A willingness on the part of friends to be flexible and available, in whatever capacity, was deemed most therapeutic and helpful.

Finally, Balmer (1992) found adolescents were disappointed in the responses of *teachers*. In most cases, this was for not acknowledging the death. This lack of a response, often interpreted as indifference, was particularly poignant when participants had a close relationship with a teacher or the teacher knew the deceased sibling and remained silent. Invariably, when teachers and school personnel did respond, whether by sending a card, attending the funeral, or simply mentioning the death, it was warmly appreciated.

In summary, family climate—and more specifically levels of cohesion, conflict, and expressiveness—exerts a considerable influence on adolescent adjustment following death (Balk, 1981; Balmer, 1992). Lower levels of attachment to parents have also been found to be predictive of higher self-esteem scores and lower anxiety/insomnia levels in the bereaved participants but not the matched controls. This finding suggests that it may be adaptive for sibling-bereaved adolescents to distance themselves from their grief-stricken parents for a period following the death (Balmer, 1992).

Regarding rating the helpfulness of family members, bereaved adolescents found their mothers to be most helpful in dealing with their grief. More specifically, it was the willingness of mothers to share their grief, as well as to share memories of the deceased, that proved to be most helpful. Although mothers were typically described as coping by expressing their grief, fathers were characterized as either not verbalizing their loss or immersing themselves in work. For adolescents who are already attempting to protect their parents by not discussing personal concerns and fears, communication with fathers rarely involved discussion of the deceased family member.

Friends were viewed as helpful when they were willing to be flexible and available to the bereaved adolescent in whatever capacity that individual needed. Finally, Balmer reported that many teachers were not viewed as supportive because, in most cases, they did not acknowledge the death, an omission that was interpreted as reflecting indifference.

ADOLESCENTS AND LOSS:
TWO PROMINENT DEPENDENT VARIABLES

In addition to the previously discussed independent variables, two prominent dependent variables have frequently been cited in probing the impact of death on adolescent functioning. These are school performance and self-esteem.

School Performance

As noted by Krupnick (1984), within the childhood grief literature there is evidence to suggest that the death of a significant person greatly increases a child's susceptibility to school dysfunction (usually measured in terms of a drop in academic grades). The few studies that have addressed this issue in adolescence appear to support this finding.

Balk (1981) found that changes in study habits after the death were reported by 23 participants (or 70% of his sample). For 19 of the participants, this change in study habits resulted in lower grades. For most, however, grades and study habits returned to their original levels over time (length of time unspecified). Gray (1987a), in his investigation of parentally bereaved adolescents, found an age-related difference in school performance. Participants 15 years of age or younger at the time of the death reported grades that were significantly lower than those older at the time of death. However, Gray did not make use of a control group in this study and thus these results must be interpreted with caution.

Although many of the participants in Balmer's (1992) research reported concentration problems in school, this did not translate into a drop in school grades. In her study, Balmer noted the grade average of each adolescent for the semester before and then following the death of a sibling. The difference between these marks was compared with the difference in marks for the matched nonbereaved adolescents over the same period. This finding is at odds with other research that has consistently reported poorer academic performance after the death of a sibling (Balk, 1981) or parent (Gray, 1987a). However, the latter research is based on self-reports, not objective data from report cards, which may in part explain the discrepancy in results.

In general, it would seem that, at least over the short term, grades alone are not necessarily good indicators of adjustment levels following the death of a sibling. Although further and perhaps more complex systematic analyses need to be conducted, it would be a mistake for parents, teachers, and mental health professionals to assume that merely maintaining school performance reflects positive adjustment to loss.

Self-Esteem

An often-discussed concern regarding psychological functioning following the death of a loved one is the issue of negative shifts in self-concept and self-esteem (Krupnick, 1984). For example, it has been noted by several authors that children have a tendency to view themselves more negatively after the death of a parent (Kliman, 1980; Rochlin, 1959). Also LaGrand (1981), in a large sample of university students, found that lowered self-confidence was a common response to a major loss. However, several empirical studies specific to adolescence have contradicted these findings.

Balk (1981) reported that the adolescents' self-concept scores on the Offer Self-Image Questionnaire (OSIQ; Offer, Ostrov, & Howard, 1981) were similar to those of norm groups for the OSIQ. Moreover, on the Morals subscale of the OSIQ, respondents showed significantly greater maturity than the scaled norms. Guerriero (1983), using the Tennessee Self-Concept Scale (TSCS), tended to support Balk's results. That is, there were no significant differences in Guerriero's study between the self-concept scores of bereaved adolescents and those of nonbereaved controls. In addition, on several dimensions of the TSCS, such as self-satisfaction, the sibling-bereaved group scored significantly higher than the comparison groups.

Hogan and Greenfield (1991) used the OSIQ in their study of grief-related symptomatology in sibling-bereaved adolescents. For their respondents, whose siblings had died more than 18 months earlier, self-esteem levels were a function of the intensity of reported grief-related symptoms. Bereaved adolescents who reported only mild intensity scores were above the mean on all subscales of the OSIQ with the exception of the sexual attitudes subscale. Adolescents with moderate or severe intensity scores were below the mean on most scales indicating low self-esteem. Martinson, Davies, and McClowry (1987) used a different self-esteem instrument in their study of the long-term effects of sibling death on self-concept. Comparison of the bereaved group's mean score with the normative data on the Piers-Harris Self-Concept Scale indicated the former reported significantly higher levels of self concept.

Balmer (1992) found both time since death and gender to be significant predictors of self-esteem as measured by the Rosenberg Self-Esteem Scale (Rosenberg, 1965). More specifically, adolescents in their 1st year of bereavement suffered lower self-esteem. In the second and third year following the death of a sibling, their self-esteem scores were indistinguishable from those of their matched controls. Females reported lower self-esteem levels, suggesting this group more so than males may be prone to adjustment problems in bereavement.

Although the previously noted studies all used standardized scales to measure self-esteem in bereaved adolescents, several retrospective investigations using semistructured interview techniques have reported similar results. For example, Davies (1991) found the long-term impact of a sibling's death was positive in nature and participants' reports reflected a sense of having personally grown from the experience. Respondents in this study also felt more mature than their same-age peers. However, some respondents did suggest that this sense of being "different" resulted in withdrawal from their friends. Finally, most participants in the Martinson and Campos (1991) study believed the death of their sibling precipitated personal growth.

In summary more recent empirical investigations regarding self-esteem and adolescent bereavement have contradicted earlier findings by suggesting that adolescents may experience either no shift or in some specific areas may report both an increase in feelings of self-worth (Balk, 1981; Guerriero, 1983; Martinson, Davies, & McClowry, 1987), as well as a sense of increased personal maturity (Balk, 1981; Davies, 1991; Martinson & Campos, 1991) following the death of a loved one. Moreover, Hogan and Greenfield (1991) have reported that self-esteem may be closely linked to the intensity of reported grief-related symptomatology.

CONCLUSION: FUTURE DIRECTIONS

There is much that is known about adolescent adjustment to death, particularly the death of a parent or sibling. But clearly there is also much that we do not know. For example, there is a marked lack of knowledge and research into how adolescents react to other loss experiences, such as the death of a friend, suicidal death, AIDS, death by violence, and adjustment to multiple deaths. We lack theory-guided research on adolescent adjustment in the face of death and know virtually nothing about relationships among surviving siblings.

Intuitively, one would expect a clear correlation between grief symptomatology and time since death, but the available data are somewhat equivocal. Two investigations employing standardized methods reached similar conclusions. Balmer's (1992) results are consistent with Hogan and Greenfield's (1991) findings that recently bereaved adolescents exhibited more grief-related symptoms than those more distantly bereaved. One must be cautious, however, in the interpretation of data gathered during semistructured interviews for it could be argued that the very process of the interview itself, in which one is asked to discuss painful memories surrounding death, precipitates emotionally intense responses not representative of the day-to-day emotional life of the participant.

Balmer (1992) observed emotional disturbance as a result of discussing a sibling's death during the semistructured interview segment of her study. This response was as likely to occur with participants whose sibling had died 3 months previous as it was with those who were bereaved for longer periods. Although this emotional turmoil is an accurate reflection of the adolescent's grief-related feelings, it does not necessarily reflect overall adjustment.

Further, research needs to be directed toward a virtually untested relationship, namely, that of personality and adjustment to loss. One of the few efforts to explore this association found that high-risk, bereaved adolescents: (a) viewed themselves as outsiders and unpopular in social situations; (b) held a world view consistent with an externalized locus of control (i.e., the victim role); (c) reported feeling disoriented; and (d) stated they were bothered by disturbing and problematic thoughts (Balmer, 1992). In contrast to their low-risk counterparts, it is suggested that these adolescents may be susceptible to self-related cognitive distortions (e.g., "no one likes me; therefore, I am worthless"), a generalized sense of being vulnerable (e.g., "I have no control over anything that happens in my life"), and bereavement-related cognitive distortions (e.g., "I sometimes see the deceased and hear them; therefore, I must be going crazy"). The most appropriate treatment intervention with this group may involve the use of cognitive-behavioral and educational strategies (Fleming & Robinson, 1991).

Perhaps the most salient feature of adolescent adjustment following death is the resiliency evidenced by the bereaved participants in the face of traumatic loss. Although participants in their first year of bereavement were often less well adjusted than nonbereaved matched controls, research has consistently shown that by the second and third year of bereavement, the adjustment scores of bereaved and nonbereaved participants were indistinguishable (e.g., Balmer, 1992). In addition, most adolescents presented as "wise beyond their years," which they attributed to a newfound emotional strength and maturity resulting from surviving the death of their family member. This finding supports Moos and Schaefer's (1986) conceptual model, which emphasizes the growth potential of a life transition or crisis. It is imperative that parents, friends, teachers, and mental health workers appreciate not only that adolescent bereavement represents a serious life crisis but that there also is potential for growth and maturity as a consequence of surviving a death-related loss.

There is a caution, however, as both Balmer (1992), and Hogan and Greenfield (1991) identified a subgroup of vulnerable bereaved adolescents at risk for long-term negative outcomes. Such individuals tend to show a pattern of low self-esteem and significantly higher scores on measures of depression, anxiety, and somatic symptomatology. Hogan and Greenfield (1991) concluded that 25% to 50% of their respondents appeared to be at risk for developing long-term, bereavement-related difficulties. In her study, Balmer (1992) reported 30% of the bereaved participants fell into the high-risk group; when the same standards were used to assess those who were potentially at risk in the nonbereaved group, 20% also fell into this high-risk category. This percentage is consistent with the findings of Offer, Ostrov, and Howard (1981) who found that 20% of all adolescents were experiencing a crisis in their behavioral or emotional state. Adolescents in this developmental group, which Offer and his colleagues termed the "tumultuous growth group," were introspective and highly sensitive, and had less developed defenses for handling emotionally difficult situations.

Therefore, when addressing the issue of high-risk or vulnerable bereaved adolescents, one must be cognizant that a percentage of these adolescents would have experienced adjustment difficulties in their adolescent years without encountering death. Results from the Balmer study suggest that this number is approximately 20%, a figure supported by Offer, Ostrov, and Howard's (1981) research. An additional 10% of the bereaved respondents in Balmer's (1992) investigation were part of a high-risk group reporting significantly higher levels of depressive symptomatology and anxiety/insomnia symptoms than did the comparable high-risk, nonbereaved group. Viewed in context, this percentage seems rather small given the trauma that bereaved adolescents have endured. This finding emphasizes the importance of a control group in future investigations of adolescent bereavement, particularly in those studies that attempt to delineate variables associated with high-risk bereaved adolescents.

8

Adolescent Responses to the Death of a Parent

Kirsten J. Tyson-Rawson

The world of adolescence is a relational world. Its primary themes are separation from and connection to others. Its central tasks are the establishment of a stable self-identity and the development of mature, intimate relationships with others. When the death of a parent occurs, the intricate web of relationship that has been a source of stability, helping to define the self by contrast and by continuity, is broken.

The death of a parent during or before the adolescent years is "off time," that is, it occurs during a stage of the parent's and adolescent's life cycle that violates expectations in our society about the ordinary human life span. The culturally accepted meaning of death as the natural end of a long and fully lived life no longer applies. As a result, the central questions of adolescence regarding separation and connection are rendered more affectively intense and cognitively challenging.

The qualitative change in cognitive, physical, and affective capabilities that is the hallmark of adolescence requires testing and expansion of what Bowlby (1980a) termed the "internal working model" of relationships. Developed in early life, the internal working model is composed of "mental representations of the self, other, and of the relationship" that "direct attention and organize memory in a way that guides interpersonal behavior and the interpretation of social experience" (Belsky & Pensky, 1988, p. 198).

Conceptually, then, the death of a parent means that adolescents face a need to reorganize existing elements and create new components of their internal working model without a significant person on whom to base affectional, gender, and vocational roles. Janoff-Bulman (1992), in her work on the trauma of overwhelming life events, has written that these "life experiences split open the interior world of victims and shatter their most fundamental assumptions . . . internal and external worlds are suddenly unfamiliar and threatening" (p. 63).

Exemplifying this experience, one late adolescent woman described the death of her father when she was 16 years old as:

> . . . hitting the wall. Everything just seemed to fall apart, I couldn't think and I'd look at Mom and not know how she could even—well, walk around and talk, it was so big. I don't remember much from that first year [after the death]. . . . I realized recently that I'd always thought—even when he was sick—thought that no matter what I did, no matter how we argued, he'd be there. But I was so wrong. I've had to work to put myself back together—to make sense of it so I can go on. (Tyson-Rawson, 1993a)

In the last decade there has been an increase in the amount of research on and clinical attention to the experiences of bereaved adolescents as a result of the death of a parent, sibling, other family member, or peer. This chapter addresses the effects of the death of a parent on adolescents from an individual developmental perspective and from within the context of the family. The goal of this work is to highlight findings across the empirical, theoretical, and clinical literatures to provide readers with a sense of what we now know about adolescent responses to the death of a parent.

The first section of this chapter discusses the implications of a parent's death for individual development. It delineates findings about the outcomes of this experience for adolescents, particularly the differential outcomes of pathology and accelerated maturity, as well as the possibility of developing new meanings regarding the self and the world. The second section focuses on factors within the nuclear family and the peer network that influence the course of adolescent bereavement and the possibility of an ongoing relationship with the deceased. The final section suggests directions for clinical and empirical research to increase our understanding and guide practice with bereaved adolescents and their families.

SIGNIFICANCE OF PARENT DEATH
FOR ADOLESCENT DEVELOPMENT

Parent death during or before adolescence has been connected with seemingly paradoxical outcomes, such as impairment in the ability to commit to long-term relationships, as well as accelerated maturity, major depression, and an increased appreciation for the value of important relationships. It would be impossible to say that the experience of parent death leads to any single outcome. Rather, the experience of loss during this stage of the life cycle is unique to the period, and its outcome is isomorphic to the complexity and richness of adolescence itself. Although adolescent bereavement shares characteristics with both adult and childhood response to loss, it differs because of its increased affective intensity, a product of the interaction of the loss and the developmental context within which it occurs (Meshot & Leitner, 1993).

Complicated Outcomes

One of the primary themes of research on bereavement is that of the potential for complicated or negative outcomes following parent death—outcomes such as depression and conduct disorder. Depression, including changes in sleeping, eating, activity levels, and an overall feeling of sadness and loss, is to be expected following the death of a significant person. However, the continuation of such experiences over a period without relief is a different issue. It is not uncommon for adolescents to report that they have difficulty remembering daily events—such as school—for months following the death of a parent and that periods of sadness recur at unexpected times even after the acute phase of bereavement. However, some adolescents also say that they have felt sad, anxious, and generally afraid for years following the death of a parent. A 19-year-old woman, 2 years after the death of her father, described her responses in the following way:

> After he died, I was so depressed that I couldn't go to school or sleep or anything. So they put me on an antidepressant for a while. Lately, I've been feeling that way again. I have these dreams, nightmares, and I can't stop thinking about him dying. . . . Recently I got my mom to get our doctor at home to prescribe Prozac for me. (Tyson-Rawson, 1993b, p. 52)

In studies performed with both community and clinical subjects, the risk of major depression was found to be over seven times greater for early adolescents after the death of either parent than for their nonbereaved peers (Gersten, Beals, & Kallgren, 1991; Gray, 1987b; Reinherz et al., 1989). In fact, the risk of depressive symptoms for bereaved adolescents 12 to 15 years of age was found to be twice that of children from 8 to 11 years, with girls at twice the risk of boys (Gersten, Beals, & Kallgren, 1991).

Although none of these studies found acting out behaviors to be statistically associated with parent death, school-related problems, substance abuse, and generalized anger have often been reported in the clinical literature, along with depression. Bereaved adolescents are likely to experience ambivalence in their feelings about the loss if their relationship with the deceased parent was in some way unresolved, for example, if the bereaved individual was in conflict with or especially dependent on the deceased parent. An additional factor that may contribute to both depression and acting out is an adolescent's sense of ambiguity about the relationship or about his or her own behavior at the time of death.

These factors may predispose adolescents whose parents are divorced to self-destructive behavior and may have effects even into the late adolescent or young adult years (Buschbaum, 1990; McGoldrick & Walsh, 1991; Walsh & McGoldrick, 1991a; Worden, 1991). For example, a 22-year-old woman reported her behaviors and state of mind 4 years after the death of her father:

> I used to be real outgoing in school and all, you know. I laughed a lot and wanted other people around me all the time. Now I just can't stand it. I really got crazy after he died. Drank and ran around. . . . Now I'm quieter, but I have these dreams that he's there and I'm supposed to do something. I feel guilty and I don't know why. I loved him so much. (Tyson-Rawson, 1993b, p. 186)

Similarly, the death of a parent may exacerbate preexisting conditions and lead to anger directed against others, as exemplified by the following from a 22-year-old woman whose father died 11 months previously.

> Poor [boyfriend]. I took all my feelings out on him. I just screamed at him and acted like a maniac. I didn't know I could be so mean. And then . . . my bulimia. I'd had it four years. . . . After he [father] died . . . I was living alone. . . . I was doing it [inducing vomiting] six or seven times in one day. It just got worse and worse. . . . I think that I felt so out of control, dad dying and feeling so alone. (Tyson-Rawson, 1993a)

Yet, as grim a picture as is painted by these and the words of other bereaved adolescents, it is clear that not all adolescents experience complicated outcomes. In fact, for many, the death of a parent can be a catalyst for growth, maturity, and a new sense of self-awareness. Even for adolescents who struggle with the types of feelings and behaviors described here, the opportunity inherent in crisis can give rise to a stronger sense of self and the value of others.

Maturity

The synergistic effect of affective intensity, cognitive dissonance, and changed life circumstances created by the permanent, physical loss of a parent to death can become a powerful motive for resolving the developmental tasks of adolescence. The need to accomplish these tasks is heightened by internal pressures for understanding and external forces for stability. That is, an adolescent may seek or be driven toward a more mature autonomy expressed in more independent behavior and adult thought because of a felt need from the self, coupled with demands from changed circumstances arising from the death.

The bereavement literature is replete with findings that bereavement during or before this time of life can catalyze an adolescent's movement toward maturity and a new direction to life choices; such a phenomenon has been noticed with persons at various stages in the life cycle (Balk, 1990; Carse, 1987; Parkes & Weiss, 1983; Silverman, 1987; Tyson-Rawson, 1993b). The possibility of this type of outcome is reflected in Silverman's (1987) work on late adolescent, college women who experienced parent death. Silverman (1987) conceptualized these women as "growing up before their time" (p. 393), an idea reminiscent of Elizur and Kaffman's (1986) finding of "accelerated maturity" among younger, bereaved kibbutz children. Silverman wrote that the death of a parent "meant growing up and understanding that life was more than fun and games" (p. 394). The potential for a positive outcome of bereavement—what can be thought of as an internal working model that meets the needs of the bereaved individual—is also reflected in a statement from the work of Parkes (1972): "Just as broken bones may end up stronger than unbroken ones, so the experience of grieving can strengthen and bring maturity to those who have previously been protected from misfortune" (pp. 5–6).

The idea of increased independence or autonomy resulting in the ability to meet one's own needs in the world is central to increased maturity. The discovery of capabilities that characterize adult behavior may come as a surprise to bereaved adolescents who are forced by the death of a parent to take on new responsibilities for their own welfare and, often, that of other family members. The death of a parent, then, has the potential to create a greater awareness of one's own capabilities. With greater autonomy and a clearer delineation of the self may also come the ability to discern and empathize with the pain of others.

The death of a parent creates a change in how adolescents view the world, leading them to perceive events as more random than they had previously thought and themselves as more vulnerable and less in control of their lives (Schwartzberg & Janoff-Bulman, 1991). In one study (Tyson-Rawson, 1993b), the lessons some late adolescent women learned following the deaths of their fathers changed their beliefs about the nature of the world in terms of its predictability, fairness, human vulnerability, and the degree to which they could determine the direction of their lives. Essentially, they came to view the nature of the world in a way that most people do not achieve until later in their adult lives. The following are statements they made: "I really thought the world was this dandy place and I really didn't know that bill collectors and people like that could care less" (Tyson-Rawson, 1993b, p. 233); "Anything can happen. When the next thing happens you do what you can to make it work out. If it doesn't you have to accept it"; "You can lose anybody at any time"; "I guess I've grown up since my father died, I don't get so mad about it [unfairness] anymore. I just think 'Well, that's the world.' I guess I hope that if I'm fair other people will be too" (p. 235); "There are just some things you can't control. So, I just try to keep my mind on the things I can have some control over" (p. 236). Schwartzberg and Janoff-Bulman (1991) found that both male and female adolescents grieved less, that is, they experienced less emotional distress following a death, when they were able to "maintain or redefine their beliefs about how the world works" (p. 284).

The development of new understandings about the world and the self, and the struggle to attribute meaning to the loss, are not static achievements. In fact, they are characterized by the "process" of the bereavement experience. In the Tyson-Rawson study (1993b) cited earlier, the term *process* was chosen to reflect the subjects' expressed sense that bereavement was, for them, an experience influenced by the passage of time, their interactions with others, and a sense of personal development. That is, the bereavement process was characterized by ongoing change within the person, among family members, and in relationships with peers. Changes in meaning and understanding happened with time, with the occurrence of unexpected stressor events, and with the demands for change in individual and family functioning and expectations created by the deaths of the subjects' fathers.

Some of the subjects, especially those whose grief was relatively new or those who reported they did not feel they had "really grieved" the death, appeared to be struggling with a lack of movement. One 18-year-old woman, whose father died unexpectedly 3 months before, said: "I don't know if I'm always going to feel like this. It seems like I'm stuck and something ought to change. . . . I don't know what's supposed to happen now but there's got to be something" (Tyson-Rawson, 1993b,

p. 152). In contrast, another woman who lost both her father and her brother during the 2 years before her interview, described the changes in her responses to events that created distress for her:

> I thought that it was extremely unfair that I had to go through two [deaths] and especially in such a short period of time. But then, after I readjusted my thinking I realized that sometimes things just happen and whether or not there's a reason for them you have to go on and suffer them. So you know I try to think that way when there's problems that arise. Either there's a reason for what's happening or if there's not a specific reason things will get better and I'll just have to do the best I can in a specific situation. (Tyson-Rawson, 1993b, p. 152)

Examination of these statements reveals an underlying theme about the development of belief and attitude, of a process of movement and change, whether expected or unexpected, in the midst of loss. The idea of "process" can serve as a reminder that the development of meaning and maturity in bereavement are not predictable, stage-specific events, nor is resolution of grief an end in itself (Silverman, 1987; Walsh & McGoldrick, 1991a). In bereavement, past, present, and future are intermingled. Grieving creates meanings for the person, and those new meanings require activity and response. Responses and activity create new meanings, which must be addressed in turn. Inherent in all discussions with the bereaved young women in this study was the assumption that past, present, and future were and would be colored by the loss of their fathers.

Ongoing Attachment to the Deceased

The work of Klass (1987, 1988) on parental grief, and research by others such as Hogan and DeSantis (1992; see also chapter 9 in this book) on sibling bereavement, strongly suggests the need to revise existing theory regarding the nature of bereavement resolution. The work of these scholars counters the prevalent theoretical tenet that the primary indicator of resolution of grieving involves the individual's adaptation to changed social circumstances. Klass (1987, 1988) posited that of equal importance is the internalization of the lost person into the self of the bereaved such that an ongoing relationship is a part of the survivor's life. Klass found that resolution includes not only the establishment of social equilibrium by investment in new relationships and tasks, but also incorporation of an "identification" with the deceased within the survivor's self-image.

Silverman's findings in a study of parental death among college women (1987) also raised important questions regarding the ongoing relationship between deceased and bereaved:

> Although it is true that the bereaved cannot live in the past, is it appropriate invariably to talk of the need for the bereaved to break with the past? Are some bereaved telling us instead that although they recognize that they must change their relationship to the deceased, they do not necessarily break the connection? (p. 403)

Klass's inclusion of a "new sense of self" and Silverman's emphasis on the continuation of connection to the deceased are especially salient when considering the tasks, both individual and family related, facing bereaved adolescents. In addition, Silverman and Silverman (1979) found, while studying communication between bereaved children and surviving parents, that children who were able to develop a way of keeping a sense of the lost parent in their lives were also better able to accept the reality of the death. The relationship to the deceased continued even though the person was dead.

One of the most intriguing findings in the Tyson-Rawson (1993b) study was late adolescent women's reports of an ongoing attachment to the deceased father. Many of the women in the study reported that relationships with their deceased fathers continued and even developed following the death. In fact, the group of women who reported the existence of the father as a welcome presence in their lives were those most likely to report they had come to some resolution regarding the death. By contrast, those who reported either emotional cutoff from the deceased or who experienced thoughts and feelings about the deceased as intrusive and distressing were most often those who felt they had not "really grieved" the loss. Although detachment from the deceased was helpful in matters related to the practical realities of life, an ongoing emotional attachment was associated with personal growth and positive outcomes for these late adolescent women.

The need to integrate the loss into one's internal world is especially relevant during this stage of the life cycle. In the case of adolescents, the pressures to separate from the nuclear family and form new, more intimate, peer relationships—issues to which attachment and loss are salient—continue to exert influence during the grieving process. The death of a significant person causes a break in the network of relationships and a concomitant loss of meaning previously derived from interactions with the other and the stable foundation such interactions can provide for interpretation of the larger world. The creation of a new model of relational meaning is necessary if the bereaved person is to reestablish stability and order in his or her life. The changes in adolescents' perceptions of the nature of the world and of themselves are part of the meaning they derive from the death of a parent. Another part of establishing meaning for the death is trying to find an explanation for the event itself and the effect it has had on their lives and the lives of those close to them. A primary arena in which a new model will be developed is in the intimate relationships of the family and peer network.

FAMILY FACTORS AND PEER RELATIONSHIPS

Multiple findings in the empirical and clinical literatures stress the importance of family variables that mediate between the experience of the death and the outcome for an adolescent. In fact, the primary trend in the current bereavement literature is to attribute adolescent symptomatology, whenever it exists following the period of acute bereavement, to factors other than the death alone. Variables influencing the nature of bereavement outcome following death include (a) the availability of social support resources perceived as familiar and safe, and the adolescent's willingness to use such resources when available; (b) the openness of communication within the family including the availability of appropriate information about the death and the deceased; (c) the ability of the surviving parent and other family members to provide stability and continuity in day-to-day life; (d) the existence of an emotional context in which the distress of bereavement may be expressed, which also involves the cohesiveness and warmth of the family; and (5) subsequent hardships or benefits affecting the adolescent's life that accrue from the presence or absence of the above factors (Berlinsky & Biller, 1982; Elizur & Kaffman, 1986; Lyon & Vandenberg, 1989; Reese, 1987; Silverman & Worden, 1992; West, Sandler, Pillow, Baca, & Gersten, 1991).

The movement of adolescents toward a new identity, characterized by separation from the family of origin, is facilitated by a known, stable, and dependable family system. Ideally, the family of origin provides a base from which adolescents can venture to explore new roles and relationships, and to which they can return for validation of triumphs and consolation for losses. The family's ability to provide this support for an adolescent is a critical factor in the outcome of bereavement following the death of a parent, as is the availability of support from peers and important others in the community.

Social Support and Communication

A primary finding in the bereavement literature is the significance of the availability, or lack thereof, of social support from, and open communication with, significant others for the bereavement process. Open communication among and social support from family members and peers are two resources that are frequently cited as important in the crisis and bereavement literature. Social support has been defined as those behavioral and attitudinal communications that convey "emotional," "esteem," and "network" support (McCubbin et al., 1980). In the case of bereavement, social support lets the bereaved know that they are part of a larger community that values, understands, and cares about their loss and is available to them in time of need. Effective social support is facilitated by open communication, both verbal and nonverbal, and can have a buffering effect on the distress of bereavement.

However, adolescents, like bereaved individuals of other ages, must be willing to accept the support of family and friends at a time when reminders of the loss and its distress can be experienced as not only painful, but also dangerous. Some adolescents may choose to cope with death by avoiding the grieving process. In addition, covert or overt rules in the family regarding the appropriateness of accepting help from others or the communication of intense affect may complicate difficulties with grieving and intensify the sense of loneliness and difference experienced by the bereaved adolescent.

The importance of open communication is highlighted by La-Grand's study (1981) of bereaved, late adolescent, college students. He reported findings that emphasize the importance of talking about both the death itself and the emotions experienced as a result of the loss: "The power for resolving loss seems to lie in the strength of the self-image, the quality of interpersonal relationships . . . the ability to communicate on an intimate level with others, and feelings of acceptance by friends and family" (p. 247).

In the case of late adolescent students who experience the death of a significant other while they are at college, open communication with peers in the university setting is critical—and often, unavailable. In many cases, these adolescents are geographically separated from family and peers in their home communities and fear being perceived by others in the college community—both students and teachers—as different and difficult. Student participants in bereavement support groups at Kansas State University (Balk, Tyson-Rawson, & Colletti-Wetzel, 1993) found that trying to talk with their peers about the death was one of many dismaying experiences following the death of a significant other. They often expressed relief following talking in the group about their grief and the changes they experienced in themselves and in their perceptions of the world. Talking with others whose experiences were similar seemed to validate and normalize their experience and provided them with a sense of hope for the future.

These findings emphasize the importance of the existence of a supportive network surrounding bereaved adolescents and the presence of communication skills that allow supportive messages to be sent to, and received by, such adolescents. Support from family and peers that communicates validation of a bereaved adolescent's experiences and self is a critical element in the resolution of bereavement and the recreation of an effective internal working model of attachments.

Family Relationships and Environmental Stability

Worden (1991) noted that "each change that occurs following the death of a family member is symbolic of the death of the family itself, leaving the primary task of establishing a new family from the old" (p. 118). That is, after a death within a family, its members are faced with altering the basic, interactional structures of their lives. At a time when individuals may be most vulnerable, when resources may seem least, choices are made that influence the future of all family members. The loss of a parent creates a mandate for change in the structures that underlie familial stability. These changes parallel those experienced by adolescents in their developmental struggle to develop a new model for understanding the world. Within the family context, the entire range of responses typical of bereavement at the death of a parent may be manifested at different times by different family members, and each response will influence reciprocally the responses of all other members.

Environmental tasks are focused on providing consistency in the family at a time when the essential nature of that network has been disrupted. The ameliorative effect of maintaining a sense of normalcy regarding family routines and rituals at times of crisis permits family members to have a sense of stability during a period of intense change (Imber-Black, 1991). Such consistency needs to be balanced, for adolescents, with acknowledgment that real-world changes have occurred.

Role reallocation within the family is required when the death of a parent occurs. Not only must other members take on the responsibility of providing for the family financially and supporting the needs of daily living, they must also address the familial roles that maintain family relationships. "Real-world" concerns, such as earning a living, may dimin-

ish the availability of the surviving parent to an adolescent in terms of
his or her physical presence as well as emotional and material support.

Between the ages of 25 and 50, the years during which people are
most likely to parent, twice the number of men as women die
(Kochanek & Hudson, 1994). Therefore, given the differential earning
power of men and women in the United States, financial difficulties
may become a fact of life for adolescents whose fathers died. Six years
after the death of her father, one woman described the changes that occurred, not only immediately following the death but also during her
college years:

> Different if he were alive? Oh, really different. . . . I wouldn't have to work
> to be in school. . . . Mom does everything she can but there's just so much
> a teacher's aide makes you know, even if she's just as good as the teacher.
> . . . My grades would be better, a lot I'll bet. 'Cause I'd have time to study
> more. (Tyson-Rawson, 1993b, p. 203)

Although the death of a spouse may place increased financial and
emotional burdens on the survivor, it also offers the opportunity for
children to see their surviving parent function outside of the roles that
have been traditional in their families. Seeing a parent take on new
nurturing or instrumental tasks can offer adolescents a new understanding of the potential for flexibility in adult roles. Although the possibility does exist that an adolescent will be pulled into roles in the
family that interrupt his or her development, the potential for growth
in terms of responsibility and empathy for others is also present. Older
adolescents, who are out of the home or working in the community,
may also find themselves acting as caretakers for their bereaved parents
in the aftermath of the death.

The coexistence of a developmental mandate for adolescents to separate with the felt need to take care of others in the family of origin can
create feelings of guilt and anger. Such feelings can lead adolescents to
avoid interaction with the family or to fail to return to their activities
outside of the family after the acute phase of bereavement is past. However, the same situation offers the parent and child an opportunity to
renegotiate their relational roles, thereby giving each an occasion to
struggle with developmental issues of separation and connection in a
context that highlights the need for both.

Postdeath Parenting and the Emotional Context

One of the most critical issues in this area is the ability of the surviving
parent to provide care for the surviving children while attending to per-

sonal needs as well as the practical needs of survival. Not only must care be provided for children, it also must be provided at a developmentally appropriate level. Maintaining a delicate balance between authority and flexibility challenges parents of adolescents under normal circumstances. The death—whether sudden or anticipated—of the person who was both spouse and parent demands that the surviving parent incorporate respect for the adolescent's increasing autonomy and cognitive abilities as well as creating an intimate environment within which grief may be expressed and meaning may be found for the loss. The difficulty and importance of such a task cannot be overestimated. Compared with younger children, adolescents have the capacity to develop a more integrated picture of the life, and circumstances of the death, of the deceased parent (Buschbaum, 1990).

Family members not only experience their own grief but are sensitive to and worried about the grief of other members. This reciprocity of concern is particularly salient in adolescent experiences of bereavement because of the increased capabilities of adolescents for empathy and understanding of the experience of others. Silverman and Worden (1992) stressed the importance of surviving parents helping children "develop a language" (p. 103) to talk about the deceased. Such conversations between parent and adolescent may take on diverse forms. They may involve the "reflecting and remembering" that Silverman and Worden (1992) have cited as critical to the bereavement process for children or they may center on the sharing of the affective aspects of grieving such that the emotional experiences of parent and adolescent can be better understood by both. In addition, adolescents need to be involved in the negotiations and decision-making processes related to reallocating family responsibilities and responding to other bereavement-related demands. When this occurs, the time of grief and loss can become an opportunity for helping adolescents learn ways to cope effectively with loss and crisis.

In all of this, the surviving parent is primarily responsible for balancing the level of adolescent involvement in a way that is developmentally appropriate. Ordinarily, the level of involvement for a child in the early adolescent stage will need to be less than that of the late adolescent or young adult. However, including even young adolescents in these daily-life decisions can provide them with a sense of stability and control based on having some influence on the changes that are made and an understanding of why they are necessary. The surviving parent is the primary person required to regulate the intensity of these conversations and experiences, and needs to find ways to tolerate the affective intensity of an adolescent's grief, thereby providing an emotionally safe environment. Although the adolescent should understand that the parent also grieves, the adult should not expect the adolescent to be the parent's primary source of support and comfort.

The distress of the bereaved spouse may reduce his or her availability to an adolescent. Not only may the parent be unable to attend to the adolescent's grief, but the adolescent may avoid talking about his or her feelings, for fear of distressing the parent further. In turn, the parent may interpret the adolescent's silence as a message that he or she does not want to talk about the death or the deceased (Tyson-Rawson, 1993b; West et al., 1991). In this case, the reciprocity of concern between parent and adolescent means that neither has the opportunity to work together to develop a safe, intimate environment for the grieving process.

No parent can be ever present or always available for his or her children, let alone when grieving the death of a partner. Most bereaved spouses, whose personal and material resources may be stretched to the limit, will be forced to make some choices about how they will spend their energies. As Rosenblatt (1988) has written, "the family rules that govern how a loss is dealt with must inevitably slight some possible responses in a way that may be frustrating and costly to some family members" (p. 72).

The gender roles enacted in the family context also influence the bereavement experience. That is, the gender roles seen as appropriate in the family before the death will continue to influence—to some extent—the need for restructuring and the way grief is expressed. In one study of 15- to 18-year-old adolescents, Youniss and Smollar (1985) found differences in the roles played by mothers and fathers. Fathers were most often seen as authoritarian and responsible for the material well-being of the family. Fathers and adolescents most often spent time together in shared activities and primarily discussed the adolescents' educational or vocational futures. It was in the latter arena that adolescents reported receiving the most emotional support from their fathers. In contrast, adolescents viewed their mothers as intimately involved in both their day-to-day behavioral and affective/intimate lives. In contrast to fathers, relationships with mothers were viewed as both authoritative and equal.

In general, empirical findings reveal that children talk more about their feelings regarding the loss when the surviving parent is female. Children whose fathers, rather than their mothers, had died were found to have experienced fewer changes in day-to-day routines, a factor consistently cited in the bereavement literature as requisite to optimal outcome of bereavement. Boys report being less comfortable discussing their feelings about the death than do girls, which is understandable given the greater stigma attached to male expression of emotion in terms of gender role socialization. Girls may be given more opportunities to grieve openly than boys who are more likely to be praised for self-control and "strength." Conversely, girls may face greater expectations that they will become caretakers for other family members. Such expectations may curtail other relationships and activities outside of the family (Cook & Dworkin, 1992; Silverman & Worden, 1992; Walters, Carter, Papp, & Silverstein, 1988).

Peer Relationships

Not only do many bereaved adolescents perceive themselves as different individuals than they were before their parents' deaths, but many also experience the difference as separating them from their peers. Balk (1990) described adolescents bereaved by sibling death as having "learned a lesson about tragedy spared most persons until later in life, and they now know life can be unfair and sorrowful" (p. 129). The discrepancy between what these bereaved adolescents know, and their peers do not, can create a rift across which adolescents sometimes feel they cannot reach. However, when the gap between the old world and the new is bridged, friendships can serve as an important part of the structure supporting the resolution of bereavement.

Tyson-Rawson (1993b) found, with one exception, that the nature of adolescent women's interactions with friends soon after the loss of their fathers predicted the type of relationships reported at the time of the interview, from 3 months to 11 years after the death. Subjects whose friends offered support at or close to the time of the death were the same subjects who reported that friendship sustained them throughout the bereavement process. They were also the individuals who were able to risk talking with new people about their experiences with their fathers. The single exception to this rule was reported by a 20-year-old woman whose father died when she was 9 years old. Her experience underlines the interactive nature of friendships, that is, emphasizes how the behavior of the bereaved individual can influence the behavior of her or his peers:

> When dad was killed, I . . . didn't tell anyone about it. I felt so alone and I really didn't want people to even know. . . . In high school I had friends I partied with but then when we came to college I wasn't so interested in them anymore. . . . They knew dad died but they didn't know anything more. . . . But just recently, when I've started to talk about it, to my roommate, she really helped me. . . . She just listened and let me cry and she

still asks about dad and what he was like. So now I've told a few more
people and they seem to think I had reasons to feel bad. It's really different now, it's a relief. (Tyson-Rawson, 1993a)

However, none of the women in this study felt that they could share
their bereavement with all of their peers. Friendships were conducted
within an environment that many of the women felt was, at least, un-
sympathetic and, at worst, hostile. For some adolescents the behavior
of peers tended to make them feel, in the words of one woman, "like
a freak." Many questioned the importance of a previously active social
life, especially in terms of the frequency with which their peers
"partied."

In general, the adolescent peer group mirrors the larger society in its
attitudes toward death. Some peers will not only fail to understand the
loss and avoid the subject of the death, but will also avoid the adolescent himself or herself, thus emphasizing the "difference" described
earlier (Silverman, 1987). Social support from peers can enable bereaved adolescents to function better as it communicates that the bereaved person is cared for, valued, accepted, and, to some degree,
understood. In essence, appropriate social support from friends allows
the bereaved adolescent to have his or her perceptions of the event validated by valued peers—an important element in adolescent development. An overall theme regarding friendships with peers following the
death of a parent is that bereaved adolescents may begin to select
friends whose behavior and attitudes reflect a greater maturity and a
willingness to take the death more seriously.

The peer network is not only the context for friendship. It is also the
arena within which intimate, sexual/romantic relationships are developed. The changes in themselves and their perceptions of the nature of
the world that bereaved adolescents report are readily apparent in the
attitudes they display toward dating. The increased sense of vulnerability and unpredictability in the world they experience, coupled with a
new understanding of the possibility of losing someone close, influences how willing adolescents will be to enter into and maintain committed relationships. Hepworth, Ryder, and Dreyer (1984) found that
those who lost a parent to death in late adolescence subsequently responded to these relationships in one of two ways. Adolescents either
moved more quickly into committed relationships or avoided such relationships entirely. This polarization of response exemplifies the
study's finding that adolescents who experienced loss by death were
more likely to exhibit extreme reactions in the quality of intimate relationships than were their nonbereaved peers or their peers who experienced parent loss because of divorce.

Adolescents' changed view of the nature of the world clearly informs the way they feel about making interpersonal commitments. When adolescents feel more vulnerable, as they become more aware of the transitory nature of human life, they develop a model of relationships that includes their experiences of loss. Not only do adolescents have their own experiences on which to draw following the death of a parent, they also draw on what they see of the experiences of their surviving parent. The loss of a partner by a parent provides a model of how relationships can end, and illuminates both their potential for pain and the need to value them while they exist.

CONCLUSION

There are many questions left to be answered in the field of adolescent bereavement. The nature of those questions is illuminated by what is left unanswered in the current research. The state of the field is now such that a focus needs to be on expanding and refining models of bereavement that specify the differential effects of loss. For example, we need to explore more fully bereavement experiences for males versus females; death of a father versus that of a mother; intact versus divorced families; or early versus middle versus late adolescents. Our questions need to be related to a specific area but consider the work that has been done by other scholars.

In the area of issues related to gender: What is most helpful for male versus female adolescents in terms of offering support for the bereavement experience? Should we attempt to teach boys to be more emotionally expressive of their grief, or is their grieving process equally effective in dealing with grief as that of their female peers? Are girls and boys actually employing different strategies in the grieving process, and, if they are, what are they? Beyond the effects discussed earlier, what are the differences in the bereavement experience when a boy versus a girl loses a mother or a father?

Another area that needs exploration is the loss of a biological parent by death following a divorce. Findings in the literature are clear that divorce and death are two different types of loss, so what happens when one type of loss follows another? Does it matter if the lost parent is the mother or the father? The noncustodial or custodial parent? How is the experience of this double loss influenced by the gender of the surviving adolescent?

Finally, what about the way in which we have done, and will do, research on bereavement during adolescence? The earlier mention of this issue labeled it "early versus middle versus late adolescence." However, the cross-sectional design implied by this phrasing may be inadequate to answer our questions about developmental differences, and it may ignore the issue of change over time. One idea that may prove fruitful is the development of cross-sequential designs in which the benefits of both longitudinal and cross-sectional models can be gained (D. E. Balk, personal communication, December 21, 1994). The advantage of using this more sophisticated design is that change over time and cohort comparison data can be integrated to yield a more reliable picture of the experience of bereavement during adolescence as well as more effectively controlling the costs associated with the longitudinal and cohort effects of cross-sectional research.

Theoretical models of bereavement during adolescence need to continue to be built, then tested and rebuilt. This will only occur if we continue to ask the questions that are difficult to answer and thereby challenge assumptions about the nature of death and grieving.

9

Adolescent Sibling Bereavement: Toward a New Theory

Nancy S. Hogan and Lydia DeSantis

In the United States alone, approximately 1.8 million siblings from birth to 19 years of age experience the death of a brother or sister. The number of children and adolescents experiencing sibling death around the world can only be expected to increase well into the next century as a result of (a) escalating social violence, such as child abuse and homicide; (b) increasing incidence of HIV/AIDS, suicide, accidents, and drug-related deaths in preadolescence and adolescence; and (c) spreading civil, ethnic, and international conflict putting more children at risk because of refugeeism, displacement, homelessness, and orphaning (Balk, 1991; Kellerman, 1994; Pappas, 1994; Parkes, 1993; Shelov, 1994; United Nations Children's Fund, 1994). The large and ever-increasing number of bereaved siblings indicates a need for research-based interventions that have been verified through evaluation of their clinical appropriateness and effectiveness.

Approximately 10 years ago, an Institute of Medicine (IOM) report on the process and impact of bereavement on general and mental health identified the need for research related to adolescent sibling

The authors thank Eric Soldau for calculating the figure of 1.8 million. The datum was abstracted from United States Department of Commerce child and adolescent mortality statistics (United States Bureau of the Census, 1993).

bereavement (Osterweis, Solomon, & Green, 1984). This more than 300-page report contained only one citation (Balk, 1983a) on adolescent sibling bereavement. The purpose of the present chapter is to (a) discuss the need for adolescent sibling bereavement research; (b) identify and critique the research literature pertaining to adolescent sibling bereavement since the IOM report; and (c) provide recommendations for future research on the topic.

The bulk of this chapter focuses primarily on research conducted and data collected when bereaved adolescents (11–19 years of age) experienced the loss of a brother or sister. Although there has been a plethora of research dealing with sibling bereavement and adolescent bereavement, much of it (a) has dealt with comparing sibling responses to the death of parents and other significant members of their interpersonal network; (b) had data collection occur during preadolescence or postadolescence; and (c) was based on other persons' (e.g., parents, peers, or professionals) perceptions of the sibling's or adolescent's grief.

NEED FOR RESEARCH ON ADOLESCENT SIBLING BEREAVEMENT

There are three basic reasons adolescent sibling bereavement research is needed. If those involved with ministering to, maintaining, and promoting the health and well-being of adolescents are to be effective, they must have an empirical (research) database that delineates the "normal" process (characteristics, intensity, and duration) of bereavement before they can differentiate resilient and vulnerable pathways through grief reactions.

Without a database grounded in research, essentially similar sets of reactions can be used to identify both functional and dysfunctional grief. A case in point is the criteria used by the medical profession to define uncomplicated grief in the *Diagnostic and Statistical Manual* (3rd ed., rev., American Psychiatric Association, 1987) and the criteria used by the nursing profession to define dysfunctional grief in the taxonomy of nursing diagnoses (Kim, McFarland, & McLane, 1987). The same cluster of reactions presents conflicting models for physicians and nurses for differentiating between normal and pathological grieving, that is, "the symptomatology described in the nursing diagnostic category as dysfunctional grief is practically identical to the symptoms described in medical literature as uncomplicated grief" (Hogan & Greenfield, 1991, p. 99).

Research on adolescent sibling bereavement is also needed for a second and closely related reason. In the search for theory or research articles and other publications for this chapter, the authors noted an emergent trend in the clinical literature of the 1990s toward the advocacy of bereavement programs for and interventions with bereaved families (Cooley, 1992; Glass, 1993; Heiney, Hasan, & Price, 1993; Johnson, Rincon, Gober, & Rexin, 1993); bereaved parents (Murphy, 1990; Murphy, Aroian, & Baugher, 1989); and bereaved adults (Barbato & Irwin, 1992; Buell & Bevis, 1989; Davis, Hoshiko, Jones, & Gosnell, 1992). A few studies have focused on providing direct care for children who experienced the death of a parent (Siegel, Mesagno, & Christ, 1990; Zambelli & DeRosa, 1992). One intervention article described a single case study of a bereaved adolescent sibling (Heiney, 1991).

Despite the increasing number of publications related to bereavement intervention programs, only two articles describing such programs included any evaluation of their effectiveness (Davis et al., 1992; Murphy, Aroian, & Baugher, 1989). In view of the fact that there are no accepted criteria for differentiating "normal" (functional) from "abnormal" (dysfunctional) adolescent sibling grief, failure to ground interventions in research data or to evaluate intervention programs empirically makes the diagnosis of functional or dysfunctional grief idiosyncratic to each individual practitioner, therapist, or clinician.

The third reason for the need of an empirical database is the effect of sibling death on adolescent development. Adolescence is the critical time of identity formulation and development of self, that is, adolescents seek to answer the questions: "Who am I?"; "Where am I going?"; and "How will I get there?" (Erikson, 1963, 1968). Siblings play a vital role in identity formation for each other via intimate personal exchanges through which they define each other (Bank & Kahn, 1982; Provence & Solnit, 1983). The sibling relationship provides the context for acquiring life skills such as "learning cooperation, practicing negotiation skills, competing and establishing territoriality, and learning that others have rights and needs at different times" (Nadelman as cited in Lamb & Sutton-Smith, 1982, p. 15). In the process of acquiring such life skills, siblings develop a mutual core identity (Bank & Kahn, 1982). The core identity emerges from a constant, interactive, dyadic comparison of one sibling's personal identity with the other sibling's personal identity (Bank & Kahn, 1982).

Although the sibling relationship is founded on a constant, interactive dyadic comparison, it is a relationship fraught with the potential for conflict and rivalry because of such factors as envy and jealousy. Research has shown that strained relationships that existed before the moment of death have resulted in some bereaved siblings expressing an ongoing regret and "sorrow for the way they had acted toward their now deceased sibling or wished that their relationship had been a closer, less conflicted one" (Hogan & DeSantis, 1992, pp. 165–166).

The death of a sibling profoundly and irrevocably alters the pathway toward an adolescent's identity formation. Surviving siblings must now redefine their roles and relations in the absence of their primary referent—the deceased brother or sister (Balk, 1991; Bank & Kahn, 1982; Hogan, 1987; Hogan & DeSantis, in press; Osterweis, Solomon, & Green, 1984; Provence & Solnit, 1983). The *situational* crisis of sibling death compounds and confounds the usual and necessary *developmental* crisis of adolescence.

Bereaved adolescents also grieve as individuals within the context of family and their interpersonal network (Blankemeyer, 1993; Hogan & Balk, 1990; Hogan & DeSantis, 1994; Krell & Rabkin, 1979). The alteration of family structure and function that occurs with sibling death is especially significant in the United States where the average family size is 3.17 persons (U.S. Bureau of the Census, 1993). Loss of a brother or sister makes the surviving sibling an only child in the majority of U.S. families. Being an only child is a "deeply lonely experience" for a surviving adolescent sibling. One bereaved adolescent described the experience of becoming an only child as follows: "I can't even express how much I hate being an only child . . . it was like my mom and dad had each other, and I had no one" (Hogan & DeSantis, 1994, p. 140).

ADOLESCENT SIBLING BEREAVEMENT RESEARCH

This section reviews research from the 1980s and 1990s in terms of themes that emerge in each decade. Because some themes that emerged in the 1980s continued to be investigated in the ensuing decade, there will be citations from the 1990s included in the decade of the 1980s and vice versa.

The major foci of adolescent sibling bereavement research done in the 1980s centered on the surviving sibling's psychosocial and cognitive development following the death of a brother or sister. In the 1990s, the major foci were centered on the bereaved sibling's self-concept, grief, personal growth, and ongoing attachment to the deceased sibling.

Decade of the 1980s:
Research Since the IOM Report

Before the seminal study by Balk (1981) done with a community-based sample to describe the impact of adolescent sibling bereavement on self-concept, other studies of sibling bereavement were done with psychiatric populations of widely mixed age groups (Binger et al., 1969; Blinder, 1972; Cain, Fast, & Erickson, 1964; Krell & Rabkin, 1979, Pollock, 1962). Most such studies relied on retrospective analysis of case studies and clinical interviews, and focused on identifying grief pathology.

In the 1980s, the studies of sibling bereavement used primarily nonpsychiatric populations and concentrated on identifying the variables and conditions of the bereavement process (Davies, 1983, 1988, 1991; Demi & Howell, 1991; Leder, 1992; Martinson, Davies, & Mc-Clowry, 1987). Several of the research studies used parents' conceptions of the sibling bereavement process rather than studying the bereaved siblings directly (Davies, 1983, 1988; Leder, 1992). Others studied the long-term outcomes of adolescent sibling death in adulthood or studied adolescent sibling bereavement when the surviving sibling was an adult rather than an adolescent (Davies, 1991; Demi & Howell, 1991).

Adolescent sibling bereavement research done with the surviving adolescent sibling in the 1980s also used community-based samples. This research focused on investigating the effect of sibling death on self-concept, depression, and academic performance (Balk, 1983a, 1983b, 1990; Birenbaum, Robinson, Phillips, Stewart, & McCown, 1990; Demi & Gilbert, 1987; Hogan, 1987; Martinson, Davies, & McClowry, 1987; McClowry, Davies, May, Kulenkamp, & Martinson, 1987; McCown & Pratt, 1985; Michael & Lansdown, 1986).

Self-Concept. Martinson, Davies, and McClowry (1987) used the Piers-Harris Self-Concept Scale with 29 bereaved siblings (age 8 to 18 years) to measure the long-term effects on their self-concept following the loss of a brother or sister to cancer. Measurement occurred 7 to 9 years after sibling death. Results showed that the bereaved siblings scored significantly higher on self-concept than the populations on which the Piers-Harris was normed.

Balk (1981, 1983a, 1983b) administered the Offer Self-Image Questionnaire for Adolescents (OSIQ-A) to 42 bereaved adolescent siblings (aged 14–19) 4 to 84 months with a mean of 22.7 months following their siblings' death. Focused interviews were also done. Results revealed that the study participants had scores similar to the groups on which the OSIQ-A was normed except for the Morals Scale, which was significantly higher than the normed group. Balk inferred that the value development of the bereaved siblings had been positively affected by the death of a brother or sister. Balk also found that approximately 33% to 50% of the participants experienced enduring reactions to grief, such as anger, guilt, confusion, depression, and shock. Acute grief was reported to be transitory and to diminish in intensity over time.

In another study of 42 bereaved adolescent siblings (aged 14–19), Balk (1990) used cluster analysis procedures to analyze data gathered 4 to 84 months postsibling loss. He determined that there were different clusters of reactions associated with scores of high, average, and low self-concept on the OSIQ-A. During the first weeks after death, the high self-concept group was more likely to experience confusion, have a decreased appetite, feel less depressed, and have less difficulty sleeping. However, later in the bereavement process, the high self-concept group was "much less likely" to experience confusion, loneliness, fear, or depression than the average or low self-concept groups.

Bereaved adolescent siblings who had average self-concept scores on the OSIQ-A experienced more anger and less trouble eating than the high or low self-concept groups (Balk, 1990). As the bereavement process progressed, the average self-concept group experienced more anger, loneliness, and depression than the other two self-concept groups.

Members of the low OSIQ-A self-concept group were initially depressed and afraid, had suicidal ideation, experienced sleeping difficulties, and were preoccupied by thoughts of their dead brother or sister (Balk, 1990). Over time, members of the low self-concept group reported greater confusion about the circumstances surrounding their sibling's death but identified less anger than the high or average self-concept groups.

Hogan and Greenfield (1991) studied 87 adolescents (aged 13–18) 18 months to 5 years postsibling death. The participants were divided into high, moderate, and mild levels of intensity of bereavement. Scores on the 11 subscales of the OSIQ-A were correlated with scores from the Hogan Sibling Inventory of Bereavement (HSIB) instrument. A multivariate analysis of variance (MANOVA) was done using the OSIQ-A as the dependent variable. The omnibus MANOVA was highly significant ($F[22,146] = 3.1$; $p < .001$), which confirmed that the three groups differed across the 11 subscales. Findings revealed that (a) the low intensity of grief group correlated with high self-concept scores; (b) the moderate intensity of grief group correlated with the moderate self-concept scores; and (c) the high intensity of grief group correlated with low self-concept scores. Hogan and Greenfield concluded that dysfunctional patterns of self-concept were associated with adolescents who continued to experience intense grief for 18 months or more since the death of their brother or sister.

Depression. The most widely reported effect of the bereavement process is depression (Abraham & Whitock, 1969; Alexander & Adlerstein, 1958; Beck, Seshi, & Tuthill, 1983; Birtchnell, 1970; Bowlby, 1963; Brent et al., 1993; Clayton & Darvish, 1979; Dyregrov, Kristoffersen, Matthiesen, & Mitchel, 1994; Freud, 1957; Hilgard, 1969; Jacobs, Hanson, Berkman, Kasl, & Ostfeld, 1989; Leahy, 1992; Lindemann, 1944; Robinson & Fleming, 1989). Demi and Gilbert (1987) studied 18 bereaved siblings (aged 10–21). They compared scores of the bereaved siblings on the Children's Depression Inventory with the scores of their parents on the Hopkin's Symptom Checklist. The deceased sibling/child had died 4 to 24 months before data collection. Results showed a positive relationship between the emotional distance scores of both parents and children.

Demi and Gilbert (1987) also administered the Impact of Events Scale to the bereaved parents and siblings to determine if a relationship existed between the way parents and siblings coped with subjective stress. Results revealed that parents had high scores on the intrusion of subjective stress subscale, whereas the siblings had high scores on the avoidance of subjective stress subscale. The investigators concluded that the surviving siblings/children responded by avoiding thoughts about their sibling's death and its aftermath as an "attempt to soothe and comfort the parent" (Demi & Gilbert, 1987, p. 389).

Hogan and Greenfield (1991) found that bereaved adolescent siblings with high intensity of grief levels on the HSIB had scored over 2 standard deviations below the norm on the emotional tone (depression) subscale of the OSIQ-A questionnaire. They also scored 1.5 standard deviations below the norm on the psychopathology subscale of the OSIQ-A. The investigators concluded that the passage of time did not decrease the level of depression or ameliorate the intensity of grief, making the bereaved adolescents with high intensity of grief particularly vulnerable to long-term negative outcomes.

Other studies of bereaved adolescent siblings have identified symptomatology indicative of depression (Balk, 1981, 1983a; Hogan, 1987, 1988; Martinson, Davies, & McClowry, 1987; Michael & Lansdown, 1986). Such symptomatology included sleep disturbances and nightmares, poor concentration, feelings of powerlessness, helplessness, and decreased self-worth, and suicidal ideation.

Researchers and clinicians who have studied the responses of children to death have also found symptomatology of depression (Binger et al., 1969; Cain & Cain, 1964; Kaffman & Elizur, 1979; Kliman, 1968; Van Eerdewegh, Bieri, Parrilla, & Clayton, 1982). The symptomatology included feeling sad, crying, enuresis, withdrawal, insomnia, and disturbances of affect.

Academic Performance.   Balk (1981, 1983a) and Hogan (1987) reported that bereaved adolescent siblings experienced difficulties in concentration and altered study habits. Both the amount of time bereaved adolescent siblings spent studying and the grades they achieved showed a decline after the death of a brother or sister. Balk (1981, 1983a) reported that grades and study habits eventually returned to normal for most of the bereaved adolescent siblings. No obvious reason was found why the academic performance of the remaining bereaved siblings did not return to their previous levels.

The only instrument that directly measures the bereavement process in adolescents who have experienced the death of a brother or sister is the HSIB (Blankemeyer, 1993; Hogan, 1987, 1988, 1990; Hogan & DeSantis, in press). Hogan constructed the HSIB by conducting community-based child and adolescent bereavement groups for surviving siblings over a 4-year period. Items in the HSIB represent the actual statements of the bereaved siblings. The items were derived from content analysis of statements made during the bereavement sessions and interviews with the participants as well as with other bereaved siblings. The items were then refined and validated through focus groups of bereaved siblings and panels of bereaved parents and experts on bereavement and adolescent development. The original HSIB had a total of 109 items using a 5-point Likert scaling. Two factors (grief and personal growth) were retained from the original five that emerged during factor analysis.

The other three factors were related to sibling perceptions of parental grief and parental cohesion, and sibling perceptions of the grief of their other surviving brothers or sisters. These three factors were ultimately deleted because they presumed an intact family of at least five members (two parents and three siblings/children). By eliminating the three factors, the instrument could be used with one-parent families and with the more typical family of two children, which constitutes most families in the United States today.

The revised HSIB has 47 items. The Cronbach alpha for grief is .95 and .90 for personal growth. The internal consistency coefficient for the total revised HSIB is .92 (Hogan & DeSantis, in press). Content validity of the revised HSIB was further confirmed by the finding that mild, moderate, and high intensity of grief on the HSIB predicted high, moderate, and low levels of self-concept, respectively, on the OSIQ-A (Hogan & Greenfield, 1991).

Decade of the 1990s

Three literature reviews were done in the 1990s on childhood and adolescent bereavement (Balk, 1991; Davies, 1994; Walker, 1993). None focused exclusively on siblings who were bereaved and studied during adolescence.

In his literature review, Balk (1991) concluded that there was a dearth of research on adolescent bereavement before 1980 but that a "plethora" of studies had been done since 1981 in three general areas: (a) adolescents grieving over the death of a parent; (b) adolescents bereaved over the death of a brother or sister; and (c) adolescents experiencing their own impending death. Balk also reviewed research done on adolescents bereaved over the death of a friend/peer but noted that there is a paucity of such studies.

Walker (1993) summarized literature on sibling bereavement from 1950 through 1992. She stated that the early studies (1950–1985) of sibling bereavement concentrated on identifying "pathological grief responses." Walker concluded that studies since 1985 came to view bereaved siblings and siblings with terminally ill brothers or sisters as individuals at risk for social and emotional problems that did not necessarily result in psychopathology.

Walker separated the studies done since 1985 into three categories for discussion: (a) age-specific studies (e.g., preschool, school age, and adolescence); (b) the impact of the family on bereaved siblings; and (c) clinical intervention studies that centered primarily on children with a sibling who was dying. Walker concluded her review with implications for nursing interventions for siblings with terminally ill brothers or sisters.

Davies (1994) evaluated studies of childhood bereavement since the 1970s. She focused the review on the "mediating variables" (individual, situational, and environmental characteristics) that interact to affect the "behaviors" and "competencies" of the bereaved siblings.

Davies (1994) delineated the individual characteristics as the age and gender of the surviving child that are generally viewed as influencing the "intensity of association, identification and competition generated" (Blinder, 1972, p. 173).

Situational variables defined by Davies are disease characteristics and the time that has elapsed since death (trajectory). Disease characteristics include life-threatening illness, illness duration, suddenness of death, and site of the death. Davies concluded that there is insufficient evidence to determine empirically the degree of importance that a sibling's disability or illness has on the surviving sibling's "development, adjustment, and subsequent bereavement" (Davies, 1994, p. 182).

Environmental factors refer to those aspects in the surviving siblings' environment that affect them socially and emotionally, that is, family relationships, characteristics of parents, nature of the communication between parents and the surviving siblings, and the degree to which the surviving and deceased siblings were part of each other's life (shared life space).

These literature reviews by Balk (1991), Davies (1994), and Walker (1993) are an excellent compendium of the complex and multidimensional phenomenon of childhood and adolescent bereavement. Taken together, they constitute the most comprehensive resource to date on how adolescent sibling bereavement research has served to broaden the conceptualization of the adolescent sibling bereavement process. Research in the 1990s has centered on refining the characteristics, intensity, and duration of the process (Balk, 1990; Balk & Hogan, 1995; Hogan & DeSantis, 1992, 1994, in press; Hogan & Greenfield, 1991).

Characteristics.   Several of the studies related to the characteristics and intensity of the bereavement process have been discussed in the previous section. Balk (1990) was cited in relation to confirming the impact of grief on self-concept and symptomatology of depression. The Hogan and Greenfield (1991) study was reviewed in relation to self-concept and to the intensity and duration of depression.

Intensity and Duration.   Factors that helped or hindered the ability of bereaved adolescents to cope with the intensity of grief from the death of their brother or sister were investigated by Hogan and DeSantis (1994). The researchers analyzed the content of the written responses to the semistructured questions concerning: (1) What helped you cope with your sibling's death?; and (2) What made it more difficult to cope with your sibling's death? Responses were from a community-based sample of 140 bereaved adolescents (aged 13–18) who had experienced the death of a brother or sister an average of 2.6 years (range, 3 months to 5 years) before to data collection.

There were five categories that contained descriptions of things that helped the bereaved adolescents cope. The categories were self, family, friends, social system, and time.

Category 1: Self. The bereaved adolescents used two forms of personal coping. They relied on their own inner strength or undertook stress-reducing activities, such as keeping busy, playing musical instruments, or releasing pent-up emotion by crying or screaming.

Category 2: Family. Parents, other kin, and pets were seen as providing comfort and care. Parents were especially helpful in assisting the surviving adolescents to see the normalcy of their grief through sharing memories about the deceased sibling/child.

Category 3: Friends. The bereaved adolescents perceived friends to constitute a peer support network that was always unconditionally there for them.

Category 4: Social system. The bereaved adolescents cited professionals, such as ministers and psychologists, and organized support groups of bereaved siblings as assisting them to feel less alone through the sharing of common experiences and helping them to answer questions about the death of their brother or sister.

Category 5: Time. For some, only the passage of time could help them cope with the death of their sibling.

Three of the same categories that contained things that helped the bereaved adolescent siblings cope with grief also contained content that hindered their coping. The categories were self, family, and social system. Although the category of "friend" was saturated with data related to "things" that helped them to cope with their sibling grief, none of the bereaved adolescents reported that friends hindered their bereavement process. Apparently for these adolescents, by definition friendship required another to be helpful and to be "there for them" during the life crisis of sibling death.

Category 1: Self. The ability of the bereaved adolescents to cope by themselves was compromised by "spontaneously occurring, painful, uninvited, intrusive thoughts and feelings related to the circumstances and events surrounding their sibling's death" (Hogan & DeSantis, 1994, p. 139). Such uninvited thoughts and feelings were engendered by (a) feelings of guilt, shame, and blame over their inability to help their dying siblings or prevent their death; (b) feeling a deep sense of loneliness that followed their sibling's death; (c) experiencing events that aroused thoughts of their deceased siblings; and (d) coming to realize that their sibling's death was final and irrevocable.

Category 2: Family. The bereaved adolescents stated that they were caused additional grief and anger by fights with or among family members, and by seeing the distress of their parents over the death of their brother or sister.

Category 3: Social system. The bereaved adolescents felt that their grief was exacerbated by the insensitivity of other people, and by rumors and gossip that were spread about their sibling's life and death. They also perceived a lack of justice in the world when those responsible for their sibling's death were not punished or when the sibling was killed in an accident.

The five factors that helped the bereaved adolescents cope with their sibling's death provided them with a sense of resourcefulness, "those things (attributes, people, or events) which increased . . . [their] sense of resiliency and ability to effect and to anticipate events associated with sibling death" (Hogan & DeSantis, 1994, p. 142). The three factors that hindered the bereaved adolescents in coping with the death of their brother or sister gave them a sense of helplessness, "those things (attributes, people, or events) which increased . . . [their] sense of vulnerability and exacerbated grief" (Hogan & DeSantis, 1994, p. 142).

The variables of intensity and duration of the adolescent sibling bereavement process were further clarified by the concept of "ongoing attachment," i.e., the continuing presence of the social and emotional bond with the deceased sibling in the face of his or her physical absence (Hogan & DeSantis, 1992). Ongoing attachment challenged the heretofore prevailing medical science view of bereavement being time bound (Bowlby, 1980b; Freud, 1957; Lindemann, 1944) and that its healthy resolution required survivors to sever or relinquish ties to the deceased (Freud, 1957; Lindemann, 1944).

Scholars in the area of death and dying have hypothesized or speculated about an ongoing relationship survivors often describe or feel that they continue to have with the deceased. For example, Klass (1993) described parental bereavement to include parents remaining connected to their dead child by maintaining an "inner representation" of the child that transcends the momentary fleeting nature of human experience. Klass (1993) concluded that "the child remains immortal, in the sense that the inner representation of the child remains a real, living presence in the parent's inner and social world" (p. 360).

Participants in several research studies on childhood or adult bereavement also mentioned the idea of remaining "connected" to the deceased, but the dimensions, characteristics, or functions of such connectedness were not explored by the investigators. McClowry and her colleagues (1987) described the ways bereaved parents attempted to keep "connected" to their deceased child (e.g., joining bereavement support groups where they could talk about their deceased son or daughter).

In a study of 125 children (aged 6–17) who experienced the death of a parent within 4 months of data collection, Silverman and Worden (1992) identified "efforts" bereaved children made to "stay connected" to their deceased mother or father. The children "stayed connected" through having dreams of their parents, talking about their parents, keeping mementos that had belonged to their deceased parents, visiting the parents' gravesites, talking to or thinking about the dead parents, and believing their dead parents were "watching" them (Silverman, Nickman, & Worden, 1992; Silverman & Worden, 1992). The investigators concluded that the bereaved children's "staying connected" behaviors were an attempt either to "keep the deceased parents alive or to make the loss real" (Silverman & Worden, 1992, p. 100).

Smith, Range, and Ulmer (1992) studied the possible relationship between degree of belief in an afterlife and perceived bereavement recovery for 121 bereaved individuals between the ages of 16 to 68 years. Results revealed that a high belief in an afterlife was associated with greater recovery from bereavement. These findings were consistent irrespective of death from natural causes, accidents, suicide, or homicide.

Although previously cited studies had identified aspects of certain characteristics of the continuing presence of the deceased in the lives of their survivors, Hogan and DeSantis (1992) were the first to derive empirically and describe comprehensively the construct of "ongoing attachment." Content analysis was done on the written responses to the question, "If you could ask or tell your dead sibling something, what would it be?" Data were collected from a community-based sample of 157 bereaved adolescent siblings. Findings yielded six mutually exclusive categories of a taxonomy of bereavement. The phenomenon that emerged from the analysis was termed "ongoing attachment." A brief description of each category follows.

Category 1: Regretting. The bereaved siblings expressed sorrow over the things they had done or said to their deceased brother or sister, wished they had been closer and more loving, and missed their shared life together.

Category 2: Endeavoring to understand. The bereaved adolescents attempted to find answers to the questions of how and why their brother or sister died.

Category 3: Catching up. The bereaved adolescents kept in touch spiritually with their dead sibling by telling them current events, inquiring about their well-being, assuring them all was well with their survivors, and asking what heaven/afterlife was like.

Category 4: Reaffirming. The bereaved adolescents continually expressed their ongoing relationship with their deceased sibling by stating how much they loved and missed them, and that they would never, ever forget them.

Category 5: Influencing. The bereaved siblings continually sought advice and guidance from their deceased brother or sister, wanted assurance that they were living up to their dead sibling's expectations, and expressed an intent to carry on their dead sibling's works and fulfill their dreams.

Category 6: Reuniting. The bereaved adolescents expressed an anticipation of meeting or seeing their deceased brother or sister again in heaven/afterlife.

When viewed together, these categories and their content demonstrated clearly that the sibling relationship (bond) "supersedes and transcends death" (Hogan & DeSantis, 1992, in press). In their bereavement, the surviving adolescents

> . . . learn to live with the physical absence and the simultaneous emotional presence of their deceased brother or sister. At the same time, the surviving siblings are anticipating a physical and social reunion in heaven with their deceased sibling. The simultaneous interaction of the phenomena of timelessness and ongoing attachment results in a sense of "everywhen" (Stanner, 1965, p. 271), a sense in which the past, present, and future are blended into a oneness. They are at one together (Stanner, 1965, p. 271). In the timeless gestalt of "everywhen," the bereaved adolescents experience a sense of conceptual, emotional, and social eternity with their deceased siblings in the face of their physical absence. (Hogan & DeSantis, 1992, p. 174)

NEW THEORY OF ADOLESCENT SIBLING BEREAVEMENT

Hogan and DeSantis (in press) have put forth a theory of adolescent sibling bereavement based on the triangulation of quantitative and qualitative data from a community-based sample of 157 bereaved adolescents (Hogan & DeSantis, 1992, 1994; Hogan & Greenfield, 1991). The three constructs of grief, personal growth, and ongoing attachment are the basis of the theory and form a complex phenomenon and process with multiple pathways through bereavement and toward personal growth.

Construct of Grief

The construct of grief was derived from the 24 items (properties) that constitute the grief factor of the HSIB (Hogan, 1987, 1990). The construct of personal growth was derived from the 23 items that constitute the personal growth factor of the HSIB (Hogan, 1987, 1990). Information on the constructs, factor analysis, and parametrics of the HSIB has been presented earlier (Blankemeyer, 1993; Hogan, 1987; Hogan & Balk, 1990; Hogan & Greenfield, 1991). The constructs of grief and personal growth were further described through content analysis of responses to the semistructured questions related to things that helped or hindered the abilities of bereaved adolescents to cope with the death of a brother or sister (Hogan & DeSantis, 1994).

The derivation of the construct of ongoing attachment has been described earlier (Hogan & DeSantis, 1992). It was further validated through the quantitative portion of the HSIB relating to the anticipation by bereaved adolescents of a reunion with their deceased sibling in heaven/afterlife (Hogan, 1987; Hogan & DeSantis, in press).

The 24 items from the HSIB yielded six categories that constituted the construct of grief (Hogan & DeSantis, in press).

Category 1: Permanently changed reality of self and family. Bereaved adolescents feel that the death of their sibling has "irrevocably altered their lives and those of their family members." The family has quantitatively decreased in size and been qualitatively changed by the loss of their "hopes, wishes, and dreams of an anticipated shared life with the [deceased] child/sibling" (Hogan & DeSantis, in press). The bereaved adolescents feel a lack of wholeness about themselves and their families, and they believe life will never again be "normal." The sense of an incomplete family is similar to the concept of "empty space" described by McClowry and her colleagues (1987).

Category 2: Physical effects. Following their sibling's death, the bereaved adolescents have a sense of being less well physically and more vulnerable to illness. Guerriero (1983) also reported that bereaved adolescents have more symptoms of illness and that their physical health declined over time when compared with the health of nonbereaved adolescent controls.

Category 3: Increased vulnerability. The bereaved adolescents fear that they will not regain their psychological equilibrium, experience a sense of helplessness, and are worried and anxious that death may occur to others they love. They also experience a sense of guilt when feeling happy or having fun, and about being alive when their brother or sister is dead. Osterweis, Solomon, and Green (1984) have described survivor guilt related to child survivors. Balk (1983b, 1990) has described feelings of guilt in surviving siblings, and Demi and Miles (1988) discuss it in relation to bereaved adults.

Also contributing to their sense of increased vulnerability are the bereaved adolescents' feelings of depression (sleeplessness, nightmares, and profound sadness), increased apathy and indifference toward life, and isolation (being exceptionally alone). Life seems hopeless and meaningless, and no one else can comprehend the depth of their grieving. Literature related to depression in bereaved adolescent siblings has been discussed previously (Balk, 1981, 1983b, 1990; Demi & Gilbert, 1987; Hogan, 1987; Hogan & Greenfield, 1991; Martinson, Davies, & McClowry, 1987; Michael & Lansdown, 1986).

Category 4: Cognitive interference. The bereaved adolescent siblings experience an inability to concentrate. Concentration "is sacrificed for the task of maintaining control over uninvited, intrusive thoughts and feelings associated with fear, guilt, and depression" (Hogan & DeSantis, in press). The inability of bereaved adolescents to concentrate has been found in other sibling bereavement studies (Balk, 1981, 1983b; Hogan, 1987).

Category 5: Desire for reunion with sibling. The bereaved adolescents express "wanting to die in order to reunite with their sibling" (Hogan & DeSantis, in press). The desire was most intense in the early phase of the bereavement process. Desire for reunion with their deceased brother or sister in heaven/afterlife was also a key category in the construct of ongoing attachment (Hogan & DeSantis, 1992).

Category 6: Coping behavior. To help distract themselves from the pain of their grief, the bereaved adolescents engage in high-risk behavior, such as driving too fast, consuming alcohol, or taking mind-altering drugs.

Construct of Personal Growth

The idea that individuals can experience personal growth following life crises has been theorized for many years for adolescents and adults (Collins, Taylor, & Skokan, 1990; Lopata, 1973, 1975; Offer, 1969; Taylor, Lichtman, & Wood, 1984). Research with bereaved siblings has shown that they feel they become more mature than friends and peers, can cope better with stress, develop closer relationships with family members, are able to reassess their priorities, and become more other centered (feel increased empathy, compassion, and tolerance for themselves and others) (Balk, 1981, 1983b; Bank & Kahn, 1982; Hogan, 1987; Hogan & DeSantis, 1994; Martinson, Davies, & McClowry, 1987; Offer, 1969; Oltjenbruns, 1991). Many of these characteristics are also reflected in the five categories that comprise the construct of personal growth.

Category 1: Permanently changed reality. Bereaved adolescent siblings experience a new sense of the impermanence of life, that is, relationships are fragile and precious, and nothing can be taken for granted. That which gives value and meaning to life often must be reprioritized.

Category 2: Increased sense of others. Bereaved adolescent siblings express a greater sense of love and responsibility for the well-being, rights, and needs of family members and others. Their sense of ultracentrism is reflective of the higher sense of morality found in other studies of bereaved siblings using standardized instruments, such as the OSIQ-A (Balk, 1981, 1983a, 1983b, 1990; Hogan, 1987; Hogan & Greenfield, 1991) and the Moos Family Environmental Scale (Davies, 1988).

Category 3: Increased resiliency. The bereaved adolescent siblings believe they are stronger, have an increased ability to cope with life, and have greater self-worth and self-awareness because of the grief they have endured. They experience a sense of renewed optimism about life and the future.

Category 4: Increased faith. There is an increase in the "faith consciousness" (Fowler, 1976, 1991a) of the bereaved adolescents as they reexamine and revaluate their values and beliefs. They develop "a new personal belief system or faith in their own inner strength to cope with the death of their sibling and future life events" (Hogan & DeSantis, in press). The "faith consciousness" embodies and stimulates their ultracentrism; for some, it includes a strengthening of religiosity (Balk & Hogan, 1995; Hogan & DeSantis, 1994). The increase in religiosity related to adolescent sibling death was also found by Balk (1981), and Hogan and DeSantis (1994). It is discussed in depth by Balk (1991), and Balk and Hogan (1995).

Category 5: Ability to receive and give help. The bereaved adolescents feel that peers and family members are "there for them" by comforting them, sharing memories of the dead sibling/child/friend, and letting them grieve on their own terms (Hogan & DeSantis, 1994). They also see themselves as "being there" for family and friends, and helping them with their bereavement process (Hogan & DeSantis, 1994).

In the theory, the constructs of grief and personal growth are seen as curvilinear trajectories that are independent in nature (Hogan & DeSantis, 1992, 1994, in press; Hogan & Greenfield, under review). There was a .19 intercorrelation between the grief and personal growth factors on the HSIB used with the sample of bereaved adolescent siblings (Hogan & DeSantis, in press). Lehman and his colleagues (1993) also empirically identified the independence of grief and personal growth in parental and spousal bereavement.

Trajectory of Grief.   Before the death of their sibling, adolescents are experiencing a shared life (physical, social, and psychological proximity) with their brother or sister. Life is normal and the world is understandable, that is, the world works. At the death of their brother or sister, all that is normal and understandable ceases. "The previous naive assumptions and 'working models' (Bowlby, 1969) of their lives are no longer valid" (Hogan & DeSantis, in press).

The bereaved adolescent siblings experience life as being hapless and are encompassed by feelings of hopelessness, despair, and profound loneliness. They are powerless to change their irrevocably altered reality. At the most intense point of grief, bereaved adolescents who become resilient survivors come to two simultaneous realizations: (a) Their deceased sibling will never return, and (b) they must regain control of their lives despite the "permanent lack of proximity" to their dead brother or sister.

The simultaneous dual realization signals a turning point in the trajectory of grief and the regaining of a sense of hope for the future. Their grief reactions lessen. They start the process of reconstructing their lives "and creating a revised model of the world based upon a new reality and normality" (Hogan & DeSantis, in press). However, feelings of bereavement will continually reemerge in significant life events in which their deceased brother or sister would have normally participated (e.g., weddings, graduations, and family holiday celebrations and milestones).

Trajectory of Personal Growth. Before the death of their sibling, the bereaved adolescents had taken their world and the people in it for granted. They were engaged in developing a sense of personal identity and seeking answers to the questions: "Who am I?"; "Where am I going?"; and "How will I get there?" Answers to the questions were sought in the life they shared with members of their interpersonal network and had been partially answered through their sibling relationship.

At the death of their brother or sister, the bereaved adolescents can no longer take life for granted, must redefine the roles and relationships in their interpersonal network, and seek answers to identity questions that have changed to: "Who am I *now?*"; "Where am I going *now?*"; and "How will I get there *now?*" Answers to the revised questions have to be sought without their primary referent, i.e., their dead brother or sister.

The search for answers to the revised identity questions leads to a reprioritization of their lives, and a transcendence of self and others as the bereaved adolescent siblings shift to ultracentrism from the usual adolescent posture of egocentrism. The transcendence of self results in personal growth and ultimately the construction of "a new model and meaning of life in the proximal absence of their dead brother or sister" (Hogan & DeSantis, in press).

The resultant outcome of the new normality is an ever-evolving recognition of the finiteness of life, and the preciousness of relationships that are "here today" and "gone today" (Hogan & DeSantis, in press). Further, the new normality for the surviving sibling and family is distinctly different from their previous sense of normality because of the physical absence of the deceased sibling/child.

Construct of Ongoing Attachment

The construct of ongoing attachment (Hogan & DeSantis, 1992) is conceptualized "as a type of motivational energy that assists in transforming bereaved adolescent siblings into resilient survivors" (Hogan & DeSantis, in press). It becomes manifest when grief is most intense, and all "expectations and anticipations" the bereaved adolescents had of a shared life with their sibling are shattered permanently and irrevocably. The bereaved siblings must replace their profound sense of helplessness, hopelessness, and meaninglessness with a sense of help, hope, and meaning. They do so through the phenomenon of ongoing attachment by anticipating the possible reunion with their deceased sibling in heaven/afterlife.

Ongoing attachment also assists the bereaved adolescent siblings to "undertake an introspective scrutiny" that results in the ultimate realization that the life they shared with their deceased sibling cannot be recovered. Accepting the irrevocability of their sibling's death frees the energy of the bereaved adolescents to "reformulate a reality that includes the spiritual presence of their deceased sibling" (Hogan & DeSantis, in press).

Ongoing attachment helps the process of personal growth to occur by leading to an expansion and transcendence of a sense of self, others, and responsibility for others. As personal growth continues, it helps the bereaved adolescent siblings to redefine their identity and world.

> Ongoing attachment, then, is the silent variable that mediates the construct of grief and the construct of personal growth. While ongoing attachment becomes manifest when grief is at its most intense, it begins to emerge at the death of a brother or sister in the construct of personal growth. This emergence of ongoing attachment accelerates and expands the process of personal growth across time. The interaction between ongoing attachment and the construct of grief, and the interaction between ongoing attachment and the construct of personal growth are bidirectional. However, in adolescent sibling bereavement, grief and personal growth remain independent despite the fact that they occur during the phenomenon of sibling death (Hogan & DeSantis, in press).

Hogan and DeSantis (in press) emphasize that the interactions between the constructs of grief, personal growth, and ongoing attachment will likely vary because of factors, such as culture, cause of death, the circumstances surrounding sibling death, the nature of the affectional bond, characteristics of the siblings, and belief in the concept of an afterlife. They call for comparative and longitudinal studies to test the theory empirically to help differentiate between normative and nonnormative adolescent sibling bereavement (Hogan & DeSantis, in press).

RECOMMENDATIONS FOR FURTHER RESEARCH

Balk reviewed current research in adolescent bereavement in 1991 and made three major recommendations to adolescent bereavement researchers. His suggestions are presented and the progress that has been made during the last four years assessed. Balk (1991) made the following recommendations:

> Research needs in this [adolescent bereavement] field of inquiry include (a) longitudinal investigations to study the trajectory of adolescent bereavement, (b) development of theoretical models to explain adolescent bereavement, and (c) integration with the traditional areas of adolescent inquiry, such as cognitive development, moral reasoning, gender socialization, and identity formation (p. 7).

Regarding the first recommendation, no published longitudinal study of adolescent sibling bereavement was found. Without longitudinal data, it is not possible to delineate empirically the bereavement trajectory for bereaved adolescents.

The lack of longitudinal studies may be due to an assumption on the part of bereavement researchers that there is an adequate and empirically derived database from which to understand the characteristics, intensity, and duration of the adolescent sibling bereavement process. This assumption would appear invalid. Since the 1991 review by Balk, there have been only two articles (Hogan & DeSantis, 1992, 1994) and one chapter in a book (Hogan & DeSantis, in press) that describe how adolescents cope with sibling death.

The development of longitudinal research will permit researchers to delineate a trajectory of adolescent sibling bereavement and to differentiate on an empirical basis functional from dysfunctional bereavement. This could assist practitioners, therapists, and clinicians to screen bereaved adolescent siblings to identify those at risk for dysfunctional outcomes, and to evaluate and modify intervention programs where and when necessary.

Longitudinal research studies would also help to determine if the catastrophic event of the death of a brother or sister serves to attenuate or buffer the process of grieving over subsequent losses. In other words, will the new working model of the world ameliorate the severity, intensity, and duration of grief experienced when additional losses occur during adolescence and adulthood.

The second recommendation by Balk (1991) concerned the need for development of theoretical models to explain adolescent bereavement. Hogan and DeSantis (in press) have recently formulated a theoretical model of the adolescent sibling bereavement process using triangulation of data from qualitative and quantitative research findings. The need for comparative and longitudinal testing of the theory has been delineated earlier. No other published, empirically based, theoretical models of adolescent sibling bereavement were found.

Balk (1991) also invited researchers to integrate cognitive development, moral reasoning, gender socialization, and identity formation into their research objectives. These important areas of study have not been addressed to date. There is, however, continuing reference by bereavement researchers to the importance of recognizing identity formation as a vital developmental task that is believed to become disrupted for surviving adolescents following sibling death. Researchers further hypothesize that having to cope with the situational crisis of sibling bereavement creates an altered pathway through the developmental tasks of adolescence. Empirical research is needed to confirm or disconfirm this hypothesis.

CONCLUSION

During the last 14 years, adolescent sibling bereavement research has been defined as an important area of study and has earned its place in the bereavement research enterprise. Considerable work has been done to define the characteristics of sibling grief using data from nonpsychiatric populations of adolescents. Researchers have continued to emphasize the necessity of understanding the bereavement process of adolescents within the developmental framework of adolescence and to understand that adolescents grieve within grieving families.

Beginning efforts have also been made to identify how groups of adolescents with low levels of grief have qualitatively and quantitatively developed more self-esteem and less depressive symptomatology than adolescents with high levels of grief. Conversely, adolescents with high levels of grief have significantly lower levels of self-esteem and more depressive characteristics than their low-grief-intensity bereaved peers. These findings provide a basis for beginning to differentiate normative from non-normative grieving. Such research-based findings can also be used by those working with bereaved adolescent siblings to (a) screen for those adolescents who would benefit from intervention; (b) construct age-appropriate interventions; and (c) evaluate and validate the effectiveness of interventions.

Findings from qualitative studies have provided a rich, in-depth description of how adolescents describe becoming survivors and how they appraise the things that help or hinder them as they cope with and adapt to their sibling's death and its aftermath. Finally, there have been valuable breakthroughs in understanding the nature of the ongoing attachment of many surviving siblings to their dead brother or sister, and how this spiritual bond sustains and nourishes the survivor adolescents.

In summary, adolescent sibling bereavement research is a recent area of study for life-event researchers. The researchers cited in this chapter are to be commended for their commitment to adolescent sibling bereavement research and for the considerable body of knowledge that they have accumulated toward understanding the adolescent sibling bereavement process. Nevertheless, many challenges lie ahead. It is important that researchers do not become complacent with the excellent progress made to date. The approximately 1.8 million bereaved children and adolescents in the United States and countless others in the world who experience the death of a brother or sister are an underserved population who remain "silent grievers." It is incumbent on bereavement researchers not only to remain advocates for these "silent grievers" but also to provide those dedicated to helping them with a scientific basis for effective interventions.

10

Death of a Friend During Adolescence: Issues and Impacts

Kevin Ann Oltjenbruns

Adolescence is often described as the "best time of our lives," but this descriptor belies the commonality of loss and the resultant grief during this life stage. Estimates of individuals who experience the death of a peer during adolescence range from 36% (Balk & McNeil, 1989, unpublished manuscript as cited in McNeil, Silliman, & Swihart, 1991) to 87% of all adolescents (Schachter, 1991). Further, Dise-Lewis (1988) found that 12% of the 681 11- to 14-year-olds she studied reported that they had lost a friend to death during the previous 1-year period. Regardless of the precise statistic, each of the individuals who died left behind many to grieve—including acquaintances, best friends, team members, classmates, romantic partners, gang members—in addition to their own family members.

McNeil, Silliman, and Swihart (1991) noted that the death of a friend, at any age, is a significant event; however, the death of a friend during adolescence "can be especially profound, due to the fragility of the youthful ego and the intense relationships adolescents have with their friends" (p. 133). Given the commonality of loss resulting from death during adolescence and the impact of the ensuing grief, it is important that parents, teachers, counselors, youth leaders, and others

The author would like to thank the following individuals for their assistance: Jill Kreutzer, Alicia Cook, and Joyce Caufman.

who interact with teens understand the significance of the loss and issues related to the bereavement process.

Typical types of losses commonly experienced by today's adolescents are the following:

- Twelve-year-old Marla died in a head-on collision when a drunk driver hit the car in which she was riding. She had just won first place in a local gymnastics meet. Marla was captain of her middle school team and was much beloved by her classmates.
- Thirteen-year-old Abbey died of leukemia; her recent bone marrow transplant was unsuccessful. In the months just before her death, Abbey attended school whenever she could. Her peer group there was important to her and supportive during her illness.
- Fourteen-year-old Alan was killed in a drive-by shooting on his way home from school. He lived in a neighborhood marked by increasing violence and was known to be a member of a gang involved in various drug-related crimes. Fellow gang members were Alan's best friends.
- Fifteen-year-old Juan died of AIDS after a 4-year struggle with the disease. He was infected by a blood transfusion given during an operation to save his leg that had been badly severed in an accident. Juan had only one true friend; other classmates were fearful of interacting with him.
- Sixteen-year-old Tad drowned after falling off a boat. Friends with him at the time of the accident were unable to save him. Tad and five of his friends had been drinking; Tad's blood alcohol level was found to be extremely high.
- Seventeen-year-old Maria committed suicide in her home after saying goodbye to her boyfriend an hour earlier. They had just come from a school dance where she had been crowned as part of the homecoming celebration's royalty.
- Eighteen-year-old Ahman was the star of the local high school basketball team. He collapsed during practice and died shortly thereafter. During the autopsy, the coroner found that Ahman had a severe heart blockage that had never been detected.

ADOLESCENT PEER RELATIONSHIPS

The examples in the previous section illustrate many different types of peer groups. Friendship networks and peer groups perform many different functions during the adolescent years. For example, peers provide the opportunity to experiment with different roles, gain feedback about one's own characteristics and abilities, test out various ideas and belief systems, contribute to a sense of identity, provide emotional support, and much more (Bigner, 1994).

Friendships during childhood are defined by many characteristics, including enjoyment of common activities or characteristics such as "fun," "nice," "helpful," or "considerate." During adolescence, as the meaning of friendship matures, other characteristics become important as well. These include acceptance of one another, loyalty and commitment, intimacy potential, ego reinforcement, and helping (Balk, 1995; Bigelow & LaGaipa, 1980). Reciprocity is a key element because feelings must be mutual if the relationship is to be truly regarded as a *friendship.* "The growth of friendship appears to be facilitated by the exchange of intimate information, emotional support, and doing things together" (Bigelow & LaGaipa, 1980, p. 36).

"Intimacy" is also a measure used to describe friendships. Intimate relationships are mutually recognized as such and intimate friends are characterized by "mutual trust and loyalty . . . they feel free to be sincere, spontaneous, and open about themselves. . . . They tend to know each other's feelings, preferences, and life facts . . . they enjoy doing things together. . . . Finally, they help and support each other by giving and sharing emotionally as well as materially, feeling free to impose on each other. A greater intensity of these dimensions marks a higher degree of intimate friendship" (Sharabany, Gershoni, & Hofman, 1981, pp. 800–801).

Relationships built on such a foundation of closeness and terminated through death constitute a significant loss. Many variables have an impact on an individual's grief responses including the centrality of the relationship, defined in terms of the role that each person plays in the other's life; time spent with one another; and emotional closeness. The death of a friend who was regarded as an intimate, a confidant, and a major source of support is likely to have a much greater impact on an adolescent than would the death of someone who is merely an acquaintance (Cook & Oltjenbruns, 1989). This is not to say, however, that the death of an acquaintance has no impact.

Some relationships are defined as ambivalent in that they are marked by contradictory feelings. Although an individual may have regarded another person as a friend, some interactions at the core of the relationship can include significant levels of anger, hostility, annoyance, intolerance, and frustration. What is known as "conflicted mourning" arises after the loss of highly troubled, ambivalent relationships. After a brief initial absence of grief—even relief—the mourner [often] experiences severe grief, with sadness, lack of acceptance of the loss, anxiety, guilt, self-reproach . . . along with a persistent need for and sense of connection to the lost person marked by remorse as well as by many of the same mixed feelings" before the death (Rando, 1993b, p. 171).

Many adolescents find themselves in relationships marked by some degree of ambivalence. Conflicts with others are frequent during this life stage and may be caused by various factors including perceived rejection by another, volatile emotions leading to hostile outbursts, or power struggles. These may be tempered, however, by a strong desire to be liked or accepted, feelings of affection, and value placed on the other's status.

When a relationship that has been ambivalent in nature is terminated through death, the survivor's grief may be complicated in nature. Typically an increased level of guilt is tied to a strong feeling that there is unfinished business and a loss of opportunity to reconcile differences (Rando, 1993b). An extremely high-risk situation for negative bereavement outcome is the case whereby a peer is murdered by one's own action. The murdered individual—a person presently characterized as being a strong adversary—may, in fact, at one time have been a friend. This situation is characteristic of numerous gang-related murders.

ADOLESCENTS' COGNITIVE DEVELOPMENT

Adolescence is a period of significant change in several developmental arenas. One of the most significant shifts is in the area of thinking processes. Piaget (1972), the cognitive theorist, identified the ability to think abstractly as one of the hallmarks of formal operational thinking that typically unfolds during the adolescent years. Adolescents are also able to think hypothetically and are more flexible in their thinking capacity than are younger children.

Adults are often dismayed over the intensity of a grief response that adolescents sometimes exhibit after the death of a classmate whom they barely even knew. This seemingly exaggerated grief reaction is related to the adolescent's unfolding intellectual capabilities. "The cognitive process . . . influences the ability to comprehend complex concepts, determines the types of questions and concerns adolescents may have about death, and modifies their own experience of the death of a loved one" (Cook & Oltjenbruns, 1989, p. 221).

With the ability to think in the abstract, which develops during adolescence, comes the ability to face one's personal mortality. This is of significance in understanding why some adults believe adolescents overreact to the death of someone the teenager hardly even knew. Perceived similarity to the person who has died may magnify a grief experience (Barnes, 1978). Teenagers may perceive themselves to be similar to adolescent agemates merely as a result of shared youth or group membership. Therefore, some teens may exhibit an intense grief reaction to the death of an age-mate—even when the deceased was a distant acquaintance or classmate rather than a true friend.

Another characteristic of adolescent thinking is a strong sense of egocentrism (Elkind, 1967). As adolescents develop abstract thinking capabilities, they are able to evaluate their own thought processes as well as conceptualize other peoples' thoughts about them. Many adolescents believe that others around them—peers in particular—are extremely interested in all they do and, as a result, may believe that others are continually judging them. This sense of egocentrism contributes to self-consciousness and a preoccupation with one's own appearance as well as with other people's reactions toward and interactions with the adolescent (Vander Zanden, 1989).

Adolescents' egocentrism sometimes causes them to personalize various thoughts and behaviors. One example is the situation wherein a teenager who can no longer remember a deceased friend's face or voice or laughter becomes overwhelmed and even frightened by the belief that others would forget him if he also were to die.

A by-product of adolescent egocentrism is termed the *imaginary audience*. Teenagers regard the world as a stage and themselves as the primary actors. What is known as behavior contagion may then be the outcome. Rather than basing one's own actions on clear thought and careful decision making, some adolescents react by copying what others in their social environment are doing. For example, when a teacher entered a ninth-grade classroom to share the news that a student in another home room had been killed in an auto accident over the weekend, six students who knew the deceased through club activities and were good friends got up and ran out of the room crying. A moment later, Misha did the same. However, Misha did not even know the person who was killed. In the days that followed, she continued to be distressed and cried often when others were around. In this situation, Misha was not engaging in a personal grief reaction to this death, but rather was mirroring the reactions of her friends who did know the deceased individual and were truly grieving his death.

Adolescents often think they are being watched carefully by others and judged by those around them. As a result, many teenagers who are dealing with a significant and painful loss following the death of a friend are hesitant to show their grief for fear they will be judged negatively, condemned, or ostracized. Although there has been an increasing understanding of normal grief processes and a heightening awareness of the need to be supportive of the bereaved, many in our society still believe that persons should grieve privately and come to terms with the death of a loved one quickly. In that context, many adolescents may be ashamed or fearful of asking for help, feeling that to do so is to show a sign of weakness.

Another aspect of the egocentrism typical of adolescents is known as the "personal fable" (Elkind, 1967). Many adolescents regard themselves as unique; as a result, these teenagers act as if they do not understand that the rules that govern others also govern themselves. Accordingly, young people often do not seem to realize that certain high-risk behaviors may have serious consequences. The personal fable, then, may contribute to many adolescents' engaging in activities (e.g., experimentation with drugs or driving at extremely high speeds) that may potentially result in death.

Once teenagers are faced with the death of an age-mate, they may be overwhelmed by the sense that the world has let them down, that it is no longer predictable. Their personal fable has been severely challenged. These adolescents are called on to face their own mortality and realize that they, too, are vulnerable to death (O'Brien, Goodenow, & Espin, 1991; Podell, 1989). Another consequence of adolescent egocentrism and the related personal fable arises from the belief that many adolescents have about their own sense of uniqueness (Fleming & Adolph, 1986). When adolescents experience the death of a loved one and grieve that loss, the personal fable may lead them to believe that their grief is so personal and unique that no one can possibly understand what they are going through. This belief, in turn, may contribute to their turning inward after a loss rather than seeking help from others (Corr, Nabe, & Corr, 1994).

PSYCHOSOCIAL TASKS OF ADOLESCENTS

As they mature, adolescents engage in various psychosocial processes including a search for individuation and strengthening a sense of personal identity. Each of these is experienced within the context of peer relationships; therefore, the death of a friend may have a significant impact on these normal developmental processes of adolescence.

Achieving Individuation

Young persons struggle to develop a clear sense of being psychologically separate from their parents through a process known as individuation (Steinberg, 1990). Encouragement to confront one's parents' rules, beliefs, and values is often provided by the adolescent's peer group. When conflict is the result, it is one's friends who offer their emotional support. "As adolescents strive to relinquish psychological dependence on parents, peer groups become a temporary replacement until fully autonomous (psychological) functioning is possible" (Brown, 1990, p. 180). It is important to understand that the process of individuation does not inevitably lead adolescents to negate all that their parents have taught them. For example, research indicates that most adolescents ultimately come to share their parents' political, religious, and moral values (Brown, 1990).

The goal of the individuation process and the struggle to become autonomous ensures that adolescents come to personal conclusions in certain arenas and that their beliefs do not simply mirror parental dictates. Recall that one of the functions of a peer group is to provide support for this process of individuation. The death of a friend who questioned one's beliefs and values, debated one's ideas, and encouraged one to challenge adult authority may leave a profound void, at least for a time, in the psychosocial support network necessary to continue the individuation process.

Strengthening a Sense of Identity

Erikson (1963) defined a variety of developmentally based psychosocial crises that arise throughout the human life cycle. The adolescent stage is marked by the need to achieve a sense of personal identity. This process involves the integration of one's prior experiences, self-evaluation, and feedback derived from the social environment consisting of family and friends. Answers to the question "Who am I" depend on this input (Bigner, 1994).

When a friend dies, there are many associated losses. These include loss of a significant companion; an important confidant; love and personal support; an information resource; a person who provided positive feedback; an individual who challenged one's ideas; and an age-mate who mirrored one's emotions or behaviors. As a result of these multiple losses, bereaved adolescents may not feel as secure as they had before the death of a friend. Thus, they may be more fearful and hesitant in challenging themselves to seek experiences that continue to promote personal growth. When the friend has committed suicide, many teenagers perceive a loss in their own ability to "measure" or evaluate a person they thought they knew.

The death of a friend may affect the development of identity in numerous ways (Podell, 1989). As noted earlier, adolescents who experience the death of an age-mate must now integrate an understanding of personal mortality into their belief systems about themselves. Although this concept may be understood much earlier in an intellectual way, it is often during adolescence that young persons come to appreciate emotionally that they, too, will die and integrate this realization into their sense of personal identity.

Further, the death of a friend provides bereaved adolescents with new experiences and additional insights about themselves, thus expanding the information base used to define a sense of identity. These insights involve personal definitions of heightened loss, appreciation of the intensity of emotions, understanding of the impact of loss on thoughts and behaviors, better understanding of one's coping strategies, insight about one's level of resiliency to crisis situations, and much more.

LOSS OF A FRIEND

Impacts on the Individual

Since the early 1980s, increased attention has been paid to the impact of death on adolescents. Nevertheless, research related to adolescent grief has focused more on bereavement caused by the death of a sibling (Balk, 1983a, 1990; Hogan, 1988) or bereavement resulting from the death of a parent (Gray, 1988) than on grief related to the death of a friend. Notable exceptions include work by O'Brien, Goodenow, and Espin (1991), and Podell (1989).

An important question, then, is whether we can legitimately turn to the literature related to adolescents' grief following the death of a family member when trying to derive insight about normal grief reactions following the death of a friend. A study done by Lurie (1993) found that there are more similarities between these two grief experiences than there are differences. Using the Grief Experience Inventory (Sanders, Mauger, & Strong, 1985), Lurie found only one significant difference between the "friend loss" group and the "family loss" group. These findings suggest that the loss of a close friend precipitates a grief reaction similar to that of the loss of a close family member. The one significant difference found was on the anger/hostility scale, with bereaved friends scoring higher on that scale than did bereaved family members. Lurie (1993) tied this finding to causality of the deaths—adolescent friends more often died from sudden, and often preventable, causes, such as suicide, homicide, or accidents. It is common to see increased anger resulting from these types of deaths.

In a study of 53 adolescents who had experienced the death of a peer, most experienced sadness, shock, disbelief, surprise, anger, and confusion. Other common responses were numbness, fear, and guilt (Schachter, 1991). Because each relationship is unique, we must be sensitive to the fact that no person's grief experience is identical to another's. However, there are commonalities that do allow understanding of typical manifestations, intensity, and duration of grief (Cook & Oltjenbruns, 1989; Podell, 1989).

Although a grief reaction can be described as "normal," it is crucial to understand that a given individual's grief is deeply personal in nature and may be affected by several variables. One variable known to have a significant impact on bereavement reactions is the cause of death. Certain causes, particularly those that are regarded to be somehow preventable, may complicate the grief reaction (Cook & Oltjenbruns, 1989). Deaths resulting from accidents, suicides, homicides, and AIDS are often thought to have been preventable. It is important to note that these particular causes—accidents, suicides, homicides, and AIDS— currently account for most adolescents' deaths. Unique issues also arise during the bereavement period if the death is sudden or violent. Again, these often characterize the deaths of today's adolescents (Schachter, 1991). When a death is thought to be preventable, feelings of guilt and anger are often exacerbated. A violent death often heightens the survivor's preoccupation with the death event itself. Thoughts of the deceased person's last few moments of life intrude on the grieving person's thoughts, together with questions regarding whether the person was in great pain or experienced much fear.

Another factor impacting many adolescents' grief following the death of a friend is the phenomenon of "survivor guilt," which is characterized by the belief that one should have died with, or instead of, the person(s) who died (Cook & Oltjenbruns, 1989). For example, Josh felt extremely guilty after four of his friends were killed in an automobile accident on the way to their homecoming game in a neighboring community. Although he was to have gone with them, he did not because his boss needed him to close the store and had asked him to stay late. For years, Josh struggled with the question of why he was the one who survived.

When an individual is responsible for the death of a friend, the personal sense of guilt may be almost overpowering. In addition, guilt may be exacerbated by blame expressed by others who also cared for the person who died. For example, a rather common death-related occurrence among adolescents is the situation in which a friend is killed at the hand of another who is driving recklessly or unsafely. Not only are these adolescent drivers left with their own personal grief and feelings of guilt, they may also be overwhelmed by the sense of blame and ostracism aimed at them by other community members. In these circumstances, professional intervention is advised.

Personal Resources

Coping Strategies. Throughout childhood and into adulthood, individuals develop a broader range of increasingly mature coping strategies. These are often categorized as emotional, practical, or cognitive coping strategies (Hoffman, Levy-Shiff, Sohlberg, & Zarizki, 1992). During the adolescent years, as there is an increased ability to think abstractly, anticipate future events, construct hypotheses, and evaluate consequences, young persons develop enhanced abilities to use cognitive coping strategies (Phelps & Jarvis, 1994). These new cognitive strategies are then often used in combination with emotional strategies and practical strategies. All three can be helpful in various situations, but there is some indication that those using "higher levels of cognitive coping tended to be more resilient to stressful events" (Hoffman et al., 1992, p. 464). Adolescents should be given information about death, related rituals, bereavement, factors that influence outcomes of grief, and so forth. Certainly many resources are helpful in this regard. These include educational units about death and grief included in the curriculum; conversations with caring, supportive, and knowledgeable adults; and books appropriate for adolescent readers, such as *How to Survive the Loss of a Love* by Colgrove, Bloomfield, and McWilliams (1991) or *Straight Talk About Death for Teenagers: How to Cope with Losing Someone You Love* by Grollman (1993).

Grief is fundamentally a multifaceted reaction to loss; the emotional response is the core of the bereavement experience. It is important to keep in mind that although adolescents do possess many coping strategies, they do not have the same repertoire as do adults nor do they necessarily have any past experience with death to draw from to understand the normalcy of their own grief reactions and the responses of others. To cope more effectively with their powerful emotions and thoughts, it is critical that adolescents find support from those in their social environment.

Social Support.   The adolescent who grieves after the death of a friend has sometimes been described as a disenfranchised griever (Doka, 1989). In this context, disenfranchisement refers to the expectation of the greater society that a particular group or individual has not experienced any significant loss and therefore should not experience a grief reaction. Unfortunately, many adults do not understand the significance of the adolescent friendship relationship that is lost through death and, therefore, do not fully understand the extent of adolescents' grief following the death of a friend (O'Brien, Goodenow, & Espin, 1991). If the centrality or closeness of many adolescent friendships is not appreciated, adults may not understand that intense grief responses are a natural outcome.

In instances in which disenfranchisement occurs, social support is minimized. Lack thereof may have serious outcomes. There is strong indication that social support does help moderate some manifestations of grief and also ultimate resolution of the loss (Balk, 1990; Floerchinger, 1991; Lurie, 1993; Rando, 1993b). Lurie (1993) found that those late adolescents who perceived that they had greater social support from parents, friends, and support organizations had lower levels of despair, anger and hostility, social isolation, somatization, depersonalization, and guilt following the death of a loved one than did those individuals perceiving lower levels of support.

Potential Impacts on Surviving Friendships: A Model of Secondary Loss and Incremental Grief

Until recently, the study of bereavement has focused on the grief of the individual who has experienced the loss. It is crucial to realize, however, that "important losses of mutual significance tend to have immediate and powerful repercussions in interpersonal relationships" (Derdeyn & Waters, 1981, p. 483). When exploring the impact of the death of a friend during adolescence, one must look beyond an individual's grief response and also examine the impact of the death on surviving friends' relationships. To accomplish this, a model of secondary loss and incremental grief is presented in the context of adolescents who are experiencing the death of a friend.

For the sake of simplicity, the explanation presented here focuses on dyadic friendship relationships; however, the model is helpful in understanding larger peer group networks as well. By definition, a peer group is a social system; systems theory, then, may provide helpful insight into understanding the impact of an adolescent's death on the group members who survive. A system has intertwining emotional, communicational, and cognitive aspects. Any change in one component of the system affects the functioning of each of the other components.

Secondary Loss and Incremental Grief. Most individuals expect to receive support from their friends during stressful life events (Berndt & Perry, 1986). Level of support is perceived to vary in relationship to the perceived closeness of the individuals involved (e.g., friends are expected to provide more support than acquaintances). If two friends are grieving the death of another peer, it may be difficult—if not impossible, at least in the short run—to provide the mutual support that had earlier marked their friendship. If even one person in a friendship dyad is grieving the death of another person, the stress on the surviving relationship may be so significant that yet another loss occurs when the two surviving friends withdraw from one another.

To understand this phenomenon better, a model of secondary loss and incremental grief is presented, together with illustrative case studies. Secondary loss is defined as a stressful change in a surviving relationship as a result of a grief experience; this stress is marked by changes in interaction style, perceived closeness, comfort, and support. If the stress is significant enough, the surviving friends may withdraw from one another for a period, and, in some instances, the friendship is ended. Incremental grief is defined as the additive factor of grief resulting from multiple related losses—loss of earlier closeness, comfort, and support—and, possibly, the loss of the friendship itself.

Jack, Paulo, and David had played together since the 3rd grade. They lived in the same neighborhood, biked to school together, played on the same teams at school, and were known to many as the "three musketeers." During the 10th grade, Paulo died in a boating accident while on a family vacation.

During the months following Paulo's death, the school counselor noticed that Jack and David no longer spent time together outside of class and seemed hostile toward one another. The counselor then spoke with each individually about what had unfolded in their relationship.

Jack described his anger toward David after Paulo's death. "Dave must not have been as good a friend as I thought. He left when I needed him most; he wouldn't even listen when I wanted to talk about Paulo. When I cried in front of him once, he got up and left the room. . . . I don't understand; I thought we were friends . . . and now I think I hate him. . . . Even though being around David is hard since he reminds me of all the good times we had with Paulo, I do need him back! . . . How can I hate him and need him all at the same time?"

In a parallel conversation with David about what had happened to his friendship with Jack after Paulo's death, Dave shared the following with the school counselor.

"I hurt so bad that I couldn't even listen to someone else who was hurting. Particularly to Jack. . . . He was the only best friend I had left and I couldn't bear to feel his hurt, too. . . . Now he's cut me off, he is totally cold towards me and he usually blows up when I do try to say something. I guess he doesn't want to be friends anymore. When I think about this, and I do a lot, I feel even worse. And I didn't think that was possible . . . 'cause I honestly thought my heart had been torn out of my chest when I heard that Paulo had died. Now sometimes I think Jack is also dead and gone—he may as well be, we are so far away from each other any more. It's awful; I don't understand what is going on. . . . If Jack cared about our friendship, he'd reach out. He must not care! I know he doesn't understand me any more and some days I think my heart is exploding all over again. I'm not sure I can take it!"

Discussion. Paulo's death comprises the primary loss component of this model. Jack and David responded to Paulo's death differently; that is, there was a dissynchrony of grief responses (i.e., variability of grief-related experiences and time taken for resolution of the grief). Jack and David also had discrepant coping styles (i.e., different strategies for coming to terms with the death).

As illustrated in the case study, Jack and David experienced a secondary loss—a stressful change in their previously close relationship. In turn, this secondary loss triggered yet another grief reaction. David felt as if he had lost "another best friend" and that he hurt all the more as a result. This outcome comprises the incremental grief component of the model.

The previous example illustrated the case where two surviving friends both knew the individual who had died. Secondary loss and the resultant incremental grief may also be the outcome of a situation in which only one of the two friends knew the deceased individual. The following is an example of this latter case.

Cari and Tammy lived next door to each other and had been friends for 6 years. They were in the same Girl Scout troop, had slumber parties together, and frequently ate at each other's homes. When 16-year-old Cari was killed by a hit-and-run driver, Tammy was devastated by her friend's death.

Tammy had also been friends with Leah for quite a long time. Tammy and Leah had gone to church camp together for several years, saw each other every Sunday at church, and played together frequently since their parents were close friends. Although Tammy and Leah had known each other for an extended time period, Leah had never even met Cari.

Leah was saddened to hear of Cari's death and was very concerned for her friend, Tammy, who was clearly grieving the loss. However, Leah did not truly understand the impact of the death on Tammy and ultimately expressed anger that Tammy refused to "get over it." After observing the stress on their relationship and overhearing an angry interchange between them, the youth minister at their church finally asked both Tammy and Leah to explain what they were feeling.

Tammy shared the following: "Cari was like a sister to me. I could tell her all my secrets, and she would always cheer me up when I was down. . . . She always made me laugh, and I helped her with her homework. One of the reasons we were such good friends was the fact that we were good at different things and didn't ever compete. . . . Cari told me I was so smart I would probably get a scholarship and be accepted into any college I wanted to attend. When Cari told me things like that, I believed her and was proud of myself. Now that she is gone, I can't even concentrate. I keep flunking tests; Cari was wrong, I guess I am actually stupid! It feels like I don't know who I am anymore or what I am good at. . . . And now things are even worse, Leah wants me to be just like I used to be. Level-headed and happy. I can't! I keep seeing Cari in my mind; I close my eyes and see a car hitting her. I am so angry . . . it didn't have to happen.

I try to tell Leah what I need—I need a friend who will listen, be there, let me cry. . . . And I am sick of Leah telling me to get over it. She just doesn't understand! She didn't even know Cari. Leah doesn't even know she is hurting me, and now I have lost another friend because of it. It isn't fair. Now there is no one to talk to; what am I going to do—Cari is dead, and now I can't even relate to Leah."

From her perspective, Leah shared the following with the youth minister:

"It's been two months since Cari died. I know Tammy loved her, but I can't understand why she keeps crying. She used to be happy and I want her to be that way again. We had such good times together, and now there is nothing. I feel like I am avoiding her at church, and I make excuses when her folks plan to come over to see my parents. They always used to bring Tammy, too. But now I don't know how to act around her. We used to tell jokes and talk about boys when she was at my house, but now she hardly says anything. I don't understand. . . . When Tammy lost a friend, I lost one, too! I didn't even know Cari, but I feel her death changed my life. I am pretty shy, and I don't have many friends. To lose Tammy this way is one of the worst things I have ever had to deal with. She is alive, but our friendship is almost dead. . . . It hurts

so bad, and I don't even know what to do about it. I am not sure Tammy even notices or cares, she is so wrapped up in her own feelings that it may not even matter to her."

Discussion. Leah supported Tammy immediately after Cari's death. After a few weeks, however, Tammy perceived that Leah no longer seemed to understand that she still needed to grieve and that she needed Leah's support. Tammy expressed frustration about Leah's perceived lack of sensitivity in such statements as "Leah does not understand why I still need to cry." "She wants me to be my 'old' fun self and that just makes me mad." "I don't think she really cares about me or our friendship or she'd understand."

Ultimately, Tammy and Leah did terminate their interactions with one another, causing a secondary loss. Tammy believed that no matter how much she explained her feelings and no matter how explicitly she described her needs for support, Leah would not or could not understand. Losing each other's friendship caused both Leah and Tammy much anger and pain, components of the incremental grief reaction.

When others in their social network do not understand the grief process (e.g., common manifestations, and the duration and intensity of grief), bereaved individuals often conclude that others are not supportive in the desired fashion. This is reflected in the second illustration. Conversely, the nongrieving individual, Leah, felt rebuffed when Tammy did not appreciate the help that Leah did offer to her. When Tammy vented her anger and withdrew as a result of her deep sadness over Cari's death, Leah withdrew from the relationship as well.

In a crisis situation, when individuals begin to distance themselves from a social network, the network is likely eventually to withdraw from the individual as well. In this case, Leah and Tammy's mutual withdrawal after Cari's death created a secondary loss and triggered grief reactions resulting from the ultimate severing of what had earlier been close friendship ties.

Some Implications of Secondary Loss and Incremental Grief. When there is a stressful or negative change in peer relationships following the death of a friend, the ultimate outcome varies from situation to situation. In some instances, the survivors who experienced secondary loss and the resultant incremental grief may ultimately reconcile and rebuild a bond between them—one that becomes even stronger than it had been before. In other instances, however, the secondary loss may be so significant that the relationship is essentially terminated. Regardless of the ultimate outcome, the secondary loss phenomenon may be expected to cause, at least for a time, added pain to that already caused by the primary loss (i.e., the death of a friend). This constitutes the incremental grief phenomenon. It is important to note that, although the experience of secondary loss and its stressful aftermath is a relatively common phenomenon, it is not universal.

POSITIVE OUTCOMES

Most discussions of adolescent bereavement typically focus on powerful emotions and stressful reactions, but there often are positive outcomes for the bereaved. These positive outcomes usually are related to individual growth and also to impact on surviving relationships. Oltjen-bruns (1991) found that 96% of her sample reported at least one positive outcome to their bereavement experiences. These included having a deeper appreciation of life; developing emotional strength; enhancing problem-solving skills; showing greater caring to loved ones; strengthening of emotional bonds with others; increasing empathy for others; and developing better communication skills. Such outcomes can be particularly important for adolescents who may be encountering an awareness of these feelings, characteristics, or skills for the first time.

Many examples of positive outcomes are reflected in the following quotations, which were included in a midwestern town's local newspaper (Huckeby, 1993, pp. 15–16) printed to pay tribute to the local high school's graduating seniors. In this particular class, four adolescents died during the 3 years just before their completing school. These individuals, too, were remembered by their friends. The following are direct quotations contributed to the graduation edition of the paper by several of the 17- and 18-year-old classmates of the four who had died:

- "G. taught me, even before he died, to appreciate life, and fun, and friends."
- "Thanks for being there, and making me laugh! Thanks for wonderful memories and for the fun together. Thank you for being special, you were my best friend. We love you and miss you and we're going on in a good way, holding your memory with us."
- "I was lucky to know you. You taught me a lot about life."
- "Can't think of you and not laugh . . . appreciate getting to meet you . . . I could have passed up on your dying and leaving us but at least I have the memories and the laughter. I will cherish every day for the rest of my life."

For all the pain that the death of a friend elicits, there can be many new insights and feelings that also result. These can contribute positively to the adolescent's overall development.

IMPLICATIONS OF PEER LOSS
DURING ADOLESCENCE

Parents

Even though many believe adolescence is a time marked by much "storm and stress" between adolescents and their parents, research indicates most adolescents depend on their parents for emotional support, and turn to them for advice and counsel (Steinberg, 1990). There are, however, several factors that may threaten parents' ability to provide support needed by adolescents who have lost a friend to death.

Adolescents often do not share much informational detail or many feelings about their friends with their own parents. As a result, parents may not understand the true importance of the bond between adolescents and their peers. When adolescent children, then, experience the death of a peer, parents may not be able to understand the significance of the loss and empathize with the resultant grief. If they do not understand normal adolescent development, they may not understand the intensity of their adolescent child's reaction to the death of a friend or an acquaintance.

Further, because of membership in a particular cohort group, many parents of today's adolescents were rather protected from the death of their own age-mates during their teenage years. Many childhood diseases had been cured or controlled; many who lost friends did so to the Vietnam War. Today's parents grew up at a time when AIDS was unknown, drive-by shootings were unheard of, drunk-driving accidents claimed fewer lives, and there were fewer adolescent suicides. As a result, parents of the current adolescent generation are less likely to have had personal experiences with the death of a peer during their teenage years or personal experience with loss resulting from those causes of adolescent death that are much more common today.

For parents to be able to provide support to their teenage children, they need substantive information about factors that may complicate the normal grief process (i.e., issues of preventability, violence, and suddenness) and bereavement outcomes that are commonly tied to particular types of death. Many parents also need help in learning how to communicate with their children about the loss and need assistance in identifying specific strategies for offering support (McNeil, 1986). This is crucial given the fact that many of the parents of today's adolescents were socialized during a time when bereaved individuals were expected to be stoic and to deal with their grief in private.

Parents who show sincere caring to their adolescent children follow-ing the death of an age-mate help to counteract what might otherwise be a feeling of disenfranchisement. This support also communicates to the adolescent that parents recognize that each friend is unique and cannot be replaced quickly even though the adolescent may have sev-eral other friends as well. Parents who imply to their children that they should curtail their grief simply because they believe the deceased can quickly be replaced by another relationship are inappropriately mini-mizing the significance of the loss.

School Personnel

When an adolescent dies, many school personnel are also affected by the death. If teachers and counselors are themselves grieving the death of a student, it may make their efforts to provide support to bereaved friends and classmates more difficult (McNeil, Silliman, & Swihart, 1991). As a result, it can be helpful to prepare school personnel in ad-vance of a crisis. For example, administrators might arrange regular in-service training sessions related to the normal grief experience so that school employees can increase their understanding of common mani-festations of grief as well as factors related to intensity and duration. This insight can support the staff's efforts to assist students who are grieving the death of a classmate and may also help teachers, coun-selors, and other helpers become more accepting of their own reactions to the death of a member of their school community.

Further, many schools find it helpful to define a general approach to be taken at the time of an adolescent's death. Certainly each school's plan will be somewhat different, depending on resources available; fur-ther, each death-related situation is highly individualistic. Nonetheless, it is important to have done some planning before the crisis of a stu-dent's dying. The following are examples (McNeil, Silliman, & Swihart, 1991; Mauk & Weber, 1991) of those areas to be included in such prob-lem-solving discussions:

1. Notification of the student's death to members of the school com-munity
2. Communication with individuals outside of the school setting who are likely to interact with the bereaved students (e.g, parents, ministers, or coaches)
3. Expression of sympathy to the deceased student's family and friends

4. Methods for providing information and answering questions about the death
5. Opportunity for students and others to become involved in meaningful rituals to pay tribute to the individual, say goodbye, memorialize, and so on
6. Ongoing opportunities for students to share their thoughts and feelings related to the loss of the relationship, the death event itself, and subsequent implications, as well as methods for providing support

Additionally, a school's planning process should include discussion of how to provide support to staff members who are personally impacted by the death. Teachers, counselors, coaches, club advisers, janitorial staff, and others also experience a unique loss because of the student's death. Their grief should also be recognized. Some may desire the flexibility to take some time away from the school setting to attend the funeral or to grieve privately. Some may need counseling support or opportunities to process their own reactions to the death.

Researchers

In recent years, researchers have been increasingly involved in studying grief reactions that are the result of the death of family members—spouses, parents, children, and siblings. Although it is evident that many adolescents experience the death of a peer, little work has been done in this area. Yet for many in this age span, the death of a close friend may dissolve a relationship that is as close or closer than some family bonds.

Research focusing on adolescent grief following the death of a friend must consider variables that are integral to the study of the relationships themselves. For example, there is a developmental change over time regarding the level of intimacy in peer relationships. Adolescents usually describe their friendships as being more intimate than do younger children (Berndt & Perry, 1986). One arena needing further study is the relationship between perceived intimacy and the intensity and duration of the grief experience. Because of maturation of intimacy, does death of a friend during adolescence have a different bereavement outcome than death of a friend during childhood?

Many researchers have found that females report greater intimacy and levels of attachment in their friendships than do males (e.g., Raja, McGee, & Stanton, 1992) as well as greater affection, social support, and enhancement of self-worth in their friendships than do males

(DuBois & Hirsch, 1990; Furman & Buhrmester, 1985). Given the current literature on gender differences associated with the nature of friendship relationships themselves, researchers should attempt to measure key characteristics of the relationship lost because of the death of a friend. If possible, this factor should be examined as an intervening variable when studying male-female differences in grief reactions following adolescents' loss of an age-mate.

CONCLUSION

Many young persons grieve the death of a friend during adolescence. Developmental issues during this life stage have an impact on the significance of the loss itself. Because friends play a central role in dealing with various psychosocial tasks, the death of a friend may put at risk or delay successful completion of those tasks. Further, developmental characteristics and capabilities (e.g., adolescent egocentrism and cognitive capacity) have an impact on the manifestations of the grief response. Coping strategies and perceived support systems also have an impact on bereavement outcome.

Although death of a friend during adolescence is relatively common, little research has directly focused on this specific loss event. There are many questions yet to be answered in this arena. Insights derived from such study will be helpful to all those called on to give adolescents support after the death of a friend.

III

Interventions

Earlier chapters in this book frequently mention ways of helping adolescents who are confronted with specific types of deaths or bereavement experiences. Chapters that follow in Part III examine intervention modalities that are distinguished not by the kind of death-related encounter that has occurred in the life of an adolescent but by the way in which assistance is offered.

This discussion of ways to help adolescents who are coping with death and bereavement begins with an analysis of the families within which such adolescents live and function. In chapter 11, Marcia Lattanzi-Licht explains the importance of noting the family context of adolescent life by describing different types of family systems, their responses to loss, and ways in which families with adolescents can be helped to cope more effectively with loss.

In chapter 12, Robert and Eileen Stevenson describe ways to complement efforts undertaken in the home and by religious institutions through educational programs for adolescents about dying, death, loss, and grief. Such programs work within the school settings which play such a prominent role in the lives of adolescents to help these youngsters prepare themselves for encounters with death and bereavement before they actually take place. In chapter 12, "death education" (as it has come to be called) is shown to be valuable as a preventive enterprise specially designed to help early and middle adolescents in four principal areas: depression and suicide; HIV and AIDS; violence; and parenting skills. This chapter also examines qualifications of death educators, the curriculum for a high school death education program, central questions that need to be faced in setting up such a program, and existing models for such curricula.

Once a traumatic event has occurred, it is too late for prior preparation, but not too late to undertake "postvention" or intervention after the fact in educational institutions. This subject is explored in chapters 13 and 14 in parallel analyses of postvention at the high school and college levels. In chapter 13, David Hill and Yvonne Foster offer a rationale, structural description, and set of guidelines for establishing postvention programs at the high school and middle school levels. Similarly, in chapter 14, Ralph Rickgarn explains the value of postvention programs for late adolescents in college and offers suggestions for implementing such programs.

Interventions that can supplement short-term postvention and that are usually conducted over a longer period are represented here by support groups for bereaved adolescents and by professional counseling or therapy. In chapter 15, Richard Tedeschi describes the role of bereavement support groups for adolescents, issues to consider in establishing and running such groups, and potential benefits of such groups. In chapter 16, LaNae Valentine explains the role of a counselor, therapist, or other professional in assisting adolescents who are coping with death and bereavement. This discussion includes indicators for professional referral, factors to consider in assessing a grief response, and techniques for working with individual adolescents alone or with adolescents and members of their families together.

Finally, in chapter 17 Michael Stevens and Julie Dunsmore outline central issues and strategies for working with adolescents who are coping with a life-threatening illness. These authors are particularly sensitive to the importance of good communication in interactions with such adolescents. Also, they offer useful guidelines for helping siblings, parents, other family members, peers, and friends of such adolescents—both for their own sake and for the sake of the adolescent with the life-threatening illness.

11

Helping Families with Adolescents Cope with Loss

Marcia Lattanzi-Licht

Families with adolescents exist in a delicate balance that combines closeness and anticipated separation. Often these families experience the best and the worst of the many elements associated with human relationships and attachments. Loss and grief during this time of family life can create a complex challenge, one that is full of disruption and conflict (Carter & McGoldrick, 1988; McGoldrick & Walsh, 1991; Walsh & McGoldrick, 1988, 1991).

In understanding adolescent grief, it is essential to appreciate the influence of the family. This chapter explores the unique context and dynamics of adolescent and family responses to the death of an immediate member, such as a parent or a sibling. It also examines ways to assess family and adolescent functioning, and suggests a framework for offering effective support.

Although adolescence is a time of spreading wings and leaving the nest, young people rely on the fact that the secure nest will be there when they return. Family life is the safe foundation that adolescents count on, rebel against, and take for granted. The growing autonomy and maturing sense of adolescent identity create structural and role changes within the family. The death of a parent can pose a level of threat related to survival and developmental concerns (Meshot & Leitner, 1992; see chapter 8). Although the issues involved in the death of a sibling are different, they may also have a great impact on personality formation (Hogan & DeSantis, 1992; Rosen, 1986; see chapter 9).

Adolescents face developmental tasks that can be seen as counter to the needs of grieving people. Adolescent developmental demands can create added confusion and distress in grieving families (Mattessich & Hill, 1987; Rodgers, 1973). And yet it also is within the family that adolescents can safely work through developmental tasks and conflicts, regain their stability, and begin to integrate loss experiences.

Numerous writers and theorists have discussed the importance of the family framework in the lives of adolescents and in their adaptation to loss (Preto, 1988; Gelcer, 1983; Vollman, Ganzert, Picher, & Williams, 1971). Within the context of the family and the view of the past family life, the true picture of adolescent grief emerges.

FAMILY VIEW

A family is characterized as an entire emotional system involving three or more generations that lives through time (Terkelson, 1980). Both living and deceased persons may be included in the family, and their functioning patterns, secrets, and myths reflect a past and history that may be a powerful influence in the present (Carter & McGoldrick, 1988). Understanding of a *family system* involves viewing the structure and dynamics of interrelatedness among members, beyond the positions and responses of individuals. In summarizing the shared assumptions of family systems clinicians and researchers, Levitt (1986) emphasized the following:

1. Mutually interdependent members who are intertwined in their functioning and growth
2. Unique experiences that create unique rules (also influenced by the larger group to which the family relates)
3. Different ways families respond to change and to external influences
4. Unique ways individual families perceive and respond to stresses within and outside the family
5. Inadequate coping that demands family reorganization

After more than 40 years of research on families, future research will most likely attempt to develop a better understanding of the nature of stresses that affect families as well as more in-depth study of family resources that include coping skills, communication and problem solving, and the ability to incorporate support (McCubbin et al., 1980).

A systems perspective creates a way of viewing families as worthwhile, capable, and open to influence by their environment and circumstances (Hall & Kirschling, 1990). This humanizing perspective generates a hopeful, optimistic foundation for work with families at painful times in their history (Sills & Hall, 1985). In addition to acknowledging capacities for learning, change, and growth, a family systems orientation also positively affirms the collective nature of human experience and survival. That understanding can be a reassuring counterpoint for the assumed separateness of adolescents.

There has been an increased focus on the provision of family-centered services during critical points in a family's life. At either end of the life continuum, the birthing and dying process, helping professionals include and welcome the active participation of family members. Hospice care has been a major influence for family involvement in situations of terminal illness. With the support of hospice, family members provide care for their loved ones, typically in the home. Adolescents can be in the role of the primary person caring for a parent, or they can assume major responsibilities for the functioning of the home and care for younger siblings (Lackey & Gates, 1995).

FAMILY CONTEXT

Perhaps the most important element of family life for adolescents lies in the degree and ways that they meet their individual needs. The significant corollary is the importance of adolescents' contributions to the ways that the needs of other family members are met. Grief represents a time of disruption in the ability of a family to meet each other's needs and is by definition a time of deficit.

In general, when a family experiences loss and bereavement additional demands are often placed on adolescents to meet the needs of the surviving parent or the remaining siblings. Adolescents are frequently asked to take on more adult responsibilities and to be more involved with the family during the time of grief.

As adolescents strive for independence, parental efforts at control can exaggerate normal conflicts and ambivalence. A death in the nuclear family prior to resolution of these natural conflicts can create more guilt and complicate the family's grief. There is an increased incidence of guilt reported in families with conflicted or dysfunctional relationships (Shanfield, Benjamin, & Swain, 1988). To understand the impact of grief on families with adolescents, it is helpful to consider family roles and characteristics as well as elements that distinguish family functioning.

Roles

Roles help a family define unique ways of functioning and of valuing its members' contributions. Grief involves not just a reallocation of roles, but also a renegotiation and redefinition of behaviors and interactions (White, 1991). In smaller families, there is more difficulty in the read-justment of roles because, quite simply, there are fewer people to divide and take on the roles of the person who died. Everyday routines and rit-uals change, and adolescents can be put in the position of maintaining the emotional life of the family.

Family Characteristics

Grief is a time of unmet expectations, expectations that were realistic before the death of the family member. Vess, Moreland, and Schwebel (1986) analyzed developmental roles and the stage of the family in the life cycle related to death of a parent. In examining elements that in-cluded the type of death and previous role allocations, they suggested that the most significant influence was the "person-oriented" or "posi-tion-oriented" characteristics of the family. Person-oriented families were represented by open communication, a flexible power structure, and achieved roles. They were more able to reallocate roles effectively following the death of a parent. Families who are position oriented with closed communication, ascribed roles, a more rigid power structure, and dependent on cultural norms lacked role reallocating mechanisms needed to ensure adequate family functioning.

Partridge and Kotler (1987) suggested that family type is a limited concept in exploring the complexity of family influence on adolescent well-being following a major loss. They emphasized exploring a "family environment" model that examines the quality of family interaction and family processes, not just the general sociological classifications of families.

In healthy adolescents, the most important influence is a positive marital interaction with intimacy, trust, and mutual enjoyment. Firm generational boundaries and effective parental coalitions characterized by shared power and respect are usually present in healthy adolescent experiences (Kleiman, 1981). Although the death of a parent does not erase these elements in an adolescent's history, these considerations do give us some idea of the dynamic challenges the family faces. In gen-eral, families with good parental boundaries continue to hold to them following the death of one of the parents. The adjustment process de-mands that the distinction between the surviving parent's and teen's boundaries and roles remains clear. In general, family patterns can either help or hinder teens in the mourning process. The lack of ability to cope with loss may, in fact, be characteristic of the entire family (Krupp, 1972).

NATURE OF THE FAMILY

On the continuum of health and well being, there are many elements that distinguish family functioning. Knapp (1986) has summarized characteristics of families that can mediate and buffer the stress of loss, or that can exaggerate the distress. In labeling them "integrated" or "isolated" families, a picture of the type of family structure of each emerges.

Characteristics of "Integrated" Families

The following are characteristics of integrated families:

- Better prepared and equipped to handle stress
- Open channels of communication and cooperation
- Family-based response to stress
- Trusting of other people
- Warm interrelationships with each other
- Confidence in themselves and others
- Free interactions with the larger social system
- More personal, family, and external resources

These characteristics all hold a family in good stead in preventing crises in ordinary times, and in effectively meeting the crisis of a death of an immediate family member. On the opposite end of the continuum, "isolate" families are less able to mobilize an effective response to crisis and are limited in their abilities to deal with grief.

Characteristics of "Isolate" Families

The following are characteristics of isolate families:

- Individual rather than family viewpoint
- Devastated by the crisis of the death
- Sense of isolation

- Little or no support available
- Internally separate, lacking closeness
- Operate as a closed system
- Minimal social contacts within and outside family
- Limited resources to draw on

These polarities outlined by Knapp (1986) are probably representative of few actual families. Nevertheless, his construct of polarities identifies characteristics of families that can help to identify areas of vulnerability for teens. Although most families would operate somewhere between these two extremes of "integrated" and "isolate" families, beliefs and resources that are nurtured and supported by a family are key determinants of the responses that the family system will make to the death of one of its members. *Adolescents are influenced by their family's characteristics; their options for responding and coping are either maximized or limited depending on the family context.*

All conceptual frameworks or models of understanding families attempt to define family structure and process in the context of offering effective support in times of crisis (Levitt, 1986). Family theorists and researchers agree that well-functioning families display four characteristics:

1. Members believe that the family is a safe, accepting, loving group where expression of members is encouraged.
2. Good problem-solving and communication skills in which negotiation is a central element are employed.
3. Flexible coping styles are used within the family.
4. The family is able to work as a unit and as individuals with close ties and clear boundaries (Levitt, 1986).

RESPONSES TO GRIEF

For many reasons, grief can be an isolating, private experience for adolescents. Developmental tasks, school pressures, restricted emotional expression, and the difficulties that others have in identifying or supporting the needs of adolescents may lead to grief that is dealt with slowly or in intermittent outbursts (Raphael, 1983). This can add to family confusion and instability given the already existing levels of developmental vulnerability. In their interactions with each other, members of families with adolescents often feel a sense that "I can't do anything right."

Hankoff (1975) noted that themes and concepts of death are woven into all aspects of adolescent development. One of the accomplishments of adolescence is the development of a psychological framework for direct emotional response to loss. Grief responses are seen as a type of crisis reaction, wherein there is an initial mobilization of an adolescent's psychological coping abilities. This "crisis reactivity" is believed to be an important aspect of emotional functioning in adults.

Adolescent grief responses may differ from those of other family members in that adolescence is basically a time of transition and uncertainty. This uncertainty can lead adolescents to suppress or repress their emotional responses. Adolescents often feel unsure, hesitant, deficient, and lacking support from others. They also report heightened intense shock, disbelief, and a greater sense of loss in bereavement, along with sleep disturbances and increased dream activity. A sibling loss puts adolescents at higher risk for failing to grieve the loss because of their own internal restraints and because the communications of those around them often limit the possibilities to do so (Rosen, 1986; see chapter 9). Grieving adolescents, like adults, will experience the conflicted emotions of guilt, anger, powerlessness, withdrawal, and isolation, in addition to feelings of overprotection. The concerns of adolescents experiencing grief typically involve the degree, timing, and opportunities for expression of these difficult responses.

In the family context, adolescents may feel insecure with the death of a parent or sibling, and overly concerned about the surviving parent(s)' grief. They may not express their own responses in an attempt to spare or protect the parent(s), and may only begin to cope with their grief when the parent(s) seem stable. Also, adolescents may adopt adult roles and responsibilities in the family. That is, adolescents may strive to become like adults in their bereavement behaviors, a response that some families may welcome (Silverman & Worden, 1992). However, this is an adaptation that can lead to a denial or repression of the youth's grief as well as unproductive patterns of adult dependency on the adolescent. It is of major importance that families not put an adolescent in the roles of the deceased parent or sibling, robbing the youth of normal identity formation efforts.

Although ambivalence is present in all relationships, it can be exaggerated during adolescence, and related to the separation process. When high degrees of ambivalence are present in a family relationship and the person dies, an adolescent is faced with more complicated and complex mourning. Guilt and self-blame in these adolescents can be extreme. The acknowledgment and reassurance of other family members about the conflicted dynamic is of major importance in decreasing the adolescent's self blame.

One of the nearly universal responses to loss is the overwhelming sense of being changed by the experience of grief, the sense of never being the same again. Adolescents experience this "changed self" response to grief as a major burden. Their carefree attitude of invulnerability is lost and replaced by a more fearful, reflective, "older" self. Also, grieving adolescents may have difficulty fitting in with peers who are living in the normal dramas of adolescence. The gap between everyday adolescent concerns and the concerns of a grieving adolescent can intensify feelings of being different and isolated, feelings that are not desirable for adolescents.

A key goal of adolescence is peer identification, to belong with and be like the members of one's peer group. Feeling different and isolated are common experiences of grief, when there is a self-focusing and self-consciousness not unlike that of adolescence. These feelings are intensified and reflected in a family where grieving parent(s) and siblings also are not themselves. Adolescents react to the sorrow of their parent(s) and may avoid them, longing not only for the deceased parent or sibling, but for the surviving parent(s) to be the way that they used to be. Extreme patterns may be seen in those adolescents who spend far more time at home than before the death, or in those who avoid the home, the family, and their sorrow deliberately. In general, adolescents find greater responsibilities and fewer rewards at home during the adaptation to the loss of the parent or sibling.

Mary was 13 when her only brother, Pete, 15, was killed in an auto accident. A year later, Mary seemed depressed and spent little time with friends. She was an excellent student, and also played high school track and basketball. Mary's parents had divorced 5 years earlier, and she lived primarily with her mother and stepfather, but spent time each week with her Dad. Mary felt that she could not tell either of her parents about her sorrow over Pete's death because of the degree of their distress. She believed that she had to be "the perfect child" now and do everything that she could to make her parents happy. Her friends did not talk to her about Pete, even though they had all been close. Feeling very alone, Mary turned to her dog, Peppy, her journal, and a strong faith as her comforts. Occasionally, Mary talked to the high school counselor who sought her out, concerned over Mary's weight loss. The counselor referred Mary to a loss group sponsored by the local hospice, where meetings were held concurrently with the Bereaved Parents Group. Mary's parents alternated in taking her to the teen group and also attended the parents' group.

Mary lost her lifelong companion, her buddy, and her favorite friend when her brother Pete was killed. They had always formed a strong coalition of sup-

port for each other that was especially helpful after their parents divorced. Mary felt unable to relate to her friends and inadequate to take her brother's place with her parents. In the loss group she learned to talk directly to her parents about her feelings and concerns. She told her Dad that she did not want to go skiing every weekend of winter vacations and asked her Mom to spend more time at home.

Talking with other teens made Mary feel less like she was "the only one" with her grief. She gradually developed a friendship with a classmate whose parents had recently divorced. Mary also began a friendship with an 11th-grade boy who was caring toward her. She continued to struggle with feelings of loneliness and depression, but used her religious faith as a source of constant comfort.

Because Mary continued to struggle with moderate levels of depression in high school, her mother contacted a local counselor. Both parents shared responsibility in bringing Mary to her sessions and in assuming payment. Two-and-a-half years after Pete's death, Mary continued to miss him and struggled with her loneliness. She was getting high grades and participated in numerous school activities. She often felt that she related better to adults than she did to young people her age. However, she also felt strongly that her parents both placed high expectations on her, and did not spend time listening to her and to her concerns. Earlier in the month her dog, Peppy, was hit by a car, and Mary no longer found as much strength in her faith.

Mary was seen in individual counseling for 16 sessions during 6 months and for an additional 3 sessions before her graduation from high school. The nature and importance of the loss of her only and very close sibling was a profound one for this exceptionally bright and sensitive young woman. The care-taking roles she assumed for both her parents, as well as the assumptions that she could not express her own needs or concerns, created major conflicts for her and increased her sense of aloneness.

Counseling emphasized the need to form clearer roles and more boundaries with her parents. Each parent participated in a session during which Mary was able to express her concerns and suggest ways that she could feel more clarity in the expectations that she was experiencing in her relationships with her parents. She also explored her worries about leaving her parents when she would go away to college. Each parent offered reassurance and gave permission and encouragement for Mary to pursue her own interests.

Mary was also encouraged to spend more time with friends with whom she was comfortable, and to participate more in the activities that she enjoyed, like music and singing, rather than sports, at which she felt she "had to" excel to compensate for Pete's death and to please her parents. She also joined a youth group at church that was exploring spiritual issues in an attempt to see her faith in a different, more sustaining way.

FAMILY ADAPTATION

There are family tasks that must occur in the process of adapting to the death of one of its immediate members. The family adjustment process has been seen to include giving permission for the mourning process to occur, relinquishing the memory of the deceased as a "power" in family activities, and rearranging of roles within and outside the family (Goldberg, 1973).

Just as families are different and unique, so are the adaptations that they make to the loss of an immediate member. In a significant study of families 7 to 9 years after the death of a child from cancer, three different grief patterns were found: "getting over it," "filling the space," and "keeping the connection" (McClowry et al., 1987). Some parents and siblings in the study described an "empty space" experience that allowed them to "keep the connection," a desirable state for the families. Other families "filled the emptiness" by keeping busy or substituting other concerns to distract them from their grief. These families reported feeling the "empty space" in situations where they especially missed the deceased child. Finally, families whose adaptation was "getting over it" saw the death in the past, not as a significant influence on them in the present (McClowry et al., 1987).

This study raises numerous questions about the ways we offer support to families. Do family members each develop different patterns of dealing with the loss? If family members do develop different patterns, what are the implications for the family's functioning? As the authors have suggested, can these patterns be applied to other relationship losses within families (e.g., that of a spouse or parent)? And how does the pattern that an adolescent develops for dealing with a death affect his or her future relationships?

There are some general principles that seem to apply to families with adolescents as important influences on the grief process.

Inclusion and Involvement

For adolescents, an important element of the family's responses surrounding the death of an immediate member is to feel an ongoing sense of inclusion and involvement. Not only is this a statement of their value and importance as members of the family, but it also communicates the message of "we can handle things together." Inclusion and participation are central even when adolescents act as though they do not want to be involved, or perhaps say they are not interested in being a part of planning or activities.

For example, Jim told his mother that he did not want to visit his Dad when he was in the hospital for treatment of advanced leukemia. However, when Jim's mother did go to visit her husband, Jim was angry and withdrawn after her return, and said he had wanted to go. At home again, Jim's Dad often asked him to spend time with him, but Jim would only do so when other family members were out of the house. After his Dad's death, Jim was firm that he did not want to participate in the meeting with the minister to plan the funeral. He remained in the kitchen, although he occasionally walked in on the meeting. At one of those times, the minister asked Jim whether he had some music he would choose to have at the service. Jim responded with certainty about three songs that were important to his Dad.

Opportunities for Expression

The wide range of adolescent emotional experiences and the limited outlets for their expression can lead to an even greater feeling of restriction for adolescents. Although it is not typical for adolescents to cry a great deal around others, they are freer to release other emotions. Music is a prime source of expression for adolescents, and can offer them some release, as can sports and other physical activities. One family with adolescents regularly rented humorous movies following the father's death. As they watched these movies, friends and peers sat together laughing, sometimes close to tears.

Anger can often be the result of significant unexpressed emotion or need. It is important for family members to look past the adolescents' anger to recognize the distress that may lie underneath. Although anger is an appropriate emotional response to the abandonment felt following a death, it can also create distance and increased feelings of alienation. The anger adolescents feel can often be directed toward an awareness that normalizes it, and toward actions that are constructive and in line with the adolescents' values.

Maintaining Family Life

Adolescents have a great need to be a part of a normal life. Families can encourage bereaved adolescents to participate in all the activities that they choose to, and to keep up their responsibilities both at school and at home. In addition, families also need to make accommodations that acknowledge the distress of loss and the major changes it forces on them. The dual process of living and confirming the changes within the family while functioning in an external world that seldom recognizes the struggles of the family is difficult. It is necessary for the family to recognize and cope with the realities of the loss, and to make the necessary internal and functional changes.

Living with Limitations

One of the most difficult adaptations for families is to a diminished, lessened experience of the family life in the present. Even in circumstances where there has been a lingering illness, the family's experience after a member's death is still one of a smaller, poorer world. Adolescents, with their expansive sense of life and themselves, often have difficulty living with the limitations that death imposes on them. It is difficult for adolescents to learn about the limits of life, let alone live them so closely.

Families who face and acknowledge their deficits, and work with them as well as they can, do better than those who act as if the deficits do not exist. Because the family is the major frame of reference and source of our reality context, denial of the importance of the death of an immediate member implies that none of us matter or are important. Another implication of patterns of avoidance, denial, or overprotection of children and adolescents is the message "you/we can't handle this." This message of low confidence within the family can create increased fears across time.

Families that acknowledge the magnitude of the loss and yet continue to focus their attention on valuing and loving each other hold the best outlook for the future. This approach also includes the ability to stay connected to the family's extended social network, despite the reality that different people may not have been available or supportive during earlier points in the grief process. Working within new limitations, most families may lose parts of their extended support system, and will add new people who are able to be supportive and available. This model of practical, understanding approaches to each other and to the outside world gives adolescents the message that, despite the undesirable nature of their situation, there are ways that the family and its members can continue on and sustain each other.

SUPPORTING FAMILIES

The nature and quality of the family, and the support available to the family, are major determining factors of the outcome of adolescent bereavement. Although these factors are equally important at other times in the life span, they are more difficult realities for families with be-reaved adolescents. Because adolescents are already working at eman-cipation and being less dependent on the family, their freedom and ability to access and use outside resources is of major importance.

The nature and quality of the family with adolescents is already in transition, with considerable fluctuation in intrafamilial support. Ado-lescents are often unable to receive adequate support because it is dif-ficult to perceive their needs. There may also be greater ambivalence and fear of dependence on the part of an adolescent who is seeking support from his or her parent(s). Also, other family members may be consumed with their own grief, and peers are often fearful or avoidant (Raphael, 1983).

Sherry was a 17-year-old high school senior when her mother died after a 2-week illness. Sherry was the youngest in her family; her older sister, age 26, was out of the house and her brother, age 22, was finishing his last year at a local college. Following her mother's death, Sherry assumed all the major roles of caring for the household and of caring for her father.

Sherry found her father to be remote, or tearful and irritable. A factory su-pervisor, he expected her to care for the house and continue to do well at school. He did not want Sherry to talk about her mother and got angry if she cried, telling her that it made him more upset. Sherry turned to her friends, three classmates who lived in the neighborhood and had been close since elementary school. Two of her friends stopped coming to Sherry's house after her mother's death. The third friend, Barbara, was still available and even spent more time than before with Sherry, doing things together, listening to her, and often help-ing her with the additional responsibilities she had at home. Barbara's family continued to welcome Sherry to their home, where she could be an adolescent. She was often included in the family's activities and became their "adopted" member.

Sherry's relationship with her father was quiet but consistent. Her older sib-lings were distant and often tried to be prescriptive or parental in their inter-actions with Sherry. Sherry continued to do well at school and was able to meet the responsibilities of her expanded roles at home. Although there was little overt support at home, Sherry did know that her father cared about her. Sherry often felt alone, both at home, and with the friends she felt had abandoned her. She was able to feel support from the friendship with Barbara and her family, relationships that have continued into her adult life.

In small families, it may be necessary and healthy for the grieving adolescent to seek resources outside the immediate family. In past times, children and adolescents typically had other adult extended fam-ily members to whom they could turn for support. Today's dispersed families often lack other adult resources who would be available to bereaved adolescents. The absence of a community of caring persons to whom one can turn is a prevalent theme in our culture. Given the societal and individual family context, bereaved adolescents typically turn to peers, teachers, clergy, or parents of their friends. Adolescents are required to be more creative in seeking out support, both within and outside the family, following the death of a parent or sibling.

One of the most significant aspects of support for adolescents and families is access to needed information. Information about what has happened, what is happening, and what to expect is of major help to families. Beyond knowing all the information available as it relates to the circumstances of the death, adolescents and families benefit from knowing about grief and the mourning process. If information can be given to the entire family and with all of its members present at the time, this can help the family incorporate more components of the information, and it may also create opportunities for increasing participation and communication within the family.

While all members function outside the family, the expanding world of adolescents is especially important to them. For that reason, it can be helpful for information and support to be available in the school context, where adolescents may feel less singled out or different. Many schools now offer loss groups for adolescents led by school staff rather than referring them to outside agencies. This seems to have considerable merit because it normalizes the experiences of bereaved adolescents and offers them support within their own world.

Other Considerations

Many deaths that adolescents experience will be sudden or involve some element of trauma. By definition, sudden or traumatic deaths involve great stresses for family systems. They are outside the range of functioning for most families and involve greater demands and adaptations around family needs, vulnerabilities, and beliefs. The distress adolescents experience around traumatic deaths is increased, and their needs for support and attention increase.

The importance of support is also crucial in losses of a peer or friend. Although this chapter has emphasized the needs and responses of families with adolescents losing an immediate member, it is obvious that an adolescent and his or her family can be greatly impacted by the death of a peer or friend (see chapter 10). Adolescents usually turn first to peers for understanding; thus, the death of a friend can increase an adolescent's sense of alienation within the family.

In the context of the death of a friend or peer, Mauk and Weber (1991) emphasized the importance of appropriate affective attention for peer survivors of adolescent suicide. Postvention efforts by significant adults are seen as important to grieving adolescents. In the death of a peer from causes other than suicide, parental and professional support are often lacking or inadequate (O'Brien, Goodenow, & Espin, 1991).

This discussion has focused on a family perspective on adolescent grief; the emphasis has been on the assumption that the vast majority of adolescents and their families do not need or seek "treatment" for their grief. In fact, early support, psychoeducational assistance, and self-help approaches seem to be the best efforts. Overclinicalization of grief further isolates adolescents and families. In those instances when there are multiple losses or other vulnerabilities in the adolescent and family, it is important to refer to mental health professionals who have a clear understanding of the grief process and are able to set appropriate goals with the adolescent and family. In this context, it is desirable for the family to seek services together, or that the family be involved if the adolescent is seen individually.

CONCLUSION: PERSONAL REFLECTIONS

There is no time in life as expansive, as intense, or as promising as adolescence. Life is at its beginning bloom when everything seems possible. Death is a remote, impersonal reality for most adolescents. And families with adolescent members are consumed with the demands of separation and launching, not of death. Although death is unwelcome at most points in the family life cycle, it is especially difficult to integrate into the ambivalence and conflicts of families with adolescents. The death of a member leaves these families feeling particularly cheated out of the future they have worked so hard for and looked forward to enjoying together.

The best way that an adolescent can live through grief is to do it as a part of a family, to have a place to learn how to live with the sorrow and the changes, and to have a place to belong. Although this chapter has been written in the third person, it is based on my professional experiences of working with families in grief for many years. More important, the understandings of family responses are based on the personal experiences I have known with my family of origin and my own nuclear family.

My mother experienced the death of both her parents within 6 months' time when she was 13 years old. Her life history taught me a great deal about the importance of support and the extended family. When my daughter, Ellen, was 17 years old, she was killed by a drunk driver. My son, Steve, 16 years old at that time, taught me a great deal about the ways that adolescents struggle with grief. He has always said that he was so grateful that he had parents whom he could talk to and who tried to understand his pain. Ellen's death was *our* loss, and we have tried to live out the experience together.

I certainly do not believe that the experience of being part of a family with an adolescent in grief is the only basis of knowing what is healthy or helpful. For me, the experience is still a humbling one—one that has left me with a tenacious commitment to the wonder of families. I hold the firm belief that in attempting to understand the experiences of grief and mourning, we can be more powerful in our supportive efforts if we extend our vision to include adolescents *within* families.

12

Adolescents and Education About Death, Dying, and Bereavement

Robert G. Stevenson and Eileen P. Stevenson

Adolescence is a time filled with life. The future seems limitless and life has a potential that knows no bounds. Adults sometimes ask why these young adults should be "burdened" with dark thoughts of death and loss. Why would any adolescent want to take a course that speaks of death when adolescents are so full of vitality? Why learn about death when one is still learning to live? The question is logical but is based on an illusion that can disappear in an instant.

In Bergen County, New Jersey, there is a community that could easily be seen as an example of small-town America. The 17,000 people who reside in this middle-class, suburban area go about their routine by coping with life's issues on a day-by-day basis. As one watches family members pursue careers, education, or family matters, the thought of "death" can seem quite remote. The high school did not have a death education course, because there was no need for one. In just a few months, that illusion was shattered by a series of tragic deaths.

A high school freshman was accidentally shot and killed by a classmate as they examined his father's off-duty revolver, and the gun went off. The community was shocked, but they expressed their grief and tried to move on. After all, this death of a young person, although tragic, was a rare and isolated occurrence. Less than 2 months later, the young son of one of the high school coaches died after a battle with leukemia. Many of the residents, as well as people throughout the area, had raised money for a bone marrow transplant and the young man's untimely death came as an emotional blow.

The impact of such a death touched countless people beyond the young man's immediate family and friends. Losses such as this, where so many are affected, can result in what is called "community grief." This type of grief raises issues that go beyond a single individual's grief experience. Again, high school students were among those most affected. Because the young man's death was not entirely unexpected, school officials believed that the young people in their care were "handling it" well. School leaders chose to believe that these bereaved youngsters needed no special support. Requests by school staff to involve others in developing a plan of support were turned down.

That summer, a teenage girl, who appeared to be responding well to treatment for a chronic illness, lapsed into a coma while on vacation at the shore. After several days on life support, she died. Several individuals stepped forward to help the young people of the town. A local priest held a prayer service while the girl was in the hospital and encouraged her friends and classmates to write letters of support. At the girl's funeral, young people played key roles throughout the ceremony (with an adult at their shoulder to offer support if it was needed). It was also announced that the public high school (located near the church) would be open after the service with cool drinks and that the high school's guidance personnel would be available to speak with any young people who wished to do so. There were many adults in this town sensitive to the needs of their young people.

Each of the deaths experienced by this community affected most, if not all of the town's young people. To plan for the aftermath of one death is important, but that alone may not be enough. There may be several losses that affect an entire community, or a "community" loss may combine with personal losses of individuals in that community. Planning for the grief that follows a single loss may not be effective when confronted by multiple grief.

The community described earlier learned through experience how to help young people who are faced with community grief. This story is typical of the way in which many communities cope with death and grief. Experiences of this type are often denied until a crisis forces us to confront their sad realities. When we finally act, mistakes are sometimes made even with the best of intentions. The lessons learned in crisis may be forgotten when we return to our normal "cocoon" of denial.

DEATH EDUCATION

Over the last quarter-century, programs have been developed to help young people and their families to cope with dying, death, loss, and grief. Family and religious institutions play important roles, but many of these programs are based in the schools and have come to be referred to collectively as "death education." Death education is that formal instruction which deals with dying, death, loss, grief, and their impact on the individual and humankind (Stevenson, 1984). This type of education may occur at home with family members, in religious instruction, or in schools.

Death education begins in the home. Parents are the first and most important teachers of their children. They model coping behaviors as they themselves try to cope with the losses they encounter in life. In an ideal situation, young people can go to family members for information and support in times of crisis, building on a foundation established early in life. However, emotional ties and concern about saying the "wrong thing" can hinder open family discussion of sensitive issues, such as the taboo topics of sex and death. If parental concern over possible "misstatements" is strong enough, such discussions may not occur at all. Parents may wish to "protect" the young person from unpleasant realities, or they may want to preserve their vision of the "innocence of childhood" for as long as possible.

It is also true that, for a variety of reasons, some families do not fulfill their potential as a safe, nurturing place for each of their members. Although the concept is overused and often misapplied, dysfunctional families do exist. The dysfunction may be in the area of communication or it may come as a result of family "secrets" (emotional baggage from the past). In such situations, family members may need help from some outside source to function more effectively in times of grief or other death-related crises.

Religious institutions also provide death education. Diversity of religious belief or lack of such belief in our pluralistic society makes it difficult to generalize about the impact of religion in the education of young people about death. Christians may view death as punishment for sin. Some Christians attribute their feelings of guilt to a traditional religious portrayal of death. Nevertheless, faith can also offer comfort in times of grief. Jesus said, "Blessed are those who mourn for they shall be comforted" (Matt. 5:4). The comfort is said to come through the belief that Jesus is the resurrection and the life, and that one who believes in him "will live, even when he dies" (John 11:25).

Eastern religions often speak of death as a "transition" in which the life force moves on to a new plane of existence or another life in this world. Eastern faiths, such as Hinduism, Buddhism, or Taoism do not speak of "personal" salvation. There is common ground, however, in religious teachings about death. In general, religious belief offers explanation for events that may otherwise seem incomprehensible (Why did he have to die?). Religion offers belief that can calm fears regarding the fate of the deceased (heaven, reunion with Brahma, movement to a new life through reincarnation). Also, religious rituals (wakes, shiva, cremation, graveside services) can be a source of communal strength. Also, when one feels hopeless, religion can be a source of hope: hope that the deceased is now beyond this "vale of tears" or that those who mourn may one day be reunited with their loved ones. Religion generally offers the belief that life continues in some form after the event of physical death and may help the bereaved to move on with their lives.

The roles of family and religion must both be taken into account when working with bereaved individuals. When death education is offered in schools, it is not done in isolation. Teachers must try to be conscious of the many influences in the lives of their students. Cultural, religious, and regional differences must all be acknowledged if death education is to be truly responsive to the needs of students.

THE ROLE OF THE SCHOOL

Death education programs in schools have developed in three areas.

> *Prevention.* Courses that present facts about the physical aspects of death, the psychosocial effects of death on the survivors, and methods of coping with dying, death, loss, and grief
> *Intervention.* School support in the midst of crisis
> *Postvention.* Continued support by the school community after a death

Death education does *not* include every course which mentions death or loss. Hamlet's soliloquy or Romeo and Juliet may well be used in a death education context, but their inclusion in a course does not, by itself, transform an English course into a death education curriculum.

In a school setting, death education includes those courses, curricula, counseling programs, and support services that offer a structured approach to issues dealing with dying, death, loss, grief, and their impact on the students, staff, their families, their friends, and society as a whole.

After a quarter-century of death education in our schools, the need for such courses and programs is clearer than ever. Although some would like to cling to the illusion that death does not touch the lives of adolescents, the reality is quite different. High school students range in age from 13 to 19 years old. The number of adolescent deaths has dropped (from a high in 1970) and is now rising again according to data in *Statistical Abstracts of the United States*. Although age ranges often include individuals 19–24 years of age as adolescents, as a general guideline it appears that about one in every 1,000 young people of high school age dies each year in the United States (U.S. Bureau of the Census, 1993, p. 87). Each of those deaths affects not just the students at one school but at schools throughout the area.

Further, 1 in 20 young people will lose a parent to death by their senior year in high school (Critelli, 1979). Sibling deaths, celebrity deaths (of adolescents' "heroes" or cult figures), and staff deaths (especially as the average age of school faculty grows older) also affect high school–age adolescents. Potentially, there are students trying to cope with loss and grief in every class in every school in this country. Thus, adolescents do not differ in whether or not they have been affected by loss and grief. They differ in their degree of success in coping with that loss and grief.

Loss and grief can have a dramatic impact on the classroom atmosphere and on the learning process. For example, grief can affect a student in a number of ways:

- *Academically*. Resulting in a shorter attention span, difficulty in remembering facts, lower grades or a lowered level of self-confidence regarding school assignments
- *Behaviorally*. As expressed in disruptive classroom behavior, poor attendance, more frequent visits to the school nurse, increased absence due to "illness" or injury, greater frequency of accidents, withdrawal from school sports or other school activities, acting out, punishment seeking, or even violent behavior
- *Emotionally*. Manifested in greater need for teacher attention and support, apathy, a general loss of interest in school, altered relationships with staff and peers, greater feelings of anger, guilt, or sadness—an inability to enjoy life including school (Stevenson, 1986)

A school or classroom can be turned upside down by the physical and emotional demands of the grief process and by the disruption caused by even a few of the possible reactions listed previously. The larger the number of students impacted by a loss and the more they have been affected, the greater the disruption of the educational process.

Further, there are some students who are "at risk" in special ways. Some bereaved students try to numb their emotional pain by self-medicating with alcohol or drugs. This attempt to cope with the pain of grief can be seen as the "cause" of problems when it may, in fact, be a manifestation of unresolved grief. Some students are coping with greater burdens imposed by more than one loss. Multiple losses are so common among contemporary high school students that they should be seen as the rule and not an exception. Multiple losses can involve personal losses of each individual, or they may arise from losses which affect an entire community.

COMMUNITY GRIEF

There are deaths and other significant losses which have an impact on an entire community. These present a special type of grief situation because an entire school, town, or region can be involved. A set of guidelines for developing a protocol for a school's response to community grief was distributed in 1986 by the National Association of Secondary School Principals (Stevenson & Powers, 1986). The protocol was developed in response to concerns voiced by death education students about the way in which the explosion of the Challenger space shuttle was dealt with (or not dealt with) in their school. It was based on questions which must be answered when a school is faced with dealing with community grief (Stevenson, 1994). These questions include the following:

- Who should inform the student(s)?
- Who else should be informed?
- Where should the students be told?
- How should the students be told?
- How might the students react?
- What issues can complicate student reaction and response?
- What support personnel are available both within and outside of the school community?

The process of developing a structured death education program within a school system can help prepare both students and staff to answer these questions and to respond more effectively in times of crisis.

In interviews with death education students, the two benefits of this type of education that were most frequently identified were (a) lessening of fear and anxiety regarding death; and (b) improved communication by students. Young people said that before taking a death education course, they believed they could not discuss the topic of death. This silence increased their fear of death and hindered communication with those, such as family members, who might have offered support. After taking a death education course, students spoke of bringing class materials home and of discussing death and grief with family members, often for the first time. As students spoke more openly about these topics, they felt that their fear and anxiety lessened. As one student said, "Before I took a death education course I thought about death all the time, but I couldn't talk about it. Since taking this course I talk about death with a lot of people . . . so I don't have to think about it any more" (Stevenson, 1984). The object here is not to eliminate a fear of death, but to bring it to a level which is less threatening to a student. It is often said that "knowledge is power"; in this case, the knowledge provided is about dying, death, loss, and grief.

Improvement also occurred in home/school communication. Parents who were interviewed said that they were more likely to notify the school after a death in the family. These same parents expressed appreciation for the assistance they felt their children had received in preparing to face the inevitable losses of life. When a death had already occurred, the school was seen as providing support that was less encumbered with personal and family grief as the student coped with the loss.

In addition to student grief, death education has come to play an important role in four areas of prevention: depression and suicide; HIV and AIDS; adolescent violence; and future parenting skills.

- *Depression and suicide.* Death education curricula have been used as a means of informing students of warning signs of suicide and symptoms of depression. In one New Jersey county, suicide prevention programs were begun in the late 1980s. Since that time the number of adolescent suicides has steadily declined, and in three neighboring counties the number of adolescent suicides has risen. The Adolescent Suicide Awareness Program has succeeded so well that it has been duplicated throughout the state.

- *HIV and AIDS.* The incidence of HIV infection and AIDS has increased dramatically among high school–age adolescents. Today, almost all health education curricula address the means of HIV transmission and symptoms of AIDS. Death education curricula discuss related issues. Issues discussed in death education courses include dealing with feelings, confidentiality, and motives behind high-risk behavior (such as drug use or unprotected sex). Death education students have often assumed a proactive stance in helping districts to develop school policies related to HIV and AIDS.
- *Adolescent violence.* The growing incidence of violence in the lives of contemporary adolescents and of violent adolescent deaths has pushed this topic to the forefront of death education. High school–age adolescents serving time for violent crimes in Bergen County, New Jersey, were five times more likely than other students to have lost a parent through death or abandonment before age 5. It is thought that unresolved childhood grief is a major source of their violent behavior. As part of their rehabilitation, a death educator was called in to consult with correctional personnel in developing ways to facilitate the resolution of their grief. Death education curricula address the causes, risks, and consequences of violent behavior, social and psychological factors behind the increase in adolescent violence, and nonviolent alternatives to violent behavior, such as peer mediation.
- *Parenting skills.* The degree of difficulty that a child experiences when coping with grief is directly related to how well the child's parents have coped and are coping with their grief. Also, young children relate to death differently than adults. Death education curricula seek to prepare adolescents to help their own present or future children understand and cope with this difficult topic.

QUALIFICATIONS OF DEATH EDUCATORS

When death intrudes in the high school routine, guidance counselors, child study team members, or the school nurse are typically the staff members expected to "handle" the situation. In many cases, they do not have the preparation or background experience for this task. Even when they have specific training, their time is limited. It would be difficult or impossible for them to find opportunities in their busy schedules to be able to plan and teach an ongoing death education curriculum.

Death educators are most often classroom teachers. At this time, death education teachers are not required to have special certification, as would be expected in other subject areas, such as health education or psychology. Part of the difficulty in requiring special certification comes from the wide variety of sponsoring disciplines in the schools. Death education curricula in secondary schools have been developed in health, family living, English, social studies, and science departments.

Death education teachers in public schools are certified as educators and have some background in child or developmental psychology, but they often have no formal training in death education. They may have difficulty in finding such training because teacher preparation programs have yet to recognize the need for preparing teachers to cope with the impact of death in the classroom. In private and parochial schools the preparation base is even more varied, since in most states less formal preparation is required of their staff members than in public schools. In addition, there may be staff members who would be uncomfortable teaching a death education curriculum because of unresolved grief in their own lives.

Staff development programs and workshops have provided an ongoing means of staff preparation for death education. Nevertheless, it should not be thought that assisting students to cope with death is a job for just one or two staff members. The entire staff should be involved at some level since there are situations where they may be needed, as in the cases mentioned earlier in this chapter. Also, because bereaved students can be found in every class, all staff members should be aware of ways in which they can be of help. If not able to help actively, they should at least be aware of how to avoid inadvertently adding to the students' problems. Staff development programs in the field of death, dying, loss, and grief have been offered to teaching staff, school nurses, guidance counselors, aides, and administrators. The involvement of administrators is important. It is these administrators who develop school response protocols related to death and other crises. They will also be the educators who evaluate the performance of the staff members who are implementing death education curricula.

In response to a lack of standardized staff preparation or teacher certification requirements, the Association for Death Education and Counseling (ADEC) has developed a program for certification of professional death educators. ADEC, headquartered in Hartford, Connecticut, is an international organization of professionals involved in the areas of death education and grief counseling. To obtain certification as a professional death educator a candidate is required to

- Demonstrate that he or she has acquired appropriate educational preparation and work experience
- Provide character references
- Supply professional references from supervisors or certified death educators who have observed the applicant's work
- Pass a comprehensive examination in death education
- Sign a copy of the ADEC code of professional ethics

Since this program was started in 1981, more than 400 candidates have received professional certification. Having an accepted standard for preparation of death educators has been an aid to administrators and a comfort to the parents of students in death education courses.

HIGH SCHOOL DEATH EDUCATION CURRICULA

Setting standards for staff selection and preparation has been difficult, but such standards now exist. Establishing standards for high school death education curricula has been an equally difficult task. A curriculum is a statement of priorities. It is important that curricula be designed and written by professional educators, but priorities must reflect those of the community as a whole. The curriculum development process should allow input by parents and concerned community members. The final death education curriculum must be accepted by the district board of education. The open nature of this curriculum development process helps to establish lines of communication between home and school. It also allows educators to address possible community concerns regarding death education.

Adolescents are not yet adults. Although they may be able to handle the intellectual requirements of college death education classes, the emotional and psychosocial components of death education mandate that high school curricula must be age appropriate in both content and methodology.

There are other decisions which must be made regarding high school death education. They can again be stated in the form of questions.

- *What will be the offering discipline(s) for the death education course or units?* The subject area in which death education takes place will shape what is taught and the manner in which it is presented. It must be determined whether death education will be placed in a single curriculum area or will be multidisciplinary involving several academic departments. This will also determine who the evaluators will be and the standards by which the curriculum and teacher will be evaluated.

* *What will be the format for the death education curriculum?* Some schools offer death education as a separate course while others have infused the death education curriculum into existing courses.
* *Will the death education course be required of all students?* The content of death education curricula may well be important for all people at some time. However, this does not mean that every student will benefit from a course offered at a set point in his/her academic experience. Potential problems in this area can be avoided by making death education courses or units elective in nature. If the background or needs of some students make it difficult for them to participate in a standard death education class, alternatives can then be made available to such individuals.
* *Are there "risks" in death education?* Even the strongest supporters of death education would agree that there are "risks" in any course with content that holds such strong potential for emotional involvement. What must be determined is to what extent these risks can be addressed in advance and possible negative effects avoided. It is also important to differentiate between real areas of concern and the "myths" about death education propagated by demagogues such as Phyllis Schlafly and her lobbying group, the Eagle Forum. Schlafly (1988) has claimed that death education is a "dirty little secret" and she often presents educators and parents as adversaries. It is her belief that death education teachers seek to undermine parental authority, act as counselors without appropriate training, and promote self-destructive behavior on the part of students. No research or statistical basis is offered for these contentions. Schlafly does not even define what she means by death education. In her writing, it remains a vague bogeyman to be feared in any form. A few anecdotal stories are manipulated to play on the fears of concerned parents.

In fact, death education as it exists bears no relationship to Schlafly's presentation. The model used by death educators seeks to reinforce the family as a positive support for students. Open home/school communication encourages parent/teacher cooperation to benefit the youngsters about whom both groups care. The counseling dimension of grief support involves certified school personnel. Knowing when to make appropriate referral of students who need additional support is part of the responsibility of every teacher.

Positive criticism of death education comes from English re-searcher Sonja Hunt (interview, Institute for Leadership Studies, Hackensack, New Jersey, July 14, 1983). She pointed out that there are events and processes in life which leave a distinct mark on an individual. Death is such an event and grief is such a process. Hunt cautioned that educators need to be aware of the possible conse-quences of their work before attempting instruction that could af-fect the grief process. She also asked educators to show clearly why schools would be an appropriate place for such interventions (Stevenson, 1984).

Basically, Hunt cautioned educators to examine death educa-tion lessons and their possible effects before implementing such lessons in the classroom. She also advised educators to maintain ongoing programs of evaluation of death education curricula and professional development programs. The last two decades have shown the wisdom in her critique. Professional journals such as *Death Studies* and *Omega* regularly publish research results evaluat-ing effects of death education. Professional organizations fre-quently offer workshops, symposia, and extension courses to develop and enhance the skills needed by death educators.

- *Is there one preferred type of death education curriculum?* The answer is a simple one: *No!* Death education curricula have developed a va-riety of models. The needs of a particular district or school and its students must be taken into account when choosing to implement one or more of these models.

MODELS OF HIGH SCHOOL
DEATH EDUCATION CURRICULA

In its earliest form, education about dying, death, loss, and grief was simply a part of everyday life and living. Death and loss were all around in the natural order of things. People died at home, and their family and friends were a part of that process. The second half of the 19th cen-tury and the first half of the 20th century saw death increasingly sepa-rated from life. It was this artificial division that was, perhaps, the major reason why death education was felt to be increasingly needed in our schools.

Death education was introduced into high schools beginning in the late 1960s. The first curriculum materials available to educators were di-vided into two categories:

- Prepared units (with supplementary materials) that were fully developed and ready-to-use lesson plans
- Unstructured "learning opportunities" and objectives to be used by educators in developing their own lessons

Perspectives on Death (1972) by Berg and Daugherty is an example of the former, whereas *Discussing Death: A Guide to Death Education* (1976) by Mills, Reisler, Robinson, and Vermilye is an example of the latter. Both types saw death education as a series of discrete topics aimed at answering student questions about death and its effects. Both relied on "outside experts" (funeral directors, doctors, nurses, clergy) coming into the classroom to supplement the work of the teacher.

As more information became available about dying, death, loss, and grief, curricula became model centered. A lesson would typically start with a psychological model, such as the "Five Stages of Dying" developed by Elisabeth Kübler-Ross (1969). The model provided a way for students to look at an experience that was new to them. The structure of a model made the topic seem less confusing and gave a basis for comparing loss experiences. Additional models of grief soon appeared.

- Westberg (1961): 10 stages
- Kries and Patti (1969): 3 stages
- Kavanaugh (1972): 7 stages
- Davidson (1975): 4 stages

These just scratch the surface (Metzgar, 1988). The drawback of these models was that as they were used more frequently they often seemed to come to have a life of their own. In extreme cases, the integrity of the model actually appeared to become more important than the individual experiences it was intended to describe.

Within each curriculum, there is a variety of themes. Some appear in almost every death education course. Others are used selectively, depending on subject area and instructor. Three widely used curricula (O'Toole, 1989; Stevenson, 1990; Zalaznik, 1992) are representative of those used in death education today. Table 12.1 lists themes in these three curricula.

The amount of time spent on an individual theme will vary based on the needs of the students involved and on significant current events. This approach is used in a curriculum developed by Concord, New Hampshire, health educator, Tom Walton. He begins with the students' expressed needs. Lessons then develop the themes in the established

TABLE 12.1   Themes in Death Education Curricula

Aging	HIV and AIDS
Change and loss as part of life	Loss experiences (permanent vs.
Children's understandings of death	temporary loss)
Chronic and life-threatening illness	Quality of life
Communication and language	Religious and philosophical views of
Cultural and historical perspectives	death
Defining death	Right to life/right to choose
Economic and legal aspects of death	Rituals of death and mourning
Euthanasia and the "right to die"	(funerals & other practices)
Family as support	Suicide prevention
Feelings	Views of life after death
Grief process	

curriculum to meet the students' priorities. Central to the process is an ongoing communication exercise which Walton calls "Circle the Wagons." Students begin by sitting in a circle and speaking about their thoughts and feelings. The instructor then uses this as a starting point for many of the lessons in the curriculum (Habib, 1993).

The latest approach to death education involves reintegration of life and death as part of a natural cycle. Stories, rather than psychological or behavioral models, are used to provide a new focal point for lessons in death education. Stories have long been used in elementary classrooms and are now being introduced on the high school level. These stories allow educators to bring a multicultural perspective to death education. Lessons can blend modern theoretical models and traditional symbols that have brought comfort to bereaved individuals for centuries. The rituals of storytelling allow an educator to move easily into an explanation of the rites of passage which have helped previous generations to cope with the same issues these students now face. Repeating the stories heard in class to parents and others continues the process of communication and brings other people and their unique points of view into the educational process. As students become more comfortable telling the stories they have learned, they are more likely to begin to piece together the stories of their own lives and to share those stories with others. This allows them to build a view of life and death on a foundation which incorporates their personal stories. Shaping and telling their personal stories has become a new method for dealing with personal grief.

CONCLUSION

High school students cannot be shielded from the realities of death in their lives. The schools which these adolescents attend can play a positive role in preparing these young men and women to cope with the realities of dying, death, loss, and grief. Such preparation has come to be called death education. When a school wishes to implement such a program, the following points should be considered:

- The process of implementing a death education curriculum should be open; input should be sought from students, parents, and community members.
- Death education instructors must be qualified, both academically and emotionally, for this challenging topic.
- Death education curricula must be age appropriate and sensitive to the varied backgrounds of individual students.
- In most cases, death education courses should be elective, with other experiences available for students who require some alternative.
- Ongoing programs of course evaluation and professional development should be established and implemented.
- Death education teachers can be valuable resources in times of crisis.
- Death education courses can impart knowledge, assist students in coping more effectively with dying, death, loss, and grief, and help to develop communication and parenting skills.

Physical illness can strike an individual at any time. For that reason society recommends, and may even require, immunization to lessen the pain and suffering caused by such illness. Treatment after the fact is often more difficult. Death and grief can also strike at any time. Death education can be viewed as a form of intellectual, emotional, and psychosocial immunization. Experience has shown that this type of education can help adolescents to cope effectively with the pain and suffering which such events can cause.

13

Postvention with Early
and Middle Adolescents

David C. Hill and Yvonne M. Foster

The experience of losing a significant other is profound and multifaceted, especially so for adolescents. If the loss involves an unexpected or nonnormative death such as that of a peer, teacher, parent, or sibling, the experience is further complicated in its emotional, psychological, cognitive, and behavioral ramifications (Neugarten & Neugarten, 1987). The effects on survivors of deaths that result from uncontrollable causes including diseases (e.g., AIDS or cancer), accidents, or intentionally inflicted death and life-threatening behaviors of suicide, homicide, parasuicide (attempted suicide), or interpersonal violence are profound. The experience of unexpected bereavement itself may have many unique and specifically traumatic aspects (Genovese, 1992). For example, suicide is certainly nonnormative and unexpected; as such, it evokes "significant symptoms of distress in most people" (Wenckstern & Leenaars, 1993, p. 153).

This chapter explores how parents and other family members, school personnel, helping professionals, community leaders, clergy, and medical professionals can ease the intensity of these responses for early and middle adolescents. Such efforts are collectively termed *postvention* (Shneidman, 1971), which refers to all the activities and support that help with the traumatic aftereffects among survivors of profound loss experiences. In this chapter, we think of postvention broadly as involving a "community-based" response rather than exclusively "school-based" programs. This follows the recommendation of the Centers for Disease Control (1988, p. 6) that a community response plan be implemented "when a potentially traumatic death occurs in the community—especially if the person who dies is an adolescent or young adult." The effectiveness of a community-based response is supported by "crisis theory," which views crises as containing both inherent dangers as well as opportunities for growth (Balk & Hogan, 1995; Nelson & Slaikeu, 1984). Our review expands the definition of postvention to include intervention after threats of death or catastrophic loss such as suicide attempt or violent aggression. In this chapter, we consider implications of unexpected loss for adolescents, postvention programs for early and middle adolescents, theoretical justifications for such programs, and recommendations for developing and implementing a postvention plan.

ADOLESCENTS' EXPERIENCE OF UNEXPECTED LOSS

Although adolescents may be more similar to other people in terms of the experience of unexpected bereavement than they are different (Kastenbaum, 1986), many aspects of the developmental status of adolescents may complicate the experience of unexpected loss. Cognitive, psychodynamic, and attachment perspectives provide special insight regarding this process.

Cognitive Developmental Theory

Elkind (1984) applied Piaget's ideas about adolescents' capacities for formal operations—the ability to engage in hypothetical-deductive reasoning in which one considers all possible solutions to a problem, evalutes projected consequences, and tests selected solutions—to the area of social cognition in ways which extend our understanding of adolescents' responses to traumatic losses. Elkind focused on adolescent egocentrism and presented an apparent paradox. Although adolescents can intellectually understand other people's perspectives (abstract thought) and feelings (empathy), they are typically so focused on themselves ("imaginary audience") that they cannot apply their empathic and hypothetical skills in interpersonal transactions. The "personal fable," the most relevant aspect of adolescent egocentrism in terms of death and loss, means that adolescents believe themselves to be invulnerable. They can abstractly consider the hypothetical reality of death, but think of it as something that will happen to someone else, not to them or their significant others. Others have agreed: "For the adolescent who views the self as indestructible, the death of a peer challenges his or her coping resiliency" (Patros & Shamoo, 1989, p. 150).

Kelly's (1955) personal construct theory is also a cognitive approach which has been applied to the experience of death anxiety (Neimeyer, 1994) and can be extended to provide insight regarding traumatic loss. "The guiding assumption of personal construct theory is that human beings construct the meaning of their own lives, by devising, testing, and continuously revising personal theories that help them anticipate their experience" (Neimeyer, 1994, p. 63). This is similar to the fundamental principle of Piaget's theory: "For Piaget, each child's mental reality is his or her own unique construction" (Berk, 1994, p. 221).

This means that adolescents' understanding of unexpected loss will involve their own personal constructs drawn from their mental and emotional experiences. Adolescent encounters with death produce rapid and continuously evolving creation of personal constructs. Death is the "prototypical example of the threatening event" (Neimeyer, 1994, p. 63) and directly challenges adolescents to create their own understanding about how death "fits" with their views of life. An unexpected death or traumatic loss can precipitate a need for revision, extension, or rejection of preexisting personal constructs. In modifying personal constructs, distortions about the future can be produced by adolescents "wherein they perceive bleak dead ends rather than bright opportunities" (Carter & Brooks, 1991, p. 205). These demands on cognitive and emotional resources can be overwhelming for adolescents who are struggling with the "normal developmental challenges" of adolescence.

Most survivors of peer suicide, homicide, or other catastrophic losses demonstrate remarkable resilience in the face of such challenges. It is sometimes true that adolescents have few previous experiences in meeting the challenges involved in such losses. However, more frequently previous experiences with loss such as divorce, geographical "relocating," and deaths of elderly family members provide the experiential foundation for resilience during early or middle adolescence (Carter & Brooks, 1990). The goal of postvention programs is to maximize resilience while reducing the risks.

Psychodynamic Aspects of Adolescence

The cognitive distortion involved in the personal fable suggests a psychodynamic dimension. The notion that adolescents respond to traumatic loss by unconsciously defending themselves against overwhelming feelings—especially anxiety, anger, and depression—suggests the dynamic concept of "defense mechanisms," providing the link between the cognitive approach and various psychodynamic models. Adolescents have developed considerable cognitive complexity in terms of conscious problem-solving and decision-making abilities. Although one might assume that they have also developed complex unconscious defense mechanisms, such as sublimation, reaction formation, identification, projection, and asceticism, this often proves to be untrue. Instead, many of the defenses involved in a traumatic crisis are primary and often fragile—including avoidance, denial, repression, regression, suppression, and acting out (i.e., anger). This provides no surprises to parents, professionals, and others with any exposure to adolescents in traumatic situations. The key point is that even as early as 11 or 12 years of age adolescents are psychodynamically complex.

Defenses and Death Anxiety. The primary anxiety evoked in traumatic loss such as death or major threat of death or physical violence is anxiety about death itself. This death anxiety can be denied, repressed, or converted to "acting out" including self-destructiveness (Firestone, 1994). Because life and death are central issues of adolescence, it follows that catastrophic loss can abruptly produce a radical encounter with death. Any combination of defense mechanisms, especially identification with a suicide completer (or attempter) and self-destructive acting out can lay the groundwork for a "contagion effect" or "suicide epidemic" (Hazell & Lewin, 1993; Petersen & Straub, 1992). The effort to interdict such an epidemic provides one part of the rationale for development of postvention programs. The psychological distress leading to this contagion effect is "specifically countermanded by the acceptance, support, and reorientation provided within suicide postvention" (Carter & Brooks, 1990, p. 387).

Death Anxiety and Individuation. A key task of adolescence is the formation of a sustained identity (Erikson, 1968). This process of individuation can be seriously hampered by excessive defensiveness surrounding issues of death and dying (Firestone, 1994). Developmentally, the experience of loss can produce many consequences for adolescents, even for those who do not engage in actual suicidal behavior such as the "copycat" or "contagion" situations. Fear of death has been recognized not only by developmental psychologists, but also in the world of popular music, for example: "It's the one who won't be taken who cannot seem to give, and the soul afraid of dying that never learns to live" (Amanda McBroom, "The Rose," 1977).*

*The Rose, by Amanda McBroom, © 1977 Warner-Tamerlane Publishing Corp. (BMI) & Third Story Music Inc. (BMI). All rights administered by Warner-Tamerlane Publishing Corp. (BMI). All rights reserved. Used by permission. Warner Bros. Publications U.S. Inc., Miami, FL 33014.

Attachment Theory

The relationship of patterns of emotional attachment in the first two years of life to later responses to traumatic loss may not seem relevant to adolescent development. The literature suggests, however, that early attachment is important to later psychosocial functioning. Based on the work of Dorpat, Jackson, and Ripley (1965), Carter and Brooks (1991) concluded that the completeness of the loss has also been associated with the degree of suicidality, with more parental death among completed suicides and more parental divorce among attempted suicides (parasuicides). Early parental loss has also been found to be a precipitating factor in parasuicide (Lester & Beck, 1976). Sroufe, Cooper, and DeHart (1992) have shown that early attachment patterns are related to various measures of social functioning in later developmental years, thus providing the basis for surviving a broken attachment, such as suicide, violent death, or disease.

The loss of a peer or significant adult represents a broken attachment even when the deceased may not seem to have been that "close" to the survivors. The loss assumes a symbolic value which can exceed the depth of the relationship to the deceased. It may symbolize other disrupted attachment experiences. In this process of symbolical generalization the potential exists for serious emotional disturbance including possible suicidality among survivors. A life event, such as the death of a student, can stir up repressed or dormant feelings left unresolved from previous losses (Nelson & Slaikeu, 1984). Thus, Bowlby (1961, p. 48) pointed out the connection of "a tendency to episodic depression or a difficulty in experiencing feelings, to a loss that occurred in the patient's adolescence or earlier childhood."

BEREAVEMENT THEORIES AND FEATURES: THEIR RELEVANCE TO POSTVENTION

Bowlby's Attachment Theory

Bowlby (1969, 1973, 1980a) combined psychodynamic, evolutionary/ethological, cognitive, and learning perspectives in developing a theory of social and cognitive development which is particularly helpful in understanding the reactions of adolescents to the experience of death and other losses. Bowlby related social competence and self-confidence to the history of a secure attachment. Attachment history produces an "internal working model" which is a cognitive set of expectations based upon experiences in significant relationships. These expectations center on the self-appraised worthiness of care and nurturing, and self-perceived effectiveness in developing emotionally sustaining relationships (Sroufe, Cooper & DeHart, 1992). This emotional and social foundation provides the capacity to experience loss, express associated feelings, resolve those feelings, and strengthen interpersonal relationships. These abilities are tested in early and middle adolescents because their developing identity and their sense of social worthiness is often so tenuous.

Genovese (1992) summarized Bowlby's theory of mourning in the following way. According to Bowlby there are four phases of the grieving process: (a) numbing; (b) yearning and searching; (c) disorganizing and experiencing depression; and (d) reorganizing. Note that most practitioners do not find that people progress sequentially and linearly through the phases of Bowlby's model. In addition, new losses can begin the process all over again.

Parkes and Weiss (1983) developed three key tasks which are part of this process. These include (a) intellectual recognition; (b) emotional acceptance; and (c) identity transformation. Adolescents experiencing unexpected death or threat of death face the challenge of working through these phases and tasks. Cognitive, psychodynamic, and behavioral dimensions discussed previously emerge clearly in this context. Intellectual recognition suggests the cognitive dimension, while numbing implies defenses such as repression, suppression, and minimization. Implications of Bowlby's theory for postvention include the value of educating the community, highlighting the complexity of the experience, and emphasizing the difficult pathway to final acceptance or learning to live with the loss and grief.

Papalia and Olds's Model

Three phases of "grief work" are outlined by Papalia and Olds (1992) in summarizing the implications of bereavement with special relevance to adolescents and postvention. The phases include (a) shock and disbelief; (b) preoccupation with the memory of the person who has died; and (c) resolution. In this model, "resolution" is akin to Bowlby's "reorganization," elusive as such an outcome may often be for many survivors. "Disbelief" parallels "numbing" to some extent. "Preoccupation," which suggests "yearning and searching," is particularly salient in considering adolescents and their responses. Often there is a tendency among adolescents to "romanticize" or "glorify" death, partly a product of their capacity for abstract thought and partly an intense form of identification in their search for meaning and identity. This tendency can feed directly into "preoccupation." Therefore, postvention programs generally need to treat issues surrounding memorial services, plaques, publications, and so forth with a great deal of care.

Self-Psychology

Carter and Brooks (1991) applied principles of self-psychology to an analysis of the emotional effects of traumatic loss. Their conceptualization of traumatic loss includes violent death and assault, as well as suicide and parasuicide. The fundamental assumption of self-psychology is that as human beings we develop a central identity, the "core self," in the process of relating to key individuals and experiences beginning at birth. This "core self" is sustained and nurtured, or possibly undermined and hampered, by the internalized representations of these significant others. These external people and experiences nurture the core self and are known as "self-objects" in the terminology of self-psychology. Development of an effective core self involves a gradual transition from infantile fantasies of omnipotence (love over death, immortality, authority figures, entitlement), invincibility, and immortality to a realistic sense of self-affirming core self.

The traumatic loss of a "self-object" causes a disruption in adolescents' narcissistic fantasies, which organize the person's sense of self, contributing to the risk of self-destructiveness including suicidality. This breaks the developmentally normal transition from "primitive" fantasies to realistic ones. Thus helping professionals and other concerned persons need to take action to prevent further losses. Carter and Brooks's emphasis on the role of fantasies of invincibility parallels Elkind's concept of the "personal fable" or "myth of invulnerability," an excellent example of the convergence of the psychodynamic and the cognitive-developmental approaches. Carter and Brooks use their model to support postvention programs for all kinds of traumatic loss including interpersonal violence.

Unexpected Grief and Posttraumatic Stress

Genovese (1992) focused attention on various approaches to understanding the impact of "unexpected" or "unanticipated" grief on survivors. His review suggests that posttraumatic symptoms which may develop into a full diagnosis of mental disorder are possible outcomes of such a loss. This is supported by other authorities (Carter & Brooks, 1991; Wenckstern & Leenaars, 1993). Post-traumatic stress symptoms generally fall into two types: hypersensitivity, on the one hand, and numbing, on the other. These apparently opposite extremes actually alternate and manifest themselves simultaneously in some survivors, producing a complex pattern of responses including the high-risk propensity for impulsive self-destructiveness. Hypersensitivity involves such experiences as sudden anger, flashbacks, nightmares, and panic reactions, while numbing produces reduced or blocked emotional responses and sometimes physical-kinesthetic numbness. Implied here is the preventive role of postvention in identifying high-risk, potentially suicidal, survivors.

Farberow's (1993) review of the empirical literature found that the impact of suicide may not differ much from that of other unexpected death. Nevertheless, many clinicians have noted important effects of suicide on survivors, and Dunne (1987) has outlined several important effects on children. These can be assumed to apply to adolescents to some extent because of their transitional nature as neither children any longer nor yet adults. These effects on children are presented as similar to posttraumatic stress disorder symptoms (Dunne, 1987) and include (a) cognitive-perceptual difficulties; (b) foreshortened sense of the future; (c) collapse of developmental accomplishments (regression); (d) dreams and nightmares; (e) contagion; (f) flashbacks; (g) preoccupation with death; and (h) pseudomaturity. This listing reinforces and extends many other concerns already described.

A common theme in all theories of bereavement is that "resolution" or the outcome of effective mourning involves detaching emotionally from the deceased. However, Balk and Hogan (1995) pointed out that a substantial body of research suggests that people do not detach, but instead maintain some form of emotional attachment to the person long after the event, in many cases for the rest of their lives. Thus, Balk and Hogan (1995) encouraged reconceptualizing continuing connectedness with the deceased as normal and expected, and not pathological. This insight should guide postvention work.

Summary: A Rationale for Providing Postvention

The preceding review has highlighted the special developmental dimensions of adolescence which make this such a pivotal life stage in which many vulnerabilities as well as many sources of potential resilience exist within adolescents' psychosocial experiences. The combination of risk-producing and resilience-supporting factors organizes our understanding of the effects of traumatic loss. Cognitive, psychodynamic, attachment, and self-psychological perspectives have been used to examine the effects of traumatic loss or threat of loss on adolescents.

The implications of these theories for the design and implementation of postvention programs have been emphasized.

We know that traumatic losses through suicide, disease, violence, accidents, and other experiences will happen. As potential postvenors we are left with two major choices: We can choose to do nothing and hope the effects will remit by themselves or we can make a plan for action to minimize negative effects and build on the growth-enhancing potential available in all crises. Our review of the developmental literature demonstrates conclusively that the first choice is untenable, and that responsible school personnel must collaborate with community and family representatives to create effective postvention plans. The projected benefits of such programs include: (a) prevention of high-risk self-destructive behavior, such as "suicide contagion" in the wake of traumatic loss; (b) reduction of the feelings of isolation and alienation that commonly pervade the student population after such an experience; (c) promotion of a sense of commonality; and (d) provision of the most effective (as well as cost-efficient) approach to suicide prevention (Hazell & Lewin, 1993). In providing such programs there is an inherent danger of glamorizing suicide or violence, and thereby encouraging further incidents of self-destructive behavior (Siehl, 1990). Nearly all authorities emphasize that the negative outcomes of postvention will only occur when the programs are designed and administered improperly.

POSTVENTION PROGRAMS

This section describes representative postvention programs and illustrates the diversity of such programs. Typical programs provide for planning, team building, media contact, teacher and staff training, classroom intervention, family involvement, and long-term follow-up. They also designate clear lines of responsibility for the various components of the postvention plan.

Representative Postvention Programs

Siehl (1990) described a postvention program which addresses the aftermath of suicide from a school practitioner's viewpoint. This 10-point program includes (a) team development; (b) in-service programs; (c) faculty contact; (d) crisis centers; (e) individual classroom procedures; (f) days following the suicide; (g) home visitation; (h) special events or memorial services; (i) media coverage; and (j) length of time for concern.

Particular strengths of this program include thorough planning in advance, the establishment of "crisis centers" at key locations throughout the school which are open to any student regardless of relationship to the deceased, continual availability of classroom consultation, and family involvement. Family members are centrally involved in deciding what information will be released to the media and in the planning of special events or memorial services. The plan also incorporates all school staff including bus drivers, food service personnel, and custodial and maintenance staff. Although media and community mental health professionals are involved in the postvention plan, apparently other community representatives (clergy, service organizations, etc.) are not specifically included. Siehl's plan focuses on suicide and does not address other forms of unexpected trauma, such as physical violence, homicide, or accidental death, to which its principles might be applied. Generally this is a well-designed and practical program.

Carter and Brooks (1990) described a clinically oriented approach based upon identifying the survivors who were closest to the deceased and therefore presumably at highest risk for self-destructive behavior. In this approach, professionally trained postvenors conduct a time-limited group process for these identified, high-risk students. This perspective is very useful for the helping professionals (e.g., school counselors, psychologists, social workers, nurses) in understanding the dynamics of recovery from traumatic loss. The model is not intended as a postvention plan for school and community leaders to use every time, but rather as an intensive individualized program focused on high-risk survivors in each particular traumatic loss event. It has the advantage of carefully assisting these survivors and increasing the probability that such individuals will seek further psychotherapy. It must be combined with a broad-based postvention plan developed at the school district and community level such as Siehl's (1990) plan.

In a study done by Hazell and Lewin (1993) the risk factors for suicidal ideation and behavior among students exposed to completed suicide were assessed. The proportion of students who chose to attend counseling and the benefits of counseling in reducing future suicidal ideation and behavior were also examined. Based on their findings, Hazell and Lewin suggested the following postvention guidelines: (a) students should be invited to select themselves for postvention counseling; (b) a brief screening of all students for the presence of risk factors for suicide should be conducted; and (c) counseling should be offered to all those who present risk factors based upon this brief screening. Empirical study found a brief 90-minute, single-session group intervention to be of no benefit; instead, follow-up sessions with the group or high-risk youth are recommended. Although this program did not target community involvement, its major strength is that counseling is offered to all students regardless of their relationship to the deceased. A simple, five-item screening questionnaire helps identify high-risk students who might not otherwise identify themselves.

Wenckstern and Leenaars (1993) outlined a postvention program which is community based and utilizes a team approach. Their multidimensional plan includes consultation, crisis intervention, community linkage, assessment and counseling, education, liaison with the media, and follow-up. The use of a traumatic events response team (TERT) is a strength of this approach. The TERT consists of critically identified school personnel, under the guidance of a mental health professional, who are available for consultation, counseling, and coordination of all aspects of the postvention. These authors offer a very comprehensive program and provide case examples demonstrating the application of their guidelines in response to an adolescent suicide, a bus accident, and an incident in which a school crossing guard was hit by a car. They believe their plan is flexible enough to deal with possible posttraumatic stress reactions and contagion effects which can occur after suicide, homicide, serious accidents, or hostage taking. Community linkage is strongly emphasized and support is extended to all students and parents through small group workshops at the school.

Guidelines for the mental health professional are suggested in a three day, school-based postvention, described by Klingman (1989). The protocol comprises: (a) the initial organizational intervention; and (b) steps for dealing with students' acute reactions to the suicide of their peer. Klingman's approach to postvention focuses on the mental health provider in the school community. This perspective is very helpful in terms of the guidance it offers to the school counselor and/or psychologist in dealing with staff, students, and parents within the first three days of a crisis.

Lamb and Dunne-Maxim (1987) recommended a proactive response to postvention which considers the needs of all students and family members in response to suicide. This model consists of two phases. In the first phase, an outside mental health consultant guides the staff through a "one time" group process in which the "fishbowl" technique is used. All faculty, including auxiliary personnel, sit in an outer circle, with those persons who feel most affected sitting in an inner circle. Persons in the outer circle are told they may also participate but must join the inner circle to speak. Survivors are encouraged to discuss their guilt, denial, distortion of facts, anxiety, anger, and grief. Guidelines for how the staff can respond to student reactions are also given. In phase two, after having incorporated what they have learned, staff help students through individual interactions.

A strength of this program is that it is an economical way to provide postvention services when resources are limited and in situations where there is no existing postvention policy and consultants are unable to work directly with students. All staff are encouraged to attend the one-time group process, a technique which can be adapted to deal with large groups of students. The authors also make valuable suggestions regarding commemorative responses in order to achieve a sense of closure for the students. They strongly discourage overdramatization, mystification, or glorification of suicide. Instead they recommend activities such as fund raising to support a worthy cause or making a contribution to a suicide prevention or youth mental health project. This is an area in which there is some disagreement among postvention professionals, although increasingly most discourage official school sponsorship of memorial services and suggest instead that such activities be done at the initiative of the family (Garfinkel et al., 1988; Lamb & Dunne-Maxim, 1987; Patros, 1989; Shipman, 1987). This approach emphasizes addressing the needs of the living (i.e., the survivors).

Patros and Shamoo (1989) described in detail the responsibilities of the principal, crisis team, faculty and staff, and the suicide consultant. They included suggestions on the availability of substitute teachers, together with an extensive list of behaviors which may be observed in students who are not dealing appropriately with the death. Also discussed is the establishment of crisis centers which are available to all students and school personnel, particularly to close friends and enemies of the suicide victim. The authors believe the focus should be on the stressors that led to the suicide rather than the suicide itself. With this guideline, and with parental permission, they suggest the use of a psychological autopsy of the suicide. Problems the youth may have been having, along with known feelings, attitudes, and behaviors before suicide, are assessed and presented to faculty for their growth and as a way to prevent future suicides. This process requires that postvention professionals demonstrate great sensitivity regarding family wishes and needs.

Hicks (1990) suggested that it is not the intent of postvention to do any type of psychological counseling. Postvention is undertaken to help students deal with their shock and grief through discussion and empathetic support. For students who may be in need of individual counseling, a student assistance program is recommended in which high-risk students are identified by team members within the school and are referred for treatment services to outside professionals. The actual services are provided by contract from a community mental health service or other providers with school funding.

In order to address the needs of other students, Hick's postvention model draws on volunteers from the community who are trained to be postventionists. Their role is to assist students and faculty in open discussion and to encourage communication and expression of feelings with the goal of preventing further crises or suicide. This model centers on community involvement and extends to various other elementary, middle, or high schools where siblings and friends of the victim may attend. All students are offered the opportunity to participate in groups which are facilitated by the volunteer postventionists. Volunteer recruitment and training are discussed, and Hicks clearly defines the roles of both postvention volunteers and the clinical crisis professionals. This is an excellent example of the importance of a community network and its linkage to the school.

Petersen and Straub (1992) noted that "the school collectively becomes a suicide survivor and, in that respect, is subject to all the emotions of any individual survivor: guilt, anger, anxiety and denial" (p. 148). They recommend a community crisis response plan with a committee made up of public and mental health personnel, suicide crisis center personnel, youth leaders, and local government officials. Duties of the community committee include reaching a consensus on a plan, periodically meeting in the absence of a crisis, and developing an effective communication network among community resources (such as police, hospital, school, and mental health agencies) to help prevent the beginning of a suicide cluster. In response to a crisis the committee provides counseling, information to the community, and a spokesperson to address the media. In addition, Petersen and Straub also suggested that teachers, coaches, deans, and counselors be trained to identify high-risk students and they offered a detailed listing of people who should be considered high-risk in the case of adolescent suicide clusters. The authors also address how to cope with a violent crisis, natural disasters, and the dying child in a classroom. This is an extensive and superbly laid-out plan which addresses the full extent of possible crises with particular emphasis on the violent crisis and its widespread effect on a school and community.

Davis and Sandoval (1991) offered guidelines for informing and responding to staff, students, and parents when a suicide has occurred. Their postvention plan encompasses four phases: initial communication with staff and the victim's parents; working with staff and crisis team; working with students and parents; and follow-up. Initial communications are made through the use of a phone tree requesting all personnel attend a planning meeting. This postvention plan, like some others, recommends that the mental health consultant focus on the feelings of faculty while educating them on how they can be helpful to the student. It is proposed that students be informed through an announcement over the intercom or a brief assembly. Parents are to be informed through a letter providing the facts of the case, information about funeral and memorial service arrangements, and an offer of consultation, support, and referrals. Davis and Sandoval suggested the use of a preselected crisis intervention team, the members of which have specialized training in crisis management. They also offer a listing to help identify youth at risk as well as adults who may be at risk. A strength of this program is its coverage of other suicides such as that of a parent, sibling of a student, or suicide of a person working in the school district, and suicide attempt.

Metzgar (1994) outlined a step-by-step, sequential, and systematic process in the design and implementation of a crisis management plan with a strong emphasis on community involvement. Metzgar defined a crisis "as any situation that causes, or has the potential to cause, a disruption of normal functioning within the school community" (p. 20). She included crises which happen within (internal) and outside (external) the school community. For both, Metzgar suggested a plan which is "flexible enough to address the full range of potential crises" (p. 21) and noted that successful crisis management is dependent on a strong internal and external support structure. Internal support includes administrators, teachers, students, and parents. External support includes crisis-trained emergency services personnel, mental health professionals, and religious and community leaders, as well as representatives of local businesses, hospitals, and media. Metzgar's plan addresses issues of cultural and ethnic diversity, political and social factors, and religious and philosophical implications, along with socioeconomic status and unique community characteristics and resources. This is an excellent source for a postvention plan flexible enough to deal with any crises which may occur.

A model proposed by Bozigar and his colleagues (1993) incorporates three goals: (a) to identify and refer students who may be at risk for depression or suicide contagion; (b) to help students begin a healthy grieving process; and (c) to return the school to an emotionally neutral environment as quickly as possible. To achieve these goals, the model sets forth a very specific postvention policy. The precise responsibilities of the postvention coordinator, mental health consultant, and crisis team are outlined in detail. Also, the model addresses issues, such as contacting the coroner, funeral home, decedent's family, other schools where the death may have an impact, students, parents, and the media. The use of an office "gatekeeper" is recommended to assure the confidentiality of students as they are summoned for individual screenings. The program also covers what should occur in the initial staff meeting, how to respond to students' questions, and procedures for student attendance at the funeral. Guidelines for educational support groups and for working with high-risk students are also provided. Consistent with other programs is the recommendation for the establishment of a scholarship or conducting a fund-raising activity in place of a memorial. The principles outlined in this model can also guide the creation of a postvention plan for other tragic deaths, making it an excellent resource for a school's response to suicide and other tragedies.

A plan recommended by the American Association of Suicidology (1990) suggests the availability of drop-in support groups throughout the school which any student may attend for two or three days following the event. The plan also recommends that open meetings for concerned parents be provided. Issues and possible strategies that should be considered during a suicidal student's hospital discharge and school reentry are also addressed.

Review of Empirical Studies of Postvention Programs

Evaluation of postvention programs is limited because of the difficulties and ethical challenges which must be considered in assessing a school in crisis. Hazell and Lewin (1993) evaluated the benefits of counseling for at-risk students following traumatic crises, either suicide or parasuicide. Their findings suggest that "proximity to attempted suicide is a more robust predictor of subsequent suicidal ideation and behavior than proximity to completed suicide" (p. 107). The intervention of a "one time," 90-minute group counseling session was found to be of no benefit; follow-up sessions with the group or selected high-risk individuals were recommended. Clearly, ongoing support is the key to effective coping with the impact of this kind of traumatic experience.

Klingman (1989) assessed the frequency of stress reactions a day after a suicide and found that classmates of the deceased exhibited significantly more psychological distress than did another group of students who did not know the person. Classmates had more discomfort over the question of their responsibility for failure to prevent the suicide, more somatic complaints, and greater overall stress reactions. This study did not examine outcome or follow-up regarding the author's reported 3-day postvention program.

Generally, the literature produced little information regarding outcome or effectiveness of postvention programs. Most of the literature involves theoretical, prescriptive, and programmatic material. Actual programs which have been implemented have rarely been examined empirically. Therefore, we are left without solid assurance that our efforts are yielding real benefits, even though they seem to be founded on both theoretical and anecdotal reports. Clearly there is a need for more research regarding effectiveness, despite logistical, design, and ethical difficulties.

RECOMMENDATIONS CONCERNING THE DEVELOPMENT OF A POSTVENTION PLAN

There are a wide array of possible approaches to postvention, from the point of view of both theory and practice. Surveys indicate that approximately half of public schools in the United States have formal or informal postvention programs (Wass, Miller, & Thornton, 1990). Clearly, we would recommend that all schools have such programs—formally developed, not simply "informally understood." Our suggestions in this section incorporate much of the work of others, while presenting as broad and flexible a plan as possible, one that is adaptable to a wide range of crises and postventions.

Make a Plan

We recommend that school personnel ally themselves with parents and other representatives of the community to develop a postvention plan that will address as many aspects of traumatic losses as possible, ideally long before any such events occur. We stress that the central role needs to be taken by the family which has suffered the loss. The school and community systems can provide support in both the planning and the implementation of the postvention plan, but our role as professionals must remain responsive to the needs of the family throughout the process. This approach is founded on our philosophy, which combines family systems' concepts and principles of adolescent development with the overwhelming need perceived by parents, teachers, and community leaders in contemporary America for close collaboration between schools and families. In a paradoxical sense, it is necessary to have a clearly conceived plan but also to be prepared to abandon it, or at least modify it, as the special dynamics of each postvention unfold. Without the clarity and sense of purpose provided by a well-developed plan, relatively manageable events can quickly become chaotic.

Development of the plan can vary depending on the organizational structure of each school system and community. Therefore, the following steps should be understood as providing a general framework, the details of which will be worked out by individuals within their own school, community, cultural, and family systems. The viewpoint represented here is that the postvention plan should be based upon a broad definition of postvention, covering school and community responses to the aftermath of the gamut of possible traumatic losses which may occur. These include all forms of unexpected death, as well as catastrophic losses like major loss of personal safety created by violence among students or in the community.

Postvention Planning Committee

A committee or task force may need to be created to develop the postvention plan. In many cases, schools will have crisis teams, multidisciplinary teams, student assistance teams, and/or other similar committees already in place that may collaborate to develop the postvention plan. While our suggestion is that a school-based team will provide the leadership in the initial planning stages, we emphasize that the first steps in forming such a committee must involve gaining participation from all potentially affected parties including parents, students, extended family members, mental health providers and organizations, family medical practitioners, drug and alcohol treatment providers, clergy, police department personnel, media representatives, members of bereavement support or self-help organizations like "Compassionate Friends," and city, county or municipal officials. Most of these groups will not be represented as members of the planning committee, but all should be contacted for ideas, suggestions, and concerns. Some of them may actually be interested enough to serve on the committee itself. In any event, all of them must be included in the ultimate postvention plan that is developed.

Education and Public Information

Once a workable plan has been developed, presented by the committee, and accepted by the school administrators, superintendents, and appropriate school board or committee, it is time to thoroughly educate school staff, students, families, and various organizations and individuals in the community about the plan. However, there is a danger that this step will not be completed thoroughly or effectively. There is a considerable level of anxiety about such topics, especially death and violence, and it may be tempting to simply file the plan hoping it will never be needed. We urge that one of the functions of the planning committee should be to educate the school and community about the plan. It is important to update the training and information dissemination processes continually with all of the constituencies listed below because staff and students constantly enter the school setting and then move on. The same is true of families, parents, and community leaders. For example, yearly inservice trainings and regular parent-teacher organization programs should include information about the postvention plan.

Students

Students are probably the first group to inform about the postvention plan. We recommend that this information be included within the context of educating students about the whole range of student support services, such as school counseling services, student assistance programs, extracurricular activities (sports, theater arts, clubs, etc.), scheduling, and college and vocational advisement. In addition, postvention information should be included in a brochure describing these student support services.

Staff

All school staff should be provided with thorough inservice training regarding the postvention plan. We prefer conducting small group trainings to allow time for all questions and concerns. Three broad groups of school personnel must be carefully trained: (a) student services and administrative staff; (b) instructional staff (teachers and others); and (c) school support staff. Student services staff personnel (guidance counselors, psychologists, social workers, student assistance or crisis team members, multidisciplinary team members, nurses, and administrators) should be trained as the key leadership group in a separate meeting or series of meetings. These people can then conduct trainings with relatively small groups of teachers, teachers' aides, and other instructional staff. This makes possible a small-group training format. The success of the entire postvention program may hinge on the depth of caring and concern, as well as the completeness of the preparation and training of the teachers. The third major group of staff members is the support staff, including maintenance, custodial, food service, transportation (bus drivers, crossing guards, etc.), playground supervisors, and others.

Parents

Parents need to be informed that the postvention plan is in place. This can be handled in much the same way that it is with the students, that is, in the context of disseminating all types of relevant information regarding school services. Again, as in the case with the students, both oral presentations such as parents' meetings and publications (brochures, quick-reference cards, etc.) need to be used. In addition, media cooperation can be used to publicize available services including postvention services.

Media

Representatives of the media also need to be informed about the postvention plan. This is of critical importance in the successful management of traumatic loss crises that will inevitably occur. Media representatives will require training and information regarding the need for sensitivity and discretion in the presentation of information regarding a crisis. The profound importance of empathy, confidentiality, and sensitivity to family priorities needs to be emphasized repeatedly with news media personnel, whose intentions are generally good but whose understanding of these key issues is often incomplete. Furthermore, the need to deemphasize sensationalizing and glorifying these kinds of traumatic losses cannot be underscored enough with media representatives. We must convince them to avoid the temptation to sensationalize and instead to focus on the true human needs of the survivors. We can make the media our allies in this endeavor.

RECOMMENDATIONS CONCERNING THE IMPLEMENTATION OF A POSTVENTION PLAN

We have described how to develop a postvention plan and how to educate the many possible constituencies that may be touched by a crisis. In this section, we provide a brief "generic" outline, recognizing that this will only serve as a framework, the details of which must originate in each unique school and community system. Ample resources exist to assist any school system in developing such a plan, many of which are noted in this chapter.

The following statements assume that a traumatic loss or life-threatening event has occurred which is likely to have profound impact on at least several students and in some cases on virtually all of them. Serious effects on many staff members are also assumed to occur in the aftermath of such an event. The following steps are presented in roughly chronological order of occurrence although many of them must take place almost simultaneously. Differences in the responses required for each kind of potentially traumatic event are not detailed here, nor are the many kinds of cultural and socioeconomic differences noted which may occur within the tremendously diverse American cultural fabric. We trust that readers will make the necessary modifications and adjustments needed in their particular situations.

1. *Leadership role.* A designated administrator called the "postvention coordinator" takes the leadership role in notifying postvention team members and all members of the student services staff (counselors, social workers, psychologists, nurses, etc.). A telephone tree system will accomplish this, whether the crisis should occur during school hours, after hours, or on weekends or holidays.

2. *Media notification.* The crisis leadership role as designated above includes as one of its immediate functions the handling of public information. Presumably, solid relationships with the media have been developed and information has been provided to them about the general postvention plan. The postvention coordinator notifies the media through telephone contacts, written press releases, and in some instances, a brief, carefully managed press conference. It is imperative that this step be taken quickly and handled with sensitivity to the family's needs in the situation. In some cases, the family may want to participate in some or all phases of the process. We strongly encourage this kind of alliance with the postvention coordinator.

3. *Crisis team meeting/parent inclusion.* The postvention team meets as soon as possible. The team plans the events and activities to be conducted during the first school day following the traumatic event. If possible, the postvention team will bring the key custodial persons (frequently the parents, but possibly grandparents, stepparents, aunts or uncles, older siblings, or foster parents) into the planning by including them in this meeting.

4. *Notify teachers and other staff.* The postvention team together with the student support staff (counselors, nurses, psychologists, etc.) begins informing staff members from the most senior teachers to the most newly hired custodial worker about the traumatic loss that has occurred. This is done using a telephone tree system. Notification will include instructions about how staff members

are to collect their postvention materials, the known facts about what occurred, how notification of students will be conducted, and a schedule of events for the upcoming school day. This staff notification process should include reminders to exercise discretion, promote confidentiality, encourage help seeking and social support, and discourage sensationalism and glorification of suicide or violence.

5. *Informing the students.* The method of notification should be previously delineated in the postvention plan. The postvention coordinator leads this process. We recommend having teachers and other staff members read a prepared statement in the "homeroom" at the beginning of the day. Consistency in terms of the facts and avoidance of speculation, "psychological interpretation," or professional jargon are crucial in this notification process. It is recommended that this not be conducted in a large assembly. A useful guideline is that the smaller the group size when the notification occurs, the more likely it is that school staff will be able to manage the emotions, questions, and cognitive and behavioral confusion that inevitably follow such announcements. The classroom notification system or the public address system can be used in a way that is consistent with this principle. Smaller groups greatly facilitate the process of identifying high-risk survivors for special postvention services.

6. *Immediate provision of small-group and individual counseling.* An integral part of the notification process includes information for students and staff members about all the support activities and meetings (who, what, when, and where) that will be provided. Special invitations should be extended with sensitivity and confidentiality to those students known to be at risk for suicide or other self-destructive behavior. Identification of "high-risk" students is commonly done through student assistance teams, guidance counselors, special education programs, multidisciplinary teams, and the school disciplinary process. Additionally, students who were close to the victim should be given such invitations even in the absence of any other indicators of "high-risk" status. The specific models and techniques that will be used with individuals and groups should already be well understood by teachers, counselors, psychologists, nurses, social workers, student assistance team members, and outside postvenors, such as mental health providers, drug/alcohol specialists, clergy, and hospice workers. Training and education about the postvention process and plan that we recommended previously should have covered

this material. These personnel should be "ready to go" with these supportive activities.

7. *Provision of supportive consultation to parents and families.* Many family members will be affected throughout the school's extended family network. The impact of the loss will reach into many homes in the community, affecting parent-adolescent interactions and contributing to already high levels of risk present in many contemporary American families. Postvention work must attend to these needs. Some schools may offer programs for parents and other family members within the school setting. Others may provide a referral network to mental health providers, clergy, and other competent people in the community. A combination of the two is probably best.

8. *Supportive consultation for postvention staff.* In the intensity of providing all of these activities, it is easy to lose track of the emotional needs of the postvenors, the psychologists, counselors, administrators, teachers, and others who are doing this immensely taxing postvention work. "Postvention for the postvenors" should be made available in the form of small-group supportive consultation, peer self-help, and individual consultation. School staff members who are specially trained and experienced can facilitate this process. Some school systems may enlist outside professionals for assistance here.

9. *Assessment and referral for high-risk youth.* The postvention process is an opportunity to identify people who need continued help and to connect them to appropriate sources of assistance. Judgments will need to be made during this risk-identification process that require specialized professional training and experience. The entire school staff must know how to obtain consultation and how to refer high-risk students to staff members or outside consultants who are proficient in evaluating the level of risk for suicide, depression, and other kinds of self-destructive behavior, such as drug and alcohol abuse and violence. Student assistance programs should be "in place" to help with this process of identification and referral. School staff members who do not have appropriate training and experience with these issues should never be put in the isolated position of having to make life-and-death decisions alone. When in doubt, consult!

10. *Continuing care and follow-up.* In our view, postvention is a process, not an event. The postvention team should provide for careful follow-up. Support groups and individual counseling must be long-term because all theories of bereavement converge on one

common principle: The grieving process takes a long time for any human being. In today's climate with the possibility of several serious traumatic events occurring in a single school year, it is possible that postvention efforts will be a part of the regular fabric of school life. We view this as a positive and preventive situation that will reduce the level of risk for suicidal, homicidal, and other life-threatening and self-destructive behavior.

CONCLUSION

This chapter has examined the impact of unexpected or traumatic loss and death on early and middle adolescents. In response to such experiences, we have outlined a rationale for establishing community-based postvention programs and described representative postvention programs for early and middle adolescents. In addition, we have offered recommendations concerning both the development and implementation of a postvention plan. We emphasize that within the throes of crisis, adolescents and other humans demonstrate remarkable resilience to recover, live, and even prosper. Effective postvention is our best effort to support that marvelous human quality.

14

The Need for Postvention on College Campuses: A Rationale and Case Study Findings

Ralph L. V. Rickgarn

> All relationships end in parting.
> There are no exceptions.

For many college and university students the possibility that significant relationships in their lives may come to an end may seem antithetical to their experience and all that they believe about life. These young people are just beginning a new chapter in their lives—one that should be filled with anticipation, hope, and high aspirations. Thoughts of loss, bereavement, grief, and mourning are intrusive in such a context. The actuality of such terminations and separations may seem offensive and shocking.

Nevertheless, loss, death, and related issues do intrude into the lives of college students. These occurrences present challenges, uncertainties, and fears to older adolescents who may have encountered few, if any, similar experiences from which to have developed constructive responses. Lack of a suitable repertoire of effective coping mechanisms may create significant concerns or render the individual unable to know how to behave. Fear of appearing to act inappropriately in the eyes of peers may even provoke a paralysis of emotion in college-age adolescents.

Accordingly, college students who are confronted with challenges associated with loss and grief will require assistance from college staff, faculty, and others who are involved in the lives of these students. If appropriate assistance is not forthcoming, these challenges may significantly affect the mental and physical health of students, as well as their ability to function effectively in an academic environment. In some cases, challenges may be of such a magnitude as to create the possibility of a disturbed student or group of students—a situation inimical to them and the institution.

This chapter examines support for students facing significant losses and grief. In order to do so, it explores loss-related issues in the lives of college students, implications of disenfranchised grief for college students, and community responses to collegiate grievers. Thereafter, the concepts of intervention and postvention are introduced to guide discussion about to whom supportive responses should be directed and how they should be conducted. Special attention is given to the idea of a collegiate Death Response Team (DRT) and guidelines for its operation. A DRT has been functioning at the University of Minnesota since 1984. Brief comments on its history and activities illustrate how this form of postvention can be applied to assist older adolescent grievers in college settings.

LOSS IN THE LIVES OF COLLEGE STUDENTS

In February 1981, *The Personnel and Guidance Journal* devoted a special issue to the subject of loss (Rupert, 1981). In that special edition, the guest editor made the following comment: "I believe this collection just scratches the surface of the implications for our profession" (p. 325). That was obviously true. Although the special edition focused on many loss-related topics and many groups affected by loss, there were no articles directly concerned with college students. In retrospect, that really was no surprise.

In 1972, Shneidman edited *Death and the College Student,* a volume of brief essays by Harvard undergraduate students on the subjects of loss, suicide, and death. These essays were the result of a 1969 course that Shneidman taught on the psychology of death. The class attracted more than 200 students, a surprising enrollment that caused Shneidman to reflect on the "popularity" of the course. He noted that there were "some discernible social and psychological forces which give impetus to this new orientation toward death" (p. xvi). The essays in the book reflect students' perspectives on these issues and are a first recognition of the impact of loss, death, and grief on college students. However, the "impetus" must have remained with the students because it was another 10 years before attention to losses experienced by college students and their grief responses became a phenomenon of interest to researchers and others working with college students.

One of the early researchers in this field was LaGrand (1981, 1982, 1985, 1986) who devoted significant time and effort to surveying college students' experiences of loss and to reporting what they said about their responses to such experiences. LaGrand (1986) noted that college students—the quintessential late adolescents and young adults in our society are "victims of a culture which refuses to recognize the magnitude of their losses, suffering, and the emotional pain that accompanies these tragic experiences. They are the hidden mourners of an affluent society" (p. ix).

We might ask: What is there about this group of individuals that results in these reactions to their losses and grief? One answer is that college students are thought to be experiencing "the best years of their lives." That description may simply reflect adult fantasy, a denial of the experiences adults had encountered in their own earlier years, or perhaps even envy on the part of adults who are so immersed in their daily endeavors that the seeming carefreeness of youth creates "blinders" to the totality of the experiences which they encounter. This devaluation of loss and grief in the lives of college students may also be the result of a youth-oriented society that would like to deny or delay the processes of aging, the inevitability of death, and the pain of grief. Such a society may not permit itself to consider ways in which these dimensions of all human experience are part of the lives of older adolescents. Similarly, the supposed invulnerability and perceived personal immortality of youth may lead college students not to believe or want to believe that any form of pain from loss or death could or should enter into their worlds.

In fact, however, college students are not unfamiliar with issues of loss, death, and grief. LaGrand's (1982) study of recent major losses revealed that 28.4% of his respondents had experienced the death of a loved one or a sudden death, 25.4% the end of a love relationship, 10.8% the end of a friendship, and 9.1% separation from loved ones. Individuals who had experienced such losses constituted a total of 73.1% of LaGrand's sample of 2,049 college students. Almost 70% of these students reported feeling depressed. Sixty percent experienced shock, 55% experienced feelings of emptiness, and 52% experienced feelings of disbelief. Helplessness and anger were present in approximately 43% of the respondents, and about one third experienced feelings of loneliness. This broad spectrum of emotional responses to loss was reported to be accompanied by both immediate and long-term physical reactions. The dominant physical response was crying (79%), but one third of the students also reported headaches, insomnia, and exhaustion.

College students in LaGrand's study reported varying coping responses to the death of a loved one. Crying and talking about the death were the responses of 70%, while 60% found accepting the death to be a positive response. The value of time well used, and the support of family and friends, were commented upon by approximately 50% of these students. It is interesting that LaGrand (1982) noted "relatively few students used the counseling center as a major support in their grieving unless they became desperate and unable to cope" (p. 25). Consequently, it is apparent that even though college students are likely to encounter significant experiences—often their first such experiences—with loss and the death of a significant person in their lives during their collegiate years, they may not recognize their own need for professional help in coping with such events.

Almost ten years after LaGrand's work, Thornton, Robertson, and Gilleylen (1991) undertook to determine the level of intensity of the grief process among college students, together with their perceptions about the availability of social support. These researchers found that students systematically underestimated the intensity of the grief process. In addition, they found another phenomenon: "Counselors should be alert that with disenfranchised losses grievers may need additional support because members of their social support networks may not provide the support" (p. 10). Clearly, college students do experience important losses, deaths, and grief, even though such experiences may not be widely recognized as a part of their overall lives, even though they may fail to appreciate the intensity of their responses to such events, and even though both college students and those around them may not recognize their needs for suitable assistance and support.

DISENFRANCHISED GRIEF AND COLLEGE STUDENTS

The concept of disenfranchised grief provides useful insights into the inadequate appreciation of and response to grief and loss experienced by college students. Doka's (1989) definition of this concept and explanation of reasons for its occurrence sheds light on key elements of these experiences in the lives of college students. Doka defined disenfranchised grief as "grief that persons experience when they incur a loss that is not or cannot be openly acknowledged, publicly mourned, or socially supported" (p. 4).

College students may experience the death of a significant person in their lives during their collegiate years. Often, this is the first encounter which they will have had with such a loss. Without a broad or helpful foundation in similar experiences and in coping with such losses in constructive ways, college students may be unsure of the legitimacy of their reactions (both whether and how they should react), even though they will know how they feel emotionally and physically. In many college students, there is a keen awareness of not wanting to engage in inappropriate behavior in the company of their peers—even though it may not be clear to the individuals in question what will or will not be regarded as inappropriate in such circumstances. Likewise, their peers, who may themselves have little or no experiential base in coping with significant losses, may be unaware of the impact of such losses on an individual or may not know how they themselves should also act or react. Both college students who experience significant losses and other students around them may be unprepared to cope with such experiences in constructive ways. Such individuals often become incapacitated and are unable to respond to each other in a helpful manner. As a result, disenfranchisement in these circumstances may arise from sources both within and outside of the individuals immediately concerned.

Doka (1989) has observed that disenfranchisement may also occur for three reasons that are clearly applicable to college students. The first of these is that *the relationship may not be recognized.* A student's grief over the death of a grandparent, parent, sibling, or other blood relative is most likely—although not always—to be viewed as appropriate. But other emotionally based relationships formed in a college setting may not be recognized. These can include relationships between roommates, sports team members, close friends, and lovers (particularly homosexual lovers). In these and other situations, a close and intense relationship may have developed, even though it has not been known to or recognized by others.

The second reason for disenfranchisement is that *the loss may not be recognized.* For college students, losses which commonly fall into this category may include the separation or divorce of parents. Disruption in relationships between parents will often be recognized as having an effect on the adults concerned, but it may only be acknowledged as affecting a college student if there is an accompanying loss of an anticipated financial base for funding that individual's continuing education. Even in instances of abusive families, the dissolution of familial relationships may result in significant grief on the part of a college student over the loss of a cohesive, although dysfunctional, family unit.

Another area in which loss is often discounted is that of pet loss. For a college student, the family dog or cat may have been with the family for "as long as I can remember." Loss of such a pet can be significant and can result in intense feelings of loneliness and sorrow. However, "under the laws of most states, pets are still considered merely items of personal property rather than objects of affection with a value beyond a market appraisal. From that perspective, how can grieving be justified for dogs and cats" (Nieburg & Fischer, 1982, p. xiv)? Many college students may be intimidated and unable to grieve the loss of their pets openly because these are losses that are not recognized or sanctioned by much of society.

A third reason for disenfranchisement is that *the griever is not recognized*. Doka (1989) noted that people who are often placed in this category include the very young, the aged, and persons with mental disabilities. Such individuals are viewed as having little comprehension of the concept of death. Consequently, many in our society appear to believe that such individuals cannot experience grief. This view is maintained even though there may be substantial evidence to show otherwise.

Although college students are not usually described as very young, aged, or mentally disabled, there are situations in which they may not be recognized by society in their capacity as rightful grievers. One circumstance in which this often occurs involves the death of a homosexual lover. The surviving partner in such a relationship may not be recognized as capable of grief while in an "illegal and immoral relationship."

One example of this is Robert, who had been living with his lover, Charlie, since their freshman year in college. In their senior year, Charlie was killed in a motorcycle accident. Charlie's parents immediately claimed the body, had it cremated, had a private funeral, removed everything they thought belonged to their son from the apartment, and asked never to be contacted. Robert's relationship with Charlie and his grief over Charlie's death were recognized by a few gay friends, but his parents told him not to "rock the boat." Others simply avoided the subject when they met Robert.

In this example—as in many real-life situations—the relationship between Robert and Charlie, Robert's loss, and Robert's grief all went unrecognized by members of Robert's immediate society. Thus, the three principal reasons for disenfranchised grief overlap and interrelate in such circumstances. This multifaceted quality of disenfranchised grief is often found in loss and grief among college students. Whatever the roots of the disenfranchisement, there is a need to rectify the situation and recognize the right of students to grieve and mourn the significant losses in their lives. Similarly, there is a need to provide such individuals with the respect, recognition, and support which they deserve and require. Without appropriate enfranchisement and assistance, such college students may experience an exacerbation, intensification, and complication of their grief and mourning.

COMMUNITY RESPONSES TO COLLEGIATE GRIEVERS

Although the potentially traumatic effects of grief have been recognized since the pioneering work of Lindemann (1944), it is only relatively recently that any attention has been focused on college students as grievers. For example, Donohue (1977) wrote one of the first articles that dealt with student deaths. Most of his article focused on administrative efforts following the death of a student and on contacts with the family. However, in a section on memorial services, Donohue noted that "a memorial does respond to the needs of local students and friends and at the same time gives the campus an opportunity to share a mutual grief with the family" (p. 30).

Similarly, Hipple, Cimbolic, and Peterson (1980) reported on the response of a student services program to a death by suicide, while Halberg (1986) developed a similar account of coping with a death from natural causes on campus. Although these reports devoted much attention to administrative matters, they also recognized the needs of students as exemplified by the following comment from Hipple, Cimbolic, and Peterson (1980): "Realizing that grief reactions can take some time to surface, contact was continued by the dormitory staff with all of the students primarily involved in the incident" (p. 457). In addition, one of the substantive recommendations in this report was that a "referral network for long- and short-term psychological support and consultation needs to be clearly identified" (p. 458).

In a broader account of death-related losses on college campuses, Stephenson (1985) recognized both needs, the organizational realities and the consequences for student survivors on the campus, as significant and essential to the development of a caring community. Stephenson also observed that there is a therapeutic value in community, and he urged institutions to identify those groups that were most affected by the loss in order to be able to work to assist them. "The appropriate resources of the university system should be identified, and efforts should be undertaken to ensure that a student's death is responded to in ways that not only recognize the impact of the loss on the survivors but also work to assist those survivors in coping with their grief both individually and in community" (p. 12).

Stephenson and others who contributed to Zinner's (1985) *Coping with Death on Campus* became a catalyst for the publication of journal articles describing how campuses responded to student deaths and an impetus for establishing appropriate response mechanisms on college campuses (e.g., Furr & Simpson, 1989; Halberg, 1986; Rickgarn, 1987). Recognizing and enfranchising loss and grief among college students has become a legitimate issue for student services professionals and others on college campuses.

In order to determine the appropriateness of a community response to collegiate grievers, each institution needs to assess its own campus climate in relationship to the developmental needs of its students, situational needs arising from traumatic life events, and how these needs are or are not being met. This assessment may be guided by the following questions:

- What is known about college student loss and grief issues (or grief and loss issues in general) on the campus, who knows it, and what is done with the information?
- Does the campus actively seek to foster the psychosocial development of its students, who is responsible for those overall efforts, and what is done in that area?
- Are efforts in this area coordinated throughout the institution or are they assumed to be one individual's responsibility, with other staff and faculty having little or no investment in them?
- Are these efforts formalized or do they exist as an ad hoc enterprise with little or no support or interest from the institution as a whole? If formalized, is there genuine support from the upper echelons of the administration?
- Are there training programs for both paraprofessional and professional staff focusing on issues of bereavement, grief, and mourning?

INTERVENTION AND POSTVENTION WITH COLLEGE STUDENTS

Why Should Institutions Intervene?

The major focus of most colleges and universities is on the curricular aspects of the institution. Promotional materials and other literature most often display the academic credentials and accomplishments of the faculty. These are the individuals who will be lecturing in the classroom, working in the laboratories, and advising students on their academic progress. Promotional materials also display the physical plant of the campus, focusing on the "eye appeal" of unique or historical buildings and areas where students will learn. Often, these materials present only a cursory overview of what is available on the campus to aid in the psychosocial development of students. In fact, in most instances, it is material that is related to the residence life program on the campus that focuses most closely on student development issues. While references to the various student services that are available for the noncurricular or the cocurricular aspects of the institution are becoming more apparent in college recruitment materials, only rarely will one find within these materials any information on counseling or other services for students related to issues of loss and death.

Since intervention is not likely to be one of the major components of an institution's public relations effort, why should there be intervention on the campus on behalf of students experiencing loss and grief? The answer encompasses three basic reasons. First, as a matter of principle *institutions should be committed to student development beyond the curriculum.* Counseling and student personnel programs cannot be maintained merely as theoretical efforts. Student affairs offices must be willing to engage students in all aspects of their lives. To do otherwise is to ignore the concept of the total student as espoused in the student development literature. One hopes that holistic development is not merely a subject for such literature; that it is accepted as an integral part of each campus' student affairs program and of each institution's comprehensive policy.

The second reason is more pragmatic. *Students who are distressed are at risk and cannot fully participate in either the curricular or co-curricular activities of the institution.* A loss of productivity in classroom, work, or any other aspect of college life may affect the student's ability to succeed, as well as his or her decision to remain at the institution. Students who are under pressures arising from loss and death-related experiences may engage in disturbing behaviors, become mentally disturbed, or both. Students in such perilous situations cannot be of benefit to themselves or to the institution.

The third reason for intervention is that *the institution should develop and maintain a genuine caring attitude toward students and all of the members of its community.* Unless such an attitude exists and unless it is expressed in concrete action on behalf of the institution and those who are its constituents, no college can hope to achieve its mission and stay in operation. This attitude and these actions are nowhere more relevant than in relation to those older adolescents and young adults who form the student body of a college or university and who have been impacted by loss and grief.

To Whom Is Intervention Directed at the College Level?

When college students suffer a significant loss or the death of someone who is important to them, the nature of that loss or their relationship to the person in question is not of primary importance for intervention. Whether the death is that of a member of the student's family, a room-mate, classmate, friend, or lover, intervention needs to be available. The type of intervention that is offered may differ. The important point is that it helps to begin the process of enfranchising student grief through understanding the effects of loss and grief, and appreciating that which will be involved in effective grief work.

Nevertheless, in some cases the nature of the death raises specific issues that require additional attention. Deaths of this sort include cata-strophic deaths, suicide, and deaths from HIV infection and AIDS. Catastrophic deaths occur when substantial numbers of individuals die, usually in a sudden, unexpected, and traumatic manner. Such deaths might result from a plane crash (e.g., when the plane was carrying the institution's sports team), a mass murder on the campus, or a series of interrelated homicides. Deaths of this sort create a profound impact beyond those individuals who were personal friends of the deceased. Typically, the enormity of the catastrophe quickly envelops the entire campus. Clearly, this type of event requires a campuswide intervention effort.

Suicidal deaths also create circumstances in which it is important to engage in postvention efforts for the survivors and sometimes to counter inappropriate media reporting. The possibility that such deaths may be seductive and influence vulnerable individuals to engage in a similar course of action in an attempt to resolve perceived prob-lems creates a situation in which concerted effort is required to en-courage potentially suicidal individuals to obtain counseling assistance.

Student deaths from HIV infection and AIDS are probably relatively rare on college campuses because the illness is likely to force with-drawal from the institution long before the death occurs. Nevertheless, the impact of the deaths of former students cannot be discounted. In addition, it is also possible that the significant other of the deceased is present on the campus. Clearly, the social stigma associated with AIDS must be addressed in working with student survivors of a person who died from HIV infection and AIDS.

How Should Intervention be Conducted at the College Level?

It is always better to be prepared and to adopt a proactive stance rather than a reactive stance. Interventions may take the form of regularly conducted programs that may focus on issues of loss and death, bereavement, or grief and mourning. These presentations can prepare students by discussing emotional, physical, and other responses that are encountered by survivors. They can also give permission to students to confront and express the feelings they have. Such students need to understand that each person reacts to loss and grief in his or her own individual way, depending on his or her prior relationship with the lost person or object, the way in which the loss or death occurred, the coping mechanisms which he or she has developed, and the availability and nature of the support which he or she receives.

To promote such understandings, developmental workshops and courses have been developed (Eckstein, 1982) which address the crucial existential aspects of loss and grief in relationship to life and living. In a similar way, others (Jacobs & Towns, 1984; Charles & Eddy, 1987) have undertaken to teach residence hall staff about issues of loss, death, and coping with a death. A survey of residence hall training materials suggests that where programs of this sort have been implemented residence life staff have become the most knowledgeable campus group as they provide direct services to and work with students in their daily lives.

Wrenn (1992) has adopted a proactive approach by arguing that "every institution of any size has the responsibility to delegate to one of its members the task of coordinating the psycho-social needs of the survivors of a death" (p. 33). In addition, Doka (1985) noted that an effective death education program not only involves courses and programs, but it also seeks to infuse the entire curriculum with content on loss and death.

Whether an individual, or preferably a group, has developed institutional protocols, workshops, training materials, or courses on death and dying, the important principle is that there are in place activities and courses that enable students to begin an understanding of life and death as a continuum instead of separate entities, and then to develop effective coping mechanisms for bereavement, grief, and mourning.

INTERVENTION AND POSTVENTION

The term "intervention" comprises all of the activities undertaken to assist someone who needs help. The term *postvention* refers to that form of intervention which occurs after the fact, after the event of some loss or death. The term postvention was first introduced by Shneidman (1973; see also 1975) who defined it as "those things done after the dire event has occurred that serve to mollify the aftereffects of the event in a person who has attempted suicide, or to deal with the adverse effects on the survivor-victims of a person who has committed suicide" (1973, p. 385). Shneidman coined this term in the context of his concern for individuals who were bereaved as the result of the death by suicide of a significant other, but the concept obviously has broader application to other sorts of deaths and losses.

The first point to note about postvention is its particular relevance to unexpected or unanticipated deaths and losses. The second point is the implicit reminder carried with this concept that even when there is nothing that we are able to do to be of help before a dire event, there is still much that can be done afterwards to assist survivors. And a third point to note is that postvention is more than merely a reactive form of intervention. It is also a proactive, forward-looking form of prevention intended to mitigate future mental health problems.

There is an old Chinese proverb which states, "You cannot prevent the birds of sorrow from flying over your head, but you can prevent them from building nests in your hair." This wise observation recognizes that sorrow is inevitable in human life, even as it suggests that effective coping with loss can mitigate present and future pangs of grief. The goal of postvention efforts on college campuses is to combine recognition of the inevitability of the ending of relationships with efforts to provide members of the campus community with the means to cope effectively with their loss and grief.

POSTVENTION STRATEGIES

Many of the authors cited earlier in the discussion of community responses to collegiate grievers (e.g., Donohue, 1977; Halberg, 1986; Hipple, Cimbolic, & Peterson, 1980) described various forms of postventive intervention, including direct intervention tactics used by one counseling center (Corazzini & May, 1985) and the development of an interdisciplinary group whose primary objective is to work with survivors (students, staff, and faculty) and respond to their needs (Rickgarn,

1987). Here, it may be helpful to formalize our discussion of postvention efforts by dividing them into three working categories: individual counseling; group counseling; and a response team working with survivors in their living or working environments. Each of these can be an effective part of a total campus response.

Individual counseling is probably the most highly developed form of response to loss and grief on many campuses. In this mode of postvention, an individual student typically makes an appointment with a counselor and discusses his or her concerns. This approach is best suited to situations involving highly individualized needs. One drawback is that it depends on the motivation and ability of the student to seek individual counseling. It is also the most costly and time-inefficient method of postvention.

The development of *survivor groups* has been a hallmark of the suicide and grief support programs that have sprung from crisis centers, religious groups, and community agencies. Some campus survivor groups that have been developed include those described by Zinner (1985), Berson (1988), Balk, Tyson-Rawson, and Colletti-Wetzel (1993), Janowiak et al. (1993), and Rickgarn (1994). These groups provide members with "the realization that they are not unique in their needs or interests, that there are others who also experience similar types of pain or discomfort and want to make changes in their lives, to eliminate adverse situations" (Rickgarn, 1994, p. 186).

Drawing on Yalom's (1985) description of "therapeutic factors" in a model taken from group therapy, McNurlen (1991) described a series of helping factors that characterize the operation of effective support groups. These factors include: identification; universality; catharsis; guidance; instillation of hope; existential issues; cohesiveness; and altruism. Support groups are certainly not therapy groups. Members of support groups come together voluntarily because of the difficulties they are encountering in coping with a shared life experience. Before their encounter with loss, such persons were, for the most part, ordinary individuals who were generally functioning normally in living. They seek not to be changed but to find assistance in coping with losses that have taxed their capacities.

For individual members and for the support group as a whole, the helping elements in the group experience can often be effective and productive. Whenever it is possible to establish generalized grief support groups (or specialized groups for those with more specific interests, such as suicide survivors), there is a saving in staff time and resources that is both good management of resources and welcome on campuses experiencing retrenchment and reallocation. More important, through the support group there is an opportunity to develop a sense of belonging and care on the campus. This arises as grieving students come to realize that not only can they obtain assistance from the group but through the group they can also engage in an important learning process about themselves and others. This realization can be shared with peers in discussions in residence halls, fraternities and sororities, and other living units on and off the campus, as well as in informal settings on the campus.

In support groups, as in individual counseling, grieving students must, on an individual basis, take the initiative to seek assistance in coping with their loss and grief. However, some students may find themselves too paralyzed by the tragic event to seek relief, or they may be unwilling to seek assistance for various reasons. Others may simply decide "it'll go away" or "I can handle it, no big deal!" Still others may believe that they do not have time in their hectic schedules to take on additional engagements. Finally, some simply do not know that resources are available to them. Even though there may be a distinct and pressing need for assistance, potential ways of obtaining that help may seem to be unavailable to or inappropriate for many students even in their greatest moments of emotional crisis.

When students will not, cannot, or do not know how to seek assistance in coping with loss and grief, what can be done? The *death response team* is a third mode of postvention, especially well suited to such circumstances.

THE DEATH RESPONSE TEAM: OPERATIONAL GUIDELINES

The basic premise of the DRT is that support can and should be brought to grieving college students, staff, or faculty where they live and work (Rickgarn, 1987). The DRT's objectives are to (a) provide a trained volunteer group that can respond to groups that have encountered a death among their members; (b) facilitate individual and group reactions to the death in an informal group setting; (c) supply initial telephone and onsite consultations for staff who are responsible for living or collegiate units; (d) offer follow-up consultation or counseling services for the group or its individual members; and (e) arrange referrals for individuals who may require short- or long-term counseling in order to address specific issues.

The DRT is composed of individuals from the counseling center, the campus mental health clinic, the residence life staff, the office of the

Vice President for Student Affairs, the university police department (officers and chaplain), campus religious centers, and public health faculty. This interdisciplinary group provides a broad spectrum of approaches by individuals who are all trained in counseling services. On campuses where there are fewer staff, a team could be supplemented with individuals from the local community who are also trained in counseling. The training and use of peer counselors can also be an effective adjunct to team membership. Within the DRT, members are responsible for recruitment, development, and training of additional persons. The DRT is administratively located in the campus counseling center where a staff member coordinates efforts. Brochures that describe the purpose of the DRT and provide the 24-hour contact number (the university police department) are available throughout the campus. The brochures advertise the availability of the team, and, more important, incorporate the DRT as an established part of campus life.

The context of an actual intervention provides a concrete example of students' reactions to the loss of a classmate and the operation of the DRT. A student's personal point of view was presented in a University of Minnesota newsletter article, "Grief in the classroom: When a student dies" (Garrott, 1994). This article records the events that occurred when two graduate students were involved in a car accident on their way to class. One of them, Abby, was killed. The article begins with the announcement of her death to her fellow students at the beginning of the class. Reflecting on the events of the afternoon, Garrott (1994) presented the following observation.

> I remember this afternoon as a series of disjointed events shrouded in feelings of confusion. This stood in contrast to the regular flow of class time where roles are well-defined and occurrences predictable. But in this situation, the usual structure was missing. The instructors were not in their usual leadership roles. They, too, were in shock and emotionally affected by the news. Classroom leadership is different when the instructor participates emotionally with the students. To lead a class in a moment when human emotion is the focus is much different from leading a cognitive inquiry. I can imagine that this is an unfamiliar and uncomfortable role for many university instructors. In this situation, it was not clear what we should do. The actions we undertook were tentative and groping. This was not solely the result of an unfamiliar situation, but due to the shock and the sorrow. (p. 2)

As the students gathered for a second class period, they began to talk about their emotional and physical reactions, beginning to understand the multiple perspectives of their classmates in grieving this death. But other issues also arose within the group.

The issue of whether to alter our schedules to grieve or to carry on with our routines arose in this meeting. We faced a major conflict within ourselves: Do we take the time and energy to grieve, recognize that our lives have been changed and admit that we are not capable of performing academically as we had before? Or, do we get "back to business" and carry on with our studies without much disruption? At this early point in the grieving process, we took space and time away from our regular schedule to grieve. I personally did not want or need to have that hour of class. I don't remember much about it. I do remember looking around, missing Abby and Carmen. (Garrott, 1994, p. 2)

Although these students had an understanding of some of their emotional responses and needs, in two class sessions after the funeral they found they were still unable to concentrate on their usual routines (e.g., schoolwork, housework, and personal relationships). They found themselves experiencing conflicting internal voices. One voice said, "In my grief, I simply can't carry on with my normal work." The other said, "What is the matter with you? You are just making excuses for not getting your work done." These inner conflicts and other unresolved issues resulted in a decision by the students and instructor to arrange for an intervention by the DRT.

Operational Guidelines

The operational guidelines that follow were used in the development of the intervention with this class and are recommended as a basis for the work of a death response team.

Contact.   Once a death has been reported to a contact point, DRT members are contacted to determine who is available to work with the situation. In most instances, two team members are engaged to work with the survivors' group, particularly if it is a large group, such as the members of a residence hall floor or a fraternity house.

Assessment.   One team member contacts the person who made the initial contact and determines what has occurred. The same individual requests other information needed to make an assessment of the situation. As a response strategy is developed, a determination is made concerning the immediacy of the needed intervention. In some instances it may be necessary to make an immediate intervention because of the emotional distress of the survivors or to deter rumors. Rumor control by team members (and others such as residence hall staff) can reduce distortions, ascertain the validity of information, and, at times, provide a mechanism for law enforcement and other departments to offer accurate information to the group. In other instances, it may be more productive to allow a day to elapse so that the shock of the event may subside and individuals may be more capable of responding to assistance. This assessment is made jointly by the person who called and the team members.

Preintervention. Upon arriving at the site, DRT members consult with the staff or other leader(s) for the group. This allows team members and the group leader(s) to become acquainted if they are not already familiar with each other. Team members also can learn of any further information that has been developed or consequences that might affect their actions, such as the group's or some individual's emotional reaction or attitude. The group leader(s) introduce the team members to the assembled group in order to provide some initial trust and rapport.

Intervention. Initially, DRT members focus on their purpose, clarify the known facts of the death(s), and discuss loss and grief reactions with an emphasis on the individual nature of those reactions. The team members also discuss emotional and physical reactions that are commonly experienced by persons who are bereaved, reassuring members of the group that a wide range of emotional reactions is normal and to be expected. Group members are encouraged to share their reactions and to allow their emotions to show, as they feel comfortable. These assurances are particularly important with students (and sometimes with adults as well) for they are often shocked by the death of a peer and may feel isolated in their reactions. This is particularly true if their emotional reactions do not appear to be synchronous with those of other members of their group. Students need to be assured that different relationships, different levels of intimacy, and their own value systems all combine to produce differing reactions. Participants are also encouraged to ask questions that may be on their minds.

As the interaction changes from the didactic to the experiential, it is important for one DRT member to quietly observe and assess individuals while the other team member deals with questions and emotional responses. This allows other individuals who may be more reticent to be drawn into the conversation or to note unusual reactions that will need individual attention after the group session. Usually these group sessions last for two hours, although this depends on the resilience of the group.

DRT members conclude by summing up what has happened during the intervention, providing referral numbers for individuals who wish to engage in further counseling and noting that they will remain for a short time should anyone wish to talk with them individually. There inevitably are a few individuals who want to share some feelings in private or ask for referrals.

Garrott's (1994) observations on this intervention show that even in a short period of time, in this case somewhat under two hours, a well-planned intervention can have a significant impact even with a group that has been attempting to resolve grief issues among themselves and their instructors.

> One of the counselors served as a facilitator and asked us to share how we were feeling. He assured us after each response that such feelings were common symptoms of grieving. These included undirected anger and frustration, a low tolerance level for one's own foibles and those of others, lowered self-confidence, inability to focus on work, the re-experiencing of past pain and grief, and inattention to daily routines such as washing dishes and clothes, preparing meals, and exercising. Also included is a new-found awareness that human life is delicate and fragile, and that loved ones are to be cherished and protected. . . .
>
> I valued the presence of the counselors, for they provided us with a knowledgeable perspective on grieving. They were not grieving Abby's death themselves, and this brought a certain objectivity to their listening skills. In some ways, it was comforting to have someone from outside the group lead our discussion. This I found similar to the structure of the funeral, where I felt able to focus on my own grief instead of worrying about the needs of others. The counselors also let us know that we were not isolated in our grief and that resources were available to us. . . .
>
> Though we are all earnest students, every aspect of the student role has been affected by our grief. Concentrating on lectures, completing routine assignments, coming up with novel ideas, making presentations, problem solving, reading, and in our case, student teaching, have all become more difficult. Having time and permission to discuss these difficulties as well as our feelings of grief has been a great help. I believe we will all be better teachers for having known Abby and for having shared our grief in losing her. (pp. 5, 7)

Postintervention.   DRT members again meet with the leadership of the group to quickly assess the intervention and determine what follow-up might be needed. Individual concerns may be presented and options offered. The group leadership is given telephone numbers for any subsequent meetings that might be needed. DRT members also recapitulate their impressions between themselves for their own evaluation and feedback. As soon as possible, DRT members call the campus counseling service and the mental health clinic in order to alert them to the possibility of walk-in clients following the intervention—which often occurs. This advance notice not only serves to alert the clinics to the possibility of greater walk-in numbers, but also provides clinic staff with some background information about the event, thereby enabling them to work with clients more effectively and with greater immediacy.

Evaluation. Meetings of DRT members are held quarterly for several purposes. Those members who have been involved in interventions report on the events which required their assistance and their observations of what happened. In addition, they describe feedback that they have received from the group or its leaders. As these experiences are shared, other members provide feedback and future intervention tactics are considered. DRT members also discuss proactive efforts that can be undertaken to alert the campus community to issues of loss and grief.

THE DEATH RESPONSE TEAM AT THE UNIVERSITY OF MINNESOTA

Originally, members of the DRT at the University of Minnesota had planned to work only with student groups in residence halls, sororities, and fraternities. However, in the 10 years of the DRT's existence at this university, the DRT has been called upon to work with sports teams, staff, and faculty groups where students, staff, and faculty are present for a session. The DRT's work has expanded to encompass any group that wishes to have the team conduct an intervention with them.

This effort has proved to be effective at the University of Minnesota where volunteer DRT members have provided the university community with an almost no cost service (departments usually allow compensatory time for DRT members equaling the intervention time, but many members do not use this time). However, for the campus community there have been significant rewards beyond the monetary. "Most of all, the team has provided a mechanism that takes the university beyond its routine and rather impersonal roles and procedures when a student dies. The team's members enter into a true involvement with the men and women of the university whose lives have been diminished by the death of a friend" (Rickgarn, 1985, p. 198).

CONCLUSION

When death intrudes into the usual vibrancy of a campus, it often happens suddenly and produces a significant impact on students, staff, and faculty. Whether the death results from natural causes, an accident, a suicide, or a homicide, it creates powerful emotional reactions among the survivors. Among students, their sense of invulnerability and immortality is rudely shattered. They are likely to experience emotional responses that they may never have previously encountered and may well not understand. Faculty and staff are often left feeling hopeless, particularly in the wake of a catastrophic event.

Precisely at these moments, the need for developed and prompt postvention efforts is most strongly felt. Such efforts are required to empower the members of the campus community at a time when incapacitation becomes the more normal state of affairs. Empowerment of students, staff, and faculty which enables them to begin interactions and to develop a genuine caring about each other before a death happens can create a climate that gives permission for empathic caring when a death does occur. Without a core group of committed persons on the campus, institutional programs—whatever their level of excellence—will take on aspects of a Hollywood movie set. "We look beautiful from the outside, our claims to fame are presented for everyone to admire. It all looks so wonderful and real until someone reaches for the doorknob and opens the door to what they believe is reality only to find that it is a fiction, a mirage. It takes much work, many dedicated people, and significant resources to create reality behind the door. If reality isn't there the student's perspective will be of the desert, not the promised land" (Rickgarn, 1994, p. 230).

Research to understand the losses of college students and their response to such losses is at a bare minimum. The development of organizational responses is in its infancy; it may not even exist on many campuses. Even with these minimal efforts, we know the powerful effects of loss, death, and grief on the campus community in general and on students in particular. In order to meet our obligations to the development of students, academically and psychosocially, further and more in-depth research must be conducted. Meanwhile, all campuses need to organize response units to cope with these issues in a proactive manner. To do otherwise is to risk disturbed students and disturbing actions on the campus, as well as the potential loss of excellent students who have become temporarily disabled by loss and grief.

15

Support Groups for Bereaved Adolescents

Richard G. Tedeschi

In the 1960s, it became apparent that an increasingly mobile, secular, and anonymous society was spawning groups of people who were meeting together for the purpose of finding ways to address and bear life problems they had in common. Alcoholics Anonymous had existed since the 1930s, but other groups were being formed to address issues that were not appropriate for 12-step treatment, had not been satisfactorily dealt with by existing organizations and professionals, and had been traditionally addressed within tight-knit communities, extended families, and religious congregations. Estimates of "mutual-help" or "self-help" group membership now range from 10 to 15 million in 500,000 to 750,000 groups (Katz, 1993).

These groups originate in a variety of ways: formation by persons who met because of common problems; spin-offs from existing groups to address more specific needs; sponsorship by professionals or community entities that identify a need among people they serve. Some groups have endured over many years and developed a professional leadership and organization; others exist only to serve the needs of the original members, then dissolve. There are different degrees of "self-help" involved in the functioning of these groups. Some are truly grassroots entities with no professional or organizational ties where mutuality is most highly valued. Some have charismatic leaders who, while not professionals, direct activities and form the group ideology. In still other groups, members are encouraged to make use of mutual help by professional leaders who provide the structure for the group.

The purposes of self-help groups include social and political action, establishment of community in a hostile social environment, and obtaining emotional support in coping with life circumstances and traumas. When emotional support is the most important purpose of a group, it is often called a "support group." These have been characterized by the presence of group leaders, regular meetings, and a focus on sharing of painful feelings, problems, and new approaches and solutions to the difficulties members have in common (Silverman, 1980).

BEREAVEMENT SUPPORT GROUPS

Among support groups, some formed for the purpose of addressing bereavement issues are very well known. These include The Compassionate Friends (for bereaved parents), Widow-to-Widow programs, NAIM and THEOS (they help each other spiritually) (for the widowed) (Videka-Sherman, 1990). Studies have shown that persons join these groups in order to be with others who share the same life experience and to learn how others cope with their bereavement. Although group members make it clear that they are not seeking psychological help, the stated reasons for joining involve aspects of psychological help (Videka-Sherman, 1990). This may indicate that support group participants, though distressed and confused, wish to see themselves as essentially healthy and normal. In turn, the ideology of the bereavement support groups is that the personal reactions are the result of the extraordinary stress, and these reactions are quite normal.

Participants in bereavement support groups generally report that they become freer in expressing feelings, more in control of their lives, and more confident, happy, and connected with others (Videka-Sherman & Lieberman, 1985). But positive changes have also been reported by bereaved persons not participating in such groups (Barrett, 1978; Marmar et al., 1988), and positive effects beyond self-report can be difficult to discern (Videka-Sherman & Lieberman, 1985; Sabatini, 1989).

BEREAVEMENT SUPPORT FOR ADOLESCENTS: DEVELOPMENTAL TASKS, BEREAVEMENT TASKS, AND SOCIAL SUPPORT

In contrast to the considerable attention given to bereavement support groups for adults in the professional literature, there is little mention of support groups for adolescents. There is no national organization providing such groups, although individual Compassionate Friends chapters may decide to form groups with siblings under the direction of a professional (Peterson, 1984). Most reports of adolescent support groups describe a local effort (e.g., Fox, 1989), usually initiated by school personnel or other professionals. Adolescents must rely on adults to recognize their distress and need for support, and for these adults to make the efforts to organize a support group for them. Fortunately, most professionals have been taught about the importance of the peer group for adolescents, making support groups an obvious way to address adolescents' distress.

The link between social support and the adjustment of adolescents can be understood when consideration is given to the utility of peer relationships in particular to the developing cognitive and social skills of adolescents. Peer interaction helps adolescents learn to observe and evaluate the self, and to develop empathy. It also provides opportunities for developing skills, such as reciprocity, that will create relationships with others, and adds stability when family life is disrupted (Gottlieb, 1991). Self-regard seems to be closely tied to peers' regard and parental support (Harter, 1987). When parents' support is lacking, support from persons outside the family becomes even more crucial (Beardslee & Podorefsky, 1988). Peers may play an increasingly influential role in the development of an adolescent's ideology, philosophy of life, or assumptive world. When this is disrupted by bereavement (Schwartzberg & Janoff-Bulman, 1991), peer support may be valuable. Social support may also be crucial for adolescents undergoing stress because they may not have the coping resources and capacity for emotional regulation found in most adults. Negative life events and dissatisfaction with social support are related to at least temporary psychological dysfunction in adolescents (Compas et al., 1986).

At the crucial ages when adolescents are learning about self-identity, how to cultivate relationships, and how to understand life events, bereavement may remove from the world of adolescents the very people who play important roles in this learning. Death may take parents, siblings, or friends. The grieving of others may make it difficult for them to provide the support needed by an adolescent. Adolescents may assume (often correctly) that peers are unlikely to have had much experience with such an event and would not be understanding of their situation (Gray, 1988). Adolescents' grief may make them difficult to approach for family and friends who have never related to adolescents in times of such emotional intensity, and who have been hearing adolescent messages of separation in recent times. Self-consciousness and the need to be accepted may make it difficult for adolescents to solicit help (Gottlieb, 1991). Males in particular may have a limited support system (LaGrand, 1985). Support groups can be invaluable in overcoming this isolation (Tedeschi & Calhoun, 1993) and in providing an arena to continue the developmental tasks of adolescence while coping with the tasks of mourning.

ESTABLISHMENT OF ADOLESCENT BEREAVEMENT SUPPORT GROUPS

Recognition of the Need

Circumstances sometimes make it virtually impossible to fail to recognize the need for support for bereaved adolescents. Ad hoc groups are often formed because of the effects on a large group of adolescents of the deaths of persons known to all, for example, a counselor (Hickey, 1993) or a fellow student (Haran, 1988; Zinner, 1985). But even when these clear cases of bereavement among a large group of adolescents have not occurred, there will be a significant percentage of adolescents in any population coping with individual losses. Statistically, the most frequent experiences are deaths of parents and grandparents. Deaths of siblings and friends are rarer. Deaths of adolescent friends are most likely to arise from automobile accidents, homicide, and suicide—all unexpected deaths (Corr, Nabe, & Corr, 1994). These trends are reflected in the circumstances of younger bereavement support group members in contrast to older adults (Davis & Jessen, 1982). A casual poll of teachers, siblings, and friends may reveal a surprising number of bereaved adolescents (Krysiak, 1985).

When a group of adolescents is bereaved by the death of an individual known to all, they may begin helping each other informally, since the death is on the minds of all at the same time. But when individuals are suffering through their personal experiences of bereavement not shared by others, help may be more difficult to find. In either case, adolescents, even older ones, can benefit from the willingness of an adult to organize and facilitate a bereavement support group.

Site and Sponsor

Where group meetings will be held can be crucial to participation. Things will work better if the group meets in a setting that is comfortable and familiar to the adolescents, and in a place where they already gather. A hospital or mental health clinic may be alien and uninviting. Churches may be comforting for some but not others. School is ideal for most, making it easier to resolve issues of meeting times, transportation, familiarity, and comfort with the site.

Formation of the Group

If the formation of the group is announced generally and people in contact with adolescents are invited to refer participants, it should be made clear who is appropriate for participation. For example, Gray (1988) reported that more than 90% of adolescent bereavement support group participants he interviewed felt that it is inappropriate to include students who lost parents through divorce rather than death. A colleague of the author was surprised by a school counselor's referral of a participant to an adolescent bereavement group who was "mourning" the loss of his drugs!

Initial Contact and Screening of Potential Members. Invitations to participate are best extended personally and individually, if possible, except in cases when large groups are bereaved. A simple question about a death can yield quite intense responses and eagerness to talk. Of course, there is substantial variation among individuals regarding readiness to disclose, especially in a group setting. Also, adolescents who are trying to express autonomy as a developmental task can feel that accepting help is a substantial stigma (Fleming & Adolph, 1986). But initial hesitancy should not be taken immediately to be an indication of lack of interest or suitability. A private, initial interview can clarify matters of readiness for support group participation and ease anxieties in the potential participant. It is also important to recognize that even though some adolescents may not wish to participate, they may accept or prefer individual counseling (Baxter, Bennett, & Stuart, 1987).

Although each experience with bereavement occurs within the context of an adolescent's views of self, relationship with the deceased, reactions of family, and role in the family, there may be certain contexts that complicate bereavement. These can make a good support group experience more difficult. When stigma is attached to the death (e.g., suicide, AIDS, or drug overdose), care must be taken to assure that the group membership will be able to respond positively to the bereaved adolescent and that disclosure is not too difficult. These deaths can also produce a tendency to avoid disclosure outside the group, focusing all the emotional energy on the group itself. For example, Baxter, Bennett and Stuart (1987) reported the case of a girl whose sister committed suicide, and whose reaction was so strong that she tended to dominate the group.

The amount of time that has elapsed since the death may not be as important a variable as it first seems. Although some groups are formed immediately after a death (especially the crisis intervention groups that are arranged after the death of a teacher or classmate), most bereavement groups will be composed of adolescents for whom the deaths have occurred weeks, months, and years ago. Sometimes unexpressed grief can be prompted by a more recent death or a story read in class, and the group will become a place where this issue can finally be aired. Often, this unresolved grief in adolescents has been the result of information being kept from them, their relatives being reluctant to speak of the dead, or their being barred from taking part in rituals of mourning. The group gives permission to talk, gather information, and mourn. The explicit message of the invitation to participate in such a group is that it is a good thing to deal with these issues openly.

Generally, the way an adolescent and his or her support system has handled the death should be explored in the initial interview. Those adolescents who have had a family who was open intellectually and emotionally in dealing with the death, and who state that they have dealt with it satisfactorily, should not be pressured to join. By contrast, adolescents whose support network has failed them and who seem reluctant should be encouraged to try the group. Also, adolescents who have behavior problems (e.g., poor school performance, legal difficulties, drug problems, promiscuity, etc.) should not be excluded, but the focus should be maintained on the bereavement issues for the purposes of the group. Some adolescents may be having so many behavior problems that individual counseling or psychotherapy may be appropriate, sometimes in conjunction with the group. Behavior problems are sometimes ameliorated by the more constructive approach of the group, and the acceptance and the cohesion that develops.

Despite the variation in personal characteristics and circumstances found among group members, by focusing on bereavement, similarities are emphasized rather than differences. This sense of "we-ness" is essential for the group, and some writers recommend giving some attention to the composition of the group in order to encourage this. For example, deaths of grandparents may be less traumatic than deaths of parents, and many adolescents may need more time and support to deal with the latter. This may indicate separate groups for adolescents who are coping with more substantial issues (Baxter, Bennett, & Stuart, 1987).

Age Range.   Given that adolescent groups are most often formed within their naturally occuring settings, usually schools, the age range of the group may not become an important issue. However, given the developmental differences between the youngest and oldest adolescents, it is best in most cases to establish separate groups for adolescents at the extremes of the age range. Also, attention must be paid to the maturity level of young adolescents, some of whom may not be ready for a more verbal, adult group experience, and who would be more comfortable with younger children who are encouraged to express their grief in nonverbal group experiences. Discussion with potential members about what they would be comfortable with and would be willing to try can help in these decisions.

Some groups function very well with a wide range of ages, with older adolescents providing tender support for younger ones. Some groups have included children as young as five or six together with adolescents (Haasl & Marnocha, 1990; Masterman & Reames, 1988), and there are also groups which do not divide by age or relationship, e.g., the Suicide Survivors Grief Group (Wrobleski, 1984) that includes parents, spouses, siblings, children, and friends, and the Family Bereavement Program (Sandler et al., 1988), which is a combination of workshop and group activities for family members.

Group Size and Member Mix.   Because most adolescent bereavement groups are composed of peers, in thinking about the composition of the group it may be most crucial to consider the particular mix of personalities and the need to avoid one or more group members who are clearly very different from the others. Perhaps the group most likely to provide a good deal of interaction and successful support is one where there is a good balance of gender, age, and personalities (talkative and reluctant, emotionally expressive and intellectual, leader and follower), but with some homogeneity regarding the seriousness of the loss for the participants.

The group should probably be composed of at least five members in order to ensure that a sense of a group will develop, even with absences, while restricting the maximum size to 10 to ensure that each person will have an opportunity to talk. This is assuming a 90-minute meeting time, which allows ample opportunity for emotional expression before having to close up intense emotions and return to the outside world. Adolescent bereavement groups have been described as running one hour (e.g., Masterman & Reams, 1988) to more than two hours (Balk, Tyson-Rawson, & Colletti-Wetzel, 1983). With shorter meeting periods, smaller groups would be appropriate.

RUNNING OF THE GROUP

Structure

Two of the fundamental decisions to be made about the character of the group are to either structure it as a closed, time-limited group, or as an open, on-going group, and to emphasize a didactic, psychoeducational approach to bereavement or a process-oriented, experiential approach. Unless there is a large population of adolescents always available to feed into the group in order to keep the group at a workable minimum size of five, a closed, time-limited group is the best choice. In this type of group, a decision is made at the outset about the number of sessions and who will participate. The number of sessions can be planned to follow a school term or other schedule in the lives of the participants, and in the literature there are references to groups lasting from one (Haran, 1988, describing a crisis intervention in a school) to 12 weekly sessions (Baxter, Bennett, & Stuart, 1987; Gray, 1988). A smaller number appears to be appropriate for less intense grief, while the longer schedule is useful for recent and intense bereavement experiences. Group members can, of course, be given an option to join succeeding groups at a later date, and ongoing support after the formal group termination may be important for a number of participants (Gray, 1988).

Open groups (Berson, 1988) have certain advantages as well. They can accommodate individual differences in need to attend the group over a period of time, and newcomers can benefit from the wisdom of veteran group members who will tend to assume some facilitator functions and serve as models for how grief can be handled successfully over time (Tedeschi & Calhoun, 1993). However, it is important that members commit to a certain number of sessions, perhaps something like four to six, because the initial meeting may feel more painful than supportive, and it will take some time to experience some relief and learn the difficult lessons of bereavement. Group members should commit to notifying the group in advance of a decision to leave so that good-byes can be said rather than leaving group members with questions and concerns about what might have happened (Berson, 1988).

Most groups appear to be a combination of didactic and experiential, structured and process oriented. Some group members want and need information about the grief experience, what to experience, and how to cope. Especially in time-limited closed groups, some information and encouragement may need to be provided by facilitators, because there are no veteran group members who can do this or model changes in bereavement that occur over time. Sometimes group members report that they prefer more direction and structure from the facilitators in order to prevent dominant group members from exerting too much control (Baxter, Bennett, & Stuart, 1987); at other times the group sets its own agenda and the facilitators must be comfortable enough to follow that agenda, rather than slavishly attend to a planned lesson in bereavement. A facilitator who is familiar with didactic material and attentive to group needs can integrate the material with a naturally progressing group process (Balk, Tyson-Rawson, & Colletti-Wetzel, 1993).

Group Activities

There are a number of sources describing didactic material and group exercises that can be used with adolescent groups (Balk, Tyson-Rawson, & Colletti-Wetzel, 1993; Baxter, Bennett, & Stuart, 1987; Gray, 1988; Haasl & Marnocha, 1990; Haran, 1988; Masterman & Reams, 1988), and some exercises designed for individuals (Worden, 1991) can be adapted to groups. Several activities appear to be commonly used. One is letter writing, for the purpose of expressing emotions, resolving issues with the deceased, and maintaining a connection with the deceased. Letters may be written to friends, describing the grief experience, or to the deceased in order to express feelings and issues that were not explored sufficiently in life. Letters can also be composed that come from the deceased addressing these issues. Many other writing exercises are possible, focusing on such issues as the feelings involved in grieving, what kind of support has been helpful, what has made grieving more difficult, and what has been learned from these experiences.

Art and creative activities have been used as well to encourage expression of emotion and telling of stories about the deceased, the adolescent's relationship with the deceased person, and the death. These activities include drawings, collages, poems, stories, songs, and group murals. Another activity that can facilitate discussion is the bringing to the group of an item that is an important possession of or that represents the deceased, and telling about the relationship between the item and the person. Readings by facilitators or group members of stories about grief and death can also prompt discussion.

The use of any activities should be determined by the composition, needs, and reactions of the participants. Some groups will welcome them enthusiastically; others will find them to be an obstacle to the freedom to talk that they can generate for themselves. Activities should be considered a means to promote constructive interaction, not an end in themselves.

Facilitator Role

The term *facilitator* has been used here and in several other reports to describe the adult, professional leaders who organize adolescent support groups. It is useful for leaders to think of themselves as facilitators in order to emphasize to group members that the group members themselves are responsible for the group process and its success. By doing this, facilitators place groups into the hands of the participants, creating more of a "mutual-help" atmosphere rather than a "group therapy" atmosphere, even though the professionals have organized the groups rather than the adolescents themselves.

The term "facilitator" also implies that each group member remains the expert on his or her own grieving process, and the facilitator and other participants support the creation of an individualized approach to addressing grief. This can offset the proscriptions and expectations that seem to exist about how long people should grieve and in what ways they should mourn. Instead, this gives participants permission to use various ways of mourning that are beneficial to them. Facilitators can keep in mind that their primary task is not to teach about grief or to help participants to get over it, but to help each group member consider various ways to address his or her grief and mourn as he or she wishes.

To accomplish this task, facilitators work in adolescent bereavement groups to maintain the focus on the participants rather than themselves, while creating a safe atmosphere by addressing process issues (e.g., encouraging passive members and controlling dominant ones), adhering to limits and rules (e.g., time limits, confidentiality, etc.), and introducing activities. They maintain the structure and fill in the gaps left by the participants. These may be gaps in information, attention to certain members, or a focus on certain issues. Facilitators should first direct attention to certain group members who might have information or advice, identifying resources in the group before assuming the expert role.

Adolescents have reported that peers have been more helpful than other people during bereavement, although only within the context of a support group where their peers have experienced similar losses have they been perceived to be understanding (Gray, 1989). The ideology that facilitators should encourage and express is the one that emerges from the group itself (Sherman, 1979) or a positive, constructive version of it, emphasizing that the participants are the experts on bereavement. The paradox for the professionals is that they negate their own power by supporting this mutual-help ideology (Klass & Shinners, 1983). But by using their understanding of mutual help and group process, facilitators help group members rediscover their own strengths. Adolescents also appreciate being listened to and respected by adults, because this often has not been their experience.

From this description of the facilitator role, it should be clear that effective adolescent bereavement group facilitators may need certain personal and professional characteristics: They need to be knowledgeable about the experience of bereavement while not adopting the role of a sage, be comfortable with emotional expressions of grief, be able to maintain limits and challenge adolescent lapses in judgment while trusting group members and the group process to produce change, and be tolerant of individual differences in bereavement based on family, religious, and cultural context.

Effective facilitators must also be accepted into this role by the adolescents in the group. A stranger would be better than a person the adolescent already knows and dislikes, does not respect, or who does not fit the role. Even though the facilitator remains somewhat separate from the group to allow it to develop an atmosphere of mutual help, there is a great deal for the facilitator to attend to, and group members can sometimes challenge facilitators to be quite self-disclosing (Berson, 1988) about experiences with grief and expertise in dealing with these issues. Given the topics discussed and the emotional intensity generated, facilitators must be able to acknowledge comfortably and manage their own emotional responses, and have access to support for themselves (Balk, Tyson-Rawson, & Colletti-Wetzel, 1993).

Cofacilitators may be useful in providing this support and sharing the work of attending to the often highly emotional group process. This is one of the reasons that having two facilitators is most useful. Debriefing by cofacilitators after the group sessions can provide relief, support, and perspective.

Possible Problems

In running support groups, there is a self-correcting tendency that tends to keep most potential problems from getting out of hand. Facilitators must remember to trust the group members and the process, and not use too heavy a hand in addressing apparent difficulties. The members themselves can often address problems within the group. Many problems can be prevented by remembering the proper role for a facilitator, keeping the group attractive by making sure everyone talks and limiting those who talk excessively, having a reasonable agenda, and making judicious use of humor (Rose & Edleson, 1987). However, there are certain problems that can occur. Some common ones will be mentioned here along with brief suggestions about addressing each of them, with the caveat that specific approaches to these problems should be considered within the context of the particular group membership and the comfort of facilitators with these approaches.

Nonproductive Silences or Discussing Superficial Things.   Silence
will be fairly common during many bereavement groups, especially
when sad circumstances are described. During many silences, there is a
great deal of emotion being felt, and it is appropriate to allow this to
"sink in." After a while, facilitators can encourage the expression of the
felt emotion, saying that the group is a place where it is safe to say what
is only privately felt in other circumstances. However, facilitators may
sometimes determine that a silence is not a productive one, and that
the group is "stuck."

Some ways to approach this include suggesting a group exercise, as
mentioned above, especially one that gets group members out of their
seats and interacting with each other. Another possibility is to make a
statement about the fact that things seem stuck, and ask the group
members what might be helpful to do to move forward. The group can
also be asked to invite a member to serve as a temporary facilitator
(Kymissis, 1993). Sometimes facilitators can induce silences by playing
too dominant a role in the group, taking responsibility off group members for initiating things.

Discussion of superficial topics can be normal and useful, reminding
adolescents that it is acceptable to have other concerns beyond bereavement and grief. However, if most group time is devoted to such issues, it may be a signal that the work of the group is completed, or that
the work is being avoided. The history of the group will allow for such
a determination by the facilitator. If there is avoidance, it is usually effective for the facilitator to make a statement about the process: that the
group has been concentrating on other things besides grief. This will
usually initiate discussion about discomfort of grief, the relief that
comes with avoidance, and how to keep the issue of grief before the
group.

Attendance Problems.   When members are missing a significant number of meetings, it may be an indication that they have obtained the
help they need and are ready to leave. This time will come at different
points for different group members; even in a time-limited group, the
specified time may be too long for some or too short for others. The
issue can often be directly raised in the group, with no implied criticism. Failure to keep regular attendance or apparently premature termination could also be an indication that some group members are
having difficulty in facing some of the material.

Often it is not a good idea to invite an adolescent into a group immediately after a death. The pain may be too intense, conflicting with
the adolescent's need to maintain some dignity in front of peers. Honor
this, and invite the member to participate in individual sessions for a

while, until a group is a comfortable place to be. Sometimes group members are the best judge of their readiness to participate, and will leave and then return when they are more ready (Berson, 1988).

Attendance problems can also be an indication of a failure on a member's part to feel supported or connected, perhaps because of differences in circumstances of the death or for other reasons. Airing these apparent differences often can bring statements of unity from other members. Discomfort with what is happening in the group may also be usefully addressed in individual sessions.

Finally, facilitators should consider the degree to which they have made each group member feel welcome and important.

Domination or Criticism by a Group Member and Bad Advice. Certain persons will feel more comfortable speaking out in the group, and facilitators should make sure that quieter individuals are given the floor by directing the "traffic" in the group and insuring that issues do not get lost in the sometimes rapid interactions among members (Schwab, 1986). If one group member dominates, it is usually comforting for other members when a facilitator is able to direct the conversation elsewhere, or makes a direct statement about giving another member an opportunity to speak.

Criticism of one group member by another is something to be avoided in bereavement groups, even though it might be appropriate for therapy groups. Bereaved adolescents are often vulnerable and may find criticism hard to bear. Facilitators can remind the group that this is a time when support is more useful, that there may be more supportive ways to make suggestions to group members, and that each person has his or her own way of grieving, which is normal and understandable. This kind of statement can also be useful in the case of bad advice being given by one group member to another. In addition, a focus on the consequences of certain suggestions will usually produce corrections to bad advice from the group members themselves. Facilitators can suggest other approaches to counteract bad advice without staking out the turf as the expert and dominating the group themselves.

Psychological Disorder in a Group Member. Some degree of psychological disorder is tolerable in members of a bereavement support group, but a judgment needs to be made by facilitators whether a member is so clearly different that he or she is not getting support from the group, even if the disturbed member does not realize this. If the group cannot empathize with this person, the member is unlikely to benefit much from the experience, and the group will become an uncomfortable place for the other adolescents. This is a situation facilitators seek to avoid during the screening interviews for the group, but if it arises, a private suggestion of individual counseling or therapy would be best for all involved.

The remaining group members should have an opportunity to discuss the fact that a group member was offered more appropriate intervention. If the difficulties were apparent to everyone, the facilitator can refer to the "difficulties" that the former member was having, and how individual attention is now being given to this person. Confidentiality must be respected by the facilitator, even while encouraging honest discussion about the difficulties the member was having with bereavement in particular.

In bereavement support groups, suicidal ideation will be quite common (Schwab, 1986). Given that adolescents have a tendency to consider suicide in many difficult circumstances, it is useful to raise the issue directly if it does not come up spontaneously. Facilitators must carefully judge the degree to which suicidal ideation is a rather normal response on the part of group members, or whether there is a dangerous situation that needs to be addressed in certain cases.

Running Overtime.   This is a facilitator problem. Rules should be set at the beginning stating that the group will start and end on time. Not to do so can create all kinds of difficulties. Members who have other commitments after the group become anxious and angry, there can be a sense of things getting out of control and therefore becoming potentially unsafe, and if running late is an option, starting late becomes an option, too. Facilitators can issue a 10-minute warning before the end of the meeting, so that members can plan to complete their talk, calm their emotions, and leave comfortably. A simple statement that the group has used up its time for the day is sufficient to end a group session. Sometimes, it might be suitable for the facilitator to recognize briefly one or two key points that were central to the session. However, facilitators must recognize that not every meeting can be tied up neatly, and the messy business of grieving will be taken up again next time.

ISSUES AND BENEFITS IN A SUPPORT GROUP FOR BEREAVED ADOLESCENTS

Facilitators should expect certain issues to be raised by bereaved adolescents. Many are not exclusive to adolescents, and it is striking how many parallels can be found in the literature on adult bereavement. Despite this, adults often overlook the issues with which adolescents are grappling, assume that an adolescent's experience may be quite different from theirs, or even that it is not so difficult. But bereaved adolescents often take on great emotional, social, and cognitive challenges within the encouraging and secure atmosphere of a support group. Although life crises of this kind have been called "opportunities" for growth, for the adolescents who are confronting intense grief, the work they do in the group seems more like a necessity. In the process, they get more comfortable with death and grief, learn how to grieve, and develop skill at supporting others.

Overcoming Isolation from Others

Bereavement appears to be an inherently isolating experience in our culture (Tedeschi & Calhoun, 1993). This may happen because many people are poorly skilled at approaching people in grief, anxious about death, or have little empathy. Most often, there is a failure simply to take the time to listen. When a death has occurred within a family, other family members may grieve differently or be emotionally unavailable to an adolescent because of their own grief. It appears that approximately half of all bereaved adolescents report disruption in family and peer relationships as a result of bereavement (Balk, 1983b).

Support groups provide an avenue to begin to overcome this isolation. There is often a good deal of discussion of responses from others that have led to a sense of isolation, especially that the rest of the world is moving on and keeps suggesting that it is best to "get over it" (Balk, Tyson-Rawson, & Colletti-Wetzel, 1993; Berson, 1988; Wortman & Silver, 1989). But even when the responses are constructive, there may still be a sense of something being missing (Dakof & Taylor, 1990; Lehman, Ellard, & Wortman, 1986), perhaps an empathy born of direct experience. So there is a comfort in being with others who have had similar experiences.

This sense of "universality," that is, that the experiences one is having are common to others, is often cited by adolescents in group therapy as an extremely helpful aspect of their participation in the group (Holmes, Heckel, & Gordon, 1991) and appears to operate in bereavement support groups as well. Furthermore, emphasis on the normality of grief and the variety of forms it takes allows group members to talk about their experiences freely and accept the differences they will notice within the group.

Information Sharing

In crisis intervention groups where all participants are grieving the death of the same person, groups are often the most efficient ways to share information about the death and to dispel rumors. In support groups where several different deaths are represented, the information that is most valued has to do with the new and powerful emotional reactions that are experienced, how much time is involved in bereavement, and how to handle certain situations that are likely to arise. These situations include what to say if someone who does not know about the death asks about the deceased, if it is right to enjoy oneself after a loved one has died, and how to maintain concentration on schoolwork. Bereaved adolescents may also discuss dreams they have had about the death and what these might mean, medical issues and causes of death, funeral and burial arrangements, and other things that are unfamiliar and confusing for them.

Often, there will be other group members who have useful perspectives on these matters or information to share. Sometimes the facilitator can provide what is needed. At other times, plans will be made to obtain missing information that might be useful in moving the bereavement process along. Since information about a death and the bereavement process is often unavailable to adolescents because adults are reluctant to disclose what they believe the adolescent could not cope with, the information-sharing aspect of the group process is often a source of great relief and clarification.

Containing Emotions and Expressing Emotions

Some adolescents choose not to express emotions because they are so painful, and many adolescents seek ways to distract themselves from emotional pain rather than face it (Gray, 1988). Bereavement experiences during adolescence may represent the first time traumatic events have occurred for these young people. These intense emotional experiences may be confusing, frightening, and for self-conscious adolescents, embarrassing. There also are adolescents who will find themselves having difficulty controlling their emotions.

The empathy and shared understanding found in a bereavement support group can encourage emotional expression, help to contain it, and allow participants to examine the emotions to determine their acceptability. Among the emotions often considered in this way are guilt, relief, and anger toward the deceased. There may have been some turmoil or conflict in relation to the deceased, spurring some guilt. This can happen when a family member dies after the adolescent had been moving away from this person or had been relatively uninvolved with the individual as a result of increasing needs for independence. Adolescents may also feel guilty that they are relieved that a death occurred, as in cases of chronic illness. They may be angry at the deceased for directly (in cases of suicide) or indirectly (e.g., in the cases of heart attacks, and alcohol- or drug-related deaths) contributing to their own deaths. Anger is commonly expressed toward family members, peers, or authorities who have not been supportive or understanding. Very often there is indignation at the messages from others that emotions should be suppressed. Through the presence of other members who are having similar experiences, groups seem to be particularly helpful in lending support to adolescents who are experiencing strong, unfamiliar emotions. Quickly the ideology of bereavement groups becomes "emotions of all kinds are OK."

Confronting Life Lessons

Adolescents have been described as having illusions of invulnerability, and those who have been asked to imagine their own deaths have reported brief, distress-free experiences at odds with the reality of most deaths (Kastenbaum, 1992). Experiences with death can shatter these pleasant illusions, especially in a group where stories are told about a variety of deaths. Reactions of family or others whom adolescents may never have seen coping with such difficult circumstances before can also be surprising. Spiritual and existential issues are of concern to many adolescents, and their experiences with death can heighten these concerns (Balk & Hogan, 1995). Such concerns are now no longer abstract; the fate of their loved one is involved. Bereaved college students have reported that their world view and general beliefs have been challenged and substantially changed by dealing with parental death (Schwartzberg & Janoff-Bulman, 1991). These changes include priorities in life, religious beliefs, assumptions about invulnerability, and a general sense of the meaningfulness of life.

A support group can be an arena in which these issues are considered more comfortably and where adolescents can develop and advance the "unseasoned" adolescent constructs of life and death (Kastenbaum, 1992). Much of this work may advance an adolescent's understanding of developmental issues of this era in the human life span—separation, identity, and intimacy—through the focus on loss, one's own vulnerability to it, and the feelings one has about it. Responding to other bereaved adolescents also brings intimacy and another look at one's identity in relation to others. Although adolescents appreciate being distracted from their grief and having time to be just like their nonbereaved friends (Gray, 1989), support groups can allow time for revision and development of evolving constructs considering the perspective of a new reference group (Gottlieb, 1981). The presence of an adult facilitator, especially one trained in grief issues, can allow a consideration of these issues from the perspective of experience. Sensitive social support may also bolster a benevolent world view at a time when this could easily be questioned (Schwartzberg & Janoff-Bulman, 1991), and help develop empathy and altruism (Berson, 1988) because of the powerful experience of providing help to other bereaved people.

The issues adolescents confront in a bereavement support group are unlikely to be neatly resolved by the end of their time in the group. Facilitators have done a good job when group members leave with a good strategy for continuing their attachment to the deceased while going on with life. As a result of the support group experience, the adolescent should be better equipped to find support from group members, family, literature, or other sources, so that they can constructively address issues that remain unresolved after the end of the group experience.

CONCLUSION: RESEARCH

In reviews of outcome studies of bereavement support groups, Lieberman (1993) cited six studies, and Zimpfer (1991) cited nine. All but one of these studies had adult group members; the exception was a child's bereavement group. Although there is an absence of controlled outcome studies, there are indications of positive outcome for participants in adolescent bereavement support groups based on surveys and anecdotal evidence from group members (Baxter, 1982; Berson, 1988; Gray 1988, 1989). In addition, one outcome study has shown the short-term superiority of a peer support group over social skills training in depressed adolescents (Fine et al., 1991). Evidence is needed to confirm that support groups for bereaved adolescents reduce distress over the short and long term, and perhaps allow developmental issues and existential issues to be addressed more successfully, producing personal growth.

At present, we can say with some confidence that there are no reports that these groups have made bereavement more difficult for adolescent participants, but it is unclear how many members drop out of bereavement support groups, what their reasons might be, and what happens to them. Groups may be helpful for adolescents lacking other sources of support, they may reduce initial distress but have minimal effect on long-term adjustment, or they may be effective in assisting adolescents to cope with grief who have been unable to address certain issues. It is also unclear what forms of bereavement support groups are most effective for various adolescents, given their personal characteristics and circumstances. If benefits are achieved as a result of these groups, it would be helpful to know what aspects of the process or what information might have the greatest impact. Hypotheses can be drawn based on the literature on group therapy and some of the information we have about adult bereavement support groups, but only research will show if such generalizations hold for adolescent bereavement support groups. Virtually any research on adolescent bereavement support groups would be enlightening at this point.

16

Professional Interventions to Assist Adolescents Who Are Coping with Death and Bereavement

LaNae Valentine

Loss is both a common and a unique component of human existence. It is common in the sense that all human beings undergo separation and loss of significant relationships throughout the course of their life experiences and share a collective need to learn ways of coping with the impact and aftermath of serious losses. Yet, at the same time, loss is unique in that each individual has a distinct life history of contact with loss and develops a particular set of beliefs about loss which reflect that life experience. In our society today, adolescents face a number of actual and potential losses. These losses are significant because they affect an adolescent's ability to cope with and adapt to subsequent and major losses such as death.

Grief is primarily concerned not with understanding, but with forming attachments and responding to loss (Wolfelt, 1983). If this is correct, any adolescent who is mature enough to feel love is mature enough to grieve. In other words, both young and old alike are capable of experiencing the full range of grief responses to the loss of a loved one. Like adults, adolescents experience grief, but often adolescents are not acknowledged in their grief and mourning in the same way as adults are. For example, adolescents may not be included in decisions such as funeral arrangements, burial preferences, and mourning rituals. This lack of participation and inclusion often leaves adolescents confused, bewildered, and alienated—making it more difficult to cope with their grief (Schachter, 1991).

This chapter examines professional interventions in the form of counseling or therapy that are designed to help adolescents who are coping with death and bereavement. Topics discussed include: the difference between "normal" and "disabling" grief in adolescence; indications for professional referral; factors to consider when assessing an adolescent's grief responses; grief counseling and grief therapy for adolescents; interventions with individual adolescents; and interventions with adolescents and their families. Two extended case studies and their discussion identify techniques that might usefully be employed in individual or family settings. In all of this, the basic goal is to enhance an adolescent's current well-being and to forestall future problems, such as poor self-esteem, problems with personal identity, or difficulties in forming close attachments for fear of once again experiencing loss and abandonment.

WHEN DOES A "NORMAL" GRIEF REACTION BECOME "DISABLING"?: INDICATIONS FOR PROFESSIONAL REFERRAL

A very broad range of responses may be part of an adolescent's normal grief and mourning. If that is correct, then what are the indicators that an adolescent should be referred for an evaluation by a mental health professional? Many years ago, Grollman (1967, p. 21) suggested:

> The line of demarcation between "normal psychological aspects of bereavement" and "distorted mourning reactions" is thin indeed, just as is the division between "normality" and "neurosis." The difference is not in symptom but in intensity. It is a *continued* denial of reality even many months after the funeral, or a *prolonged* bodily distress, or a *persistent* panic, or an *extended* guilt, or an *unceasing* idealization, or an *enduring* apathy and anxiety, or an *unceasing* hostile reaction to the deceased and to others. Each manifestation does not in itself determine a distorted grief reaction; it is only as it is viewed by the professional in the composition of the total formulation.

Further, Lindemann (1944, p. 147) emphasized that "not only over-reaction but under-reaction of the bereaved must be given attention, because delayed responses may occur at unpredictable moments and the dangerous distortions of the grief reaction, not conspicuous at first, may be quite destructive later."

For these reasons, Webb (1993) proposed that the important point is to evaluate the degree of intrusiveness into the person's life created by the grieving. Those seeking to help must determine the extent to which an adolescent can carry out his or her usual activities and proceed with his or her developmental tasks despite the grief. When the adolescent's social, emotional, or physical development shows signs of interference, the grief process can justifiably be considered "disabling." In such circumstances, "the grief has become all-encompassing and detrimental" (Webb, 1993, p. 21). Any adolescent who experiences a disabling grief of this sort may be in a situation in which assistance is needed that goes beyond that which family members are able to provide.

Fox (1985) noted that professional services are indicated if there are questions about suicidal risk or if the adolescent has been involved in some way in the death of the deceased. There is evidence that adolescents who lose a parent, sibling, or friend to suicide are at greater risk for suicide and depression than those in the general population. Other "red flags" that might indicate a need for professional help include psychosomatic problems, difficulties with schoolwork, nightmares or sleep disorders, changes in eating patterns, suicidal hints, and temporary regressions. In addition, behaviors such as angry acting out, destruction of property, decline in school performance, truancy, substance abuse, and depression should be noted. None of these on its own necessarily suggests a diagnosis of dysfunctional grieving, but each could be a possible indicator that the adolescent's grief work may be complicated and that professional intervention is indicated.

FACTORS TO CONSIDER WHEN ASSESSING A GRIEF RESPONSE

The intensity and duration of grief and mourning are influenced by several factors, such as who the person was that died, the nature, strength, and security of the attachment to the deceased, and the presence and intensity of ambivalence in the relationship. Other significant factors include early childhood experiences around loss, kinship, timeliness of death, previous warning, preparation for bereavement, and the need to hide feelings, as well as the blame the adolescent feels for bringing about the death.

In trying to assess how an adolescent is responding to a loss it is also important to look at historical antecedents, such as the number of previous losses experienced by the survivor and how they were grieved. If previous losses were not grieved adequately, the present loss will be more difficult to grieve. The survivor's mental history is important to consider as well. Adolescents with a history of depression usually have a more difficult time grieving than those without such a history. Also of importance are personality variables, such as how inhibited survivors are about expressing feelings, how well they handle anxiety, and how they cope with stressful situations. Persons diagnosed with certain personality disorders, or those highly dependent or who have difficulty forming relationships, tend to have a more difficult time handling loss.

One should also consider the position of a bereaved adolescent within his or her family system. The degree to which that family system is disrupted by the death of a member will largely depend upon the timing in the life cycle, the nature of the death, the openness of the family system, and the family position of the dying member. For example, the death of a parent, especially the parent who held the greatest family responsibilities, will leave a large hole in the family system. Similarly, when sudden death occurs, there is no opportunity for anticipatory grieving or family discussions among the children, spouse, and the dying parent. Also, if there were unresolved issues, they will become painful and will contribute to the difficulty of the surviving adolescent's grief work (Parry & Thornwall, 1992; Worden, 1991).

In addition, grief and mourning in adolescents will be influenced by broader social and cultural variables. For example, the degree of perceived emotional and social support from others, both inside and outside the family, is significant. Studies show that those who do less well with bereavement often have inadequate or conflicted social support (Worden, 1991).

GRIEF COUNSELING AND GRIEF THERAPY

What kind of professional help is appropriate for bereaved adolescents? Worden (1991) distinguished between grief "counseling" and grief "therapy" based on whether the client's grief is viewed as uncomplicated or complicated. Although Worden's distinctions were mainly based on work with bereaved adults, they appear to have some relevance to adolescents as well. According to Worden, *grief counseling* is the appropriate treatment for *uncomplicated grief* where the goal is to help the survivor complete any unfinished business with the deceased and say a final good-bye. The goal in *grief therapy* for *complicated grief* is "to identify and resolve the conflicts of separation which preclude the completion of mourning tasks in persons whose grief is absent, delayed, excessive, or prolonged" (Worden, 1991, p. 79).

By contrast, Webb (1993) referred to "therapy" as a process of help conducted by a mental health professional and "counseling" as the process of help which is provided by religious leaders and educational personnel. In any event, the goals and procedures of any professional intervention will differ according to the needs of a specific adolescent.

Grief Counseling for Adolescents

Worden (1991) defined four tasks of mourning as (a) to accept the reality of the loss; (b) to work through to the pain of grief; (c) to adjust to an environment in which the deceased is missing; and (d) to relocate the deceased emotionally and move on with life. Many adolescents and their families are able to accomplish these tasks without the need of professional assistance. Families and systems that are open and supportive of one another, open to the expression of feelings about the deceased and variables surrounding the death, and flexible in terms of role readjustment will usually be able to navigate this transition period, accept the reality of the loss, readjust to the loss, say an appropriate good-bye, and reinvest in life and other relationships.

Sometimes, however, even these "healthy" or "hardy" families will seek the services of a counselor to coach them through the grieving process. This assistance can be sought before, during, or after the death of a loved one. In the case of anticipated death, families often choose to engage a counselor to assist them to communicate about the impending death, to express feelings of love and appreciation or of ambivalence, to conduct any unfinished business, and to express and cope with fears and anxieties.

Adolescents often report that they need and want opportunities to talk about their feelings and experiences with death. They may express a need for support in assisting them to come to terms with feelings of guilt and anger, difficulties in relations with the surviving parent and other family members, memories about and hallucinations of the deceased, school problems, difficulties relating to peers following the loss, dealing with fears of one's own death and fears of losing another person close to them, or coping with the funeral and other rituals related to the loss (Gray, 1988; Schachter, 1991).

The counseling context can provide adolescents permission to address their concerns within a safe, nonjudgmental environment and to include them in decisions regarding the funeral arrangements, burial preferences, and mourning rituals. Helping bereaved adolescents communicate their thoughts without fear of upsetting other family members facilitates constructive grief work (Bowen, 1976).

Grief Therapy for Adolescents

Factors associated with death which are known to complicate mourning and often require intervention by a trained therapist include a sudden and unanticipated death; a traumatic, violent, mutilating, or random death; death from an overly lengthy illness; or a death the mourner perceives as preventable. Also deaths resulting from chronic illnesses or an illness such as AIDS, can engender additional stressors known to complicate mourning, such as, anger, ambivalence, guilt, stigmatization, and social disenfranchisement.

Other factors which may complicate grief and mourning include problematic familial relationships and the death of a sexually or physically abusive parent. The mourning process of an adolescent victim/survivor of an abusive parent is often severely complicated by many factors related to the abuse, together with anger, ambivalence, or dependence toward the deceased parent. Adolescents raised in families with one or more alcoholic parents or with one or more parents who are psychologically impaired, rigid in beliefs, compulsive, codependent, absent, neglectful, or chronically ill are also vulnerable to a difficult grieving process (Rando, 1993a).

After the death of such a parent, an adolescent may experience relief and sadness simultaneously—which can be frightening. Or the adolescent, out of guilt, may interpret the loss as a personal rejection or some kind of personal failure within the self. Such an adolescent may manifest excessive guilt for negative feelings toward the deceased which could prolong grief, depression, and thoughts of suicide (Cutter, 1974). Often, an individual adolescent is unable to sort through and resolve these confusing issues without the assistance of a therapist who understands the dynamics of abuse and how they affect the development and personality of the survivor.

These considerations lead to the recommendation that adolescents who are experiencing difficult losses or dysfunctional mourning should seek assistance from a therapist who is professionally trained in psychodynamics, psychopathology, and family systems.

PROFESSIONAL INTERVENTIONS WITH INDIVIDUAL ADOLESCENTS

Professional interventions with individual adolescents who are coping with death and bereavement involve a cognitive process which consists of confrontation with and restructuring of thoughts about the deceased, the loss experience, and the changed world within which the bereaved must now live (Stroebe, 1993). This process involves going over the events before and at the time of death, focusing on memories, and working toward restructuring the former relationship with the deceased. It requires an active, ongoing, effortful attempt to come to terms with the loss (Rando, 1991). In this process, a bereaved adolescent needs to bring the reality of loss into his or her awareness as much as possible.

Generally, difficulties during mourning which tend to involve denial of the loss and denial of the painful affects associated with it are addressed by individual intervention. Suppression of feelings, denial of the pain of the loss, avoidance of discussion of memories or feelings regarding the deceased, and a hurried reentry back to one's life deserve attention in order to forestall complicated grief and mourning.

Alex, a 17-year-old, white male was referred to therapy by his parents shortly following the death of his best friend, Bill, who was killed in an automobile accident. Alex's parents reported that since Bill's death, he had been depressed and angry. They reported that Alex was doing poorly in school, not eating or sleeping well, and had lost all interest in his other friends and previously enjoyed activities. Alex's mother reported that on several occasions she had heard Alex calling out Bill's name and talking to him in his sleep. When his parents tried to approach Alex and encourage him to talk about Bill and his feelings about his death, Alex would angrily reply, "Bill is gone. There is no use talking about him because it wouldn't bring him back." Alex finally agreed to come for help upon his parents' urging.

Talking about, remembering, and reflecting upon the deceased with others is one of the major needs of the bereaved. Alex had isolated himself from family members and friends by his refusal to talk and interact with them. Many grief theorists believe reflecting upon and communicating about remembered experiences with the deceased is a means of overcoming this separation and loss, and a means of relieving the trauma of the loss. The task of the therapist is to help the survivor acknowledge what has been lost, and to recognize that his or her pain is worthy of respect. The psychological result is "my beloved friend is not completely gone, for I now carry him within myself and can never really lose him." In this way the interpersonal relationship is maintained even though the other is dead (Nerken, 1993; Switzer, 1970).

The initial stages of therapy with Alex involved direct questioning about Bill's death, encouragement to relive past experiences with Bill, and to express memories, thoughts, and feelings regarding his life and death. Although Alex was quite closed during the first session, the therapist persisted in encouraging him to talk about anything he would. Alex showed no emotion during these sessions and his responses to questions bordered on the sarcastic and bitter. Often, he would turn the questions around and ask the therapist, "What do you think?" or "Aren't you supposed to have all the answers?" Alex was good at keeping his defenses in place so that he would not have to feel the pain of his loss. Gradually, he began talking more, but not about Bill or his death. He wanted to talk about his childhood, his parents and siblings, his school teachers. Every now and then, he would talk about Bill and his pain would emerge gradually.

Another need of the bereaved is a release of emotion, especially "negative" emotions, such as hostility, hate, and guilt (Switzer, 1970). After several sessions, Alex finally admitted that he felt extremely guilty about Bill's death. Apparently, minutes before his death, Bill had asked Alex to come with him to help him move a piano. Alex had refused, giving some excuse about having to do something else. Bill was killed in an auto accident on his way to move the piano. Rather than feeling relieved that he had not been in the car, Alex expressed that he felt selfish and guilty for not going with Bill, saying he should have been the one to die rather than Bill.

Alex continued by describing Bill's character to the therapist and expressing what a fine person and friend he had been to him. Alex struggled with making sense out of the injustice and meaninglessness of his friend's death and acknowledged aspects about himself with which he was not happy. Alex's admission of the guilt, pain, and self-hate he was holding was a turning point in his therapy. He was able to express strong emotions about his friend and to reflect about what Bill had meant to him.

At this point, Alex was freer in expressing vulnerable feelings of insecurity and fear, stating that his world had been turned upside down and questioning what to believe or trust. Nerken (1993) pointed out that a loved one's death needs to be seen as a cognitive as well as an emotional crisis. When a loved one dies, one literally does not know what to think, especially when the death is sudden, accidental, and unexpected. Alex expressed a need to reexamine everything he believed about life in the course of his therapy. He stated he felt that he was no longer certain of anything, did not really know his family members or friends, and did not know what was important anymore. His sense of coherence, purpose, values, and his understanding of his role in life was challenged.

Another essential task of grief work involves finding the meaning of the loss. This involves reflection, wherein the griever reflects endlessly upon memories, thoughts of why the death happened, the future, and the feelings of pain associated with these reflections. Some part of every grief involves dreams, hopes, and expectations arising out of the relationship that will never be fulfilled because of the death. Hopes and dreams connected to the relationship are examined and mourned after a death, together with how this affects the way the survivor reflects on himself or herself.

Feelings and thoughts about the deceased are translated into cognitions the bereaved can live with. This is achieved through a process of reflection in which meaning is found in the resulting cognition. When addressing grief within intimate relationships, Fleming and Robinson (1991) suggested that the deceased loved one be viewed as leaving a cognitive legacy, which can be retrieved by the bereaved as they address such questions as: "What lessons in living has the deceased taught me?"; "What has knowing and loving the deceased meant to me?"; "How am I different as a result of this intimate relationship?" As these questions are reflected upon and answered, the reflective self becomes more capable of doing for itself what another once did, thus achieving a transition from losing what one had to having what one has lost (Nerken, 1993).

Some of the therapeutic assignments Alex completed included writing a letter to Bill expressing to him what he appreciated about him and what he meant to him. Also, Alex wrote a letter to himself as Bill would have written, expressing what Bill appreciated about Alex. This allowed Alex a chance not only to reflect on what Bill meant to him, but what he thought he meant to Bill. Alex visited Bill's grave site, read aloud the contents of his letter to Bill, and sought to resolve any unfinished business that might have been left between them.

According to Nerken (1993), grief work is *self*-work of the most profound and intense kind. Alex matured greatly during his grieving process in that he developed clarity and understanding of his beliefs and values and his own identity. He developed a more adequate philosophy of life which incorporated the reality of death both intellectually and emotionally into his present being. Alex concluded that even though Bill's life had been short, he had influenced many people around him for good. Bill's death did not have to be a meaningless, random event. Alex reflected that he and others who knew Bill would always remember him and be better persons because of him. He resolved to be kinder, more sensitive, and less selfish—all of which would be his way of keeping Bill's memory alive. In this way, Alex's experience of grieving his friend's death suggests that effective coping with grief involves discovering that the meaning of death may be found in how our lives are influenced by the life of a departed loved one.

Techniques Used in Working With Individual Adolescents

There are a number of interventions that can be employed to assist an individual through the grieving process. In the cases of a delayed, masked, or inhibited grief reaction, the goal is to activate the grief process. Some interventions designed to further this goal include guided imagery for reliving, revising, and revisiting scenes of the loss, for example, the funeral (Cates, 1986; Melges & DeMaso, 1980; Paul & Miller, 1986). Other interventions helpful in assisting the adolescent to acknowledge the pain of the loss are direct questioning regarding the death, amassing as much knowledge of the death as possible via parents, caretakers, copies of newspaper articles, death certificates, visits to the grave site, guided imagery, and the use of notes and letters. These techniques can be coupled with encouragement to relive past experiences and to express memories, thoughts, and feelings regarding the loss.

Ramsey (1977) used behavioral techniques, such as flooding and prolonged exposure to stimuli associated with the loss. Volkan (1975) used an approach that includes identifying linking objects or reminders which link the person to the deceased, emotionally reliving the circumstances of the death, and visiting the grave site. Paul and Miller (1986) used interventions such as the genogram or family tree, visits to the grave site, videotaping pictures of the deceased, role-plays involving the image of the deceased, letter writing, a visit to the place of death, a review of hospital records, obituaries, and other details of the death, inclusion of friends, relatives, and other informants in the process, and the use of evocative music. And Worden (1991) proposed a variety of techniques, including the Gestalt "empty chair" method, role-playing, psychodrama, and focusing on "linking objects."

These techniques are vehicles to facilitate access to the client's sensory modalities and are employed "to stimulate the experience of hitherto unrecognized pain, tears, anger, and rage about the fact that someone who was so close and important is gone" (Paul & Miller, 1986, p. 445). All of the previously mentioned approaches are aimed at identifying and removing obstacles to the mourning process.

PROFESSIONAL INTERVENTIONS WITH ADOLESCENTS AND THEIR FAMILIES

Central to effective mourning is the clarification and improvement of present relationships with family members and other significant persons. An understanding of the family context is essential to appreciate the unique significance of the adolescent's bereavement. A family systems perspective maintains that the response of one family member will reverberate among all family members. Frequently, the adults in the family are also grieving and are understandably less available to comfort the adolescent while they are immersed in their own grieving processes.

Walsh and McGoldrick (1991) identified two family tasks that benefit the immediate and long-term adaption of both individual family members and the family as a functional unit. These tasks are (a) to share acknowledgment of the reality of death and to share the experience of loss; and (b) to reorganize the family system and to reinvest in other relationships and life pursuits. In connection with these tasks, however, McGoldrick and her colleagues (1991) warned that "clinicians should be careful about definitions of 'normality' in assessing families' responses to death, since the manner of, as well as the length of time assumed normal for mourning differs greatly from culture to culture" (pp. 176–177).

Though the initial impact of death on survivors may be intrapsychic, the reactions of individual survivors will affect others and will therefore trigger change throughout the family system. Assessing a bereaved family following the death of a family member means noting whether the family is behaving in ways that will ultimately promote effective coping and aid in regaining function, or in ways that will hamper or prevent these goals, and thus contribute to dysfunction in the family system. When a family member dies, it becomes difficult or impossible for the family to exist as it did before the death. Of necessity, the family must reorganize following a loss. Thus, role flexibility and openness in the family system becomes an issue when a family member dies (Lamberti & Detmer, 1993).

Katie, a 14-year-old, white female was referred to therapy by her parents, Mr. and Mrs. Dixon, for "extreme acting out behaviors." The parents reported that Katie's behavior had deteriorated over the past three years and had become "uncontrollable." They described her as belligerent, angry, disrespectful, disobedient, and uncooperative. They stated she had been skipping school, lying, and sneaking out at night, was mean and cruel to the younger children, and flew into rages when confronted with her behavior or whenever any kind of punishment or consequence was used to discipline her. Mr. and Mrs. Dixon reported that Katie's anger and rages were becoming increasingly more frightening. She was very disruptive to the whole family and it had gotten to where they were fearful for the safety and well-being of the other children. The final straw was when Katie threatened her younger brother with a knife during a fight.

Katie was the second of seven children. She had an older brother and four younger brothers and sisters. A younger brother had died three years previously. On interviewing Katie, it was apparent she was a very angry, depressed young woman. She was uncooperative and unwilling to talk initially, yet she said enough to confirm a diagnosis of depression and angrily admitted that she wished she could just go away, that suicide was something she considered often.

Mr. and Mrs. Dixon viewed therapy as their last hope before removing Katie from the home. Neither wished for that to occur, but could see no other choice unless her behavior changed. They had exhausted every means of discipline they knew. When questioning the parents as to how they might explain the deterioration in Katie's behavior, the parents both acknowledged that her behavior changed after the death of their son, Mark. When asked to review the details of Mark's death, both Mr. and Mrs. Dixon tearfully recounted the events of his death.

Mrs. Dixon had been upstairs sewing and had delegated to Katie the responsibility of taking care of 4-year-old Mark who was downstairs playing. Katie apparently had left Mark unattended for a few minutes, during which time he entangled himself in the drawstrings of the drapes. When Katie found him, he was strangled. She ran upstairs to tell Mrs. Dixon that something was wrong with Mark. Upon seeing Mark, Mrs. Dixon immediately called 911. When the paramedics arrived, they pronounced Mark dead. Mrs. Dixon contacted Mr. Dixon who arrived home shortly thereafter. She angrily stated that the only thing he said to them when he got home was "this house is a pig sty, get it cleaned up." Mrs. Dixon stated that Mr. Dixon informed the other children of Mark's death, after which there was no more discussion or expression of feeling regarding this tragic event.

Mrs. Dixon reported that Mr. Dixon had placed himself in charge of the funeral and had made all the arrangements without any input from the other family members. To her knowledge, after the funeral no one mentioned Mark's death or said anything more about him. Mrs. Dixon expressed anger toward her husband in the session, blaming him for not allowing the family to grieve openly.

In working with families, the therapist must assess the degree of openness in the family system. In an open system, all family members are free to communicate a high percentage of inner thoughts, feelings, and fantasies to another who can reciprocate (Bowen, 1976). It quickly became apparent that the Dixon family was a closed system and the family was not functioning in a manner conducive to grieving Mark's death.

One important way of helping an adolescent in therapy is to help the parents. Often, in the case of losing a child or a spouse, the surviving parent(s) do not talk with the adolescent and the other children about the deceased or about their emotions relating to the death. Or the converse can happen, when surviving parents overload or flood an adolescent with their pain which the adolescent can interpret as the burden of responsibility for that parent's emotional well-being (Warm-brod, 1986). The therapist can assist the parents in finding the right balance of emotional sharing and help them in dealing with their own anxiety and pain so that the children in the family are free to express their own.

Having Katie talk and grieve only with the therapist may still have left her unable to share her feelings with her parents. If so, that would still leave her feeling isolated from her parents and siblings. Having family sessions where parents and children attend sessions together has considerable value and is recommended in these circumstances. The parents can directly answer the adolescents' and other children's questions about what caused the death and address whatever other concerns or questions they might have. It is advisable to include such relatives as grandparents, aunts, and uncles if they are involved with the adolescent and are sources of support for him or her. One of the important aspects of seeing the whole family and the extended family together is that it supports their existence as a family, despite death, and encourages family members to turn to one another instead of isolating and withdrawing.

During the family sessions with the Dixons, the family was able to talk about Mark, talk about his death, share their feelings about missing him, and clarify their questions about his death. They talked openly about how they were informed of his death, reviewed what they were told about how he died, and discussed how they felt when they received the news. All the children admitted they sensed a feeling of fear and gloom around Mark's death, they sensed tension and anger between Mom and Dad, and they were afraid to say anything that they thought might upset their parents further.

These were emotional sessions for Katie as she was finally able to express all the guilt and self-hate she was experiencing as a result of feeling responsible for Mark's death and believing that everyone else in the family was holding her responsible as well. For the first time, family members openly shared tears and gave support to one another as they shared their grief. Family members got to see Katie in a different light as she shared her guilt and pain. Katie benefited from learning that other family members, especially Mrs. Dixon, did not blame her for Mark's death as she had assumed.

The therapist also asked the family members to recount the events following the news of Mark's death, details about the funeral, where it was held, what they thought of the service, where Mark was buried, and whether they had visited the grave site since the death. In addition to talking about the facts of the death and funeral, the therapist took the family back to the time before the death and asked each family member to review his or her memories of Mark. Questions reviewed were the following: What did Mark look like? Did he have (blue eyes, curly hair) like one of the other children? The family was asked to bring pictures to show the therapist and to express what they enjoyed about him. What was special about Mark to each of them? What did each person like or not like about him?

Many of the family members seemed to be in a numbed, shut-down state, as they had been accustomed to repressing their thoughts and feelings about Mark's death. During one session, each family member was asked to bring a picture, object, or possession that reminded them of Mark. Each person was given an opportunity to express what Mark meant to them, to express what they appreciated about him and what they miss most about him, to share their feelings about his death, and to say good-bye in whatever way was comfortable for each person.

Mr. and Mrs. Dixon also participated in a few marital sessions during which Mrs. Dixon expressed anger and frustration with what she perceived as Mr. Dixon's controlling nature. She asserted that she was tired of quietly going along with his decisions and having no voice in matters pertaining to the family. She expressed a desire to change the dynamics in their relationship and an unwillingness to remain in a passive position in their marriage. Marital therapy consisted of improving communication skills between the two and resolving these marital issues.

Other family sessions were held to assist the family in improving communication and problem-solving skills throughout the family. Each family member discussed how they were going to fill the place in their family that Mark had held. Time was spent helping family members understand that much of Katie's angry, hurtful behavior was a result of all the painful, scared feelings she had kept inside for feeling guilty about Mark's death. Several individual sessions were spent with Katie, helping her to release the guilt and forgive herself.

This family was entrenched in dysfunctional patterns, patterns that were probably in place even before Mark's death. Simply assisting the family to grieve his death did not eliminate all the problems and dysfunctional patterns. However, Katie's behavior improved greatly throughout the course of therapy. Her depression lifted and she was able to get along better with her parents and siblings. Subsequently, she did better in school. Finally, addressing and grieving the death of their son and brother helped this family to loosen some of their dysfunctional patterns, helped to break down the isolation between family members, and initiated opportunities for much needed change in this family system.

Techniques Used in Working with Adolescents and Families

It is important for the therapist to discern how family members are reacting to each other in their grief, whether negatively or positively. The therapist can model for the parents appropriate ways to talk and to listen to other family members if they are having difficulty. The aim of this modeling is to have an effect during the crisis period as well as on the future of the parent-child relationship. The therapist must model an accepting and attentive stance to strongly expressed feelings.

It is important for the therapist to note areas of confusion and ask questions which will clarify the adolescent's concerns and explore his or her feelings about the death. Other questions can include those that take the family back to the time before the person died. It is important to hear from each family member what his or her memories are and to respect each person's memories.

The therapist's interest in the deceased can give the family an opportunity to reflect on the deceased's life as well as death. For example, the family can be invited to share photographs of the deceased and to recount memories of happy times. Drawing a family genogram with detailed questions about each person can serve as a reminder of the continuance of life. The genogram helps the therapist learn more about the various people in the family's background and present life, and draws attention to possible resources in the extended family. Talking about members of the extended family can bring up issues, sometimes old ones, that may be interfering with grieving.

In cases where feelings of ambivalence, guilt, or hostility are expressed in conjunction with feelings of sadness and loss, it might be helpful to coach an adolescent in the expression of these feelings and in the expression of words that were never said or questions that were never asked. These questions and feelings can be shared with other family members as well as directly with the deceased. This can be facilitated by asking the adolescent to write a letter to the deceased person and to express in it whatever "unfinished" things are still distressing him or her. Rituals such as sending the letter, reading the letter at the grave site, talking to the deceased in an empty chair, or visiting the grave site can be used as a means to express remaining thoughts and feelings.

In cases of delayed grief, it might be helpful to ask the adolescent and family to gather information about the deceased and the death, such as a review of hospital records, obituaries, and other details of the death, a visit to the place of death, and reviewing pictures of the deceased. These experiences can help revive the memories and feelings the adolescent felt but did not express at the time of the death (Paul & Miller, 1986).

It might also be necessary to help the family restructure and reorganize after the death of a family member. In the situation where a parent dies, the roles of parenting should be handled by another adult(s). The surviving parent may choose to remain alone or to involve another adult from the extended family, a babysitter, or a good friend whose parenting expertise is respected. These options are preferable to "elevating" the adolescent into the parental subsystem.

If an older child is elevated to the role of parent, he or she has been removed from the sibling subsystem and given responsibilities inappropriate to his or her age and family position. Attempting to fill the role of parent could block an adolescent's mourning, thwart developmental tasks, and affect future relationships. Similarly, an adolescent should not be expected to fill the vacant role in the spousal subsystem. A more appropriate intervention would be discussion of the problems associated with the loss of the parental role, encouragement of expression of feelings related to the loss of the parent, and examination of suitable alternatives to fill the parental role (Lamberti & Detmer, 1993).

Likewise, the death of a sibling requires a rearrangement of the hierarchy of roles within the sibling subsystem. Changes within this system must be monitored by the therapist so that no one child is considered responsible for taking over all the tasks or identity of the deceased. Care should be taken to ensure that the surviving adolescent is not expected to "replace" a deceased sibling, thereby losing his or her own identity. Intervention in such a situation must make overt the wishes, projections, and expectations of the parent regarding the "replacement" child. This allows the parents to express their grief as they let go of the image and fantasy related to the dead child that have been placed on the replacement child. That child is free then to return to his or her place in the sibling subsystem (Lamberti & Detmer, 1993).

CONCLUSION

Research and clinical observations suggest that experiencing the death of a loved one during adolescence can result in personal growth in the survivors, the development of personal autonomy, and enhanced capacity to cope with change (Benoliel, 1985; Edmonds & Hooker, 1992). Significant losses often serve as turning points in people's lives and lead to new perspectives on the meaning of what is important in living. Narrative accounts of people's experiences with trauma and loss indicate that people have the capacity to transform personal pain and despair into contributions to the quality of their lives and the lives of others. Any model of grief counseling and grief therapy that focuses only upon negative or pathological outcomes should be examined in light of resiliency research.

Why are some adolescents highly effective in dealing with major traumas or stressors such as a death? Resiliency investigators seek to answer such questions as who remains invulnerable in the face of stress and why? These studies suggest three kinds of protective factors that assist adolescents to cope. These include family environment, support networks, and personality characteristics (Hauser & Bowlds, 1990). Professional intervention with adolescents who are coping with death and bereavement should incorporate these factors in the process. The professional can assist the adolescent in building better relationships with parents, siblings, and other extended family, and in building a better external support system in the community with ministers, teachers, and friends. Also, the professional can assist the adolescent to develop individual coping styles, social skills, communication and cognitive skills, self-esteem, self-confidence, and autonomy. In doing so, the adolescent can develop a sense of control at a time when he or she might be feeling helpless and lost.

17

Helping Adolescents Who Are Coping with a Life-Threatening Illness, Along with Their Siblings, Parents, and Peers

Michael M. Stevens and Julie C. Dunsmore

This chapter discusses ways to help adolescents who are coping with a life-threatening illness. Attention is also given to helping siblings, parents, and peers of such adolescents. The chapter takes note of the need for adolescents to take part in their own health care, emphasizes the importance of successful communication in helping adolescents who are coping with a life-threatening illness, presents strategies for improving communication with young people, and offers guidelines for working with adolescents, their siblings, parents, and friends.

PARTICIPATORY ASPECTS OF HEALTH CARE

There is a continuing trend in Western health care for patients, including adolescents with a life-threatening illness, to be more involved in the planning and delivery of their own health care and for their needs as consumers to receive more consideration, than might have occurred 10 years ago. One consequence is that the system has had to adjust to this change. Health care professionals have had to adjust their style of communication with their patients and show more respect for the patients' wishes. As the legal requirements for informed consent become steadily more stringent and patients' awareness of their rights increases, some positive effects are evident for adolescents dealing with a life-threatening illness.

Informed Consent and Rights of Youth in Decision Making

Informed consent, open communication, honest and full disclosure, and patient information all express this altered focus in doctor-patient relationships (Ley, 1988). Individuals are encouraged to play a more active role in their treatment, rehabilitation, and medical decision making. Patients who want to be involved in treatment decisions are known to be significantly more hopeful than others. Young people, particularly, prefer a participatory approach to treatment and decision making (Cassileth, Zupkis, Sutton-Smith, & March, 1980).

Patients who receive information are able to develop more accurate expectations about potential threats of physical harm. As a consequence of being adequately informed, they cope more effectively by being able to solve problems and reduce anxiety and uncertainty (Derdiarian 1987; Kellerman, Zelter, Ellenberg, Dash, & Rigler, 1980). Adolescent cancer patients with knowledge of their disease are less depressed than those who are less well informed (Kvist, Rajantie, Kvist, & Siimes, 1991). Seeking information may help the person cope better with other aspects of his or her life (Derdiarian, 1987). Often patients with an extremely life-threatening illness cope by trying to avoid being informed about their illness (Dunsmore, 1992; Carr-Gregg & White, 1987; Cohen & Lazarus, 1979; Goss & Lebovitz, 1977). Denial and avoidance tend to reduce disruptive levels of anxiety and promote normal functioning and self-image (Van Dongen-Melman, Pruyn, Van Zanen, & Sanders-Woudstra, 1986). Fluctuating episodes of denial and avoidance have been reported in adolescents with cancer (Dunsmore, 1992; Carr-Gregg, 1987). Information-seeking behavior, and the degree to which parents are relied on as a source of information, are both influenced by the stage of illness. In active phases of illness, some authors (Levenson, Pfefferbaum, Copeland, & Silverberg, 1982; Susman et al., 1982) have reported that dependence on parents increases and willingness to absorb additional information falls. However, it has also been reported that adolescents in an active phase of illness sought more information and repeated clarification of information (Dunsmore & Quine, in press).

Needs of the Ill Adolescent for Information and Assistance With Decisions

Adolescents with cancer wish to be involved in the planning and decision-making aspects of their health care to a greater extent than generally occurs (Dunsmore & Quine, in press). To enable meaningful participation by adolescents, access to clear and appropriate information is vital. Education of caregivers to promote their willingness and ability to allow adolescent participation is important in the success of such collaboration. Adolescents generally lack experience in making adult decisions, such as those typically required in planning their treatment. They can be assisted by receiving education about how the health system caring for them works, and about various options which may be available to them in deciding treatment. Ideally, health carers themselves act as models of effective communication and as guides for effective navigation through the health care system. An adolescent's need for honesty, trust, debate, and fair treatment is paramount. Participation in peer support groups is useful in helping adolescents to become aware that there may be more than one option, more than just one way of doing things. One example of such groups is CanTeen (the Australian Teenage Cancer Patients Society, Inc.) which was established in Sydney, Australia, in 1985 to provide peer support for adolescents with cancer and their brothers and sisters. CanTeen has grown to become a national organization and has recently established programs in New Zealand and Ireland.

STRATEGIES FOR WORKING EFFECTIVELY WITH ADOLESCENTS

In order to reestablish their equilibrium and maintain hope for the future, adolescents with a life-threatening illness need both information about their illness and support to cope with the implications of that knowledge. Research has shown that the type of intervention that seems most helpful focuses on facing directly the threat posed by the illness and on increasing social support (Spiegel, 1993). Both knowledge and support are required to assist in building hope and improving quality of life. However, when adolescents with cancer are asked to rank their preferences for sources of knowledge and support, striking differences in preference become apparent.

Adolescents rate doctors and other health professionals providing care as the most preferred source of knowledge about their illness. Adolescents acknowledge and respect the expertise of those responsible for their treatment, and need to feel confident that their treatment providers are competent. However, when preferences for sources of support are considered, health professionals respected for their knowledge may be surprised to find that they are not thought to be as useful as sources of support in comparison to other adolescents with cancer, family members, and friends. This may be related to adolescents' shyness and distrust of adult authority figures. There are clear implications for development of altered styles of communication and initiatives allowing for more supportive professional relationships between health professionals and their adolescent patients.

Those preferred as providers of support are perceived as being understanding and caring, and as people with whom one can talk and debate. In a recent study (Dunsmore, 1992), 96% of the members of CanTeen felt that discussions with other adolescents with cancer had been very beneficial. For both support and information, peers rated high in preferences. Parents and peers with cancer were preferred over health professionals as providers of support. Adolescents with cancer reported that they prefer parental involvement, though not parental control (Dunsmore & Quine, in press).

Providing support without taking control is seen as a challenge both by the adolescents and those supporting them. The proportion of adolescents wanting their parents involved in discussions with doctors varies from 50% (Dunsmore & Quine, 1994) to 70% (Levenson et al., 1982). In the more recent of these studies, adolescents made a distinction on the basis of what was to be discussed: for treatment-related issues, 35% wanted a parent to be present; for feelings and concerns, 50% wanted a parent to be present.

COMMUNICATION: AN IMPORTANT SKILL FOR WORKING WITH ADOLESCENTS

Guidelines from a recently published list (Stevens, 1994) for improving communication with parents of children with cancer are adapted here to apply to adolescents with a life-threatening illness:

- Conduct interviews in a quiet, comfortable room with everyone seated. Young people may be intimidated by close eye-to-eye contact ("being eye-balled"); a side-by-side arrangement may be preferred. Interviews may be held effectively in settings other than a hospital room, e.g., the hospital coffee shop or gardens.
- During important discussions, allow a relative or friend to be included who may recall information that the adolescent or parents forget.

- Give a clear description and identification of the illness (e.g., use the word "cancer"); use plain language. If appropriate to the situation, use the words "death" and "dying" to let the adolescent and family know that these words are not taboo.
- Emphasize that the adolescent or family did not cause the disease and could not have prevented it, that the diagnosis has been made without undue delay, and (if appropriate to the situation) that effective therapy is available that has cured similar patients.
- Provide enough time for questions. Avoid having the adolescent and parents feel rushed. Encourage them to write down any points of anxiety as they occur for discussion at the next consultation.
- Seek feedback about what the adolescent and parents have understood from each consultation.
- Recognize that the adolescent and family may immediately assume that the youth will die, and soon. Aim to readjust expectations to a hopeful level, in keeping with the adolescent's actual outlook.
- Provide a written summary or tape recording of the discussion.
- Be prepared to repeat information patiently over several consultations.
- Do not offer detailed technical information initially that may be misunderstood or forgotten.
- At an early stage, and with the adolescent's consent, spend time with the adolescent's partner, parents, siblings, and grandparents, and liaise with the adolescent's school or employer to help allay anxiety.
- Have the family meet another family with a similar diagnosis and a successful outcome.
- Encourage the young person to meet another young person who has or has had a similar life-threatening illness and is doing well.
- In the longer term, be easily contactable, provide a variety of opportunities for information and support, and always allow hope. What is hoped for may need to be redefined from time to time, if an adolescent's condition deteriorates.
- Appoint another member of the health care team approved by the adolescent as his or her "buddy," to be available for discussion and to act as an advocate for the youth with the rest of the team.
- Support the adolescent and family in their current hope, and help them maintain a realistic focus on what the youth can still do.
- Encourage the adolescent and siblings to join a peer support organization.
- Acknowledge that meaningful communication is often a matter of trial and error.

TABLE 17.1 Improving Communication Between Caregivers and Adolescents with a Life-Threatening Illness

Communication	Examples given by adolescents	Strategies for improved communication
*What adolescents say **inhibits** good communication*		
Impersonal, detached manner	Sounding too textbookish Appearing uncaring Using intimidating tone or body language Excluding the patient Being stuffy	Avoid "hiding" behind the patient's chart Establish what both prefer to be called Be open to use of nicknames Talk to the adolescent, not about the adolescent
Use of authority behavior	Using medical terminology or jargon without explanation Conducting large ward rounds Treating adolescents as if they are unintelligent Limiting access to results of tests	Limit size of ward rounds; introduce strangers Inform patient of results promptly Provide opportunity for questions Assist understanding by seeking feedback (e.g., "This has been a lot of information to take in. Could you let me know in a nutshell what you have understood so far?")
Lack of time, haste	Not explaining time limitations Not appearing to listen ("Having one foot out the door") Delegating care to a more junior physician Not providing time for one-to-one discussions	Agree about time available for discussions Encourage adolescents to write down their questions Organize follow-up by appropriate staff members
Generation gap	Appearing uncomfortable about spending time with patient Embarrassment when discussing sensitive issues Showing frustration with adolescents Procrastinating over decisions Trying too hard to relate at the young person's level	Be honest about issues of sex, fertility, relationships Ask young person to explain further if not understood Maintain sense of humor and be prepared for some teasing about age

*What adolescents say **facilitates** good communication*

Interactive communication	Ability to listen Seeking feedback Allowing questions	Choose an environment conducive to discussion Encourage discussion of alternatives and their consequences Encourage discussion of fears or intense emotions by legitimizing these as being "normal"
Knowledge and professional expertise	Ability to make correct decisions Demonstrations of competent skills (e.g., inserting intravenous cannulas) Being able to explain reasons underlying decisions Being confident	Provide a simple explanation for why decisions are made or information that supports a preferred choice in treatment Provide access to written information Explain all procedures clearly If unable to answer a question, acknowledge and be willing to research information required
Honesty and a straightforward approach	Providing an opportunity to discuss all related issues Not withholding information Not seeking to protect from the truth Not telling parents one thing and the patient another	Establish a direct style of communicating Adolescents benefit by receiving information about how communication may proceed (e.g., "I will be honest with you and not keep anything from you. Please ask if you think something is not being said.") Be willing to repeat information Be willing to review decisions
Professional friendship	Showing genuine concern for the adolescent as an individual, not just as a case or a disease Having a sense of humor Providing some self-disclosure Remembering small details about the patient Being there for support afterward	Respect the adolescent's privacy Maintain confidentiality Admit mistakes Treat adolescents as individuals Recognize that the adolescent's concerns and aspirations may change with time

Adolescents who participated in discussion groups conducted by
CanTeen were asked for pointers which they thought inhibited or facilitated good communication. The findings are summarized in Table
17.1, together with strategies for improved communication. Clearly, the
cognitive maturity of adolescents is important in determining how caregivers should communicate with them. Communication should be consistent with the cognitive level of the adolescent in order to have
maximum impact (Kaplan & Friedman, 1994).

CENTRAL ISSUES IN WORKING WITH ADOLESCENTS WITH A LIFE-THREATENING ILLNESS

How Attentive Listening and Improved Communication Help

Much of the tension experienced by adolescents with a life-threatening
illness can be released to assist them in successfully coping with their
predicament by simply permitting them to discuss their thoughts and
feelings, and to share their dreams and frustrations. All too often, an
issue of importance to the adolescent is ignored in the hope that it will
go away. Denial is a coping strategy used by patients and care providers
alike. Health professionals and patients each may not discuss important
issues, fearing that doing so may "open the flood-gates" and precipitate
unacceptable levels of emotion. As one young person said, "I thought if
I started crying, I'd never stop!"

To be able to listen to adolescents and to discuss death and dying
with them without putting up barriers, caregivers need to be aware of
their own beliefs and fears about death. It is normal to have uncomfortable feelings surface when working with a young person who is facing death. But if one becomes overwhelmed by these feelings, one will
have little energy left to assist others. Time out, and occasionally super-
vision, assist the caregiver to deal with a range of feelings, including sadness and anger, that emerge when dealing with the death of a young
person and with past experiences of one's own that are brought to the
surface at such times.

Negotiation and Being Offered Choices

Adolescents value opportunities for negotiations concerning their
treatment, whether early in the course of their illness, in follow-up, and,
for those who are dying, in palliative care. Being offered choices affords

them a sense of control over their situation. In early phases of treatment, better compliance with therapy is likely. For those in palliative care, adverse emotions such as anger, frustration, depression, and anxiety will be lessened. Choices in even apparently mundane matters such as what to eat, wear, or watch on television, can boost morale effectively. As a cartoon by Ashley Brilliant says, "If you cannot go over it, under it, around it, or through it, you'd better negotiate with it."

Recognition of Small Achievements

When one is required to redefine one's hopes from hope for cure to hope for prolonged survival with good quality, the positive value of small achievements becomes significant. Hope is better preserved if the ill adolescent's small achievements, from day to day, are acknowledged and respected.

Hospital and Health Care Team Issues

Adolescents prefer to be cared for in the company of their peers in an adolescent ward, rather than in a pediatric or adult ward (Tebbi & Stern, 1988). To foster a more home-like atmosphere, hospitals may need to relax rules concerning visiting hours, rooming in, decoration of the patient's room, and related issues when caring for terminally ill adolescents.

Those caring for terminally ill adolescents must face the prospect of repeated losses and will frequently experience painful emotions including sadness, anger, frustration, and guilt. Caregivers must recognize their own limitations and use appropriate support within their institution or treatment team. Death of an adolescent has been reported as being the most difficult to cope with for staff (Adams, 1979).

Jealousy and resentment may occur in staff who feel threatened by perceived intrusions into their area of responsibility by other health care professionals who are involved in the patient's care, or who feel displaced in the patient's affections. The patient's wishes and preferences should be respected and dialogue should occur between caregivers so that any conflict between caregivers may be lessened.

Occasional conflict will arise within the treatment team over whether to proceed with further attempts at curative therapy or change to palliative care. Foremost consideration must be given to the anticipated benefits and disadvantages of the proposed therapy for the patient. The need for a sensible advocate for the patient within the treatment team is vital.

Certain health professionals evoke striking affection, respect, and loyalty from their adolescent patients and develop close "professional friendships." These friendships are valued highly by patients. One adolescent said, "It makes me feel that I'm alive that I affect someone else, it's not all one-sided."

Leisure Activities

Participation in activities such as camps affords chronically and terminally ill adolescents a valuable opportunity to escape from the tedium and concerns of their day-to-day routine. Recreational camps provide an ideal opportunity to mix socially with other teenagers, and to have fun and take risks in a safe environment. Group discussions are easily arranged at camps. One-to-one discussions also are facilitated, because the adolescents are able to choose when, and with whom, they will talk. Camps afford a good opportunity for adolescents to talk informally among themselves and to become better acquainted with those who care for them, often seeing their health professionals in a different light for the first time. Self-esteem can be effectively built up by success with simple accomplishments.

Peer Support and Its Value

Improvements in coping, quality of life, and self-esteem have been noted in adults with cancer who make use of peer support (Spiegel, 1993). Research currently being undertaken is beginning to demonstrate similar benefits for young people with cancer.

In a study of long-term survivors of childhood cancer, two thirds of the subjects were evaluated as having few friends, being substantially isolated, and participating in social and leisure activities less than their peers (Zwartjes, 1980). In a contemporary study of Australian adolescent cancer patients, 65 of 86 individuals (75%) recalled serious difficulties in maintaining friendships as a result of their illness and treatment. Problems encountered varied with age: younger adolescents reported being teased at school by peers (Wasserman, Thompson, Wilimas, & Fairclough, 1987); middle to late adolescents reported feelings of rejection, isolation, and stigma associated with having cancer. Many of the subjects reported that their peers experienced difficulty in discussing cancer and their situation with them (Carr-Gregg, 1987).

In a report of a support group conducted over three months for nine adolescent cancer patients, all said that having the opportunity to talk to another adolescent who had received chemotherapy and was doing well, would have been valuable (Orr, Hoffmans, & Bennets, 1984). The founder of CanTeen, who had had cancer as a young adult, reported that adolescents expressed a desire to talk to other young people with cancer and related experiencing a special bond that had emerged between those who had experienced such contact (Carr-Gregg, 1989).

As adolescents themselves have said, "CanTeen has helped me to get problems off my chest without feeling embarrassed, which has made me feel better within myself. I feel as though I actually belong somewhere . . . we have all been through the same thing and we understand how the treatment affects us." "It's terrific to be in a supportive, understanding, and fun environment. Because everyone has been in a similar situation, there is no need to put on a facade, or feel that it's wrong to talk about cancer" (Butters, 1991). Comments such as these, made by teenage members of CanTeen, testify to the value of peer support through contact with other youths with cancer provided by such organizations.

Further research is required into the value of peer support for young people with a life-threatening illness, and into the reasons why some young people prefer not to avail themselves of peer support.

Aids to the Adolescent's Communication with Health Professionals

Adolescents often benefit from having a focus other than the health professional, when discussing difficult issues. For example, it is helpful to use photographs or photo albums which enable the adolescent to talk about his or her family and friends. Similarly, writing poems, letters (which may or may not be mailed), or a journal can assist in the release of pent-up emotions, and help clarify issues and decisions that may need to be made.

Drawing As an Aid to Expression

Drawing is a creative activity which may be very therapeutic by facilitating nonverbal communication and enabling the release of emotions. Drawing assists adolescents in telling their stories. Examples of drawings done by adolescents with cancer or their siblings are shown in Figures 17.1 to 17.3, together with explanations provided by the young people who drew them.

FIGURE 17.1 Drawing by a 14-year-old girl, diagnosed with a cerebral tumor at age 12 years and 6 months, treated with intensive radiotherapy and steroid therapy. Scalp hair had not regrown on the right side of her head. "The house is my house, and the people inside the house are my friends and family welcoming me inside, but I feel outcast and alone and don't want to come in. The colors surrounding the sad person (me) are like a happy, cheerful front that everyone always sees. Because I'm looking so much better now, apart from my hair, people don't want to know about my sadness and disbelief that this has happened. The hands in the doorway are reaching out for me, but I feel like an outsider and don't want to come in."

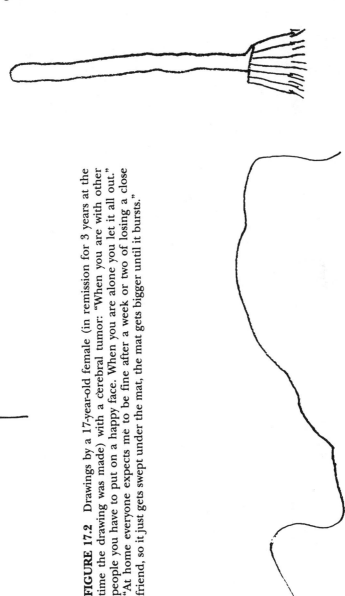

FIGURE 17.2 Drawings by a 17-year-old female (in remission for 3 years at the time the drawing was made) with a cerebral tumor: "When you are with other people you have to put on a happy face. When you are alone you let it all out." "At home everyone expects me to be fine after a week or two of losing a close friend, so it just gets swept under the mat, the mat gets bigger until it bursts."

FIGURE 17.3 Drawing by a 16-year-old girl whose brother had died 8 months earlier of osteogenic sarcoma: "I feel I'm in a straight jacket but I have a zipper over my lip. The tears won't stop. There's a dagger in my heart. Laughter is all around me."

Leaving Behind a Permanent Record

When discussing their death and the effect their death may have on those that they love, many adolescents mention the importance of leaving behind some permanent record. Although painful for some, many dying adolescents have taperecorded messages for their friends and family; some have made videos. Composing these messages in the company of a friend or counselor may be less threatening, because a two-way conversation or interview is less artificial and often results in much more of the real personality of the young person being displayed. There may be both much laughter and more serious messages.

Because hope is so important to these adolescents, preparations such as these are often best completed by putting these tasks in the "just in case" category. Discussion usually centers around all the energy that is required to suppress feelings of fear and anxiety associated with the possibility of dying. Nightmares are reported as common. Often, adolescents who have "put their house in order" find they can invest additional energy into living.

SIBLINGS OF ADOLESCENTS WITH A LIFE-THREATENING ILLNESS

The poem on page 344 was written by a teenage girl whose brother had cancer. It is a very powerful expression of the experiences of siblings of young people who are living with a life-threatening illness. When families direct most of their energy and concern into caring for a young person who is ill, the needs and experiences of the well siblings are often overlooked.

Ambivalence in Sibling Relationships

Relationships between siblings may span six or more decades and will often be the longest relationships that a person experiences. The relationship between siblings is always significant, although it may be ambivalent. Being closely related does not mean that siblings will be the best of friends. Health professionals frequently express surprise and concern at the degree of animosity that can exist between siblings. Assumptions that young patients always belong to "happy, perfect families" will not assist health professionals in working effectively with either patients or their families.

Only A SIBLING

Tammy McGowan

How do you tell someone you love
You don't want them to die
How can I try to be normal
I know I will cry

How do I cope with my anger
At life, at God and sometimes even at you
How can I put a smile on my face
While my insides are ripping in two

How can I tell you I'm frightened
Of the skeleton my brother's become
Tired and thin from your battle
A war that I'm scared cannot be won

How can I tell you I love you
When all our lives it's going unsaid
How do I stop you from drowning
When the water's already over my head

Every wince stabs me too, with pain
Why cannot I tell anyone how I feel
When I feel like I'm going insane

How can I think of my future
When it's possibly a future without you there
Why do I feel so damn helpless
And my problems too insignificant to share

How do I tell you big brother
That I'm scared of what's happening to you
Why cannot anyone seem to understand
That your dying is killing me too.

By Tammy McGowan a member of CanTeen Australia Ltd., a peer support network for teenagers with cancer and their brothers and sisters. Reprinted with kind permission of Tammy McKenzie neé McGowan and CanTeen Australia Ltd.

At time, sibling rivalry can be very pronounced. Jealousy between siblings is common. Tensions between siblings may convey confusing messages to adults. Frequently, arguments and rivalry are accepted by siblings as the norm. Reactions to each other may swing to extremes.

One of the authors' (JCD) patients with cancer was a twin who would argue and snap at his twin brother most of the time, but if another person threatened or argued with the same brother, the ill twin would defend him as if his life truly depended on it. Sibling relationships are both complex and contradictory!

Reactions of Siblings to a Life-Threatening Illness

Siblings of adolescents with a life-threatening illness often refer to the confusion and guilt experienced in acknowledging the fact that their ill brother or sister may die, and, at the same time, having to deal with thoughts of competition for the attention and love of adults. There may be feelings of unworthiness associated with being jealous but still wanting to be special. The sibling may have his or her own private version of the causation of the patient's illness. There may be misconceptions about the nature of the illness, about the hospital clinic, and about the treatment program. There may be a fear of developing the same illness. There may be compromised academic and social functioning because of preoccupation with the stress of illness. There may be guilt and shame relating to relief for not developing the illness and shame over the patient's disfigurement as marking the family as different (Rando, 1984). A 13-year-old brother of a 15-year-old girl who had a brain tumor and who had been severely affected by steroid therapy, expressed his embarrassment at her appearance, saying, "How would you feel having to walk down the street with someone who doesn't look normal, who cannot walk straight and dribbles? Everyone just stares. I feel so bad. She's my sister, but I hate everyone staring and thinking mean things."

Need to Prove One's Worth

Siblings often feel that they need to prove their worth by becoming "Super Siblings," able to take everything in their stride, overcoming problems in a minute, being patient, caring, and selfless, excelling at school, and providing love and support for their ill sibling. They are often expected to grow up over night. Many grieve their loss of innocence. It is no wonder that such siblings have a high level of depression, anxiety disorders, and school difficulties (Cairns, Clark, Smith, & Lansky, 1979; Spinetta, 1981a, 1981b).

Working with Siblings—What Helps

Siblings of a young person with a life-threatening or terminal illness are assisted by the following:

- Being given a clear and unambiguous concept of the illness and its cause
- Being encouraged to dispense with any erroneous concepts of the cause of the illness
- Being allowed to visit the clinic, meet staff caring for the ill sibling, and witness the patient's treatment program
- Being assigned helpful tasks in the ill sibling's home care
- Being reassured that they will not develop the same illness
- Being provided with appropriate opportunities for ventilation (verbal and nonverbal) of feelings of sadness or resentment toward the ill sibling or parents
- Having a liaison with the sibling's school (with the sibling's and patient's consent)
- Providing opportunities to "say good-bye" as the ill sibling's death approaches
- Being allowed to attend a sibling's funeral along with the rest of the family, if they wish to do so. Children should not be forced to attend such events; they need the freedom to participate to the degree they feel comfortable. Willingness to take part is increased by providing information about what will happen and options for participation.

When a young person is dying it is important that siblings be permitted to make informed choices about what they would like to do in order to cope. Often, simple fear of the unknown prevents them from doing what they think would be best: fear of breaking down or crying or getting angry, fear of saying or doing the wrong thing, fear of "death." Is death scary? Is it contagious? Will it make them feel sick too?

Health professionals can act as important role models in assisting siblings to find safe ways of relating to the young person who is dying, for example, by continuing to talk to the person who is dying, even after entering a coma, by gently touching the dying person, by showing respect, by being still able to respond to the humor that can so often be expressed, by showing that just being there may be the most important thing.

Many siblings who have been with their ill brother or sister during the final stages of life have reported how important it was to say to the dying sibling whatever was on their mind. Sometimes they needed privacy to do so. Sadly, some have said they wanted to, but felt unable to ask for that special time. With the support of a caregiver, young people in this situation can be encouraged to "talk" or write a letter to their deceased sibling. This can be a helpful and liberating part of the grieving process for anyone with "unfinished business."

Overprotection of Siblings

That one child in a family is in need of special care and attention will certainly change the family's dynamics. The most important message provided by a group of adolescents who each had a sibling with cancer was "Don't shut me out, I'm part of this family too." Ruses adopted by families intended to protect well siblings are common, in which the well children are kept uninformed of the true situation so as not to become upset. Many such siblings relate experiences of being sent into another room when issues to do with their ill brother or sister were being discussed.

In fact, it is difficult, and also inappropriate, to attempt to conceal the true situation from siblings. Lack of openness frequently causes needless distress and anxiety, as young people attempt to process meager information often gleaned from unreliable sources. They in turn may not feel able to disclose their feelings, for fear of upsetting their parents all the more. Much energy can be wasted in playing "the protection game."

Misperceptions by Adults of Siblings' Reactions

Fears, anger, and confusion experienced by siblings can be trivialized by adults. One sibling reported her parent saying, "What have you got to be upset about? Stop being so selfish. Think about your poor sister." In fact, many siblings of adolescents with a life-threatening illness talk about trading places with the ill sibling. Their anger often arises from a feeling of helplessness, of being unable to change the situation. One sibling said, "I feel so useless, so frustrated that I cannot help!"

It is rare, however, for adolescent siblings to make declarations of love to their ill brother or sister. One 14-year-old whose sister had cystic fibrosis said, "I've known her all my life. How can I tell her I love her? She'll think I've lost it!"

Encouraging Siblings to Express Their Feelings

Often, young people need encouragement to express their feelings toward their ill sibling, but to do so in their own way. Adolescents often express a need to be able to use humor as a means of communicating safely with their sibling. Words are not as critical as the feelings imparted (Foley & Whittam, 1990).

Siblings should be encouraged to express their love and concern for the young person who is dying, in whatever style they have previously used. Sometimes they may need to discuss some of their uncomfortable feelings with someone else, before they feel ready to express their feelings to their sibling. Encouraging them to write a letter that remains unposted may sometimes help them to clarify their thoughts and feelings. Poetry, drawing (see Figures 17.1–17.3), and journal writing can also be helpful.

Need for Honesty With Siblings

Honesty is regarded by siblings as important. Many siblings have said that the anxiety they experience often results from the unknown and from trying to best discern the truth. Many agonize for hours over something they overheard or something they misunderstood from a book. Information provided for them needs to be clear and simple. An opportunity for both questions and debate should be provided. Ignorance can cause great heartache. Many siblings worry that their own children may also become ill.

Talking about these matters with honesty and openness helps to show there is nothing of which to be ashamed. Helping siblings rehearse ways of explaining the ill sibling's current situation will enable them to handle these discussions more effectively when outside the family. They often just need reassurance that, should their sibling's condition deteriorate abruptly or other important changes occur, they will be informed immediately.

Value of Family Discussions

Sometimes important family discussions need repeating, as children and adolescents grow older and new issues are raised. There may be no rational explanation for the young person's illness and death, or for why a brother or sister developed cancer or had heart disease. Young people still need opportunities to discuss what they believe may be the explanation, and to discover what is known about their brother's or sister's illness.

Peer Support for Siblings

For the sibling, peer support has been shown to be extremely beneficial. During the adolescent years in particular, peer support is very important. Siblings often find they can talk openly with peers about the frustrations and joys of living with a sibling, because the others understand. As one adolescent expressed it, "The feeling of relief was incredible! I wasn't alone."

Relatives, friends, and teachers can also be of great assistance to siblings of terminally ill young people simply by acknowledging the difficulties they face. Siblings need opportunities to be involved in the care of their ill brother or sister if they wish, but also permission to get on with their own lives and acknowledgment that they too are important.

PARENTS AND OTHER FAMILY MEMBERS OF ADOLESCENTS WITH A LIFE-THREATENING ILLNESS

Sources of Distress for Parents and Other Family Members

Sources of distress that parents and other family members face include loss of the parental role, the unnaturalness of a child predeceasing a parent, fearful societal reactions to the young person's death, loss of support from a partner, and pain associated with parenting of the surviving children. Identifying these issues and discussing them will assist parents and other family members to focus on and talk about their feelings, and to cope more effectively with the issues confronting them.

Avoidance by Parents and Other Family Members

Terminally ill adolescents report that, frequently, one of their parents will begin avoiding them—most commonly, the father. They say parents and other family members will often demonstrate their awkwardness and uncertainty about what to say or do when in the presence of their ill son or daughter. The adult may be wanting not to show his or her emotions and may attempt to disguise them (e.g., by wearing sunglasses to mask recent crying, even at night). Parents may need to be encouraged not to begin avoiding their ill child, and be reminded that just being there can help. Exploring concrete ways of providing help can assist both parties to have a sense of doing something. Often this can also provide opportunities gently to feel okay about "just being there."

Sources of Assistance for Parents and Other Family Members

Parents and other family members may benefit from receiving additional professional counseling and, through support groups, understanding and encouragement from other parents who have had similar experiences. Young people with life-threatening illness should receive reassurance from their parents that the parents will be honest and not keep information from the youth. As has been said by adolescents in many CanTeen groups, "Banish secrets!"

Assistance in Coping by Being Prepared

Parents and other family members may need to be warned about extreme variations in mood, especially aggression, that can occur in terminally ill young people. These may be aggravated by adverse drug reactions, renal failure, or hallucinations. The anger may be against the unfairness of the situation. Parents may need to be prepared for being given disagreeable statements of fact by the adolescent that they may not have heard before. As one parent reported her daughter saying, "I've never told you this before, but you get on my nerves." Parents may need encouragement to find ways of dealing with the aggression and spite poured out at them, and to stand by the young person, rather than being driven away. Despite difficulties such as these, many parents speak of the times spent with their dying adolescent as special, as something positive. Young people who are dying feel very comforted just to know their parents are present with them.

PEERS AND FRIENDS OF ADOLESCENTS WITH A LIFE-THREATENING ILLNESS

The term *cancer patient* is regarded by many in the community as a stigmatizing label. The vocabulary used to describe cancer and the process of treatment both create distancing and a negative attitude within the very community that could best support the patient (Bartholome, 1982). However an opposing view holds that this same stigmatization is lessening, as a result of both the contemporary demystification of medicine and altered practices in schools (Hodges, Graham-Pole, & Fong, 1984; Koocher, 1986).

There is some inconsistency in studies of peers of adolescents with cancer. Patients in earlier studies reported that they thought peers avoided them because of ignorance or misconceptions about cancer being fatal and contagious. Wasserman and colleagues (1987) reported 40% of long-term survivors of Hodgkin's disease were teased about their baldness or thinness and treated as contagious or as outcasts. However, peers of adolescents with cancer in another study (Hodges, Graham-Pole, & Fong, 1984) were found to be well informed about cancer and reported that they had enjoyed positive relationships with the adolescent with cancer. The views of peers obtained directly by interview are considered to be more reliable than the perceptions of those views as provided by patients, because the patients' perceptions may have been influenced by their own avoidance behavior and negative self-image. However, the peers' responses may have been biased to be considered acceptable by the interviewer. Improved education about cancer and wider discussions in class on topics such as death and illness may also account for the differing results. Despite these differences, reports are consistent that few peers visit their friend with cancer either in hospital or at home.

Awareness of the Grieving of Peers

It is important not to underestimate the intensity of grieving by peers. Peers with a disease or situation similar to the patient need to be given the opportunity for extra debriefing, because of the implications for themselves of their friend's progress or deterioration. "Best friendships" are common during adolescence, heightening grief. The closeness of these friendships may not be understood or appreciated by caregivers and family. Referred to as disenfranchised grief (Doka, 1989), the loss that close friends feel may go unrecognized by society and may also be discounted by young people themselves. More research is required about the incidence and long-term consequences of disenfranchised grief.

Encouraging Peers to Keep in Touch
With the Adolescent

Sometimes peers with cancer will avoid coming to visit an adolescent in the hospital or at home, because of the distress and painful emotions entailed in continuing contact. Subsequently, such peers may experience marked guilt after the person's death if they were unable to keep up contact because of fear of becoming upset or being confronted with a reminder of their own situation. If this fear can be discussed with someone supportive, solutions can often be found that enable satisfactory contact to be maintained.

It is helpful to encourage peers to make arrangements for a more formalized visiting program, which allows young people to come in pairs. They usually find it easier to come with a friend than alone. They may need to be forewarned about the patient's current condition. They may need to visit only for a short period of time. They should be open to the patient's signals about wanting or not wanting visitors, and about how long the visit should last. Telephoning the home or ward before the visit is helpful. They should try not take it personally if turned away, accepting that the patient's condition may not be suitable for a visit by anyone at that particular time. An opportunity to debrief may be needed after some visits.

CONCLUSION

Adolescents who are coping with a life-threatening illness and with dying are helped most effectively by caregivers who combine professionalism and competence in their area of expertise with an ability to communicate well with young people and an ability, while offering useful support and knowledge, to impart to ill adolescents the conviction that they are "on their side."

Adolescents who are dying seem to manage best when they receive support for their own individual style of coping. Patterns of coping need to be evaluated with an open mind, and accepted if deemed workable. Caregivers need to be willing to be adaptable and flexible, because a young person's preferred method of coping may change.

As caregivers, we must constantly remember to listen to the adolescents with a life-threatening illness, their siblings, peers, and family members. It is through a willingness to listen that we will most accurately discern how to support them most effectively.

When compared to the death of an adult, the death of a young person affects a wider proportion of those connected to the person, including siblings, parents, families, peers, and, significantly, caregivers. It is essential for us as caregivers to bear in mind that expanded "ripple effect" when formulating our plans for the young person's management and support.

Caregivers working with these adolescents, while acknowledging that their work is demanding, frequently stressful, and at times unavoidably sad, will emphasize that they consider the work fulfilling, that they enjoy working with these young people and their families, and that they consider it a privilege to do so. It is vital that these caregivers avail themselves of adequate support, debriefing, and planned leave from their work in order to help maintain the enthusiasm of their long-term commitment.

References

Abraham, M., & Whitock, F. (1969). Childhood experiences and depression. *British Journal of Psychiatry, 115,* 883–888.

Adams, D. W. (1979). *Childhood malignancy: The psychosocial care of the child and his family.* Springfield, IL: Charles C Thomas.

Adams, D. W., & Deveau, E. J. (1986). Helping dying adolescents: Needs and responses. In C. A. Corr & J. N. McNeil (Eds.), *Adolescence and death* (pp. 79–96). New York: Springer Publishing.

Alexander, I. E., & Adlerstein, A. M. (1958). Affective responses to the concept of death in a population of children and early adolescents. *Journal of Genetic Psychology, 93,* 167–177.

Allberg, W. R., & Chu, L. (1990). Understanding adolescent suicide: Correlates in a developmental perspective. *The School Counselor, 37,* 343–350.

Allison, K. W., & Takei, Y. (1993). Diversity: The cultural contexts of adolescents and their families. In R. M. Lerner (Ed.), *Early adolescence: Perspectives on research, policy, and intervention* (pp. 51–69). Hillsdale, NJ: Erlbaum.

American Association of Suicidology. (1990). *Suicide prevention guidelines: Suggestions for dealing with the aftermath of suicide in the schools.* Denver: Author.

American Psychiatric Association. (1987). *Diagnostic and statistical manual of mental disorders* (3rd ed., rev.). Washington, DC: Author.

American Psychological Association. (1993). *Violence & youth: Psychology's response* (Summary Report of the American Psychological Association Commission on Violence and Youth, Vol. 1). Washington, DC: Author.

Anderson, J. E., Kann, L., Holtzman, D., Arday, S., Truman, B., & Kolbe, L. (1990). HIV/AIDS knowledge and sexual behavior among high school students. *Family Planning Perspectives, 22,* 252–255.

Ariès, P. (1962). *Centuries of childhood: A social history of family life* (R. Baldick, Trans.). New York: Random House.

Ariès, P. (1981). *The hour of our death.* (H. Weaver, Trans.). New York: Knopf.

Athens, L. H. (1989). *The creation of dangerous violent criminals.* London: Routledge.

Austin, D. A., & Mack, J. E. (1986). The adolescent philosopher in a nuclear world. In C. A. Corr & J. N. McNeil (Eds.), *Adolescence and death* (pp. 57–75). New York: Springer Publishing.

Bacchetti, P., & Moss, A. R. (1989). Incubation period of AIDS in San Francisco. *Nature, 338,* 251–253.

Bachman, J. G., Johnston, L. D., & O'Malley, P. M. (1986). *Monitoring the future: Questionnaire responses from the nation's high school seniors, 1986.* Ann Arbor, MI: University of Michigan.

Balk, D. E. (1981). *Sibling death during adolescence: Self-concept and bereavement reactions.* Unpublished doctoral dissertation, University of Illinois at Urbana-Champaign, Champaign, IL.

Balk, D. E. (1983a). Adolescents' grief reactions and self-concept perceptions following sibling death: A case study of 33 teenagers. *Journal of Youth and Adolescence, 12,* 137–161.

Balk, D. E. (1983b). Effects of sibling death on teenagers. *Journal of School Health, 15,* 14–18.

Balk, D. E. (1990). The self-concepts of bereaved adolescents: Sibling death and its aftermath. *Journal of Adolescent Research, 5,* 112–132.

Balk, D. E. (1991). Death and adolescent bereavement: Current research and future directions. *Journal of Adolescent Research, 6,* 7–27.

Balk, D. E. (1995). *Adolescent development: Early through late adolescence.* Pacific Grove, CA: Brooks/Cole.

Balk, D. E., & Hogan, N. S. (1995). Religion, spirituality, and bereaved adolescents. In D. W. Adams & E. J. Deveau (Eds.), *Beyond the innocence of childhood: Helping children and adolescents cope with death and bereavement* (Vol. 3, pp. 61–88). Amityville, NY: Baywood.

Balk, D. E., Tyson-Rawson, K. J., & Colletti-Wetzel, J. (1993). Social support as an intervention with bereaved college students. *Death Studies, 17,* 427–450.

Balmer, L. E. (1992). *Adolescent sibling bereavement: Mediating effects of family environment and personality.* Unpublished doctoral dissertation, York University, Toronto, Ontario, Canada.

Bandura, A. (1964). The stormy decade: Fact or fiction? *Psychology in the Schools, 1,* 224–231.

Bandura, A. (1992). A social cognitive approach to the exercise of control over AIDS infection. In R. J. DiClemente (Ed.), *Adolescents and AIDS: A generation in jeopardy* (pp. 89–116). Newbury Park, CA: Sage.

Bank, S., & Kahn, M. (1982). *The sibling bond.* New York: Basic Books.

Barbato, A., & Irwin, H. C. (1992). Major therapeutic systems and the bereaved client. *Australian Psychologist, 27,* 22–27.

Barnes, M. J. (1978). The reactions of children and adolescents to the death of a parent or sibling. In O. J. Sahler (Ed.), *The child and death* (pp. 185–201). St. Louis: Mosby.

Barrett, C. J. (1978). Effectiveness of widows' groups in facilitating change. *Journal of Consulting and Clinical Psychology, 46,* 20–31.

Barrett, R. K. (1991). Homicide and suicide: Who is at risk. *The American Black Male.* New York: William Pruitt Enterprises, *3*(2), 4–8; *3*(3) 4–6.

Barrett, R. K. (1993). Urban adolescent homicidal violence: An emerging public health concern. *The Urban League Review, 16*(2), 67–75.

Bartholome, W. G. (1982). Good intentions become imperfect in an imperfect world. In J. Van Eys (Ed.), *Children with cancer: Mainstreaming and reintegration* (pp. 17–33). Lancaster, England: MTP Press.

Bartol, R. C. (1991). *Criminal behavior.* Englewood Cliffs, NJ: Prentice Hall.

Baxter, G. W. (1982). Bereavement support groups for secondary school students. *School Guidance Worker, 38,* 27–29.

Baxter, G., Bennett, L., & Stuart, W. (1987). *Adolescents and death: Bereavement support groups for secondary school students* (2nd ed.). Missisaugua, Ontario: Canadian Centre for Death Education and Bereavement at Humber College.

Beardslee, W. R., & Podorefsky, D. (1988). Resilient adolescents whose parents have serious affective and other psychiatric disorders: Importance of self-understanding and relationships. *American Journal of Psychiatry, 145,* 63–69.

Beck, A. J., Seshi, B., & Tuthill, R. (1963). Childhood bereavement and adult depression. *Archives of General Psychiatry, 9,* 295–302.

Bell, H., Avery, A., Jenkins, D., Feld, J., & Schoenrock, C. (1985). Family relationships and social competence during late adolescence. *Journal of Youth and Adolescence, 14,* 109–119.

Bell, J. (1978). Family context therapy: A model for family change. *Journal of Marriage and Family Therapy, 4,* 111–126.

Belsky, J., & Pensky, E. (1988). Developmental history, personality, and family relationships: Toward an emergent family system. In R. A. Hinde & J. Stevenson-Hinde (Eds.), *Relationships within families: Mutual influences* (pp. 193–219). Oxford, England: Clarendon.

Bennett, D. L. (1985). Young people and their health needs: A global perspective. *Seminars in adolescent medicine, 1,* 1–14.

Benoliel, J. Q. (1985). Loss and adaptation: Circumstances, contingencies, and consequences. *Death Studies, 9,* 217–233.

Bensinger, J. S., & Natenshon, M. A. (1991). Difficulties in recognizing adolescent health issues. In W. R. Hendee (Ed.), *The health of adolescents* (pp. 381–410). San Francisco: Jossey-Bass.

Berg, D. W., & Daugherty, G. G. (1972). *Perspectives on death.* Baltimore: Waverly Press.

Berk, L. (1994). *Child development.* Boston: Allyn & Bacon.

Berlin, I. N. (1987). Suicide among American Indian adolescents: An overview. *Suicide and Life-Threatening Behavior, 17,* 218–232.

Berlinsky, E. B., & Biller, H. B. (1982). *Parental death and psychological development.* Lexington, MA: Heath.

Berman, A. L. (1985). The teenager at risk for suicide. *Medical Aspects of Human Sexuality, 19*(5), 123–124, 129.

Berman, A. L., & Jobes, D. (1991). *Adolescent suicide: Assessment and intervention.* Washington, DC: American Psychological Association.

Berndt, T. J., & Perry, T. B. (1986). Children's perceptions of friendship as supportive relationships. *Developmental Psychology, 22,* 640–648.

Berson, R. J. (1988). A bereavement group for college students. *Journal of American College Health 37,* 101–108.

Bigelow, B. J., & LaGaipa, J. J. (1980). The development of friendship values and choice. In H. C. Foot, A. J. Chapman, & J. R. Smith (Eds.), *Friendship and social relations in children* (pp. 15–44). New York: Wiley.

Bigner, J. J. (1994). *Individual and family development: A life-span interdisciplinary approach.* Englewood Cliffs, NJ: Prentice Hall.

Binger, C. M., Ablin, A. R., Feuersteum, R. C., Kushner, J. H., Zogler, S., & Mikkelsen, C. (1969). Childhood leukemia: Emotional impact on patient and family. *New England Journal of Medicine, 208,* 414–418.

Birenbaum, L. K., Robinson, M. A., Phillips, D. S., Stewart, B. J., & McCown, D. E. (1990). The response of children to the dying and death of a sibling. *Omega, 20,* 213–228.

Birren, J. E., Kinney, D. K., Schaie, K. W., & Woodruff, D. S. (1981). *Developmental psychology: A life-span approach.* Boston: Houghton Mifflin.

Birtchnell, J. (1970). Depression in relation to early and recent parent death. *British Journal of Psychiatry, 116,* 299–306.

Black, D. (1976). *The behavior of law.* New York: Academic Press.

Blankemeyer, M. (1993). *Adolescent sibling bereavement: Family factors associated with adjustment to loss.* Unpublished master's thesis, Oklahoma State University, Stillwater, OK.

Bleyer, W. A. (1990). The impact of childhood cancer on the United States and the world. *CA: A Cancer Journal for Clinicians, 40,* 355–367.

Blinder, B. (1972). Sibling death in childhood. *Psychiatry and Human Development, 2,* 169–175.

Block, C. R. (1986). *Homicide in Chicago.* Chicago: Center for Urban Policy.

Bliatout, B. T. (1993). Hmong death customs: Traditional and acculturated. In D. P. Irish, K. F. Lundquist, & V. J. Nelson (Eds.), *Ethnic variations in dying, death, and grief: Diversity in universality* (pp. 79–100). Washington, DC: Taylor & Francis.

Blos, P. (1941). *The adolescent personality: A study of individual behavior.* New York: D. Appleton-Century.

Blos, P. (1979). *The adolescent passage: Developmental issues.* New York: International Universities Press.

Bluebond-Langner, M. (1978). *The private worlds of dying children*. Princeton: Princeton University Press.

Blumenthal, S. J. (1990). Youth suicide: Risk factors, assessment, and treatment of adolescent and young adult suicidal patients. *Psychiatric Clinics of North America, 13*, 511–556.

Bohannon, P. (Ed.). (1960). *African homicide and suicide*. Princeton: Princeton University Press.

Bowen, M. (1976). Family reaction to death. In P. Guerin (Ed.), *Family therapy* (pp. 335–348). New York: Gardner.

Bowlby, J. (1961). Childhood mourning and its implications for psychiatry. *American Journal of Psychiatry, 118*, 481–488.

Bowlby, J. (1963). Pathological mourning and childhood mourning. *Journal of the American Psychoanalytic Association, 11*, 500–541.

Bowlby, J. (1982). *Attachment and loss: Vol. 1. Attachment* (2nd ed.). New York: Basic Books. (Original work published 1969)

Bowlby, J. (1973). *Attachment and loss: Vol. 2. Separation—Anxiety and anger.* New York: Basic Books.

Bowlby, J. (1980a). *Attachment and loss: Vol. 3. Loss—Sadness and depression.* New York: Basic Books.

Bowlby, J. (1980b). Grief and mourning in infancy and early childhood. *Psychoanalytic Study of the Child, 15*, 9–52.

Bowler, S., Sheon, A. R., D'Angelo, L. J., & Vermund, S. H. (1993). HIV and AIDS among adolescents in the United States: Increasing risk in the 1990s. *Journal of Adolescence, 15*, 345–371.

Bowser, B. P., & Wingood, G. M. (1992). Community-based HIV-prevention programs for adolescents. In R. J. DiClemente (Ed.), *Adolescents and AIDS: A generation in jeopardy* (pp. 94–211). Newbury Park, CA: Sage.

Box, S. (1987). *Recession, crime and punishment*. Totowa, NJ: Barnes & Noble.

Boyd, J. H., & Moscicki, E. K. (1986). Firearms and youth suicide. *American Journal of Public Health, 76*, 1240–1242.

Bozigar, J. A., Brent, D. A., Hindmarsh, K., Kerr, M. M., McQuiston, L., & Schweers, J. A. (1993). *Postvention standards manual: A guide for a school's response in the aftermath of a suicide*. Pittsburgh: University of Pittsburgh Medical Center, Western Psychiatric Institute and Clinic, Services for Teens at Risk.

Brazil, J., & Platte, M. (1994, September 23). Southland firms dominate market for small handguns. *Los Angeles Times*, pp. 1, 28, 29.

Brennan, T., & Auslander, N. (1979). *Adolescent loneliness: An exploratory study of social and psychological predispositions and theory* (Vol. 1). Rockville, MD: National Institute of Mental Health, Juvenile Problems Division.

Brent, D. A., Crumrine, P. K., Varma, R. R., Allan, M., & Allman, C. (1987). Phenobarbitol treatment and major depressive disorder in children with epilepsy. *Pediatrics, 89*, 909–917.

Brent, D. A., Perper, J., Moritz, G., Baugher, M., & Allman, C. (1993). Suicide in adolescents with no apparent psychopathology. *Journal of the American Academy of Child and Adolescent Psychiatry, 32,* 494–500.

Brent, D. A., Perper, J. M., Moritz, G., Allman, C., Liolus, L., Schweers, J., Roth, C., Balach, L., & Canobbio, R. (1993). Bereavement or depression? The impact of the loss of a friend to suicide. *Journal of the American Academy of Child and Adolescent Psychiatry, 32,* 1189–1197.

Bretherton, I. (1987). New perspectives on attachment relations: Security, communication, and internal working models. In J. Osofsky (Ed.), *Handbook of infant development* (pp. 1061–1100). New York: Wiley.

Brooks-Gunn, J. (1987). Pubertal pressures: Their relevance for developmental research. In V. B. Van Hasselt & M. Hersen (Eds.), *Handbook of adolescent psychology* (pp. 111–130). New York: Pergamon.

Brown, B. B. (1990). Peer groups and peer cultures. In S. Feldman & G. Elliott (Eds.), *At the threshold: The developing adolescent* (pp. 171–196). Cambridge, MA: Harvard University Press.

Brown, L. M., & Gilligan, C. (1990, March). *The psychology of women and the development of girls.* Paper presented at the meeting of the Society for Research on Adolescence, Atlanta, GA.

Buell, J. S., & Bevis, J. (1989). Bereavement groups in the hospice program. *The Hospice Journal, 5,* 107–118.

Burke, D. S., Brundage, J. F., Goldenbaum, M., Gardner, L.I., Peterson, M., Visintine, R., & Redfield, R. R. (1990). Human immunodeficiency virus infections in teenagers. *Journal of the American Medical Association, 263,* 2074–2077.

Burr, W. R., Klein, S. R., Burr, R. G., Doxey, C., Harker, B., Holman, T. B., Martin, P. H., McClure, R. L., Parrish, S. W., Stuart, D. A., Taylor, A. C., & White, M. S. (1994). *Reexamining family stress: New theory and research.* Thousand Oaks, CA: Sage.

Busch, K. G., Zagar, R., Hughes, J. R., Arbit, J., & Bussell, R. E. (1990). Adolescents who kill. *Journal of Clinical Psychology, 46,* 472–485.

Buschbaum, B. C. (1990). An agenda for treating widowed parents. *Psychotherapy Patient, 6,* 113–130.

Butters, P. (1991). *Been there done that: A resource for teenagers with cancer.* St. Pauls, NSW: CanTeen.

Cain, A. C., & Cain, B. C. (1964). On replacing a child. *Journal of the American Academy of Child and Adolescent Psychiatry, 34,* 443–456.

Cain, A. C., Fast, I., & Erickson, M. E. (1964). Children's disturbed reactions to the death of a sibling. *American Journal of Orthopsychiatry, 3,* 741–752.

Cairns, N. U., Clark, G. M., Smith, S. D., & Lansky S. B. (1979). Adaptation of siblings to childhood malignancy. *Journal of Pediatrics, 95,* 484–487.

Calhoun, G., Jurgens, J., & Chen, F. (1993). The neophyte female delinquent: A review of the literature. *Adolescence, 28,* 461–471.

CanTeen Focus Groups. (1991–1993). *Archival videotapes.* St. Pauls, NSW: CanTeen.

Campbell, E., Adams, G. A., & Dobson, W. R. (1984). Familial correlates of identity formation in late adolescence: A study of the predictive utility of connectedness and individuality in family relations. *Journal of Youth and Adolescence, 13,* 509–525.

Caplan, M. G., & Douglas, V. I. (1969). Incidence of parental loss in children with depressed moods. *Journal of Child Psychology and Psychiatry, 10,* 225–232.

Carr-Gregg, M. (1987). *The adolescent with cancer in the Australian health care system.* Unpublished thesis, University of New South Wales, Australia.

Carr-Gregg, M. (1989). CanTeen: The New Zealand Teenage Cancer Patients Society—new direction in psychosocial oncology? *New Zealand Medical Journal, 102,* 163–165.

Carr-Gregg, M., & White, L. (1987). The adolescent with cancer: A psychological overview. *The Medical Journal of Australia, 147,* 496–501.

Carse, J. P. (1987). Grief as a cosmic crisis. In O. S. Margolis, H. C. Raether, A. H. Kutscher, J. B. Powers, I. B. Seeland, R. DeBellis, & D. J. Cherico (Eds.), *Acute grief: Counseling the bereaved* (pp. 3–8). New York: Columbia University Press.

Carter, B., & Brooks, A. (1990). Suicide postvention: Crisis of opportunity? *The School Counselor, 37,* 378–389.

Carter, B., & Brooks, A. (1991). Clinical opportunities in suicide postvention. In A. A. Leenaars & S. Wenckstern (Eds.), *Suicide prevention in schools* (pp. 197–211). New York: Hemisphere.

Carter, B., & McGoldrick, M. (1988). Overview: The changing family life cycle. In B. Carter & M. McGoldrick (Eds.), *The changing family life cycle: A framework for family therapy* (2nd ed.; pp. 3–28). New York: Gardner.

Cassileth, B. R., Zupkis, R. V., Sutton-Smith, K., & March, V. (1980). Information and participation preferences among cancer patients. *Annals of Internal Medicine, 92,* 832–836.

Cates, J. A. (1986). Grief therapy in residential treatment: A model for intervention. *Child Care Quarterly, 15,* 147–158.

Cates, W., & Stone, K. M. (1992). Family planning, sexually transmitted diseases and contraceptive choice: A literature update: Part I. *Family Planning Perspectives, 24,* 75–84.

Centers for Disease Control. (1988). CDC recommendations for a community plan for the prevention and containment of suicide clusters. *Morbidity and Mortality Weekly Report, 37* (Suppl. 5–6), 1–12.

Centers for Disease Control (1991). *Morbidity and Mortality Weekly Report, 39,* 13.

Centers for Disease Control. (1994, January). *HIV/AIDS surveillance* (year-end ed.). Washington, DC: Author.

Chang, P-N., Nesbit, M., Youngren, N., & Robinson, L. (1987). Personality characteristics and psychosocial adjustment of long-term survivors of childhood cancer. *Journal of Psychosocial Oncology, 5*(4), 43–58.

Charles, K. E., & Eddy, J. M. (1987). In-service training on dying and death for residence hall staff. *NASPA Journal, 25,* 136–129.

Chesler, M., & Lawther, T. (1990). How am I different? *Candlelighters* [Youth newsletter], 7(2), 2, 7.

Chumlea, W. C. (1982). Physical growth in adolescence. In B. J. Wolman (Ed.), *Handbook of developmental psychology* (pp. 471–485). Englewood Cliffs, NJ: Prentice Hall.

Clayton, P. J., & Darvish, H. S. (1979). Course of depressive symptoms following the stress of bereavement. In J. E. Barrett (Ed.), *Stress and mental disorder* (pp. 121–136). New York: Raven.

Cohen, F., & Lazarus, R. (1979). Coping with stress of illness. In G. Stone, F. Cohen, & N. Adler (Eds.), *Health psychology* (pp. 217–224). San Francisco: Jossey-Bass.

Coleman, J. C. (1978). Current contradictions in adolescent theory. *Journal of Youth and Adolescence, 7,* 1–11.

Colgrove, M., Bloomfield, H., & McWilliams, L. (1991). *How to survive the loss of a love* (2nd ed.). New York: Bantam.

Collins, O. P. (1990). *Individual and family factors influencing probability for suicide in adolescents.* Unpublished doctoral dissertation, Kansas State University, Manhattan, KS.

Collins, R. L., Taylor, S. E., & Skokan, L. A. (1990). A better world or a shattered vision? Changes in life perspective following victimization. *Social Cognition, 8,* 263–285.

Collins, W. A. (1990). Parent-child relationships in the transition to adolescence: Continuity and change in interaction, affects, and cognition. In R. Montemayor, G. Adams, & T. Gullotta (Eds.), *From childhood to adolescence: A transitional period?* (pp. 85–86). Beverly Hills: Sage.

Compas, B. E., Slavin, L. A., Wagner, B. M., & Vannatta, K. (1986). Relationship of life events and social support with psychological dysfunction among adolescents. *Journal of Youth and Adolescence, 15,* 205–221.

Conrad, J. P. (1985). *The dangerous and the endangered.* Toronto: D. C. Heath.

Cook, A. S., & Dworkin, D. S. (1992). *Helping the bereaved: Therapeutic interventions for children, adolescents, and adults.* New York: Basic Books.

Cook, A. S., & Oltjenbruns, K. A. (1989). *Dying and grieving: Lifespan and family perspectives.* New York: Holt, Rinehart, & Winston.

Cook, J. A. (1984). Influences of gender on the problems of parents of fatally-ill children. *Journal of Psychosocial Oncology, 2,* 71–91.

Cooley. M. E. (1992). Bereavement care: A role for nurses. *Cancer Nursing, 15,* 125–129.

Corazzini, J. G., & May, T. M. (1985). The role of the counseling center in responding to student death. In E. S. Zinner (Ed.), *Coping with death on campus* (pp. 39–50). San Francisco: Jossey-Bass.

Corder, B. F., Page, P. V., & Corder, R. F. (1974). Parental history, family communication and interaction patterns in adolescent suicide. *Family Therapy, 1,* 285–290.

Corr, C. A. (1995). Entering into adolescent understandings of death. In E. A. Grollman (Ed.), *Bereaved children and teens: A support guide for parents and professionals* (pp. 21–35). Boston: Beacon Press.

Corr, C. A., Nabe, C. M., Corr, D. M. (1994). *Death and dying, life and living.* Pacific Grove, CA: Brooks/Cole.

Cosse, W. J. (1992). Who's who and what's what? The effects of gender on development in adolescence. In B. R. Wainrib (Ed.), *Gender issues across the life cycle* (pp. 5–16). New York: Springer Publishing.

Cottle, T. J. (1972). The connections of adolescence. In J. Kagan & R. Coles (Eds.), *Twelve to sixteen: Early adolescence* (pp. 294–336). New York: Norton.

Counts, D. R., & Counts, D. A. (Eds.). (1991). *Coping with the final tragedy.* Amityville, NY: Baywood.

Critelli, C. (1979, January). *Parent death in childhood.* Paper presented at the Columbia-Presbyterian Medical Center Symposium on The Child and Death, New York.

Crockett, L. J., Petersen, A. C., Graber, J. A., Schulberg, J. E., & Ebata, A. (1989). School transitions and adjustment during early adolescence. *Journal of Early Adolescence, 9,* 181–210.

Cross, S., & Markus, H. (1991). Possible selves across the life span. *Human Development, 34,* 230–255.

Curtis, L. (1975). *Violence, race and culture.* Lexington, MA: Lexington Books.

Cutter, F. (1974). *Coming to terms with death: How to face the inevitable with wisdom and dignity.* Chicago: Nelson-Hall.

Dakof, G. A., & Taylor, S. E. (1990). Victims' perceptions of social support: What is helpful to whom? *Journal of Personality and Social Psychology, 58,* 80–89.

D'Angelo, L. J., Getson, P. R., Luban, N. L. C., & Gayle, H. D. (1991). Human Immunodeficiency Virus (HIV) infection in urban adolescents: Can we predict who is at risk? *Pediatrics, 88,* 982–986.

Danish, S. J., & D'Augelli, A. R. (1980). Promoting competence and enhancing development through life development intervention. In L. A. Bond & C. J. Rosen (Eds.), *Competence and coping during adulthood* (Vol. 5, pp. 105–129). Hanover, NH: University Press of New England.

Danish, S. J., Smyer, M. A., & Nowak, C. A. (1980). Developmental interventions: Enhancing life-event processes. In P. B. Baltes & O. G. Brim (Eds.), *Life-span development and behavior* (Vol. 3, pp. 340–346). New York: Academic Press.

Dattel, A. R., & Neimeyer, R. A. (1990). Sex differences in death anxiety: Testing the emotional expressiveness hypothesis. *Death Studies, 14,* 1–11.

Davidson, G. W. (1975). *Living with dying.* Minneapolis: Augsburg.

Davidson, L. E. (1989). Suicide clusters and youth. In C. R. Pfeffer (Ed.), *Suicide among youth: Perspectives on risk and prevention* (pp. 83–99). Washington, DC: American Psychiatric Press.

Davies, B. (1988). The family environment in bereaved families and its relationships to surviving sibling behavior. *Children's Health Care, 17,* 22–31.

Davies, B. (1991). Long-term outcomes of adolescent sibling bereavement. *Journal of Adolescent Research, 6,* 83–96.

Davies, B. (1994). Sibling bereavement research: State of the art. In I. B. Corless, B. B. Germino, & M. Pittman (Eds.), *A challenge for living: Dying, death and bereavement* (pp. 173–201). Boston: Jones & Bartlett.

Davies, E. B. (1983). *Behavioral responses to the death of a sibling.* Unpublished doctoral dissertation, University of Washington, Seattle.

Davis, G., & Jessen, A. (1982). A clinical report on group intervention in bereavement. *Journal of Psychiatric Treatment and Evaluation, 4,* 81–88.

Davis, J. M., & Sandoval, J. (1991). *Suicidal youth: School-based intervention and prevention.* San Francisco: Jossey-Bass.

Davis, S. F., Bremer, S. A., Anderson, B. J., & Tramill, J. L. (1983). The interrelationships of ego strength, self-esteem, death anxiety, and gender in undergraduate college students. *Journal of General Psychology, 108,* 35–59.

Davis, J. M., Hoshiko, B. R., Jones, S., & Gosnell, D. (1992). The effect of a support group on grieving individuals' level of perceived support and stress. *Archives of Psychiatric Nursing, 6,* 35–39.

Da Silva, A., & Schork, M. A. (1984). Gender differences in attitudes to death among a group of public health students. *Omega, 15,* 77–84.

Dearing, J. W., Meyer, G., & Rogers, E. M. (1994). Diffusion theory and HIV risk behavior change. In R. J. DiClemente & J. L. Peterson (Eds.), *Preventing AIDS: Theories and methods of behavioral interventions* (pp. 79–94). New York: Plenum.

Deem, R. (1986). *All work and no play?: A study of women and leisure.* Milton Keynes, England: Open University Press.

Delise, J. R. (1986). Death with honors: Suicide among gifted adolescents. *Journal of Counseling and Development, 64,* 558–560.

Demi, A. S., & Gilbert, C. (1987). Relationship of parental grief to sibling grief. *Archives of Psychiatric Nursing, 6,* 385–391.

Demi, A. S., & Howell, C. (1991). Hiding and healing: Resolving the suicide of a parent or sibling. *Archives of Psychiatric Nursing, 5,* 350–356.

Demi, A. S., & Miles, M. S. (1988). Suicide bereaved parents: Emotional distress and physical health problems. *Death Studies, 12,* 297–307.

Derdeyn, A. P., & Waters, D. B. (1981). Unshared loss and marital conflict. *Journal of Marital and Family Therapy, 7,* 481–487.

Derdiarian, A. (1987). Information needs of recently diagnosed cancer patients. A theoretical framework: 1. *Cancer Nursing, 10,* 107–115.

Deveau, E. J. (1990). The impact on adolescents when a sibling is dying. In J. D. Morgan (Ed.), *The dying and the bereaved teenager* (pp. 63–79). Philadelphia: Charles Press.

DeVincenzi, I., for the European Study Group on Heterosexual Transmission of HIV. (1994). A longitudinal study of human immunodeficiency virus transmission by heterosexual partners. *New England Journal of Medicine, 331,* 341–346.

de Wilde, E. J., Kienhorst, I. C., Diekstra, R. F., & Wolters, W. H. (1993). The specificity of psychological characteristics of adolescent suicide attempters. *Journal of the American Academy of Child and Adolescent Psychiatry, 32,* 51–59.

Diamond, G., & Bachman, J. (1986). High-school seniors and the nuclear threat, 1975–1984: Political and mental health implications of concern and despair. *International Journal of Mental Health, 15,* 210–241.

DiClemente, R. J. (1990). The emergence of adolescents as a risk group for human immunodeficiency virus infection. *Journal of Adolescent Research, 5,* 7–17.

DiClemente, R. J. (1992). Epidemiology of AIDS, HIV seroprevalence and HIV incidence among adolescents. *Journal of School Health, 62,* 325–330.

DiClemente, R. J. (1993a). Confronting the challenge of AIDS among adolescents: Directions for future research. *Journal of Adolescent Research, 8,* 156–166.

DiClemente, R. J. (1993b). Preventing HIV/AIDS among adolescents: Schools as agents of behavior change. *Journal of the American Medical Association, 270,* 760–762.

DiClemente, R. J. (1994). HIV prevention among adolescents. In P. T. Cohen, M. A. Sande, & P. A. Volberding (Eds.), *The AIDS knowledge base: A textbook on HIV disease from the University of California, San Francisco, and San Francisco General Hospital* (2nd ed., 10.10). Boston: Little, Brown.

DiClemente, R. J., & Brown, L. K. (1994). Expanding the pediatrician's role in HIV prevention for adolescents. *Clinical Pediatrics, 32,* 1–6.

DiClemente, R. J., & Peterson, J. (1994). Changing HIV/AIDS risk behaviors: The role of behavioral interventions. In R. J. DiClemente & J. L. Peterson (Eds.), *Preventing AIDS: Theories and methods of behavioral interventions* (pp. 1–4). New York: Plenum.

Dise-Lewis, J. E. (1988). The life events and coping inventory: An assessment of stress in children. *Psychosomatic Medicine, 50,* 484–499.

Doka, K. J. (1985). The crumbling taboo: The rise of death education. In E. S. Zinner (Ed.), *Coping with death on campus* (pp. 85–95). San Francisco: Jossey-Bass.

Doka, K. J. (1989). Disenfranchised grief. In K. J. Doka (Ed.), *Disenfranchised grief: Recognizing hidden sorrow* (pp. 3–12). Lexington, MA: Lexington Books.

Donohue, W. R. (1977). Student death: What do we do? *NASPA Journal, 14*(4), 29–32.

Dorpat, T. L., Jackson, J. K., & Ripley, H. S. (1965). Broken homes and attempted and completed suicide. *Archives of General Psychiatry, 12,* 213–216.

Dubois, D. L., & Hirsch, B. J. (1990). School and neighborhood friendship patterns of blacks and whites in early adolescence. *Child Development, 61,* 524–536.

Dunne, E. J. (1987). Surviving the suicide of a therapist. In E. J. Dunne, J. L. McIntosh, & K. Dunne-Maxim (Eds.), *Suicide and its aftermath: Understanding and counseling the survivors* (pp. 142–150). New York: Norton.

Dunsmore, J. C. (1992). *Too much too young? Adolescents with cancer: An exploration of their needs and perceptions of how cancer has made them different from others their age* [Treatise]. University of Sydney, Australia.

Dunsmore, J. C., & Quine, S. (in press). Information support and decision making needs and preferences of adolescents with cancer: Implications for health professionals. *Journal of Psychosocial Oncology.*

Durkheim, E. (1951). *Suicide: A study in sociology.* (J. A. Spaulding & G. Simpson, Trans.). Glencoe, IL: Free Press.

Dyregrov, A., Kristoffersen, J. I. K., Matthiesen, S., & Mitchel, J. (1994). Gender differences in adolescents' reactions to the murder of their teacher. *Journal of Adolescent Research, 9,* 363–383.

Eccles, J. S., Midgley, C., Wigfield, A., Buchanan, C. M., Reuman, D., Flanagan, C., & MacIver, D. (1993). Development during adolescence: The impact of stage-environment fit on young adolescents' experience in schools and families. *American Psychologist, 48,* 90–101.

Eckstein, D. (1982). Reflections relative to death, dying, and grieving workshops. *The Personnel and Guidance Journal, 61,* 138–142.

Edmonds, S., & Hooker, K. (1992). Perceived changes in life meaning following bereavement. *Omega, 25,* 307–318.

Elizur, E., & Kaffman, M. (1986). Children's bereavement reactions following death of the father. In R. H. Moos (Ed.), *Coping with life crises: An integrated approach* (pp. 49–58). New York: Norton.

Elkind, D. (1967). Egocentrism in adolescence. *Child Development, 38,* 1025–1034.

Elkind, D. (1978). Understanding the young adolescent. *Adolescence, 13,* 127–134.

Elkind, D. (1979). *The child and society: Essays in applied child development.* New York: Oxford University Press.

Elkind, D. (1984). *All grown up and no place to go.* Reading, MA: Addison-Wesley.

Erikson, E. H. (1963). *Childhood and society* (2nd ed.). New York: Norton.

Erikson, E. H. (1968). *Identity, youth and crisis.* New York: Norton.

Evans, T. W. (1992). *Making a difference in our public schools.* Princeton: Peterson's Guides.

Ewalt, P. L., & Perkins, L. (1979). The real experience of death among adolescents: An empirical study. *Social Casework, 60,* 547–551.

Fanon, F. (1967). *Black skin, white masks.* New York: Grove Press.

Fanon, F. (1968). *The wretched of the earth.* New York: Grove Press.

Farber, S. S., Felner, R. D., & Primavera, J. (1985). Parental separation/divorce and adolescents: An examination of factors mediating adaptation. *American Journal of Community Psychology, 13,* 171–185.

Farberow, N. L. (1993). Bereavement after suicide. In A. A. Leenaars (Ed.), *Suicidology: Essays in honor of Edwin Shneidman* (pp. 337–345). New Jersey: Jason Aronson.

Federal Bureau of Investigation. (1992). *Crime in the United States, 1991: Uniform crime reports.* Washington, DC: U.S. Department of Justice.

Feifel, H. (1990). Psychology and death: Meaningful rediscovery. *American Psychologist, 45,* 537–543.

Feinstein, S. (1981). Adolescent depression. In L. Steinberg & L. Mandelbaum (Eds.), *The life cycle: Readings in human development* (pp. 317–335). New York: Columbia University Press.

Felner, R. D., Aber, M. S., Primavera, J., & Cauce, A. M. (1985). Adaptation and vulnerability in high-risk adolescents: An examination of environmental mediators. *American Journal of Community Psychology, 13,* 365–379.

Fine, S., Forth, A., Gilbert, M., & Haley, G. (1991). Group therapy for adolescent depressive disorder: A comparison of social skills and therapeutic support. *Journal of the American Academy of Child and Adolescent Psychiatry, 30,* 79–85.

Fingerhut, L. A., & Kleinman, J. C. (1989). Mortality among children and youth. *The American Journal of Public Health, 79,* 899–901.

Fingerhut, L. A., Kleinman, J. C., Godfrey, E., & Rosenberg, H. (1991). Firearm mortality among children, youth, and young adults 1–34 years of age, trends and current status: United States, 1979–88. *Monthly Vital Statistics Report, 39*(11), (Suppl.).

Firestone, R. W. (1994). Psychological defenses against death anxiety. In R. A. Neimeyer (Ed.), *Death anxiety handbook: Research, instrumentation, and application* (pp. 217–241). Washington, DC: Taylor & Francis.

Fishbein, M., Middlestadt, S. E., & Hitchcock, P. J. (1994). Using information to change sexually transmitted disease-related behaviors: An analysis based on the theory of reasoned action. In R. J. DiClemente & J. L.

Peterson (Eds.), *Preventing AIDS: Theories and methods of behavioral interventions* (pp. 61–78). New York: Plenum.

Fisher, J. D., Misovich, S. J., & Fisher, W. A. (1992). Impact of perceived social norms on adolescents' AIDS-risk behavior and prevention. In R. J. DiClemente (Ed.), *Adolescents and AIDS: A generation in jeopardy* (pp. 117–136). Newbury Park, CA: Sage.

Fitzpatrick, J. P. (1974). Drugs, alcohol and violent crime. *Addictive Disease, 1,* 353–367.

Fleming, S. J., & Adolph, R. (1986). Helping bereaved adolescents: Needs and responses. In C. A. Corr & J. N. McNeil (Eds.), *Adolescence and death* (pp. 97–118). New York: Springer Publishing.

Fleming, S. J., & Robinson, P. J. (1991). The application of cognitive therapy to the bereaved. In T. M. Vallis, J. L. Howes, & P. C. Miller (Eds.), *The challenge of cognitive therapy: Applications to nontraditional populations* (pp. 135–158). New York: Plenum.

Floerchinger, D. S. (1991). Bereavement in late adolescence: Interventions on college campuses. *Journal of Adolescent Research, 6,* 146–156.

Flowers, B. R. (1988). *Minorities and criminality.* New York: Greenwood Press.

Foley, G. V., & Whittam, E. H. (1990). Care of the child dying of cancer: 1. *CA: A Cancer Journal for Clinicians, 40,* 327–354.

Forrest, S. (1988). Suicide and the rural adolescent. *Adolescence, 90,* 341–347.

Fowler, J. W. (1976). Stages in faith: The structural-developmental approach. In T. Hennessy (Ed.), *Values and moral development* (pp. 173–211). New York: Paulist.

Fowler, J. W. (1981). *Stages of faith: The psychology of human development and the quest for meaning.* San Francisco: Harper & Row.

Fowler, J. W. (1991a). *Stages of faith and religious development: Implications for church, education, and society.* New York: Crossroads.

Fowler, J. W. (1991b). Stages of faith consciousness. In F. K. Oser & G. Scarlett (Eds.), *Religious development in childhood and adolescence* (pp. 27–45). San Francisco: Jossey-Bass.

Fox, S. S. (1985). *Good grief: Helping groups of children when a friend dies.* Boston: New England Association for the Education of Young Children.

Fox, S. S. (1989). Good grief: Preventive interventions for children and adolescents. In S. C. Klagsbrun, G. W. Kliman, E. J. Clark, A. H. Kutscher, R. DeBellis, & C. A. Lambert (Eds.), *Preventive psychiatry: Early intervention and situational crisis management* (pp. 83–92). Philadelphia: Charles Press.

Freud, A. (1969). Adolescence. In *The writings of Anna Freud* (Vol. 5, pp. 136–166). New York: International Universities Press.

Freud, S. (1957). Mourning and melancholia. In J. Strachey (Ed. & Trans.), *The standard edition of the complete psychological works of Sigmund Freud* (Vol. 14, pp. 243–258). London: Hogarth Press.

Furman, W., & Buhrmester, D. (1985). Children's perceptions of the personal relationships in their social networks. *Developmental Psychology, 21,* 1016–1024.

Furr, S., & Simpson, J. (1989). Responding to the death of a college student. *The Journal of College and University Student Housing, 19,* 17–21.

Fyfe, J. (1981). Race and extreme police-citizen violence. In R. L. McNeely & C. E. Pope (Eds.), *Race, crime and criminal justice* (pp. 89–108). Beverly Hills: Sage.

Gabor, T. (1986). *The prediction of criminal behavior.* Toronto: University of Toronto Press.

Gallup, G. (1991). *The Gallup survey on teenage suicide.* Princeton: The George H. Gallup International Institute.

Gans, J. E. (1990). *America's adolescents: How healthy are they?* (American Medical Association, Profiles of Adolescent Health Series.) Chicago: American Medical Association.

Garbarino, J., Dubrow, N., Kostelny, K., & Padro, C. (1992). *Children in danger: Coping with the consequences of community violence.* San Francisco: Jossey-Bass.

Garber, B. (1983). Some thoughts on normal adolescents who lost a parent by death. *Journal of Youth and Adolescence, 12,* 175–183.

Garfinkel, B. D., Crosby, E., Herbert, M., Matus, A., Pfeifer, J., & Sheras, P. (1988). *Responding to adolescent suicide: The first 48 hours.* Bloomington, IN: Phi Delta Kappa Educational Foundation.

Garfinkel, H. (1949). Research note on inter- and intra-racial homicides. *Social Forces, 27,* 369–381.

Garland, A. F., & Zigler, E. (1993). Adolescent suicide prevention. *American Psychologist, 48,* 169–182.

Garrott, H. (1994). Grief in the classroom: When a student dies. *Elsie Speaks, 4*(2), 1–8.

Gary, L. E. (Ed.). (1981). *Black men.* Newbury Park, CA: Sage.

Gelcer, E. (1983). Mourning is a family affair. *Family Process, 22,* 501–576.

Gelman, D., & Gangelhoff, B. K. (1983, August 15). Teenage suicide in the Sun Belt. *Newsweek, 102,* pp. 71–72, 74.

Genovese, F. (1992). Family therapy with adolescents in a school situation. In J. D. Atwood (Ed.), *Family therapy: A systemic behavioral approach* (pp. 298–320). Chicago: Nelson-Hall.

Gersten, J. C., Beals, J., & Kallgren, C. A. (1991). Epidemiology and preventive interventions: Parental death in childhood as an example. *American Journal of Community Psychiatry, 19,* 481–498.

Gibbs, J. T. (Ed.). (1988). *Young, black, and male in America.* New York: Auburn House.

Gilanshah, F. (1993). Islamic customs regarding death. In D. P. Irish, K. F. Lundquist, & V. J. Nelson (Eds.), *Ethnic variations in dying, death, and grief: Diversity in universality* (pp. 137–145). Washington, DC: Taylor & Francis.

Gilligan, C., Lyons, N. P., & Hanmer, T. J. (Eds.). (1990). *Making connections: The relational worlds of adolescent girls at the Emma Willard School.* Cambridge, MA: Harvard University Press.

Gilmore, M. (1994, June 2). The road from nowhere. *Rolling Stone,* pp. 44–46, 53.

Glass, B. C. (1993). The role of the nurse in advanced practice in bereavement care. *Clinical Nurse Specialist, 7,* 62–66.

Glassman, L. (1993). *Violence in the schools: How America's school boards are safeguarding our children.* Alexandria, VA: National School Boards Association.

Glick, I. O., Weiss, R. S., & Parkes, C. M. (1974). *The first year of bereavement.* New York: Wiley.

Goldberg, S. B. (1973). Family tasks and reactions in the crisis of death. *Social Casework, 54,* 398–405.

Goldscheider, F., & Goldscheider, C. (1994). Leaving and returning home in 20th century America. *Population Bulletin, 48*(4).

Goodman, P. (1960). *Growing up absurd.* New York: Random House.

Gordon, A. K. (1986). The tattered cloak of immortality. In C. A. Corr & J. N. McNeil (Eds.), *Adolescence and death* (pp. 16–31). New York: Springer Publishing.

Goss, M., & Lebovitz, B. (1977). Coping under extreme stress: Observations of patients with severe poliomyelitis. *Archives of General Psychiatry, 6,* 423–448.

Gottlieb, B. H. (1981). Preventive interventions involving social networks and social supports. In B. H. Gottlieb (Ed.), *Social networks and social support* (pp. 201–232). Beverly Hills: Sage.

Gottlieb, B. H. (1991). Social support in adolescence. In M. E. Colten (Ed.), *Adolescent stress: Causes and consequences* (pp. 281–307). New York: Aldine De Gruyter.

Gould, M. S. (1990). Suicide clusters and media exposure. In S. J. Blumenthal & D. J. Kupfer (Eds.), *Suicide over the life cycle: Risk factors, assessment and treatment of suicidal patients* (pp. 517–532). Washington, DC: American Psychiatric Press.

Gouldner, A. W. (1973). Foreword. In I. Taylor, P. Walton, & J. Young (Eds.), *The new criminology: For a social theory of deviance* (pp. ix–xiv). London: Routledge & Kegan Paul.

Graham, H. D., & Gurr, T. R. (1969). *The history of violence in America: Historical and comparative perspectives.* New York: Bantam.

Gray, R. (1987a). *Adolescents faced with the death of a parent: The role of social support and other factors.* Unpublished doctoral dissertation, University of Toronto, Toronto, Ontario, Canada.

Gray, R. E. (1987b). Adolescent response to the death of a parent. *Journal of Youth and Adolescence, 16*, 511–525.

Gray, R. E. (1988). The role of school counselors with bereaved teenagers: With and without peer support groups. *School Counselor, 35*, 185–193.

Gray, R. E. (1989). Adolescents' perceptions of social support after the death of a parent. *Journal of Psychosocial Oncology, 7*, 127–144.

Grier, W., & Cobb, P. (1968). *Black rage.* New York: Basic Books.

Grollman, E. A. (1967). Prologue: Explaining death to children. In E. A. Grollman (Ed.), *Explaining death to children* (pp. 3–27). Boston: Beacon.

Grollman, E. A. (1993). *Straight talk about death for teenagers: How to cope with losing someone you love.* Boston: Beacon.

Grotevant, H. D., & Cooper, C. R. (1986). Individuation in family relationships: A perspective on individual differences in the development of identity and role-taking skill in adolescence. *Human Development, 29*, 82–100.

Guerriero, A. M. (1983). *Adolescent bereavement: Impact on physical health, self-concept, depression, and death anxiety.* Unpublished master's thesis, York University, Toronto, Ontario, Canada.

Guerriero, A. M., & Fleming, S. J. (1985). *Adolescent bereavement: A longitudinal study.* Paper presented at the Annual Meeting of the Canadian Psychological Association, Halifax, Nova Scotia.

Haasl, B., & Marnocha, J. (1990). *Bereavement support group program for children: Leader manual.* Muncie, IN: Accelerated Development.

Habib, D. (1993, September). The boundaries fall away: Health teacher cultivates an open class atmosphere. *Concord Monitor,* (Suppl.), 1. [Special Reprint].

Hafen, B. Q., & Frandsen, K. J. (1986). *Youth suicide: Depression and loneliness.* Evergreen, CO: Cordillera.

Halberg, L. J. (1986). Death of a college student: Response by student services professionals on one campus. *Journal of Counseling and Development, 64*, 411–412.

Halporn, R. (1992). Chinese Americans in loss and grief. *The Forum, 17*(6), 1, 16–20.

Hall, G. S. (1904). *Adolescence: Its psychology and its relations to physiology, anthropology, sociology, sex, crime, religion, and education* (Vol. 1). New York: D. Appleton.

Hall, J. E., & Kirschling, J. M. (1990). A conceptual framework for caring for families of hospice patients. *The Hospice Journal, 6*, 1–28.

Hamburg, D. A. (1992). *Today's children: Creating a future for a generation in crisis.* New York: Times Books.

Handy, B. (1994, April 18). Never mind. *Time: The Weekly Newsmagazine, 143*, 70–72.

Hankoff, L. D. (1975). Adolescence and the crisis of dying. *Adolescence, 10,* 373–389.

Haran, J. (1988). Use of group work to help children cope with the violent death of a classmate. *Social Work with Groups, 11,* 79–92.

Harding, R. W., & Fahey, R. P. (1973). Killings by Chicago police, 1969–70: An empirical study. *Southern California Law Review, 4,* 284–315.

Hardt, D. V. (1979). An investigation of the stages of bereavement. *Omega, 9,* 279–285.

Harter, S. (1987). The determinants and mediational role of global self-worth in children. In N. Eisenberg (Ed.), *Contemporary topics in developmental psychology* (pp. 219–241). New York: Wiley.

Harter, S. (1990). Self and identity development. In S. S. Feldman & G. R. Elliott (Eds.), *At the threshold: The developing adolescent* (pp. 352–387). Cambridge, MA: Harvard University Press.

Haslam, M. T. (1978). A study of psychiatric breakdown in adolescence: Diagnosis and prognosis. *International Journal of Psychiatry, 24,* 287–294.

Hauser, S. T., & Bowlds, M. K. (1990). Stress, coping, and adaptation. In S. S. Feldman & G. R. Elliott (Eds.), *At the threshold: The developing adolescent* (pp. 388–413). Cambridge, MA: Harvard University Press.

Hauser, S. T., & Greene, W. M. (1991). Passages from late adolescence to early adulthood. In S. I. Greenspan & G. H. Pollock (Eds.), *The course of life: Vol. 4. Adolescence* (pp. 377–405). Madison, CT: International Universities Press.

Hawkins, D. F. (Ed.). (1986). *Homicide among black Americans.* Lanham, MD: University Press of America.

Hawton, K. (1986). *Suicide and attempted suicide among children and adolescents.* Beverly Hills: Sage.

Hazell, P., & Lewin, T. (1993). An evaluation of postvention following adolescent suicide. *Suicide and Life-Threatening Behavior, 23,* 101–109.

Hein, K. (1993). "Getting real" about HIV in adolescents. *American Journal of Public Health, 83,* 492–494.

Hein, K. (1992). Adolescents at risk for HIV infection. In R. J. DiClemente (Ed.), *Adolescents and AIDS: A generation in jeopardy* (pp. 3–16). Newbury Park: Sage.

Hein, K. (1987). AIDS in adolescents: A rationale for concern. *New York State Journal of Medicine, 88,* 290–295.

Heiney, S. P. (1991). Sibling grief: A case report. *Archives in Psychiatric Nursing, 32,* 13–17.

Heiney, S. P., Hasan, L., & Price, K. (1993). Developing and implementing a bereavement program for a children's hospital. *Journal of Pediatric Nursing, 8,* 385–389.

Henry, C. S., Stephenson, A. C., Hanson, M. F., & Hargott, W. (1993). Adolescent suicide and families: An ecological approach. *Adolescence, 28,* 291–308.

Hepworth, J., Ryder, R. G., & Dreyer, A. S. (1984). The effects of parental loss on the formation of intimate relationships. *Journal of Marriage and Family Therapy, 10,* 73–82.

Hickey, L. O. (1993). Death of a counselor: A bereavement group for junior high school students. In N. B. Webb (Ed.), *Helping bereaved children: A handbook for practitioners* (pp. 239–266). New York: Guilford.

Hicks, B. B. (1990). Postvention process. In L. W. Barber (Ed.), *Youth suicide: A comprehensive manual for prevention and intervention* (pp. 79–83). Bloomington, IN: National Educational Service.

Hilgard, J. (1969). Depressive and psychotic states as anniversaries of sibling death in childhood. *International Psychiatry Clinics, 6,* 197–211.

Hill, R. (1949). *Families under stress.* Westport, CT: Greenwood.

Hindus, M. S. (1980). *Prison and plantation: Crime, justice and authority in Massachusetts and South Carolina, 1767–1878.* Chapel Hill, NC: University of North Carolina Press.

Hipple, J. L., Cimbolic, P., & Peterson, J. (1980). Student services response to a suicide. *Journal of Counseling and Student Personnel, 21,* 457–458.

Hodges, M. H., Graham–Pole, J., & Fong, M. L. (1984). Attitudes, knowledge and behaviors of school peers of adolescent cancer patients. *Journal of Psychosocial Oncology, 2*(2), 37–46.

Hoffman, M. A., Levy-Shiff, R., Sohlberg, S. C., & Zarizki, J. (1992). The impact of stress and coping: Developmental changes in the transition to adolescence. *Journal of Youth and Adolescence, 21,* 451–469.

Hogan, N. S. (1987). *An investigation of the adolescent sibling bereavement process and adaptation.* Unpublished doctoral dissertation, Loyola University of Chicago, Chicago.

Hogan, N. S. (1988). The effect of time on adolescent sibling bereavement. *Pediatric Nursing, 14,* 333–336.

Hogan, N. S. (1990). Hogan Sibling Inventory of Bereavement (HSIB). In J. Touliatos, B. Perlmutter, & M. Straus, (Eds.), *Handbook of family measurement techniques* (p. 524). Newbury Park, CA: Sage.

Hogan, N. S., & Balk, D. E. (1990). Adolescents' reactions to sibling death: Perceptions of mothers, fathers, and teenagers. *Nursing Research, 39,* 103–106.

Hogan, N. S., & DeSantis, L. (1992). Adolescent sibling bereavement: An ongoing attachment. *Qualitative Health Research, 2,* 159–177.

Hogan, N. S., & DeSantis, L. (1994). Things that help and hinder adolescent sibling bereavement. *Western Journal of Nursing Research, 16,* 132–153.

Hogan, N. S., & DeSantis, L. (in press). Basic constructs of a theory of adolescent sibling bereavement. In P. Silverman, S. Nickman, & D. Klass (Eds.), *But it does not end a relationship.* Washington, DC: Taylor & Francis.

Hogan, N. S., & Greenfield, D. B. (1991). Adolescent sibling bereavement: Symptomatology in a large community sample. *Journal of Adolescent Research, 6,* 97–112.

Holinger, P. C., & Offer, D. (1981). Perspectives on suicide in adolescence. In R. G. Simmons (Ed.), *Research in community and mental health* (Vol. 2, pp. 139–157). Greenwich, CT: JAI Press.

Holmes, G. R., Heckel, R. V., & Gordon, L. (1991). *Adolescent group therapy: A social competency model.* New York: Praeger.

Holmes, J. (1993). *John Bowlby and attachment theory.* London: Routledge.

Howard, M., & McCabe, J. B. (1990). Helping teenagers postpone sexual involvement. *Family Planning Perspectives, 22,* 21–26.

Huckeby, G. (May, 1993). Wyoming's future—1993 graduates. Remembering friends. *The Sheridan Press* (pp. 15–16). Sheridan, Wyoming.

Huff-Corzine, L., Corzine, J., & Moore, D. C. (1986). Southern experience: Deciphering the South's influence on homicide rates. *Social Forces, 64,* 906–924.

Hurrelmann, K. (Ed.). (1994). *International handbook of adolescence.* Westport, CT: Greenwood Press.

Imber-Black, E. (1991). Rituals and the healing process. In F. Walsh & M. McGoldrick (Eds.), *Living beyond loss: Death in the family* (pp. 207–223). New York: Norton.

Inhelder, B., & Piaget, J. (1958). *The growth of logical thinking: From childhood to adolescence.* New York: Basic Books.

Institute of Medicine. (1986). *Confronting AIDS.* Washington, DC: National Academy Press.

Irish, D. P. (1993). Introduction: Multiculturalism and the majority population. In D. P. Irish, K. F. Lundquist, & V. J. Nelson (Eds.), *Ethnic variations in dying, death, and grief: Diversity in universality* (pp. 1–10). Washington, DC: Taylor & Francis.

Irish, D. P., Lundquist, K. F., & Nelsen, V. J. (Eds.). (1993). *Ethnic variations in dying, death, and grief: Diversity in universality.* Washington, DC: Taylor & Francis.

Jacks, I., & Cox, S. G. (Eds.). (1984). *Psychological approaches to crime and its correction.* Chicago: Nelson Hall.

Jacobs, B., & Towns, J. E. (1984). What residence hall staff need to know about dealing with death. *NASPA Journal, 22*(2), 32–36.

Jacobs, S. C., Hanson, F. F., Berkman, L., Kasl, S. V., & Ostfeld, A. M. (1989). Depressions of bereavement. *Comprehensive Psychiatry, 30,* 218–224.

Janoff-Bulman, R. (1992). *Shattered assumptions.* New York: Free Press.

Janowiak, S., Drapkin, R., Lear, S., and Mei-tal, R. (1993, April). *Living with loss: A support group for bereaved college students.* Paper presented at the 15th Annual Conference of the Association for Death Education and Counseling, Memphis, TN.

Jemmott, J. B., & Jemmott, L. S. (1994). Interventions for adolescents in community settings. In R. J. DiClemente & J. L. Peterson (Eds.), *Preventing AIDS: Theories and methods of behavioral interventions* (pp. 141–174). New York: Plenum.

Jemmott, J. B., Jemmott, L. S., & Fong, G. T. (1992). Reductions in HIV risk-associated sexual behaviors among black male adolescents: Effects of an AIDS prevention intervention. *American Journal of Public Health, 82,* 372–377.

Jenkins, R. L., & Crowley, E. B. (1981). *Predictions of violence.* Springfield, IL: Charles C Thomas.

Johnson, G. B. (1941). The Negro and crime. *Annuals of the American Academy of Political and Social Science, 217,* 93–104.

Johnson, L. C., Rincon, B., Gober, C., & Rexin, D. (1993). The development of a comprehensive bereavement program to assist families experiencing pediatric loss. *Journal of Pediatric Nursing, 8,* 142–146.

Jonah, B. A. (1986). Accident risk and risk-taking behaviour among young drivers. *Accident Analysis and Prevention, 18,* 255–271.

Josselson, R. (1987). *Finding herself: Pathways to identity development in women.* San Francisco: Jossey-Bass.

Jurich, A. P. (1987). Adolescents and family dynamics. In H. G. Lingren, L. Kimmons, P. Lee, G. Rowe, L. Rottmann, L. Schwab, & R. Williams (Eds.), *Building family strengths* (Vol. 8, pp. 167–181). Lincoln: University of Nebraska Press.

Kaffman, M., & Elizur, E. (1979). Children's bereavement reactions following death of the father. *International Journal of Family Therapy, 1,* 203–228.

Kagen-Goodheart, L. (1977). Reentry: Living with childhood cancer. *American Journal of Orthopsychiatry, 47,* 651–658.

Kalish, R. (Ed.). (1980). *Death and dying: Views from many cultures.* Farmingdale, NY: Baywood.

Kania, R. E., & Mackey, W. C. (1977). Police violence as a function of community characteristics. *Criminology, 15,* 27–48.

Kann, L., Anderson, J. E., Holtzman, D., Rose, J., Truman, B. I., Collins, J., & Kolbe, L. J. (1991). HIV-related knowledge, beliefs, and behaviors among high school students in the United States: Results from a national survey. *Journal of School Health, 61,* 397–401.

Kantrowitz, B. (1993, August 2). Wild in the streets. *Newsweek, 122,* 40–46.

Kaplan, M. E., & Friedman, S. B. (1994). Reciprocal influences between chronic illness and adolescent development. *Adolescent medicine: State of the art reviews, 5,* 211–221.

Kastenbaum, R. (1959). Time and death in adolescence. In H. Feifel (Ed.), *The meaning of death* (pp. 99–113). New York: McGraw-Hill.

Kastenbaum, R. (1986). Death in the world of adolescence. In C. A. Corr & J. N. McNeil, (Eds.), *Adolescence and death* (pp. 4–15). New York: Springer Publishing.

Kastenbaum, R. (1992). *The psychology of death* (2nd ed.). New York: Springer Publishing.

Katz, A. H. (1993). *Self-help in America: A social movement perspective.* New York: Twayne.

Katz, E. R., Rubinstein, C. L., Hubert, N. C., & Bleu, A. (1988). School and social reintegration of children with cancer. *Journal of Psychosocial Oncology, 6*(3/4), 123–140.

Kavanaugh, R. E. (1972). *Facing death.* Los Angeles: Nash.

Kellerman, A. L. (1994). Annotation: Firearm-related violence—what we don't know is killing us. *American Journal of Public Health, 84,* 541–542.

Kellerman, J., Zelter, L., Ellenberg, L., Dash, J., & Rigler, D. (1980). Psychological effects of illness in adolescence: 1. Anxiety, self-esteem, and perception of control. *Journal of Pediatrics, 97,* 126–131.

Kelley, P. W., Miller, R. N., Pomerantz, R., Wann, F., Brundage, J. F., & Burke, D. S. (1990). Human immunodeficiency virus seropositivity among members of the active duty US Army 1985–89. *American Journal of Public Health, 80,* 405–410.

Kelly, G. A. (1955). *The psychology of personal constructs.* New York: Norton.

Keniston, K. (1965). *The uncommitted: Alienated youth in American society.* New York: Harcourt, Brace & World.

Kerr, P. (1987, October 19). A crack plague in Queens brings violence and fear. *The New York Times,* pp. A-1 & B-5.

Kessler, R. K., Burgess, A. W., & Douglass, J. E. (1988). *Sexual homicide.* Lexington, MA: Lexington Books.

Kim, M. J., McFarland, G. K., & McLane, A. M. (1987). *Pocket guide to nursing diagnosis.* St. Louis: Mosby.

Kirby, D., & DiClemente, R. J. (1994). School-based interventions to prevent unprotected sex and HIV among adolescents. In R. J. DiClemente & J. L. Peterson (Eds.), *Preventing AIDS: Theories and methods of behavioral interventions* (pp. 117–139). New York: Plenum.

Kirby, D., Barth, R. P., Leland, N., & Fetro, J. V. (1991). Reducing the risk: Impact of a new curriculum on sexual risk-taking. *Family Planning Perspectives, 23,* 253–263.

Kirk, W. G. (1993). *Adolescent suicide: A school-based approach to assessment and intervention.* Champaign, IL: Research Press.

Klass, D. (1987). John Bowlby's model of grief and the problem of identification. *Omega, 18,* 13–32.

Klass, D. (1988). *Parental grief: Solace and resolution.* New York: Springer Publishing.

Klass, D. (1993). Solace and immortality: Bereaved parents' continuing bond with their children. *Death Studies, 17,* 343–368.

Klass, D., & Shinners, B. (1983). Professional roles in a self-help group for the bereaved. *Omega, 13,* 361–375.

Kleck, G. (1979). Capital punishment, gun ownership, and homicide. *American Journal of Sociology, 84,* 882–910.

Kleiman, J. (1981). Optimal and normal family functioning. *American Journal of Family Therapy, 9,* 37–44.

Kliman, A. (1968). Eighteen untreated orphans. In G. Kliman (Ed.), *Psychological emergencies of childhood* (pp. 74–84). New York: Grune & Stratton.

Kliman, G. (1980). Death: Some implications in child development and child analysis. *Advances in Thanatology, 4,* 18–36.

Klingman, A. (1989). School-based emergency intervention following an adolescent's suicide. *Death Studies, 13,* 263–274.

Knapp, R. J. (1986). *Beyond endurance: When a child dies.* New York: Schocken Books.

Kochanek, K. D., & Hudson, B. L. (1994). Advance report of final mortality statistics, 1992. *Monthly Vital Statistics Report, 43*(6), (Suppl.).

Koocher, G. P. (1973). Childhood, death, and cognitive development. *Developmental Psychology, 9,* 369–375.

Koocher, G. P. (1986). Psychosocial issues during the acute treatment of pediatric cancer. *Cancer, 58,* 468–472.

Koocher, G. P., & O'Malley, J. E. (1981). *The Damocles syndrome: Psychosocial consequences of surviving childhood cancer.* New York: McGraw-Hill.

Koocher, G. P., O'Malley, J. E., Foster, D., & Gogan, J. L. (1976). Death anxiety in normal children and adolescents. *Psychiatria Clinica, 9,* 220–229.

Koss, M. P. (1988). Hidden rape: Sexual aggression and victimization in a national sample in higher education. In A. W. Burgess (Ed.), *Rape and sexual assault* (Vol. 2, pp. 3–25). New York: Garland.

Koss, M. P., Gidycz, C. J., & Wisniewski, N. (1987). The scope of rape: Incidence and prevalence of sexual aggression and victimization in a national sample of students in higher education. *Journal of Consulting and Clinical Psychology, 55,* 162–170.

Krell, R., & Rabkin, L. (1979). The effects of sibling death on the surviving child. *Family Process, 18,* 471–477.

Kries, B., & Patti, A. (1969). *Up from grief: Patterns of recovery.* New York: Seabury.

Krupnick, J. L. (1984). Bereavement during childhood and adolescence. In M. Osterweis, F. Solomon, & M. Green (Eds.), *Bereavement: Reactions, consequences, and care* (pp. 99–141). Washington, DC: National Academy Press.

Krupp, G. (1972). Maladaptive reactions to the death of a family member. *Social Casework, 53,* 425–434.

Krysiak, G. J. (1985). Circle of friends. *The School Counselor, 33,* 47–49.

Kübler-Ross, E. (1969). *On death and dying.* New York: Macmillan.

Kunjufu, J. (1985). *Countering the conspiracy to destroy black boys* (Vols. 1 & 2). Chicago: African-American Images.

Kvist, S. B., Rajantie, J., Kvist, M., & Siimes, M. A. (1991). Aggression: The dominant psychological response in children with malignant disease. *Psychological Reports, 68,* 1139–1150.

Kymissis, P. (1993). Group psychotherapy with adolescents. In H. I. Kaplan & B. J. Sadock (Eds.), *Comprehensive group psychotherapy* (3rd ed., pp. 577–584). Baltimore: Williams & Wilkins.

Lacayo, R. (1994, September 19). When kids go bad. Time: *The Weekly Newsmagazine, 144,* 60–63.

Lackey, N. R., & Gates, M. F. (1995). *Experiences of the adolescent caregiver of cancer patients.* Final report of the funded study. Indianapolis: Sigma Theta Tau International.

Ladame, F. (1992). Suicide prevention in adolescence: An overview of current trends. *Journal of Adolescent Health, 13,* 406–408.

LaGrand, L. E. (1981). Loss reactions of college students: A descriptive analysis. *Death Studies, 5,* 235–247.

LaGrand, L. E. (1982). How college and university students cope with loss. In R. A. Pacholski, & C. A. Corr (Eds.), *Priorities in death education and counseling* (pp. 85–97). Arlington, VA: Forum for Death Education and Counseling.

LaGrand, L. E. (1985). College student loss and response. In E. S. Zinner (Ed.), *Coping with death on campus* (pp. 15–28). San Francisco: Jossey-Bass.

LaGrand, L. E. (1986). *Coping with separation and loss as a young adult: Theoretical and practical realities.* Springfield, IL: Charles C Thomas.

LaGrand, L. E. (1988). *Changing patterns of human existence: Assumptions, beliefs, and coping with the stress of change.* Springfield, IL: Charles C Thomas.

Lamb, F., & Dunne-Maxim, K. (1987). Postvention in schools: Policy and process. In E. J. Dunne, J. L. McIntosh, & K. Dunne-Maxim (Eds.), *Suicide and its aftermath: Understanding and counseling the survivors* (pp. 245–260). New York: Norton.

Lamb, M., & Sutton-Smith, B. (1982). *Sibling relationships across the life span.* Hillsdale, NY: Erlbaum.

Lamberti, J. W., & Detmer, C. M. (1993). Model of family grief assessment and treatment. *Death Studies, 17,* 55–67.

Laufer, M. (1980). Which adolescents must be helped and by whom? *Journal of Adolescence, 3,* 265–272.

Leahy, J. (1992). Validity and reliability of the Beck Depression Inventory— Short Form in a group of adult bereaved females. *Journal of Clinical Psychology, 48,* 64–68.

Leder, S. N. (1992). Life events, social support, and children's competence after parent or sibling death. *Journal of Pediatric Nursing, 7,* 110–119.

Lee, B. L., & Safrin, S. (1992). Drug interactions and toxicities in patients with AIDS. In M. A. Sande & P. A. Volberding (Eds.), *The medical management of AIDS* (3rd ed., pp. 129–144). Philadelphia: W. B. Saunders.

Lehman, D. R., Ellard, J. H., & Wortman, C. B. (1986). Social support for the bereaved: Recipients' and providers' perspectives on what is helpful. *Journal of Consulting and Clinical Psychology, 54,* 438–446.

Lehman, D. R., Davis, C. G., Delongis, A., Wortman, C. B., Bluck, S., Mandel, D. R., & Ellard, J. H. (1993). Positive and negative life changes following bereavement and their relations to adjustment. *Journal of Social and Clinical Psychology, 12,* 90–112.

Leigh, G. K. (1986). Adolescent involvement in family systems. In G. K. Leigh & G. W. Peterson (Eds.), *Adolescents in families* (pp. 38–72). Cincinnati: South-Western.

Lester, D. (1988). *The biochemical basis of suicide.* New York: Thomas.

Lester, D., & Beck, A. T. (1976). Early loss as a possible sensitizer to later loss in attempted suicides. *Psychological Reports, 39,* 121–122.

Levenson, P., Pfefferbaum, B., Copeland, D., & Silverberg, Y. (1982). Information preferences of cancer patients ages 11–20 years. *Journal of Adolescent Health Care, 3,* 9–13.

Leviton, L. C. (1989). Theoretical foundations of AIDS-prevention programs. In R. O. Valdiserri (Ed.), *Preventing AIDS: The design of effective programs* (pp. 42–90). New Brunswick, NJ: Rutgers University Press.

Levitt, J. M. (1986). The conceptualization and assessment of family dynamics in terminal care. *The Hospice Journal, 2,* 1–19.

Lewin, K. (1939). Field theory and experiment in social psychology: Concepts and methods. *American Journal of Sociology, 44,* 868–896.

Lewis, M., & Volkmar, F. R. (1990). *Clinical aspects of child and adolescent development* (3rd ed.). Philadelphia: Lea & Febiger.

Ley, P. (1988). *Communicating with patients: Improving communication, satisfaction and compliance.* New York: Croom Helm.

Lieberman, M. A. (1993). Bereavement self-help groups: A review of conceptual and methodological issues. In M. S. Stroebe, W. Stroebe, & R. O. Hansson (Eds.), *Handbook of bereavement: Theory, research and intervention* (pp. 411–426). Cambridge, England: Cambridge University Press.

Lindemann, E. (1944). Symptomatology and management of acute grief. *American Journal of Psychiatry, 101,* 141–148.

Litt, I. F., Cuskey, W. R., & Rudd, S. (1983). Emergency room evaluation of the adolescent who attempts suicide: Compliance with follow-up. *Journal of Adolescent Health Care, 4,* 106–108.

Lopata, H. Z. (1973). *Widowhood in an American city.* Cambridge, MA: Schenckman.

Lopata, H. Z. (1975). On widowhood: Grief work and identity reconstruction. *Journal of Geriatric Psychiatry, 8,* 41–55.

Lui, K., Darrow, W. W., & Rutherford, G. W. (1988). A model-based estimate of the mean incubation period for AIDS in homosexual men. *Science, 240,* 1333–1335.

Lurie, C. (1993). *The death of friends vs. family members in late adolescence: The role of perceived social support and self-worth.* Unpublished master's thesis, Colorado State University, Fort Collins.

Lyon, J. B., & Vandenberg, B. R. (1989). Father death, family relationships, and subsequent psychological functioning in women. *Journal of Clinical Child Psychology, 18,* 329–335.

Madhubuti, H. R. (1990). *Black men: Obsolete, single, dangerous?* Chicago: Third World Press.

Main, D. S., Iverson, D. C., McGloin, J., Banspach, S. W., Collins, J. L., Rugg, D. L., & Kolbe, L. J. (1994). Preventing HIV infection among adolescents: Evaluation of a school-based program. *Preventive Medicine, 23,* 409–417.

Majors, R., & Billson, J. M. (1992). *Cool posse: The dilemmas of Black manhood in America.* New York: Lexington Books.

Mann, J. J., DeMeo, M. D., Keilp, J. G., & McBride, P. A. (1989). Biological correlates of suicidal behavior in youth. In C. R. Pfeffer (Ed.), *Suicide among youth: Perspectives on risk and prevention* (pp. 185–202). Washington, DC: American Psychiatric Press.

Mansfield, C. J., Conroy, M. E., Emans, S. J., & Woods, E. R. (1993). A pilot study of AIDS education and counseling of high-risk adolescents in an office setting. *Journal of Adolescent Health, 14,* 115–119.

Marcia, J. E. (1964). *Determination and construct validity of ego identity status.* Unpublished doctoral dissertation, The Ohio State University, Columbus.

Marcia, J. E. (1980). Identity in adolescence. In J. Adelson (Ed.), *Handbook of adolescent psychology* (pp. 159–187). New York: Wiley.

Marcia, J. E. (1987). The identity status approach to the study of ego identity development. In T. Honess & K. Yardley (Eds.), *Self and identity: Perspectives across the lifespan* (pp. 161–171). London: Routledge & Kegan Paul.

Markus, H., & Nurius, P. (1986). Possible selves. *American Psychologist, 41,* 954–969.

Marmar, C. R., Horowitz, M. J., Weiss, D. S., Wilner, N. R., & Kaltrieder, N. B. (1988). A controlled trial of brief psychotherapy and mutual-help group treatment of conjugal bereavement. *American Journal of Psychiatry, 145,* 203–212.

Martinson, I. M., & Campos, R. D. (1991). Adolescent bereavement: Long-term responses to a sibling death from cancer. *Journal of Adolescent Research, 6,* 54–69.

Martinson, I. M., Davies, E. B., & McClowry, S. G. (1987). The long-term effects of sibling death on self concept. *Journal of Pediatric Nursing, 2,* 227–235.

Marzuk, P. M., Tierney, M., Tardiff, K., Gross, E. M., Morgan, E. B., Hsu, M., & Mann, J. J. (1988). Increased risk of suicide in persons with AIDS. *Journal of the American Medical Association, 259,* 1333–1337.

Maslow, A. H. (1970). *Motivation and personality* (2nd ed.). New York: Harper & Row.

Masterman, S. H., & Reames, R. (1988). Support groups for bereaved preschool and school-aged children. *American Journal of Orthopsychiatry, 58,* 562–570.

Mattessich, P., & Hill, R. (1987). Life cycle and family development. In M. B. Sussman & S. K. Steinmetz (Eds.), *Handbook of marriage and the family* (pp. 437–469). New York: Plenum.

Mauk, G. W., & Weber, C. W. (1991). Peer survivors of adolescent suicide: Perspectives on grieving and postvention. *Journal of Adolescent Research, 6,* 113–131.

Mazrui, A. A. (Ed.). (1977). *The warrior tradition in modern Africa.* Leiden: E. J. Brill.

McBroom, A. (1987). *The rose* (Recorded by B. Midler). Seacaucus, NJ: Warner Bros.

McClowry, S. G., Davies, E. B., May, K. A., Kulenkamp, E. J., & Martinson, I. M. (1987). The empty space phenomenon: The process of grief in the bereaved family. *Death Studies, 11,* 361–374.

McCown, D. E., & Pratt, C. (1985). Impact of sibling death on children's behavior. *Death Studies, 9,* 323–335.

McCubbin, H. I., & Patterson, J. M. (1982). Family adaptation to crisis. In H. I. McCubbin (Ed.), *Family stress, coping, and social support* (pp. 26–47). Springfield, IL: Charles C Thomas.

McCubbin, H. I., Joy, C. B., Cauble, A. E., Comeau, J. K., Patterson, J.M., & Needle, R. H. (1980). Family stress and coping: A decade review. *Journal of Marriage and the Family, 42,* 855–871.

McGoldrick, M., & Walsh, F. (1991). A time to mourn: Death and the family life cycle. In F. Walsh & M. McGoldrick (Eds.), *Living beyond loss: Death in the family* (pp. 30–49). New York: Norton.

McGoldrick, M., Almeida, R., Hines, P. M., Garcia-Preto, N., Rosen, E., & Lee, R. (1991). Mourning in different cultures. In F. Walsh & M. McGoldrick (Eds.), *Living beyond loss: Death in the family* (pp. 176–206). New York: Norton.

McKenry, P. C., & Price, S. J. (1994). Families coping with problems and change: A conceptual overview. In P. C. McKenry & S. J. Price (Eds.), *Families and change: Coping with stressful events* (pp. 1–18). Thousand Oaks, CA: Sage.

McNeil, J. N. (1986). Talking about death: Adolescents, parents and peers. In C. A. Corr & J. N. McNeil (Eds), *Adolescence and death* (pp. 185–201). New York: Springer Publishing.

McNeil, J. N., Silliman, B., & Swihart, J. J. (1991). Helping adolescents cope with the death of a peer. *Journal of Adolescent Research, 6,* 132–145.

McNurlen, M. (1991). Guidelines for group work. In C. A. Corr, H. Fuller, C. A. Barnickol, & D. M. Corr (Eds.), *Sudden infant death syndrome: Who can help and how* (pp. 180–202). New York: Springer Publishing.

Mead, M. (1930). Adolescence in primitive and modern society. In V. F. Calverton & S. D. Schmalhausen (Eds.), *The new generation: The intimate problems of modern parents and children* (pp. 169–188). New York: Macauley.

Melges, F. T., & DeMaso, D. R. (1980). Grief resolution therapy: Reliving, revising, and revisiting. *American Journal of Psychotherapy, 34,* 51–61.

Merton, R. (1952). *Social theory and social structure.* Glencoe, IL: Free Press.

Meshot, C. M., & Leitner, L. M. (1993). Adolescent mourning and parental death. *Omega, 26,* 287–299.

Metzgar, M. M. (1988). *Crisis in schools; Is your school prepared?* Seattle: Author.

Metzgar, M. (1994). Preparing schools for crisis management. In R. G. Stevenson (Ed.), *What will we do? Preparing a school community to cope with crises* (pp. 17–35). Amityville, NY: Baywood.

Michael, S., & Lansdown, R. (1986). Adjustment to the death of a sibling. *Archives of Disease in Childhood, 61,* 278–283.

Miller, K. E., King, C. A., Shain, B. N., & Naylor, M. W. (1992). Suicidal adolescents' perceptions of their family environment. *Suicide and Life-Threatening Behavior, 22,* 226–239.

Miller, W. B. (1958). Lower class culture as a generating milieu of gang delinquency. *Journal of Social Issues, 14,* 5–19.

Mills, G. C., Reisler, R., Robinson, A. E., & Vermilye, G. (1976). *Discussing death: A guide to death education.* Palm Springs, CA: ETC Publications.

Millstein, S. G., Petersen, A. C., & Nightingale, E. O. (Eds.). (1993). *Promoting the health of adolescents: New directions for the twenty-first century.* New York: Oxford University Press.

Moore, D. (1984). Parent-adolescent separation: Intrafamilial perceptions and difficulty separating from parents. *Personality and Social Psychology Bulletin, 10,* 611–619.

Moore, D. (1987). Parent-adolescent separation: The construction of adulthood by late adolescents. *Developmental Psychology, 23,* 298–307.

Moore, D., & Schultz, N. R. (1983). Loneliness at adolescence: Correlates, attributions, and coping. *Journal of Youth and Adolescence, 12,* 95–100.

Moos, R. H. (1974). *Preliminary manual for family environment scale, work environment scale, group environment scale.* Palo Alto, CA: Consulting Psychologists Press.

Moos, R. H., & Schaefer, J. A. (1986). Life transitions and crises: A conceptual overview. In R. H. Moos & J. A. Schaefer (Eds.), *Coping with life crises: An integrated approach* (pp. 3–28). New York: Plenum.

Morano, C. D., Cisler, R. A., & Lemerond, J. (1993). Risk factors for adolescent suicidal behavior: Loss, insufficient family support, and hopelessness. *Adolescence, 28,* 851–865.

Morrison, E., Starks, K., Hyundman, C., & Ronzio, N. (1980). *Growing up sexual.* New York: Van Nostrand.

Mundy, C. (1994, June 2). The lost boy. *Rolling Stone,* pp. 51–53.

Murphy, S. A. (1990). Preventive intervention following accidental death of a child. *Image, 22,* 174–179.

Murphy, S. A., Aroian, K., & Baugher, R. J. (1989). A theory-based preventive intervention program for bereaved parents whose children have died in accidents. *Journal of Traumatic Stress, 2,* 319–334.

Murry, V. M., & Bell-Scott, P. (1994). Dealing with adolescent children. In P. C. McKenry & S. J. Price (Eds.), *Families and change: Coping with stressful events* (pp. 88–110). Thousand Oaks, CA: Sage.

National Research Council. (1993). *Losing generations: Adolescents in high-risk settings.* Washington, DC: National Academy Press.

Neimeyer, R. A. (1994). The threat index and related methods. In R. A. Neimeyer (Ed.), *Death anxiety handbook: Research, instrumentation, and application* (pp. 61–101). Washington, DC: Taylor & Francis.

Neimeyer, R. A., & Chapman, K. M. (1980). Self/ideal discrepancy and fear of death: The test of an existential hypothesis. *Omega, 11,* 233–240.

Nelson, E. R., & Slaikeu, K. A. (1984). Crisis intervention in the schools. In B. Barke (Ed.), *Crisis intervention: A handbook for practice and research* (pp. 247–262). Newton, MA: Allyn & Bacon.

Nerken, I. R. (1993). Grief and the reflective self: Toward a clearer model of loss resolution and growth. *Death Studies, 17,* 1–26.

Neugarten, B., & Neugarten, D. A. (1987). The changing meanings of age. *Psychology Today, 21,* 29–33.

Nichols, S. E. (1985). Psychosocial reactions of persons with AIDS. *Annals of Internal Medicine, 103,* 765–767.

Nieburg, H. A., & Fischer, A. (1982). *Pet loss: A thoughtful guide for adults and children.* New York: Harper & Row.

Noblit, G. W. (1987). Ideological purity and variety in effective middle schools. In G. W. Noblit & W. T. Pink (Eds.), *Schooling in social context: Qualitative studies* (pp. 203–217). Norwood, NJ: Ablex.

Noppe, L. D., & Noppe, I. C. (1991). Dialectical themes in adolescent conceptions of death. *Journal of Adolescent Research, 6,* 28–42.

O'Brien, J. M., Goodenow, C., & Espin, O. (1991). Adolescent reactions to the death of a peer. *Adolescence, 26,* 102, 431–440.

O'Carroll, P. O., & Mercy, J. (1986). Recent trends in black homicide. In D. Hawkins (Ed.), *Homicide among black Americans* (pp. 29–42). Lanham, MD: University Press of America.

Offer, D. (1969). *The psychological worlds of the teenager.* New York: Basic Books.

Offer, D., & Offer, J. B. (1975). *From teenage to young manhood: A psychological study.* New York: Basic Books.

Offer, D., & Sabshin, M. (1984). Adolescence: Empirical perspectives. In D. Offer & M. Sabshin (Eds.), *Normality and the life cycle: A critical integration* (pp. 76–107). New York: Basic Books.

Offer, D., Ostrov, E., & Howard, K. I. (1981). *The adolescent: A psychological self-portrait.* New York: Basic Books.

Offer, D., Ostrov, E., Howard, K. I., & Atkinson, R. (1988). *The teenage world: Adolescents' self-image in ten countries.* New York: Plenum.

Oldham, D. G. (1978). Adolescent turmoil: A myth revisited. *Journal of Continuing Education in Psychiatry, 39,* 23–32.

Olson, D. H., Sprenkle, D. H., & Russell, C. S. (1979). Circumplex model of marital and family systems: 1. Cohesion and adaptability dimensions, family types, and clinical applications. *Family Process, 18,* 3–28.

Oltjenbruns, K. A. (1991). Positive outcomes of adolescents' experience with grief. *Journal of Adolescent Research, 6,* 43–53.

Orbach, I. (1988). *Children who don't want to live.* San Francisco: Jossey-Bass.

Orlofsky, J. L. (1978). Identity formation, achievement, and fear of success in college men and women. *Journal of Youth and Adolescence, 7,* 49–62.

Orr, D. P., Hoffmans, M. A., & Bennets, G. (1984). Adolescents with cancer report their psychosocial needs. *Journal of Psychosocial Oncology, 2*(2), 47–59.

Osmond, D. H. (1994a). Classifications and staging of HIV disease. In P. T. Cohen, M. A. Sande, & P. A. Volberding (Eds.), *The AIDS knowledge base: A textbook on HIV disease from the University of California, San Francisco, and San Francisco General Hospital* (2nd ed., 1.1). Boston: Little, Brown.

Osmond, D. H. (1994b). HIV disease progression from infection to CDC-defined AIDS: Incubation period, cofactors and lab markers. In P. T. Cohen, M. A. Sande, & P. A. Volberding (Eds.), *The AIDS knowledge base: A textbook on HIV disease from the University of California, San Francisco, and San Francisco General Hospital* (2nd ed., 1.7). Boston: Little, Brown.

Osterweis, M., Solomon, F., & Green, M. (Eds.). (1984). *Bereavement: Reactions, consequences, and care.* Washington, DC: National Academy Press.

O'Toole, D. (1989). *Growing through grief: A K–12 curriculum to help young people through all kinds of loss.* Burnsville, NC: Mountain Rainbow Publications.

Papalia, D. E., & Olds, S. W. (1992). *Human development* (5th ed.). New York: McGraw-Hill.

Papini, D. R. & Roggman, L. A. (1992). Adolescent perceived attachment to parents in relation to competence, depression and anxiety: A longitudinal study. *Journal of Early Adolescence, 12,* 420–440.

Pappas, G. (1994). Elucidating the relationships between race, socioeconomic status, and health. *American Journal of Public Health, 84,* 892–893.

Parkes, A. S. (1993). *Backlash.* Cambridge, England: Cambridge University Press.

Parkes, C. M. (1972). *Bereavement: Studies of grief in adult life.* New York: International Universities Press.

Parkes, C. M. (1985). *Bereavement. British Journal of Psychiatry, 146,* 11–17.

Parkes, C. M. (1988). Bereavement as a psychosocial transition: Processes of adaptation to change. *Journal of Social Issues, 44,* 53–65.

Parkes, C. M., & Weiss, R. S. (1983). *Recovery from bereavement.* New York: Basic Books.

Parry, J. K., & Thornwall, J. (1992). Death of a father. *Death Studies, 16,* 173–181.

Partridge, S., & Kotler, T. (1987). Self-esteem and adjustment in adolescents from bereaved, divorced, and intact families: Family type versus family environment. *Australian Journal of Psychology, 39,* 223–234.

Patros, P. G., & Shamoo, T. K. (1989). *Depression and suicide in children and adolescents: Prevention, intervention, and postvention.* Needham Heights, MA: Simon & Schuster.

Paul, N., & Miller, S. (1986). Death and dying and the multigenerational impact. In M. Karpel (Ed.), *Family resources: The hidden partner in family therapy* (pp. 438–469). New York: Guilford.

Peck, M. (1982). Youth suicide. *Death Education, 6,* 29–47.

Perry, W. G. (1970). *Forms of intellectual and ethical development in college students.* New York: Holt, Rinehart & Winston.

Peskin, H. (1967). Pubertal onset and ego functioning. *Journal of Abnormal Psychology, 72,* 1–15.

Petersen, A. C. (1983). Menarche: Meaning of measure and measuring meaning. In S. Golub (Ed.), *Menarche* (pp. 63–76). New York: Heath.

Petersen, S., & Straub, R. L. (1992). *School crisis survival guide: Management techniques and materials for counselors and administrators.* West Nyack, NY: The Center for Applied Research in Education.

Peterson, R. (1984). The Compassionate Friends. *Death Education, 8,* 195–197.

Pfeffer, C. R. (1986). *The suicidal child.* New York: Guilford.

Phelps, S. B., & Jarvis, P. A. (1994). Coping in adolescence: Empirical evidence for a theoretically-based approach to assessing coping. *Journal of Youth and Adolescence, 23,* 359–371.

Phillips, D. P., Carstensen, L. L., & Paight, D. J. (1989). Effects of mass media news stories on suicide, with new evidence on the role of story content. In C. R. Pfeffer (Ed.), *Suicide among youth: Perspectives on risk and prevention* (pp. 101–116). Washington, DC: American Psychiatric Press.

Piaget, J. (1929). *The child's conception of the world.* London: Routledge & Kegan Paul.

Piaget, J. (1972). Intellectual evolution from adolescence to adulthood. *Human Development, 15,* 1–12.

Piaget, J., & Inhelder, B. (1969). *The psychology of the child.* London: Routledge & Kegan Paul.

Plopper, B. L., & Ness, M. E. (1993). Death as portrayed to adolescents through Top 40 rock and roll music. *Adolescence, 28,* 793–807.

Podell, C. (1989). Adolescent mourning: The sudden death of a peer. *Clinical Social Work, 17,* 64–78.

Pollock, G. H. (1962). Childhood parent and sibling loss in adult parents: A comparative study. *Archives of General Psychiatry, 7,* 296–305.

Portner, J. (1994, January 12). School violence up over the past 5 years, 82% in survey say. *Education Week,* p. 9.

Poussaint, A. F. (1983). Black on black homicide: A psychological-political perspective. *Victimology, 8,* 161–169.

Press, A., McCormick, J., & Wingert, P. (1994, August 15). A crime as American as a Colt .45. *Newsweek, 124,* 22–23.

Preto, N. G. (1988). Transformation of the family system in adolescence. In B. Carter & M. McGoldrick (Eds.), *The changing family life cycle: A framework for family therapy* (2nd ed., pp. 255–283). New York: Gardner.

Provence, S., & Solnit, A. (1983). Development promoting aspects of the sibling experience: Vicarious mastery. In A. J. Solnit, R. S. Eissler, & P. B. Newbaur (Eds.), *The psychiatric study of the child* (pp. 337–351). New Haven: Yale University Press.

Pynoos, R. S. (1985). Children traumatized by witnessing acts of personal violence: Homicide, rape or suicide behavior. In S. Eth & R. S. Pynoos (Eds.), *Post-traumatic stress disorder in children* (pp. 19–43). Washington, DC: American Psychiatric Press.

Quintana, S. M., & Kerr, J. (1993). Relational needs in late adolescent separation-individuation. *Journal of Counseling and Development, 71,* 349–354.

Radelet, M. (1981). Racial characteristics and the imposition of the death penalty. *American Sociological Review, 46,* 918–927.

Raja, S. N., McGee, R., & Stanton, W. R. (1992). Perceived attachments to parents and peers and psychological well-being in adolescence. *Journal of Youth and Adolescence, 21,* 471–485.

Ramsey, R. W. (1977). Behavioral approaches to bereavement. *Behavioral Research and Therapy, 15,* 131–140.

Rando, T. A. (1984). *Grief, dying and death: Clinical interventions for caregivers.* Champaign, IL: Research Press.

Rando, T. A. (Ed.). (1986). *Parental loss of a child.* Champaign, IL: Research Press.

Rando, T. A. (1991). *How to go on living when someone you love dies.* New York: Bantam.

Rando, T. A. (1993a). The increasing prevalence of complicated mourning: The onslaught is just beginning. *Omega, 26,* 19–42.

Rando, T. A. (1993b). *Treatment of complicated mourning.* Champaign, IL: Research Press.

Raphael, B. (1983). *The anatomy of bereavement.* New York: Basic Books.

Raphael, D. (1979). Sequencing in female adolescents' consideration of occupational, religious, and political alternatives. *Adolescence, 14,* 73–80.

Raundalen, M., & Finney, O. J. (1986). Children's and teenagers' views of the future. *International Journal of Mental Health, 15,* 114–125.

Reese, M. F. (1987). Growing up: The impact of loss and change. In D. Belle (Ed.), *Lives in stress: Women and depression* (pp. 65–88). Beverly Hills: Sage.

Reinherz, H. Z., Stewart-Berghauer, G., Pakiz, B., Frost, A. K., Moeykins, B. A., & Holmes, W. M. (1989). The relationships of early risk and current mediators to depressive symptomatology in adolescence. *Journal of the American Academy of Child & Adolescent Psychology, 28,* 942–947.

Rhodes, J. E., & Fischer, K. (1993). Spanning the gender gap: Gender differences in delinquency among inner-city adolescents. *Adolescence, 28,* 879–889.

Rickgarn, R. L. V. (1987). The death response team: Responding to the forgotten grievers. *Journal of Counseling and Development, 66,* 197–199.

Rickgarn, R. L. V. (1994). *Perspectives on college student suicide.* Amityville, NY: Baywood.

Robinson, P. J., & Fleming, S. J. (1989). Differentiating grief and depression. *The Hospice Journal, 5,* 77–88.

Robinson, P. J., & Fleming, S. J. (1992). Depressotypic cognitive patterns in major depression and conjugal bereavement. *Omega, 25,* 291–305.

Rochlin, G. (1959). The loss complex. *Journal of the American Psychoanalytic Association, 7,* 299–316.

Rodgers, R. (1973). *Family interaction and transaction: The developmental approach.* Englewood Cliffs, NJ: Prentice Hall.

Roper, W. L., Peterman, H. B., & Curran, J. W. (1993). Commentary: Condoms and HIV/STD prevention—clarifying the message. *American Journal of Public Health, 83,* 501–503.

Ropp, L., Visintainer, P., Uman, J., & Treloar, D. (1992). Death in the city: An American childhood tragedy. *Journal of the American Medical Association, 267,* 2905–2910.

Rose, H. M., & McClain, P. D. (Eds.). (1990). *Race, place and risk.* New York: State University of New York Press.

Rose, S. D., & Edleson, J. L. (1987). *Working with children and adolescents in groups.* San Francisco: Jossey-Bass.

Rosen, H. (1986). *Unspoken grief: Coping with childhood sibling loss.* Lexington, MA: Lexington Books.

Rosenberg, T. (1965). *Society and the adolescent self-image.* Princeton, NJ: Princeton University Press.

Rosenblatt, P. C. (1988). Grief: The social context of private feelings. *Journal of Social Issues, 44,* 67–78.

Ross, H. M. (1981). Societal/cultural views regarding death and dying. *Topics in Clinical Nursing, 3,* 1–16.

Rotheram-Borus, M. J. (1991). Serving runaway and homeless youths. *Family and Community Health, 14*(3), 23–32.

Rotheram-Borus, M. J., Koopman, C., Haignere, C., & Davies, M. (1991). Reducing HIV sexual risk behaviors among runaway adolescents. *Journal of the American Medical Association, 266,* 1237–1241.

Rotheram-Borus, M. J., Koopman, C., & Rosario, M. (1992). Developmentally tailoring prevention programs: Matching strategies to adolescents' serostatus. In R. J. DiClemente (Ed.), *Adolescents and AIDS: A generation in jeopardy* (pp. 212–229). Newbury Park, CA: Sage.

Roy, A. (1986). Genetic factors in suicide. *Psychopharmacology Bulletin, 22,* 666–668.

Rubenstein, J. L., Heeren, T., Housman, D., Rubin, C., & Stechler, G. (1989). Suicidal behavior in "normal" adolescents: Risk and protective factors. *American Journal of Orthopsychiatry, 59,* 59–71.

Rupert, D. (Ed.). (1981). Loss [Special issue]. *The Personnel and Guidance Journal, 59*(6).

Ryan, N. D., Puig-Antich, J., Rabinovitch, H., Ambrosini, P., Robinson, D., Nelson, B., & Novacenko, H. (1988). Growth hormone response to desmethylimipramine in depressed and suicidal adolescents. *Journal of Affective Disorders, 15,* 323–337.

Rybash, J. M., Hoyer, W. J., & Roodin, P. A. (1986). *Adult cognition and aging.* New York: Pergamon.

Ryland, D. H., & Kruesi, M. J. (1992). Suicide among adolescents. *International Review of Psychiatry, 4,* 185–195.

Sabatini, L. (1989). Evaluating a treatment program for newly widowed people. *Omega, 19,* 229–236.

St. Lawrence, J. S., Brasfield, T. L., Jefferson, K. W., Alleyne, E., O'Bannon, R. E., & Shirley, A. (1995). Cognitive-behavioral intervention to reduce African-American adolescents' risk for HIV infection. *Journal of Consulting and Clinical Psychology, 63,* 221–237.

St. Louis, M. E., Conway, G. A., Hayman, C. R., Miller, C., Petersen, L. R., & Dondero, T. J. (1991). Human immunodeficiency virus infection in disadvantaged adolescents. *Journal of the American Medical Association, 266,* 2387–2391.

St. Louis, M. E., Rauch, K. J., Petersen, L. R., Anderson, J. E., Schable, C. A., & Dondero, T. J. (1990). Seroprevalence rates of human immun-odeficiency virus infection at sentinel hospitals in the United States. *New England Journal of Medicine, 323,* 213–218.

Sande, M. A., & Volberding, P. A. (Eds.). (1992). *The medical management of AIDS* (3rd ed.). Philadelphia: W. B. Saunders.

Sanders, C. M., Mauger, P. A., & Strong, P. N. (1985). *A manual for the Grief Experience Inventory.* Palo Alto, CA: Consulting Psychologists Press.

Sandler, I., Gersten, J. C., Reynolds, K., Kallgren, C. A., & Ramirez, R. (1988). Using theory and data to support interventions: Design of a program for bereaved children. In B. H. Gottlieb (Ed.), *Marshaling social support: Formats, processes and effects* (pp. 53–83). Newbury Park, CA: Sage.

Sands, R. G., & Dixon, S. L. (1986). Adolescent crisis and suicidal behavior: Dynamics and treatment. *Child and Adolescent Social Work, 3,* 109–122.

Schachter, S. (1991). Adolescent experiences with the death of a peer. *Omega, 24,* 1–11.

Schlafly, P. (1988, April 13th). Death education comes into the open. *The Brooklyn Spectator.* (A syndicated column printed in many newspapers nationwide on or about April 13, 1988.)

Schlegel, A., & Barry, H. (1991). *Adolescence: An anthropological inquiry.* New York: Free Press.

Schwab, R. (1986). Support groups for the bereaved. *Journal for Specialists in Group Work, 11,* 100–106.

Schwartzberg, S. S., & Janoff-Bulman, R. (1991). Grief and the search for meaning: Exploring the assumptive worlds of bereaved college students. *Journal of Social and Clinical Psychology, 10,* 270–288.

Selman, R. L. (1980). *The growth of interpersonal understanding: Developmental and clinical analyses.* New York: Academic Press.

Shaffer, D. (1988). The epidemiology of teen suicide: An examination of risk factors. *Journal of Clinical Psychiatry, 49,* 36–41.

Shafii, M., Carrigan, S., Whittinghill, J. R., & Derrick, A. (1985). Psychological autopsy of completed suicide in children and adolescents. *American Journal of Psychiatry, 142,* 1061–1064.

Shanfield, S., Benjamin, G., & Swain, B. (1988). The family under stress: The death of adult children. In O. S. Margolis, A. H. Kutscher, E. R. Marcus, H. C. Raether, V. R. Pine, I. B. Seeland, & D. J. Cherico (Eds.), *Grief and the loss of an adult child* (pp. 3–7). New York: Praeger.

Sharabany, R., Gershoni, R., & Hofman, J. (1981). Girlfriend, boyfriend: Age and sex differences in intimate friendship. *Developmental Psychology, 17,* 800–808.

Shaughnessy, M. F., & Nystul, M. S. (1985). Preventing the greatest loss—suicide. *Creative Child and Adult Quarterly, 10,* 164–169.

Sheley, J. F. (1985). *Crime problem: An introduction to criminology.* Belmont, CA: Wadsworth.

Shelov, S. P. (1994). The children's agenda for the 1990s and beyond [Editorial]. *American Journal of Public Health, 84,* 1066–1067.

Sherman, B. (1979). Emergence of ideology in a bereaved parents group. In M. A. Lieberman & L. D. Borman (Eds.), *Self-help groups for coping with crisis* (pp. 305–322). San Francisco: Jossey-Bass.

Shneidman, E. (1971). Prevention, intervention, and postvention of suicide. *Annals of Internal Medicine, 75,* 453–458.

Shneidman, E. S. (1972). *Death and the college student.* New York: Behavioral Publications.

Shneidman, E. (1973). Suicide. *Encyclopedia Britannica* (14th ed., Vol. 21, pp. 383–385). Chicago: William Benton. (Reprinted in Shneidman, E. [1981]. *Suicide thoughts and reflections, 1960–1980* [pp. 6–28]. New York: Human Sciences Press.)

Shneidman, E. (1975). Postvention: The care of the bereaved. In R. O. Pasnau (Ed.), *Consultation-liaison psychiatry* (pp. 245–256). New York: Grune & Stratton. (Reprinted in Shneidman, E. [1981]. *Suicide thoughts and reflections, 1960–1980* [pp. 157–167]. New York: Human Sciences Press.)

Shipman, F. (1987). Student stress and suicide. *The Practitioner: NASSP Newsletter, 14*(2), 2–11.

Short, J. F., & Stodtbeck, F. L. (1965). *Group process and gang delinquency.* Chicago: University of Chicago Press.

Shreve, B. W., & Kunkel, M. A. (1991). Self-psychology, shame, and adolescent suicide: Theoretical and practical considerations. *Journal of Counseling and Development, 89,* 305–311.

Siegel, K., Mesagno, F. P., & Christ, G. (1990). A prevention program for bereaved children. *American Journal of Orthopsychiatry, 60,* 168–175.

Siehl, P. M. (1990). Suicide postvention: A new disaster plan what a school should do when faced with a suicide. *The School Counselor, 38,* 52–57.

Silberman, C. (1978). *Criminal violence-criminal justice: Criminals, police, courts, and prisons in America.* New York: Random House.

Sills, G. M., & Hall, J. E. (1985). A general systems perspective for nursing practice. In J. E. Hall & B. R. Weaver (Eds.), *Distributive nursing practice: A systems approach to community health* (pp. 21–29). Philadelphia: J. B. Lippincott.

Silverman, P. R. (1980). *Mutual help groups: Organization and development.* Beverly Hills: Sage.

Silverman, P. R. (1987). The impact of parental death on college-age women. *Psychiatric Clinics of North America, 10,* 387–404.

Silverman, S. M., & Silverman, P. R. (1979). Parent-child communication in widowed families. *American Journal of Psychotherapy, 33,* 428–441.

Silverman, P. R., & Worden, J. W. (1992). Children's reactions in the early months after the death of a parent. *American Journal of Orthopsychiatry, 62,* 93–104.

Silverman, P. R., Nickman, S., & Worden, J. W. (1992). Detachment revisited: The child's reconstruction of a dead parent. *American Journal of Orthopsychiatry, 62,* 494–503.

Simpson, J. A., & Weiner, E. S. C. (1989). The Oxford English dictionary (2nd ed.; 20 vols.). Oxford, England: Clarendon Press.

Slaby, A. E., & McGuire, P. L. (1989). Residential management of suicidal adolescents. *Residential Treatment for Children and Youth, 7,* 23–43.

Smith, K., & Crawford, S. (1986). Suicidal behavior among "normal" high school students. *Suicide and Life-Threatening Behavior, 16,* 313–325.

Smith, K., Ostroff, J., Tan, C., & Lesko, L. (1991). Alterations in self-perceptions among adolescent cancer survivors. *Cancer Investigations, 9,* 581–588.

Smith, P. C., Range, L. M., & Ulmer, A. (1992). Belief in afterlife as a buffer in suicidal and other bereavement. *Omega, 24,* 217–225.

Speece, M. W., & Brent, S. B. (1984). Children's understanding of death: A review of three components of a death concept. *Child Development, 55,* 1671–1686.

Spiegel, D. (1993). *Living beyond limits: New hope and help for facing life-threatening illness.* London: Vermilion.

Spinetta, J. J. (1981a). Adjustment and adaptation in children with cancer: A 3-year study. In J. J. Spinetta & P. Deasy-Spinetta (Eds.), *Living with childhood cancer* (pp. 5–23). St. Louis: Mosby.

Spinetta, J. J. (1981b). The sibling of the child with cancer. In J. J. Spinetta & P. Deasy-Spinetta (Eds.), *Living with childhood cancer* (pp. 133–142). St. Louis: Mosby.

Sroufe, L. A., Cooper, R. G., & DeHart, G. B. (1992). *Child development: Its nature and course* (2nd ed.). New York: McGraw-Hill.

Stanner, W. E. H. (1965). The dreaming. In W. A. Lessa & E. Z. Vogt (Eds.), *Reader in comparative religion: An anthropological approach* (3rd ed., pp. 269–277). New York: Harper & Row.

Staples, R. (1976). *Race and family violence: The internal colonialism perspective.* Unpublished manuscript.

Staples, R. (1982). *Black masculinity: The black male's role in American society.* San Francisco: Black Scholar Press.

Staton, A. Q., & Oseroff-Varnell, D. (1990). Becoming a middle school student. In A. Q. Staton (Ed.), *Communication and student socialization* (pp. 72–99). Norwood, NJ: Ablex.

Steinberg, L. (1990). *At the threshold: The developing adolescent.* Cambridge, MA: Harvard University Press.

Steinberg, L., & Silverberg, S. (1986). The vicissitudes of autonomy in early adolescence. *Child Development, 57,* 841–851.

Stephenson, J. S. (1985). Death and the campus community: Organizational realities and personal tragedies. In E. S. Zinner (Ed.), *Coping with death on campus* (pp. 5–13). San Francisco: Jossey-Bass.

Sterling, C. M., & Van Horn, K. R. (1989). Identity and death anxiety. *Adolescence, 24,* 321–326.

Stevens, M. M. (1994). Improving communication with parents of children with cancer. *The Medical Journal of Australia, 160,* 325.

Stevens, M. M. (1995). Palliative care for children dying of cancer: Psychosocial issues. In D. W. Adams & E. J. Deveau (Eds.), *Beyond the innocence of childhood: Helping children and adolescents cope with life-threatening illness and dying* (Vol. 2, pp. 181–209). Amityville, NY: Baywood.

Stevenson, R. G. (1984). *A death education course for secondary schools: "Curing" death ignorance.* Unpublished doctoral dissertation, Fairleigh Dickinson University, Teaneck, NJ.

Stevenson, R. G. (1986). Measuring the effects of death education in the classroom. In G. H. Paterson (Ed.), *Children and death: Proceedings of the 1985 King's College Conference* (pp. 201–210). London, Ontario: King's College.

Stevenson, R. G. (1990). Contemporary issues of life and death. In John D. Morgan (Ed.), *Death education in Canada* (pp. 43–79). London, Ontario: King's College.

Stevenson, R. G. (Ed.). (1994). *What will we do? Preparing a school community to cope with crises.* Amityville, NY: Baywood.

Stevenson, R. G., & Powers, H. L. (1986, December). How to handle death in the school. In *Tips for principals* (pp. 1–2). Reston, VA: National Association of Secondary School Principals.

Stewart, K. E., & Haley, W. E. (in press). Friends, lovers, and "absent" fathers: Family caregiving in the HIV epidemic. In K. A. Johnson, (Ed.), *Men's caregiving roles in an aging society.* Newbury Park, CA: Sage.

Strauss, N. (1994, June 2). The downward spiral. *Rolling Stone,* 35–43.

Stricof, R. L., Kennedy, J. T., Nattell, T. C., Weisfuse, I. B., & Novick, L. F. (1991). HIV seroprevalence in a facility for runaway and homeless adolescents. *American Journal of Public Health, 81,* 50–53.

Stroebe, M. (1993). Coping with bereavement: A review of the grief work hypothesis. *Omega, 26,* 19–42.

Stroebe, M., Gergen, M., Gergen, K., & Stroebe, W. (1992). Broken hearts or broken bonds: Love and death in historical perspective. *American Psychologist, 47,* 1205–1212.

Sugar, M. (1968). Normal adolescent mourning. *American Journal of Psychotherapy, 22,* 258–269.

Sullivan, K., & Sullivan, A. (1980). Adolescent-parent separation. *Developmental Psychology, 16,* 93–99.

Sullivan, L. (1991). Violence as a public health issue. *Journal of the American Medical Association, 265,* 2778.

Sullivan, S. (1993, July 6). Wife beating N the hood. *The Wall Street Journal,* A-12.

Susman, E. J., Hersh, S. P., Nannis, E. D., Strope, B. E., Woodruff, P. J., Pizzo, P. A., & Levine, A. (1982). Conceptions of cancer: The perspectives of child and adolescent patients and their families. *Journal of Pediatric Psychology, 7,* 253–261.

Sweeting, H. N., & Gilhooly, M. L. M. (1992). Doctor, am I dead? A review of social death in modern societies. *Omega, 24,* 251–269.

Switzer, D. K. (1970). *The dynamics of grief.* New York: Abingdon.

Taylor, S. E., Lichtman, R. R., & Wood, J. V. (1984). Attributions, beliefs about control, and adjustment to breast cancer. *Journal of Personality and Social Psychology, 46,* 489–502.

Tebbi, C. K., & Stern, M. (1988). Burgeoning speciality of adolescent oncology. In *The adolescent with cancer* (pp. 9–20). New York: American Cancer Society.

Tedeschi, R. G., & Calhoun, L. G. (1993). Using the support group to overcome the isolation of bereavement. *Journal of Mental Health Counseling, 15,* 47–54.

Terkelson, K. (1980). Toward a theory of the family life cycle. In B. Carter & M. McGoldrick (Eds.), *The family life cycle: A framework for family therapy* (pp. 21–52). New York: Gardner.

Thornburg, H. D. (1980). Early adolescents: Their developmental characteristics. *The High School Journal, 63,* 215–221.

Thornton, G., Robertson, D. U., & Gilleylen, C. (1991, April). *Disenfranchised grief and college students ratings of loss situations.* Paper presented at the 13th Annual Conference of the Association for Death Education and Counseling, Duluth, MN.

Title, C. R., Villemez, W. J., & Smith, D. A. (1978). The myth of social class and criminality. *American Social Review, 43,* 643–656.

Tobin-Richards, M. H., Boxer, A. M., & Petersen, A. C. (1983). The psychological significance of pubertal change: Sex differences in perceptions of self during early adolescence. In J. Brooks-Gunn & A. C. Petersen (Eds.), *Girls at puberty: Biological and psychological perspectives* (pp. 127–154). New York: Plenum.

Toews, J., Martin, R., & Prosen, H. (1985). Death anxiety: The prelude to adolescence. *Adolescent Psychiatry, 12,* 134–144.

Triolo, S. J., McKenry, P. C., Tishler, C. L., & Blyth, D. A. (1984). Social and psychological discriminants of adolescent suicide: Age and sex differences. *Journal of Early Adolescence, 4,* 239–251.

Tross, S. & Hirsch, D. A. (1988). Psychological distress and neuropsychological complications of HIV infection and AIDS. *American Psychologist, 43,* 929–934.

Turner, C. F., Miller, H. G., & Moses, L. E. (Eds.). (1989). *AIDS: Sexual behavior and drug use.* Washington, DC: National Academy Press.

Tyson-Rawson, K. J. (1993a). *College women and bereavement: Late adolescence and father death.* Unpublished raw data.

Tyson-Rawson, K. J. (1993b). *College women and bereavement: Late adolescence and father death.* Unpublished doctoral dissertation, Kansas State University, Manhattan.

United Nations Children's Fund. (1994). *The state of the world's children, 1994.* New York: Oxford University Press.

United States Bureau of the Census. (1993). *Statistical abstract of the United States* (113th ed.). Washington, DC: U.S. Government Printing Office.

United States Department of Justice, Federal Bureau of Investigation. (1990). *Uniform crime reports, crime in the United States.* Washington, DC: Government Printing Office.

Vachon, M. L. S., & Stylianos, S. K. (1988). The role of social support in bereavement. *Journal of Social Issues, 44,* 175–190.

Vander Zanden, J. W. (1989). *Human development* (4th ed.). New York: Knopf.

Van Dongen-Melman, J. E., Pruyn, J. F., Van Zanen, G. E., & Sanders-Woudstra, J. (1986). Coping with childhood cancer: A conceptual view. *Journal of Psychosocial Oncology, 4*(1/2), 147–161.

Van Eerdewegh, M. M., Bieri, M. D., Parrilla, R. H., & Clayton, P. (1982). The bereaved child. *British Journal of Psychiatry, 140,* 23–29.

Vess, J., Moreland, J., & Schwebel, A. I. (1985). Understanding family role reallocation following a death: A theoretical framework. *Omega, 16,* 115–128.

Videka-Sherman, L. (1990). Bereavement self-help organizations. In T. J. Powell (Ed.), *Working with self-help* (pp. 156–174). Silver Spring, MD: National Association of Social Work Press.

Videka-Sherman, L., & Lieberman, M. A. (1985). The impact of self-help and professional help on parental bereavement: The limits of recovery. *American Journal of Orthopsychiatry, 55,* 70–81.

Volkan, V. D. (1975). "Re-grief" therapy. In B. Schoenberg & I. Gerber (Eds.), *Bereavement: Its psychological aspects* (pp. 334–350). New York: Columbia University Press.

Vollman, R., Ganzert, A., Picher, L, & Williams, W. (1971). The reactions of family systems to sudden and unexpected death. *Omega, 2,* 101–106.

Walker, C. L. (1993). Sibling bereavement and grief responses. *Journal of Pediatric Nursing, 8,* 325–334.

Walker, R. S. (1991). *AIDS: Today, tomorrow: An introduction to the HIV epidemic in America.* Atlantic Highlands, NJ: Humanistic Press International.

Walsh, F., & McGoldrick, M. (1998). Loss and the family life cycle. In C. J. Falicov (Ed.), *Family transitions: Continuity and change over the life cycle* (pp. 311–336). New York: Guilford.

Walsh, F., & McGoldrick, M. (1991a). Loss and the family: A systemic perspective. In F. Walsh & M. McGoldrick (Eds.), *Living beyond loss: Death in the family* (pp. 1–29). New York: Norton.

Walsh, F., & McGoldrick, M. (Eds.). (1991b). *Living beyond loss: Death in the family*. New York: Norton.

Walter, H. J., & Vaughan, R. D. (1993). AIDS risk reduction among a multiethnic sample of urban high school students. *Journal of the American Medical Association, 270,* 725–730.

Walters, M., Carter, B., Papp, P., & Silverstein, O. (1988). *The invisible web: Gender patterns in family relationship*. New York: Guilford.

Warmbrod, M. (1986). Counseling bereaved children: Stages in the process. *Social Casework, 67,* 351–358.

Wass, H., Miller, D. M., & Thornton, G. (1990). Death education and grief/suicide intervention in the public schools. *Death Studies, 14,* 253–268.

Wasserman, A. L., Thompson, E. I., Wilimas, J. A., & Fairclough, D. L. (1987). The psychological status of survivors of childhood/adolescent Hodgkin's disease. *American Journal of Diseases in Childhood, 141,* 626–631.

Waterman, A. S. (1992). Identity as an aspect of optimal psychological functioning. In G. R. Adams, T. P. Gullotta, & R. Montemayor (Eds.), *Adolescent identity formation* (pp. 50–72). Newbury Park, CA: Sage.

Waters, R. (1990). *Ethnic minorities and the criminal justice system*. Aldershot, England: Avebury.

Weaver, G. D., & Gary, L. E. (1993). Stressful life events, psychosocial resources and depressive symptoms among older African American men. *The Urban League Review, 16*(2), 45–56.

Webb, N. B. (1993). Assessment of the bereaved child. In N. B. Webb (Ed.), *Helping bereaved children: A handbook for practitioners* (pp. 19–42). New York: Guilford.

Wechsler, H., Davenport, A., Dowdall, G., Moeykens, B., & Castillo, S. (1994). Health and behavioral consequences of binge drinking in college: A national survey of students at 140 campuses. *Journal of the American Medical Association, 272,* 1672–1677.

Weiner, T. B. (1977). Psychopathology in adolescence. In J. Adelson (Ed.), *Handbook of adolescent psychology* (pp. 288–312). New York: Pergamon.

Weiner, I. B. (1985). Clinical contributions to the developmental psychology of adolescence. *Genetic, Social, and General Psychology Monographs, 111,* 195–203.

Weiss, R. S. (1988). Loss and recovery. *Journal of Social Issues, 44,* 37–52.

Wenckstern, S., & Leenaars, A. A. (1993). Trauma and suicide in our schools. *Death Studies, 17,* 151–171.

Wenz, F. V. (1979). Self-injury behavior, economic status, and family anomie syndrome among adolescents. *Adolescence, 14,* 387–398.

West, S. G., Sandler, I., Pillow, D. R., Baca, L., & Gersten, J. C. (1991). The use of structural equation modeling in generative research: Toward the design of a preventive intervention for bereaved children. *American Journal of Community Psychology, 19,* 459–480.

Westberg, G. (1971). *Good grief.* Philadelphia: Fortress.

White, J. M. (1991). *Dynamics of family development: A theoretical perspective.* New York: Guilford.

Wilson, A. N. (1992). *Understanding black male violence.* New York: Afrikan World Infosystems.

Winbush, R. (1988). Growing pains: Explaining adolescent violence with developmental theory. In J. Carlson & J. Lewis (Eds.), *Counseling the adolescent* (pp. 57–73). Denver: Love.

Wingood, G. M., & DiClemente, R. J. (1992). Cultural, gender and psychosocial influences on HIV-related behavior of African-American female adolescents: Implications for the development of tailored prevention programs. *Ethnicity & Disease, 2,* 381–388.

Wingood, G. M., & DiClemente, R. J. (in press). Understanding the role of gender relations in HIV prevention research. *American Journal of Public Health.*

Winiarski, M. G. (1991). *AIDS-related psychotherapy.* New York: Pergamon.

Wodarski, J. S., & Harris, P. (1987). Adolescent suicide: A review of influences and the means for prevention. *Social Work, 32,* 477–484.

Wolfelt, A. (1983). *Helping children cope with grief.* Muncie, IN: Accelerated Development.

Wolfgang, M. E., & Ferracuti, F. (1967). *The subculture of violence.* Beverly Hills: Sage.

Wolfgang, M. E., Figlio, R. F., & Sellin, T. (1972). *Delinquency in a birth cohort.* Chicago: University of Chicago Press.

Worden, J. W. (1991). *Grief counseling and grief therapy: A handbook for the mental health practitioner* (2nd ed.). New York: Springer Publishing.

Worth, L. A., & Burack, J. H. (1994). Outpatient management of HIV infection. In P. T. Cohen, M. A. Sande, & P. A. Volberding (Eds.), *The AIDS knowledge base: A textbook on HIV disease from the University of California, San Francisco, and San Francisco General Hospital* (2nd ed., 4.3). Boston: Little, Brown.

Worth, L. A., & Volberding, P. A. (1994). Clinical applications of antiretroviral therapy. In P. T. Cohen, M. A. Sande, & P.A. Volberding (Eds.), *The AIDS knowledge base: A textbook on HIV disease from the University of Cali-*

fornia, San Francisco, and San Francisco General Hospital (2nd ed., 4.5).
Boston: Little, Brown.

Wortman, C. B., & Silver, R. C. (1989). The myths of coping with loss. *Journal of Consulting and Clinical Psychology, 57,* 349–357.

Wrenn, R. L. (1992). Educating the educators. *Thanatos, 17*(1), 33–35.

Wright, B. (1990). *Black robes, white justice.* New York: First Carol.

Wrobleski, A. (1984). The suicide survivors grief group. *Omega, 15,* 173–183.

Yalom, I. D. (1985). *The theory and practice of group psychotherapy* (3rd ed.). New York: Basic Books.

Young, T. J. (1985). The clinical manifestation of alienation. *High School Journal, 69,* 55–60.

Youniss, J., & Smollar, J. (1985). *Adolescent relations with mothers, fathers, and friends.* Chicago, IL: University of Chicago Press.

Zalaznik, P. H. (1992). *Dimensions of loss and death education* (3rd ed.). Minneapolis: Edu-Pac.

Zambelli, G. C., & DeRosa, A. P. (1992). Bereavement support groups for school age children: Theory, intervention and case examples. *American Journal of Orthopsychiatry, 62,* 484–493.

Zimpfer, D. G. (1991). Groups for grief and survivorship after bereavement: A review. *Journal for Specialists in Group Work, 16,* 46–55.

Zimring, F. E. (1984). Youth homicide in New York: A preliminary analysis. *The Journal of Legal Studies, 13,* 81–99.

Zinner, E. S. (1985). Group survivorship: A model and case study application. In E. S. Zinner (Ed.), *Coping with death on campus* (pp. 51–68). San Francisco: Jossey-Bass.

Zinner, E. S. (Ed.). (1985). *Coping with death on campus.* San Francisco: Jossey-Bass.

Zuckerman, B. S., & Beardslee, W. R. (1986). The impact of the threat of nuclear war on children and adolescents. *Developmental and Behavioral Pediatrics, 7,* 383–384.

Zwartjes, W. (1980). The psychological costs of curing the child with cancer. In J. Van Eys & M. P. Sullivan (Eds.), *Status of the curability of childhood cancer* (pp. 277–284). New York: Raven Press.

Author Index

A

Aber, M. S., 147
Ablin, A. R., 177, 180
Abraham, M., 179
Adams, D. W., 105, 106, 337
Adams, G. A., 12
Adlerstein, A. M., 23, 179
Adolph, R., 6, 23, 140–141, 144, 145, 146, 147, 201, 297
Alexander, I. E., 23, 179
Allan, M., 71
Allberg, W. R., 72, 73, 75, 76, 77
Alleyne, E., 89, 91
Allison, K. W., 34, 35
Allman, C., 71, 80, 179
Ambrosini, P., 71
American Association of Suicidology, 264
American Psychiatric Association, 174
American Psychological Association, 45
Anderson, B. J., 38
Anderson, J. E., 87, 88
Arbit, J., 55
Arday, S., 88
Aries, P., 4
Aroian, K., 175
Athens, L. H., 62

Atkinson, R., 14
Auslander, N., 33
Austin, D. A., 31
Avery, A., 12

B

Baca, L., 163, 168
Bacchetti, P. 86
Bachman, J., 31
Bachman, J. G., 27–28
Balach, L., 179
Balk, D. E., 1, 7, 9, 11, 13, 14, 139, 141, 142, 144, 145, 146, 147, 149, 150, 151, 152, 159, 164–165, 169, 172, 173, 174, 176, 177–178, 179, 180, 181, 182, 188, 189–190, 192–194, 196, 198, 203, 206, 251, 257, 285, 299, 301, 303, 307, 309
Balmer, L. E., 143, 145, 146, 147, 148, 149, 150, 151, 152, 153,
Bank, S., 175, 176
Bandura, A., 14, 89
Bank, S., 189
Banspach, S. W., 89
Barbato, A., 175
Barnes, M. J., 200
Barrett, C. J., 294
Barrett, R. K., 2, 43, 44, 45, 47, 49, 51–52, 53, 54, 57, 58, 60

Subject Index